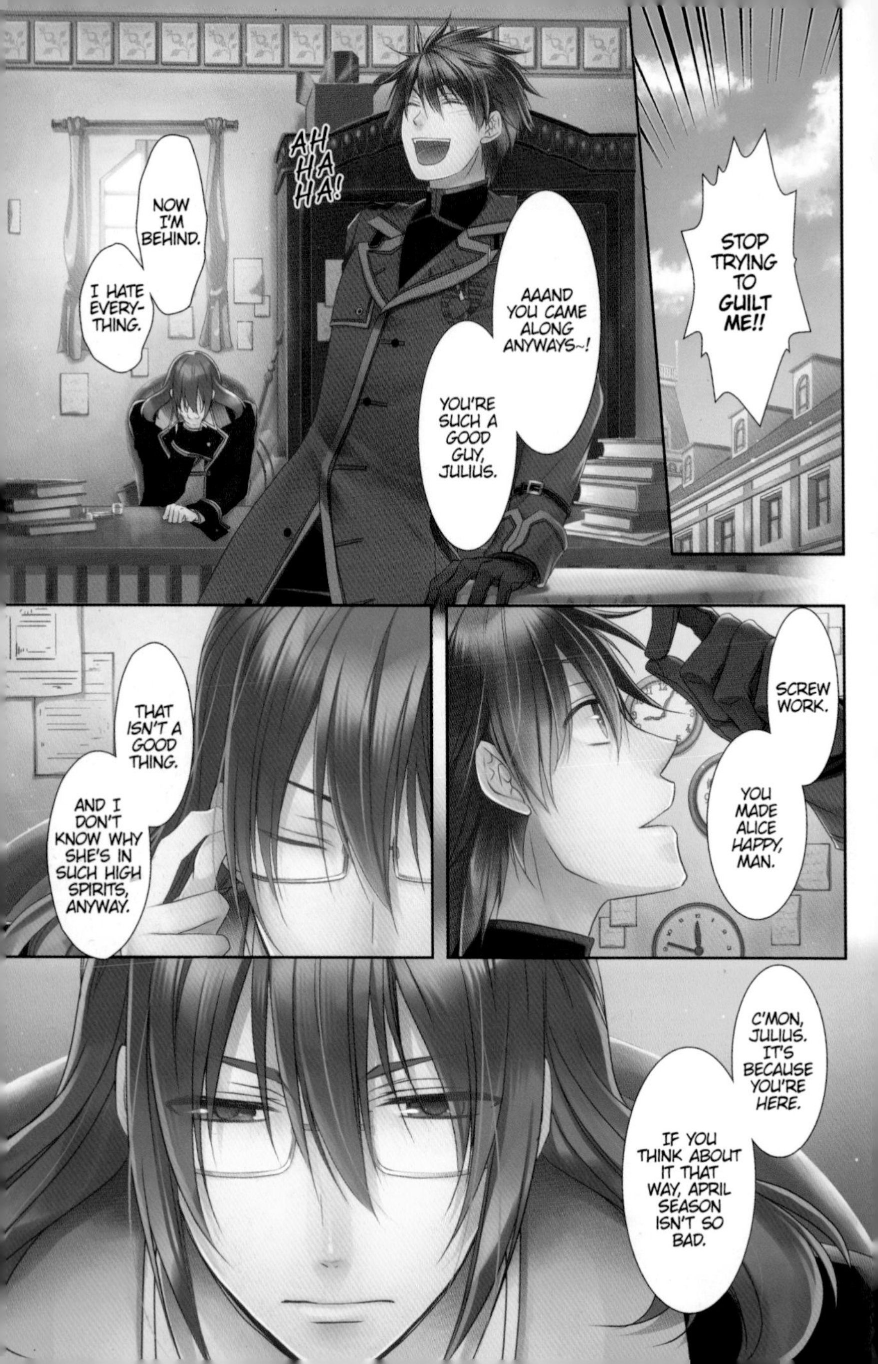
STOP TRYING TO GUILT ME!!
AH HA HA!
AAAND YOU CAME ALONG ANYWAYS~!
YOU'RE SUCH A GOOD GUY, JULIUS.
NOW I'M BEHIND.
I HATE EVERY-THING.
SCREW WORK.
YOU MADE ALICE HAPPY, MAN.
THAT ISN'T A GOOD THING.
AND I DON'T KNOW WHY SHE'S IN SUCH HIGH SPIRITS, ANYWAY.
C'MON, JULIUS. IT'S BECAUSE YOU'RE HERE.
IF YOU THINK ABOUT IT THAT WAY, APRIL SEASON ISN'T SO BAD.

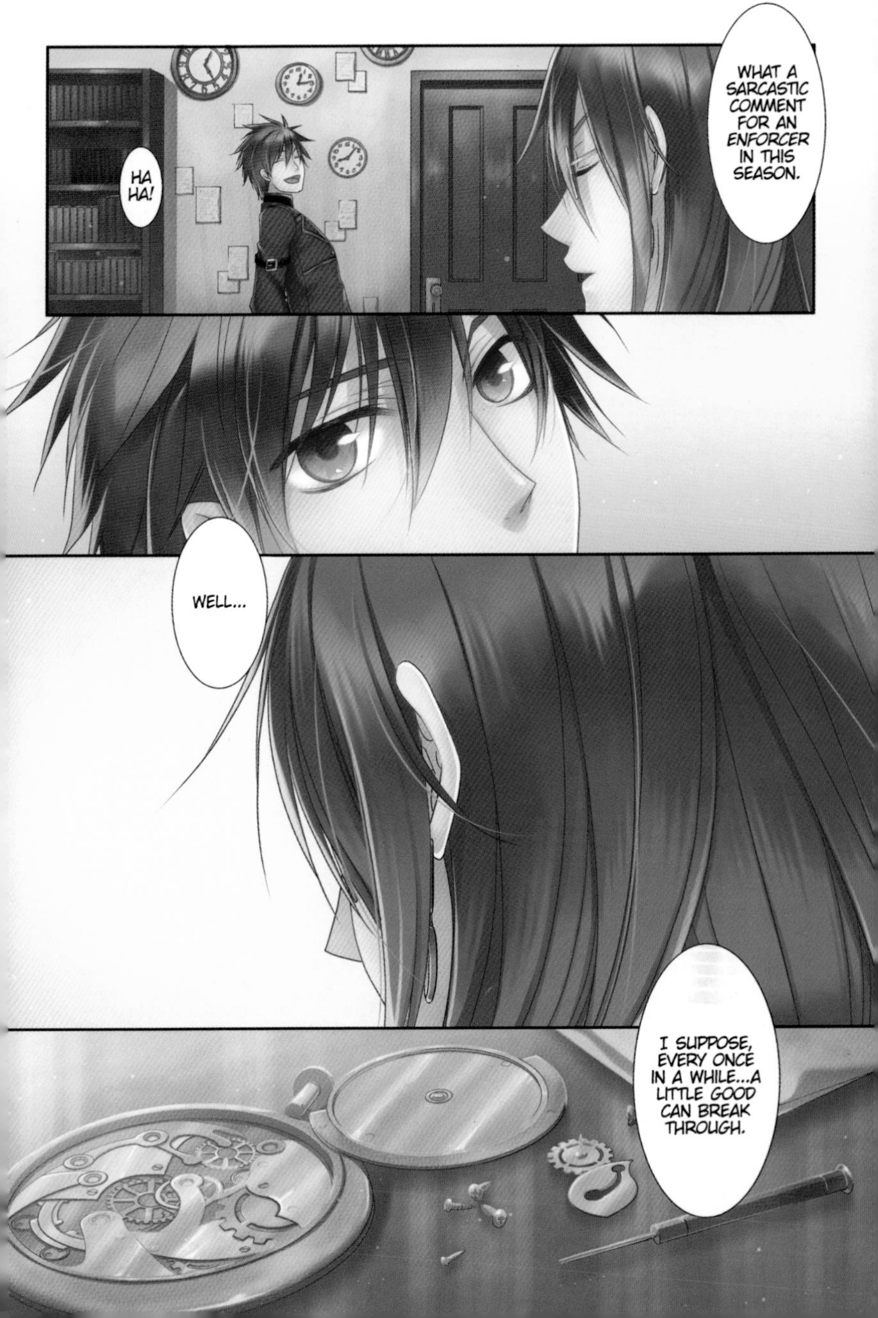
WHAT A SARCASTIC COMMENT FOR AN ENFORCER IN THIS SEASON.
HA HA!
WELL...
I SUPPOSE, EVERY ONCE IN A WHILE...A LITTLE GOOD CAN BREAK THROUGH.

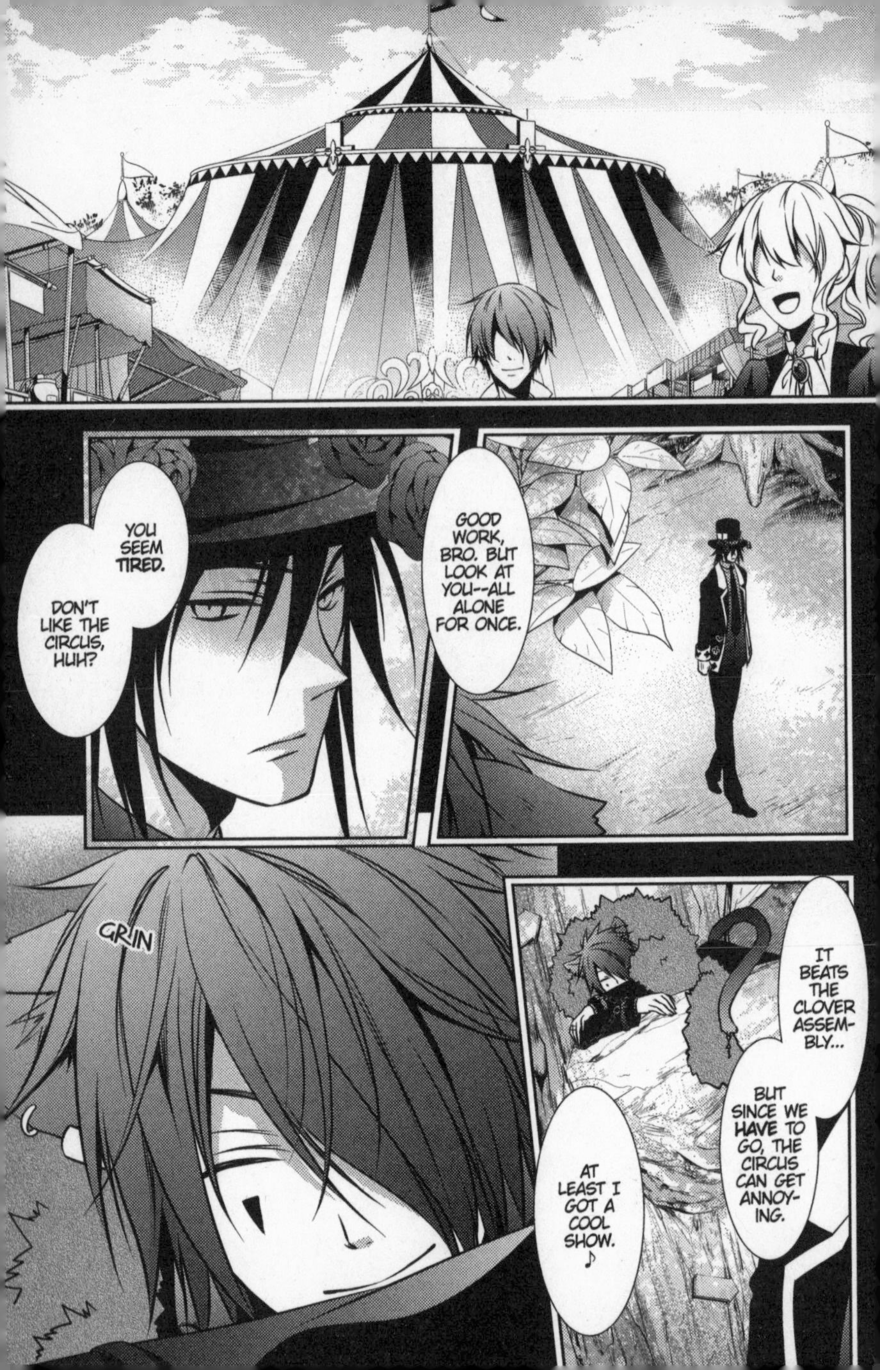
GOOD WORK, BRO. BUT LOOK AT YOU--ALL ALONE FOR ONCE.
YOU SEEM TIRED.
DON'T LIKE THE CIRCUS, HUH?
IT BEATS THE CLOVER ASSEM-BLY...
BUT SINCE WE HAVE TO GO, THE CIRCUS CAN GET ANNOY-ING.
AT LEAST I GOT A COOL SHOW. ♪
GRIN

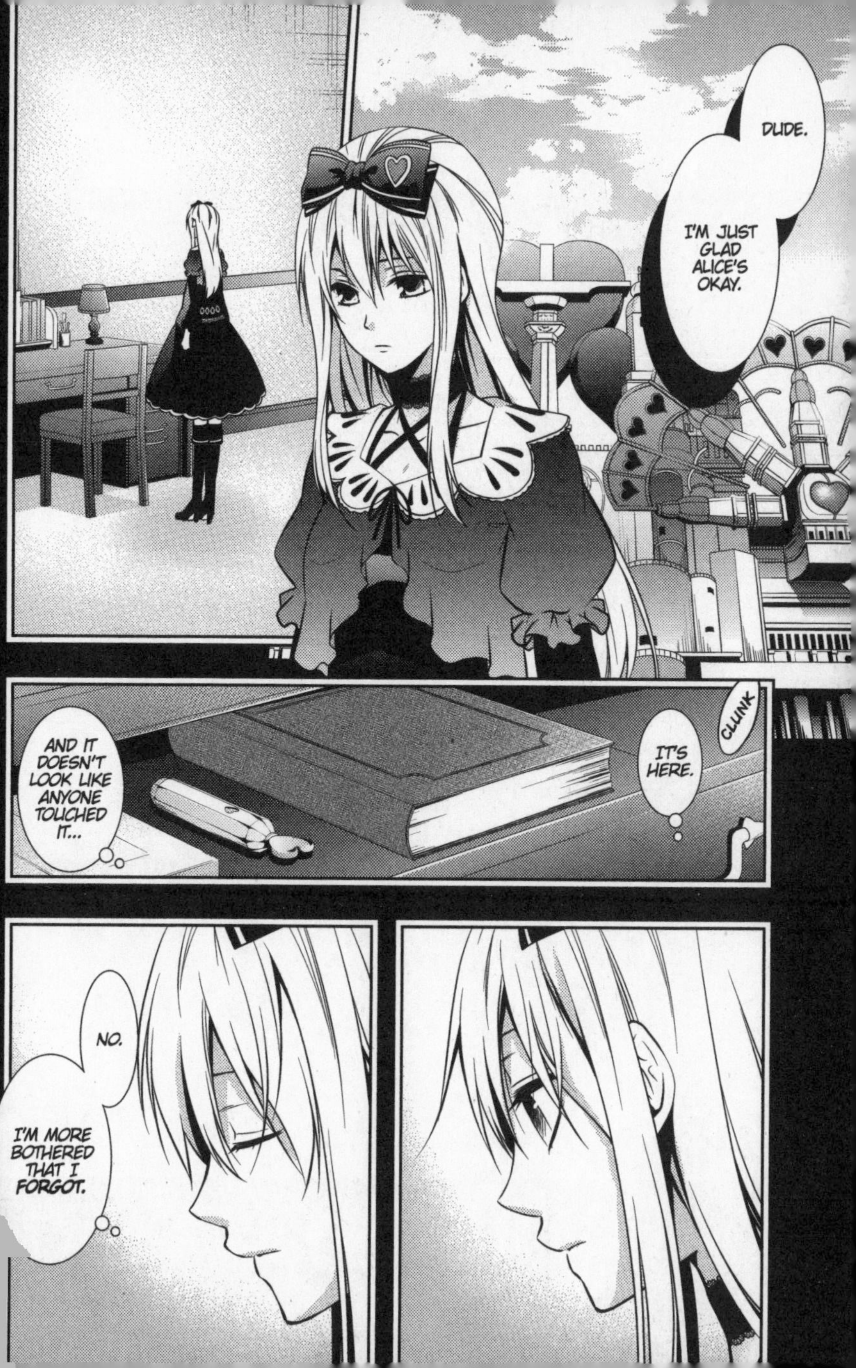
DUDE.
I'M JUST GLAD ALICE'S OKAY.
CLUNK
IT'S HERE.
AND IT DOESN'T LOOK LIKE ANYONE TOUCHED IT...
NO.
I'M MORE BOTHERED THAT I FORGOT.

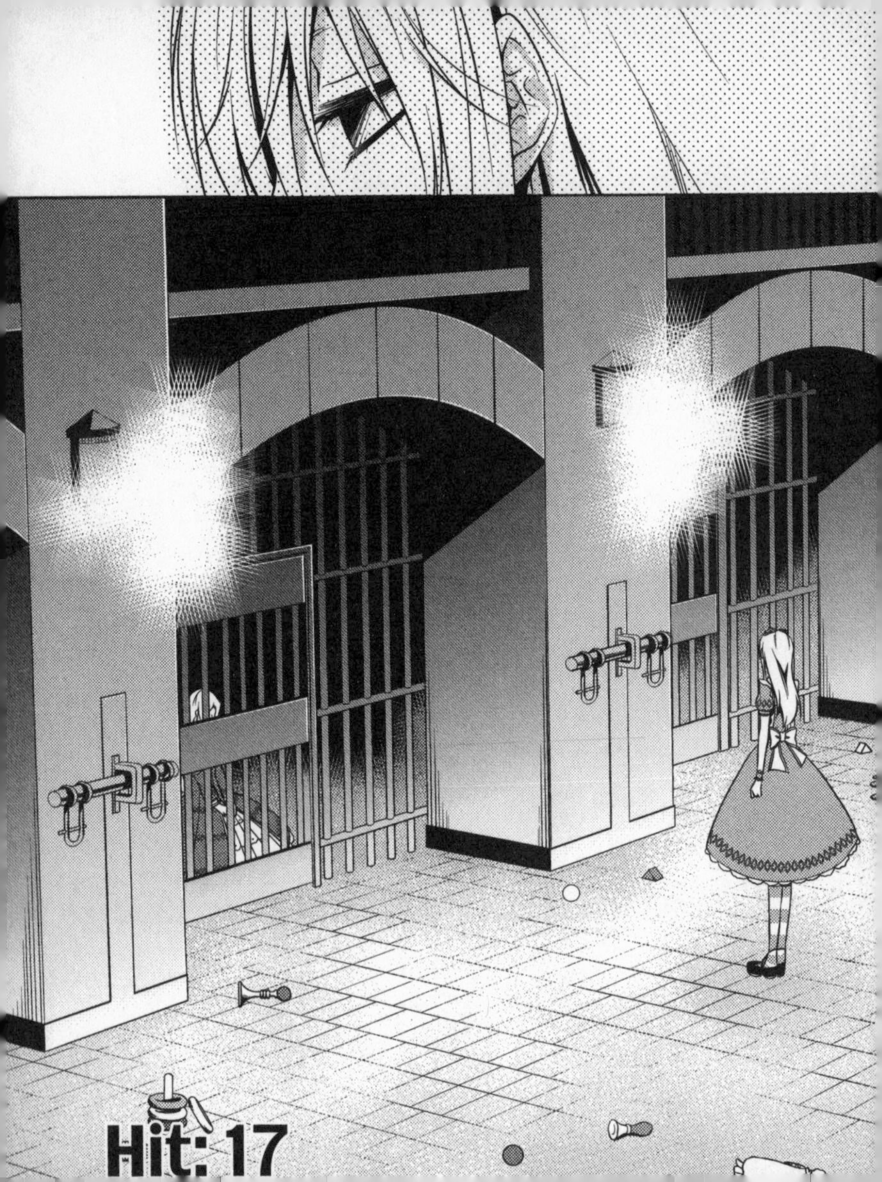
Hit: 17

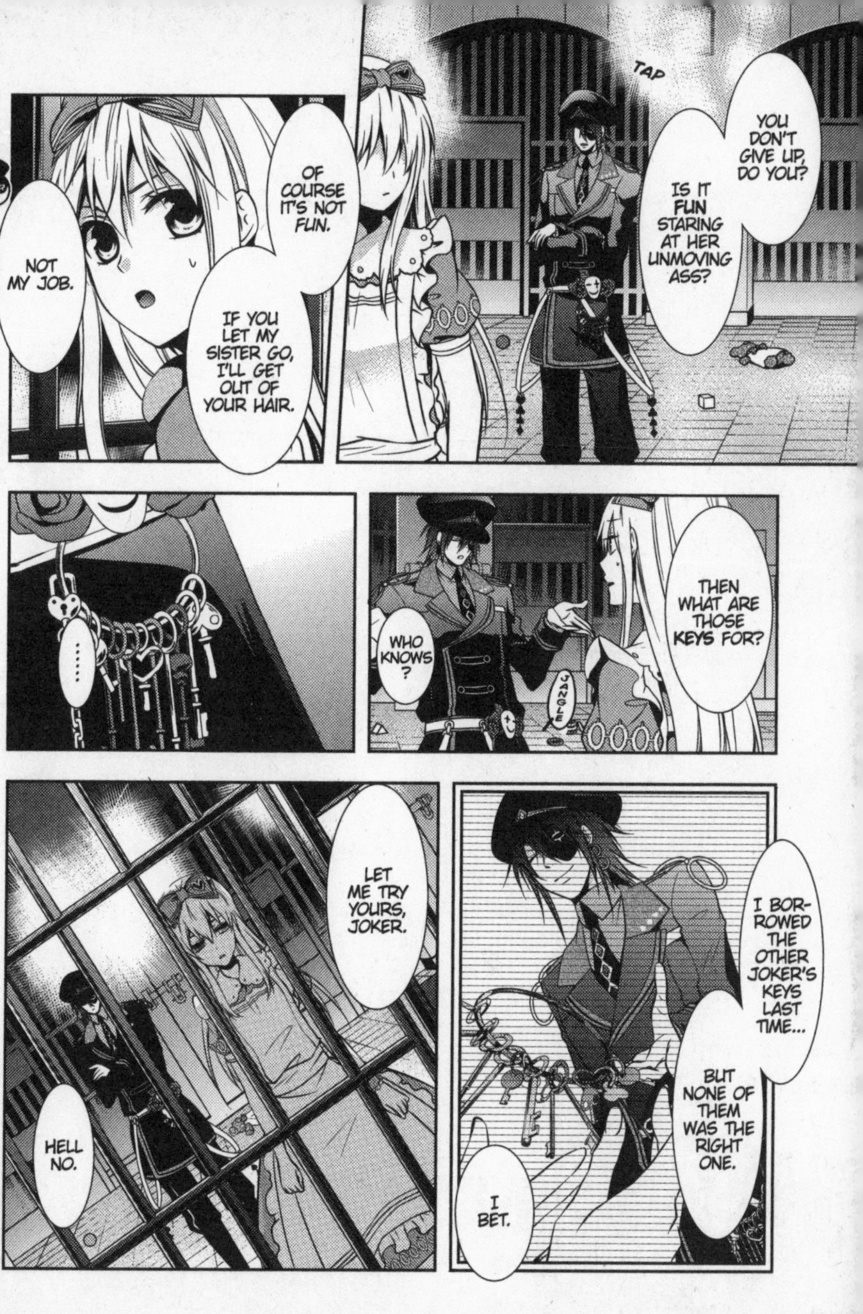
TAP
YOU DON'T GIVE UP, DO YOU?
IS IT FUN STARING AT HER UNMOVING ASS?
OF COURSE IT'S NOT FUN.
IF YOU LET MY SISTER GO, I'LL GET OUT OF YOUR HAIR.
NOT MY JOB.
THEN WHAT ARE THOSE KEYS FOR?
JANGLE
WHO KNOWS?
......
I BOR-ROWED THE OTHER JOKER'S KEYS LAST TIME...
BUT NONE OF THEM WAS THE RIGHT ONE.
I BET.
LET ME TRY YOURS, JOKER.
HELL NO.

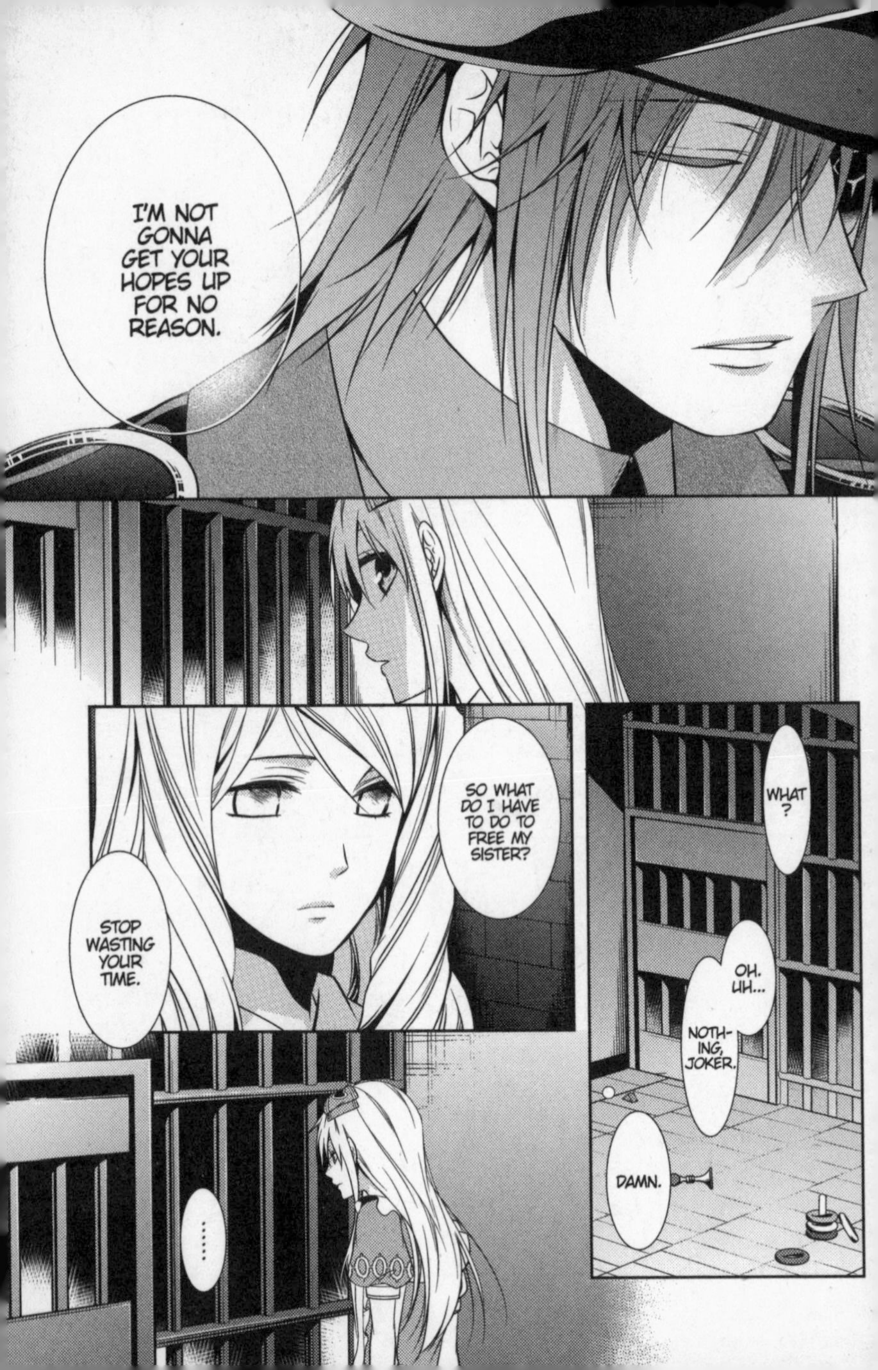
I'M NOT GONNA GET YOUR HOPES UP FOR NO REASON.
WHAT?
OH. UH...
NOTH-ING, JOKER.
DAMN.
SO WHAT DO I HAVE TO DO TO FREE MY SISTER?
STOP WASTING YOUR TIME.
......

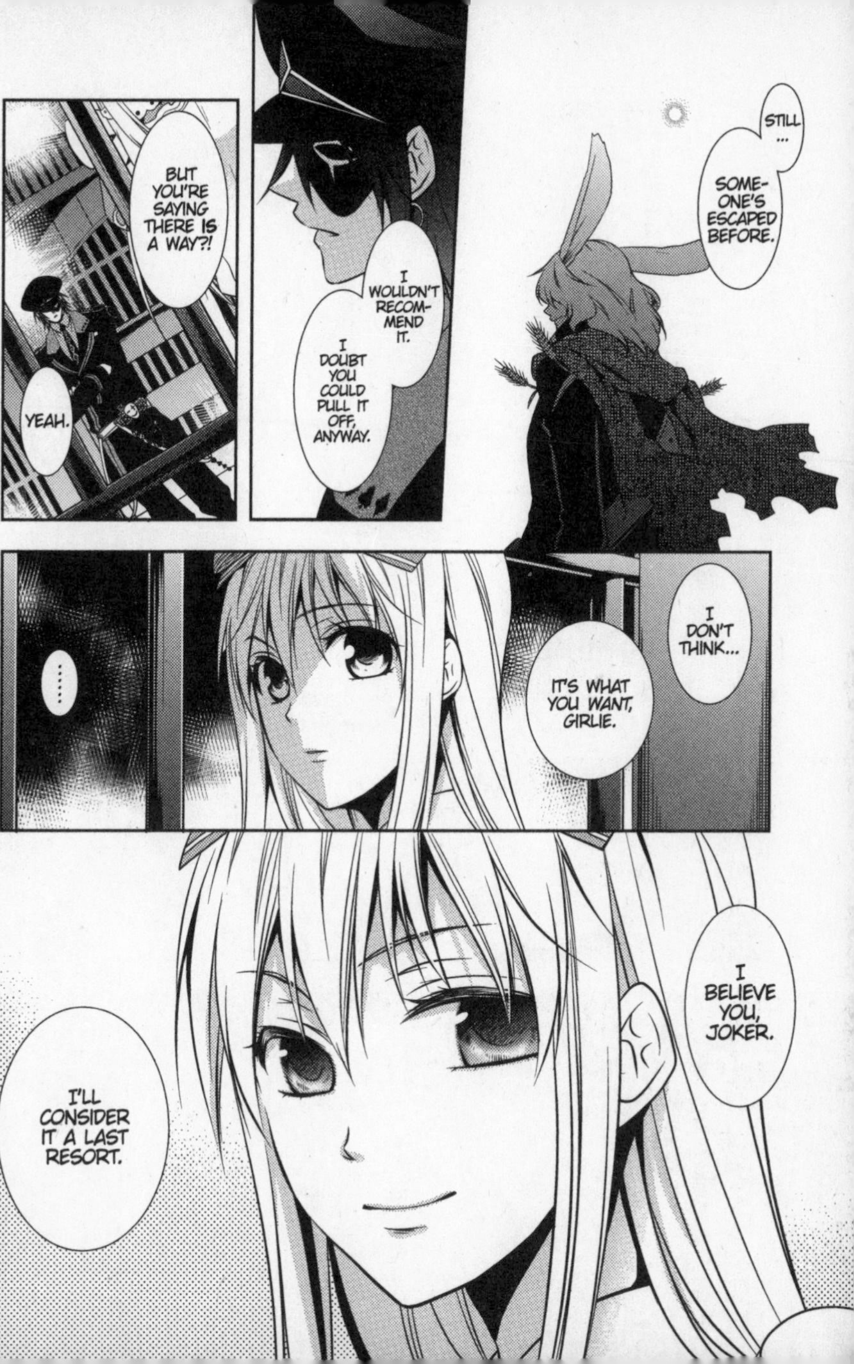
STILL ...
SOME-ONE'S ESCAPED BEFORE.
I WOULDN'T RECOMM-MEND IT.
I DOUBT YOU COULD PULL IT OFF, ANYWAY.
BUT YOU'RE SAYING THERE IS A WAY?!
YEAH.
I DON'T THINK...
IT'S WHAT YOU WANT, GIRLIE.
......
I BELIEVE YOU, JOKER.
I'LL CONSIDER IT A LAST RESORT.

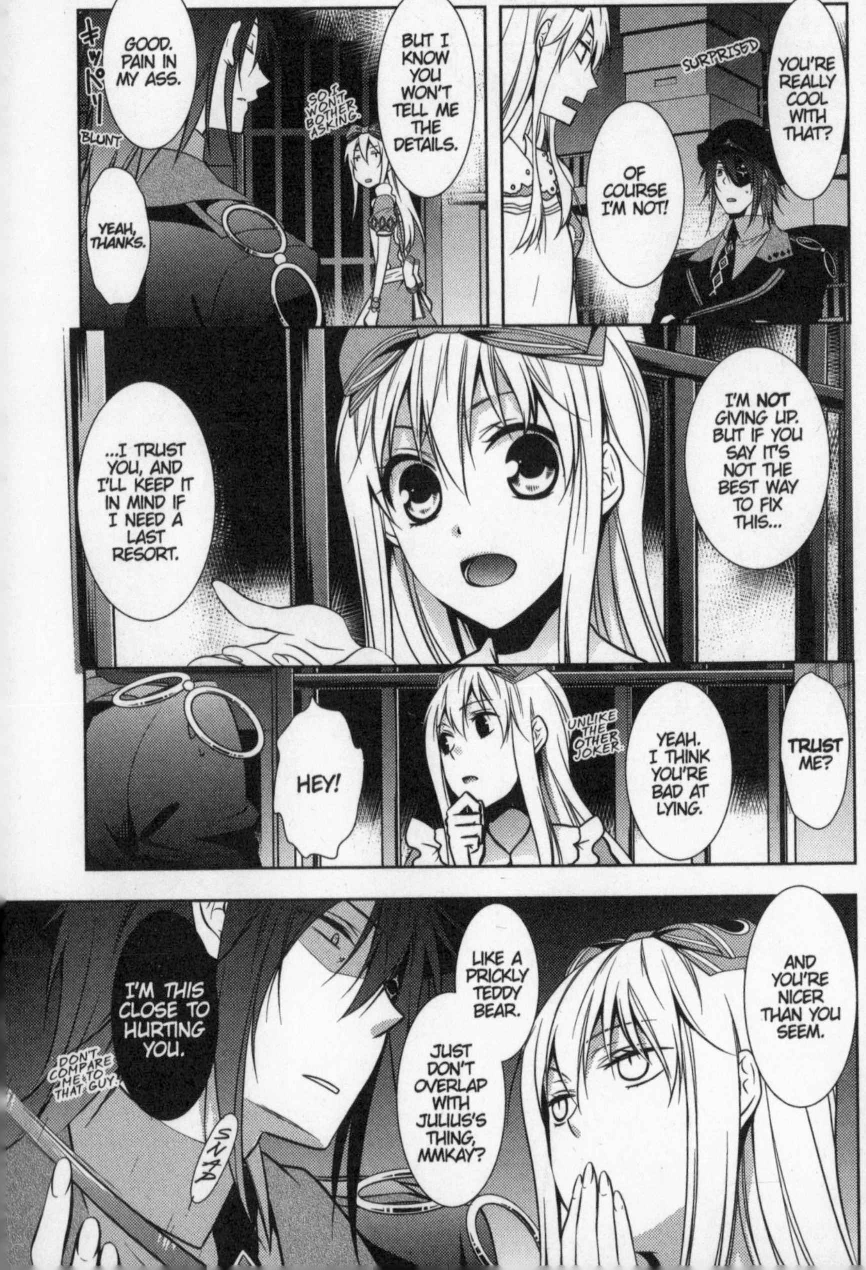
YOU'RE REALLY COOL WITH THAT?
SURPRISED
OF COURSE I'M NOT!
BUT I KNOW YOU WON'T TELL ME THE DETAILS.
SO I WON'T BOTHER ASKING.
GOOD. PAIN IN MY ASS.
キッパリ
BLUNT
YEAH, THANKS.
I'M NOT GIVING UP. BUT IF YOU SAY IT'S NOT THE BEST WAY TO FIX THIS...
...I TRUST YOU, AND I'LL KEEP IT IN MIND IF I NEED A LAST RESORT.
TRUST ME?
YEAH. I THINK YOU'RE BAD AT LYING.
UNLIKE THE OTHER JOKER.
HEY!
AND YOU'RE NICER THAN YOU SEEM.
LIKE A PRICKLY TEDDY BEAR.
JUST DON'T OVERLAP WITH JULIUS'S THING, MMKAY?
SNAP
I'M THIS CLOSE TO HURTING YOU.
DON'T COMPARE ME TO THAT GUY.

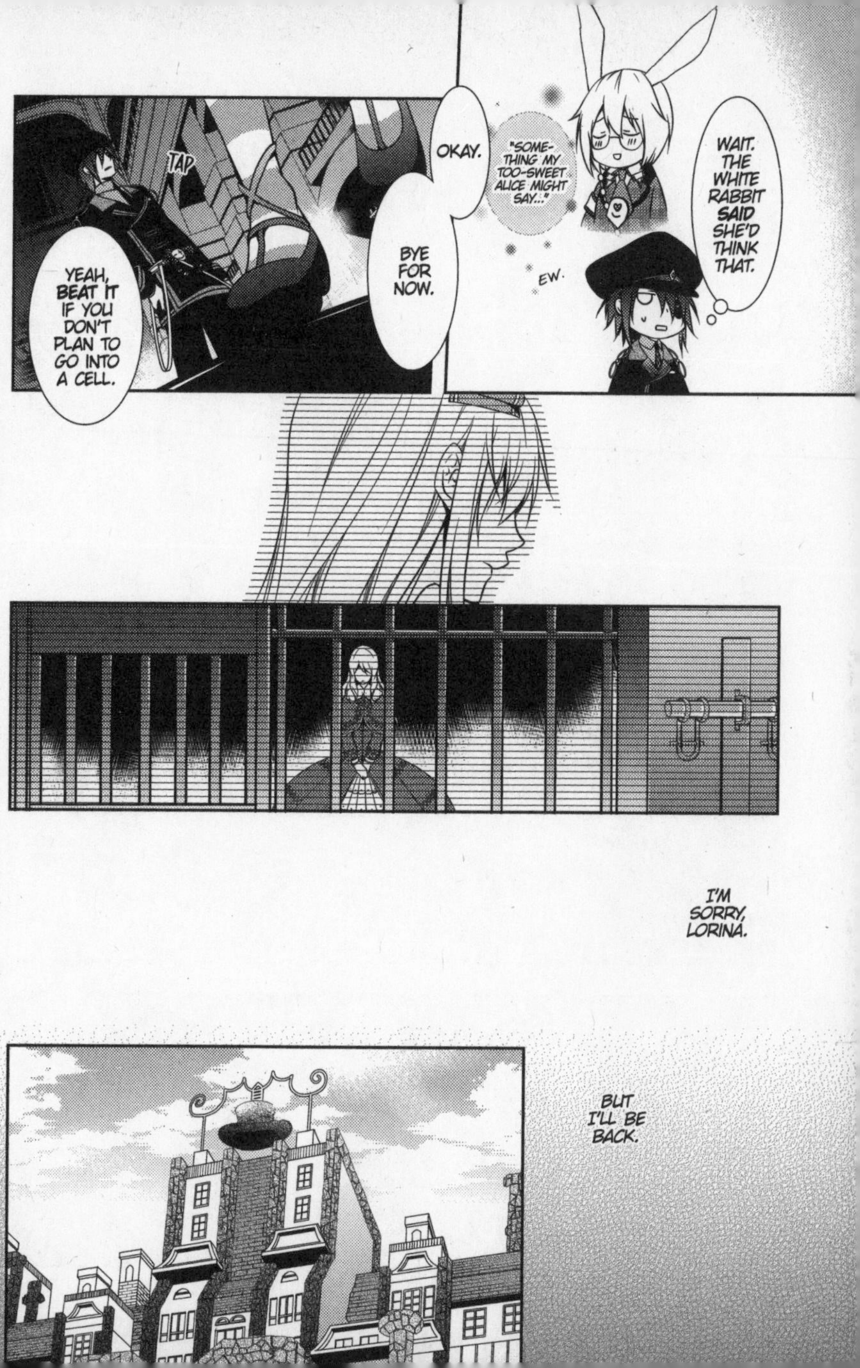
WAIT. THE WHITE RABBIT SAID SHE'D THINK THAT.
"SOME-THING MY TOO-SWEET ALICE MIGHT SAY..."
EW.
OKAY.
BYE FOR NOW.
TAP
YEAH, BEAT IT IF YOU DON'T PLAN TO GO INTO A CELL.
I'M SORRY, LORINA.
BUT I'LL BE BACK.

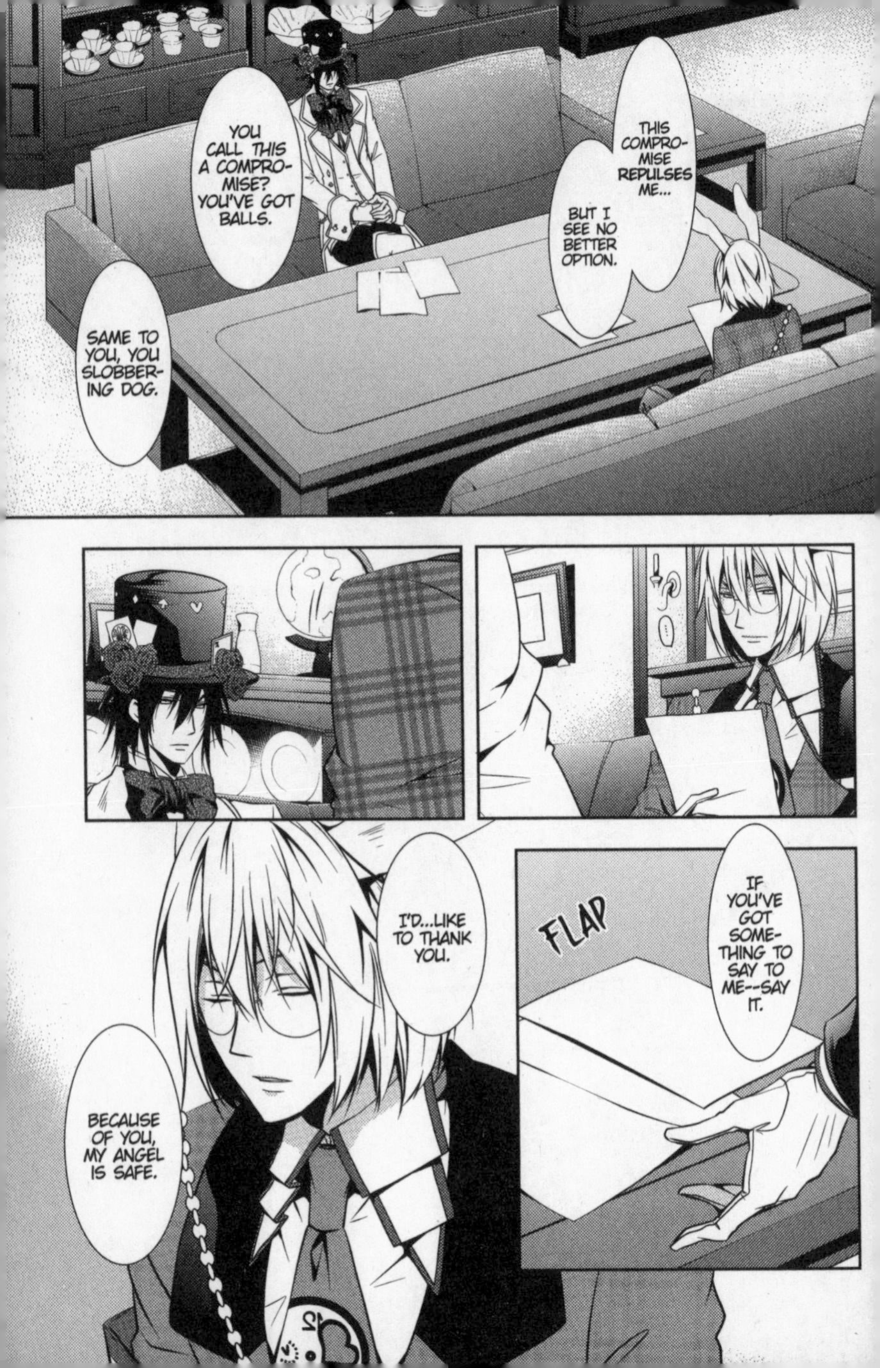
THIS COMPRO-MISE REPULSES ME...
BUT I SEE NO BETTER OPTION.
YOU CALL THIS A COMPRO-MISE? YOU'VE GOT BALLS.
SAME TO YOU, YOU SLOBBER-ING DOG.
IF YOU'VE GOT SOME-THING TO SAY TO ME--SAY IT.
FLAP
I'D...LIKE TO THANK YOU.
BECAUSE OF YOU, MY ANGEL IS SAFE.

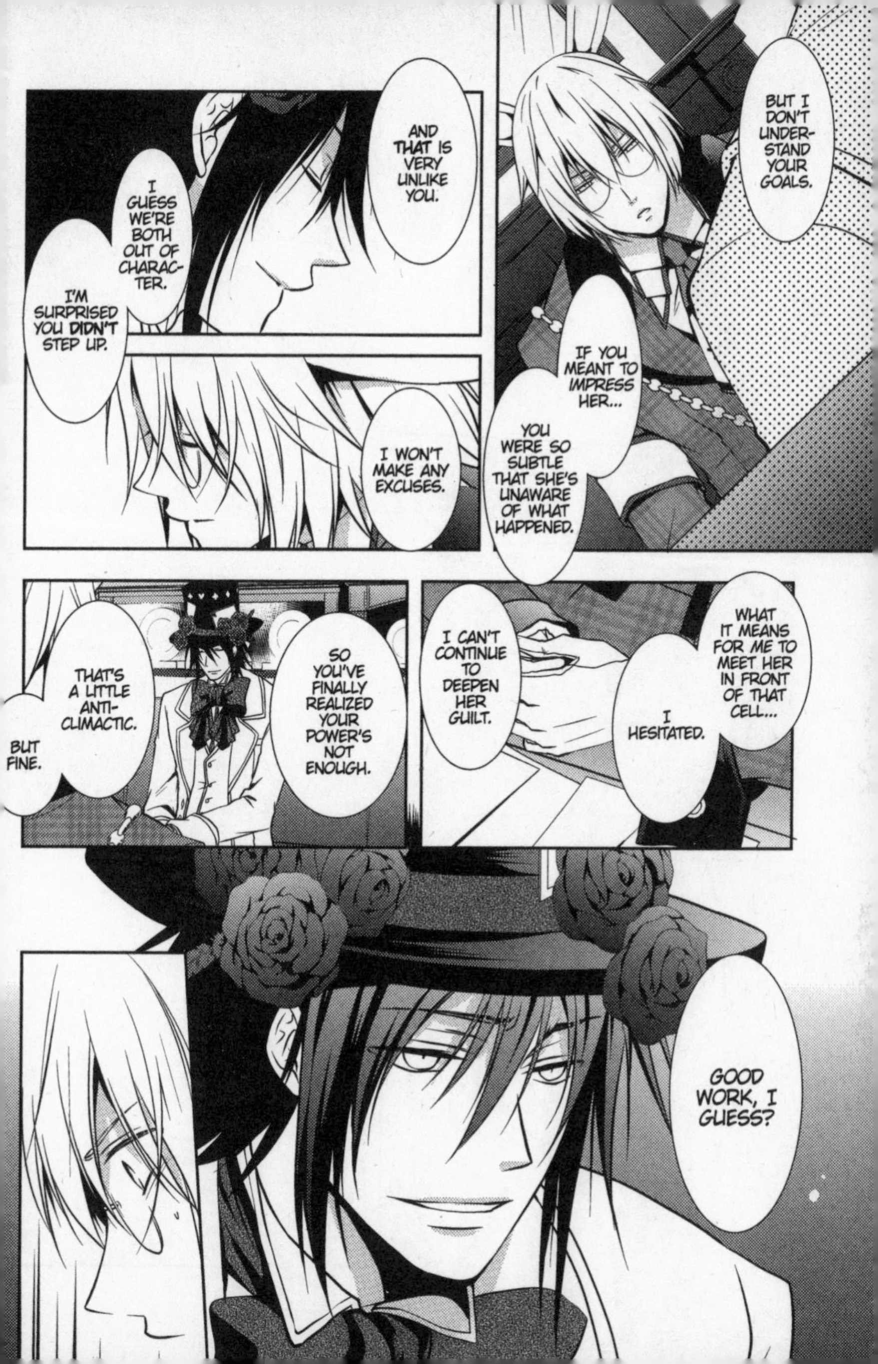
BUT I DON'T UNDERSTAND YOUR GOALS.
IF YOU MEANT TO IMPRESS HER...
YOU WERE SO SUBTLE THAT SHE'S UNAWARE OF WHAT HAPPENED.
AND THAT IS VERY UNLIKE YOU.
I GUESS WE'RE BOTH OUT OF CHARACTER.
I'M SURPRISED YOU DIDN'T STEP UP.
I WON'T MAKE ANY EXCUSES.
WHAT IT MEANS FOR ME TO MEET HER IN FRONT OF THAT CELL...
I HESITATED.
I CAN'T CONTINUE TO DEEPEN HER GUILT.
SO YOU'VE FINALLY REALIZED YOUR POWER'S NOT ENOUGH.
THAT'S A LITTLE ANTI-CLIMACTIC.
BUT FINE.
GOOD WORK, I GUESS?

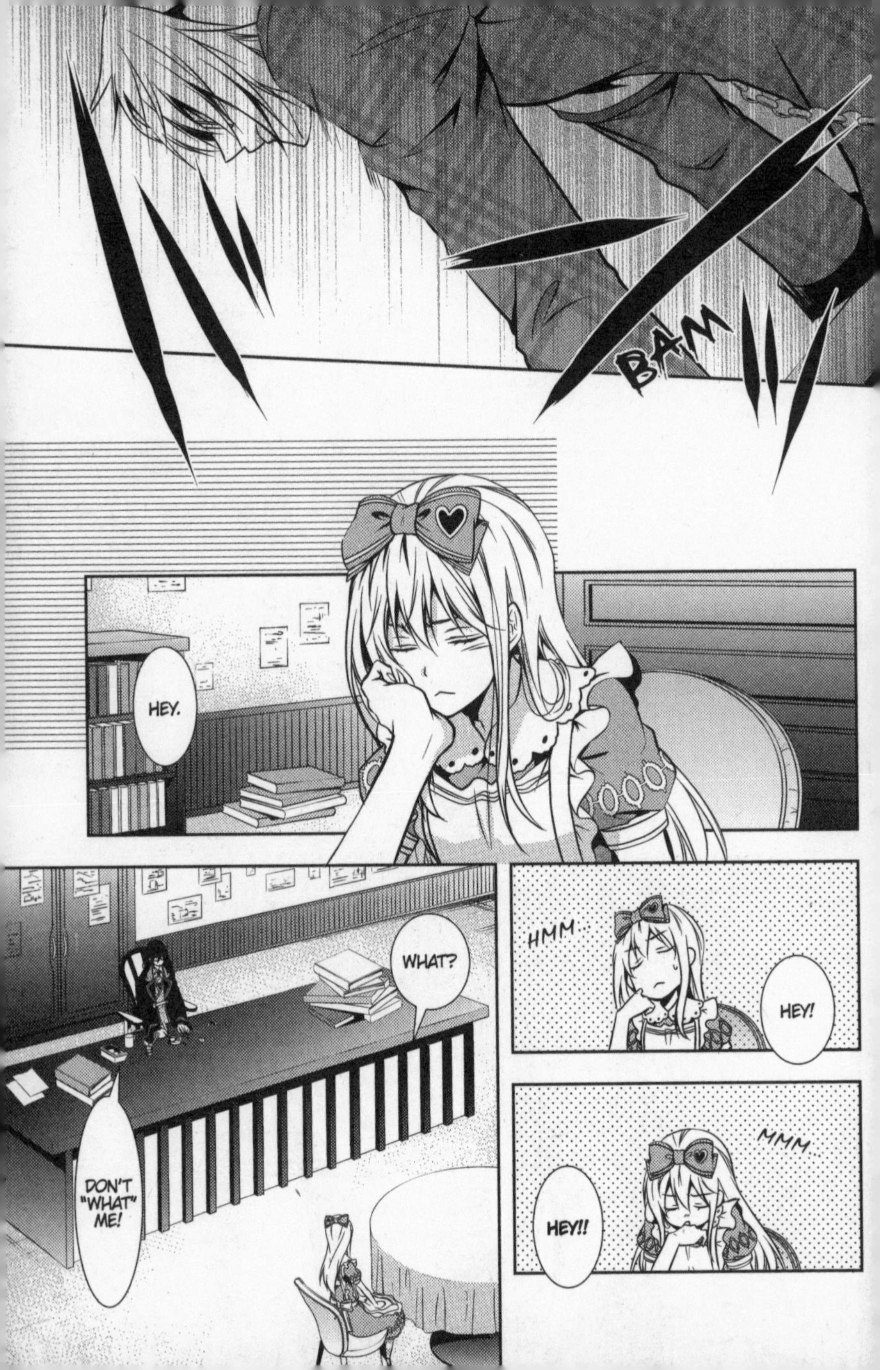
BAM
HEY.
HMM
HEY!
MMM
HEY!!
WHAT?
DON'T "WHAT" ME!

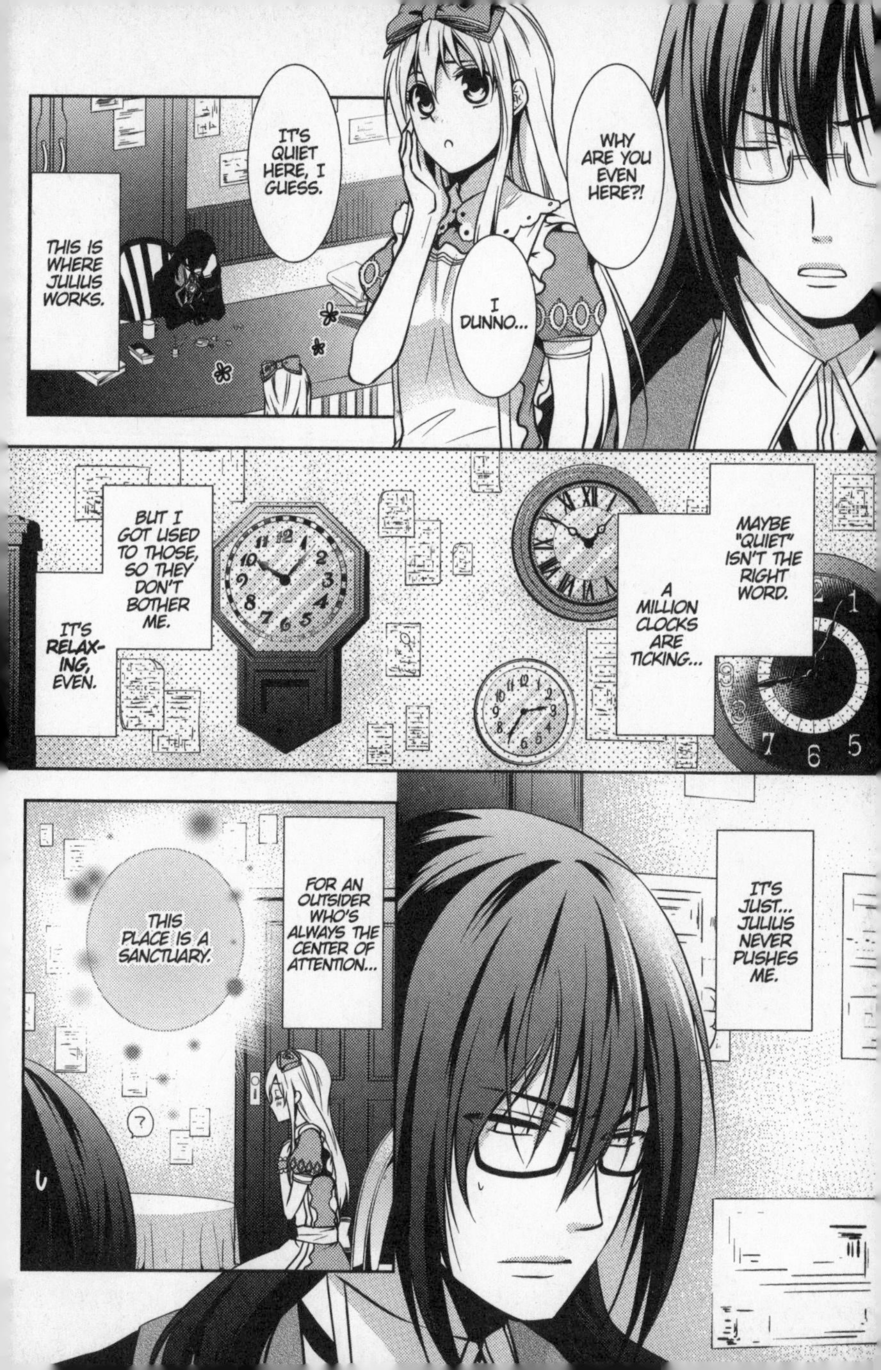
WHY ARE YOU EVEN HERE?!
I DUNNO...
IT'S QUIET HERE, I GUESS.
THIS IS WHERE JULIUS WORKS.
MAYBE "QUIET" ISN'T THE RIGHT WORD.
A MILLION CLOCKS ARE TICKING...
BUT I GOT USED TO THOSE, SO THEY DON'T BOTHER ME.
IT'S RELAX-ING, EVEN.
IT'S JUST... JULIUS NEVER PUSHES ME.
FOR AN OUTSIDER WHO'S ALWAYS THE CENTER OF ATTENTION...
THIS PLACE IS A SANCTUARY.
?

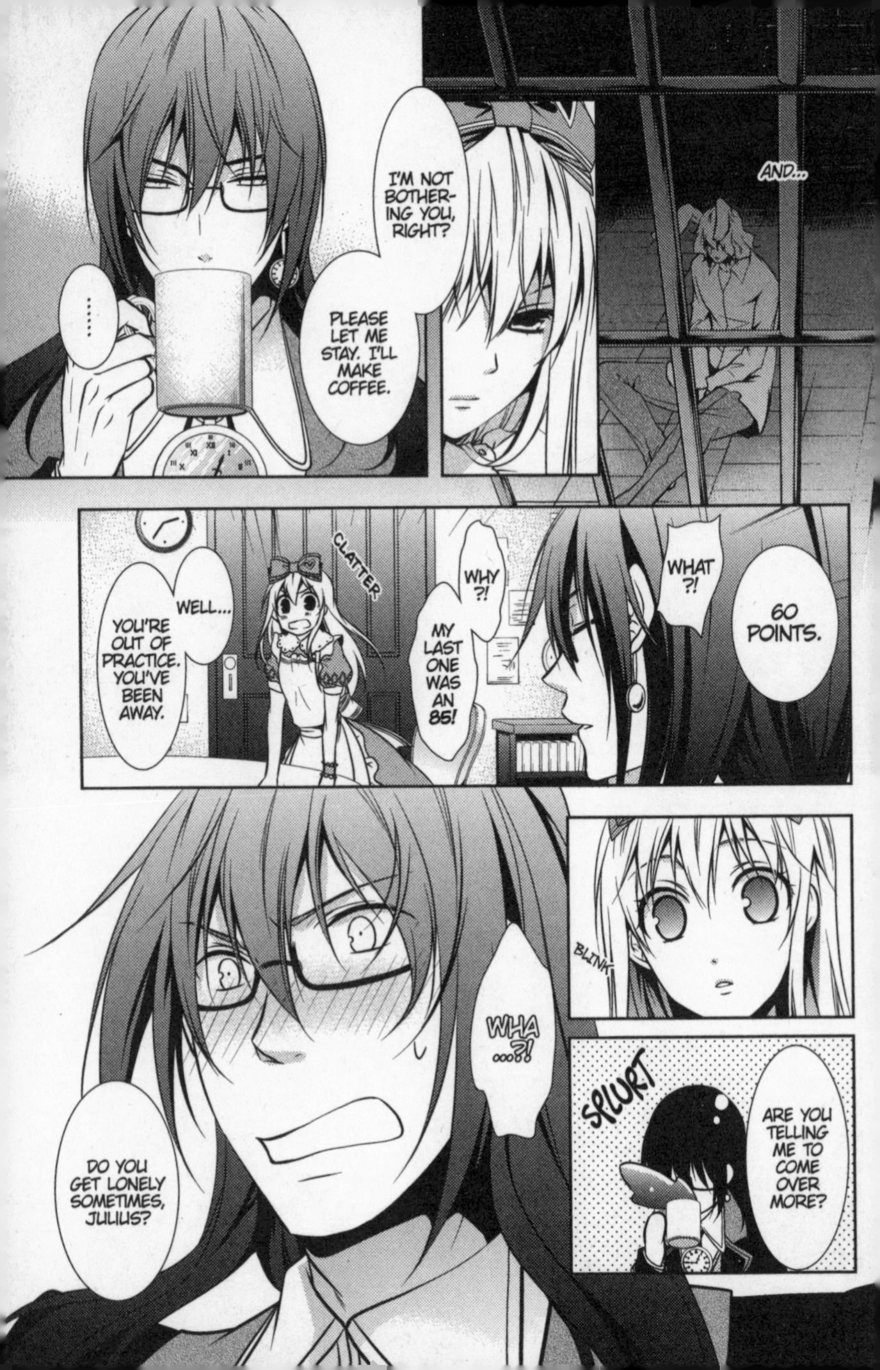
AND...
I'M NOT BOTHERING YOU, RIGHT?
PLEASE LET ME STAY. I'LL MAKE COFFEE.
......
60 POINTS.
WHAT?!
WHY?!
MY LAST ONE WAS AN 85!
CLATTER
WELL...
YOU'RE OUT OF PRACTICE. YOU'VE BEEN AWAY.
BLINK
ARE YOU TELLING ME TO COME OVER MORE?
SPLURT
WHA...?!
DO YOU GET LONELY SOMETIMES, JULIUS?

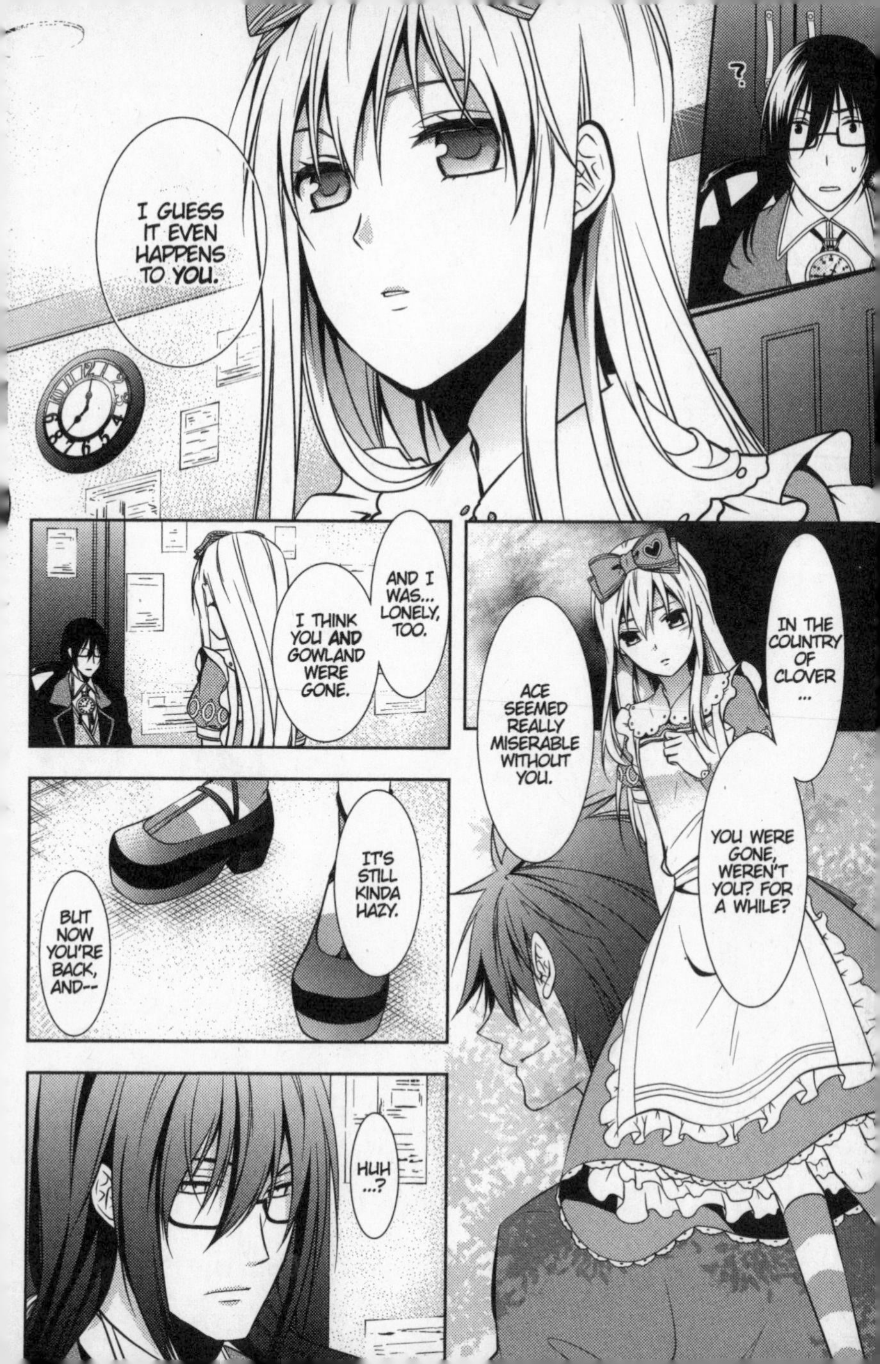
?
I GUESS IT EVEN HAPPENS TO YOU.
IN THE COUNTRY OF CLOVER...
ACE SEEMED REALLY MISERABLE WITHOUT YOU.
YOU WERE GONE, WEREN'T YOU? FOR A WHILE?
AND I WAS... LONELY, TOO.
I THINK YOU AND GOWLAND WERE GONE.
IT'S STILL KINDA HAZY.
BUT NOW YOU'RE BACK, AND--
HUH...?

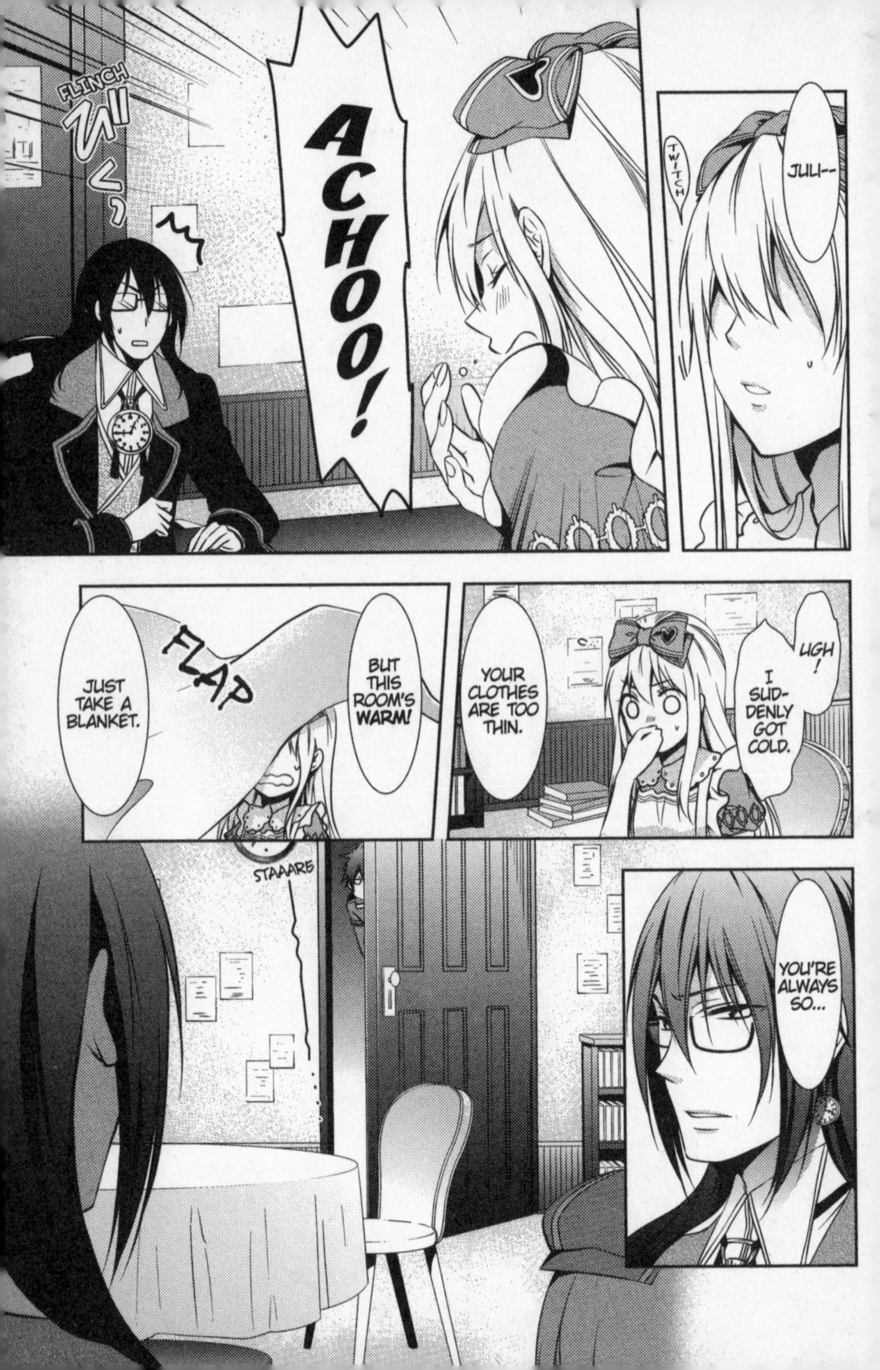
TWITCH
JULI--
ACHOO!
FLINCH
UGH! I SUDDENLY GOT COLD.
YOUR CLOTHES ARE TOO THIN.
BUT THIS ROOM'S WARM!
FLAP
JUST TAKE A BLANKET.
YOU'RE ALWAYS SO...
STAAARE

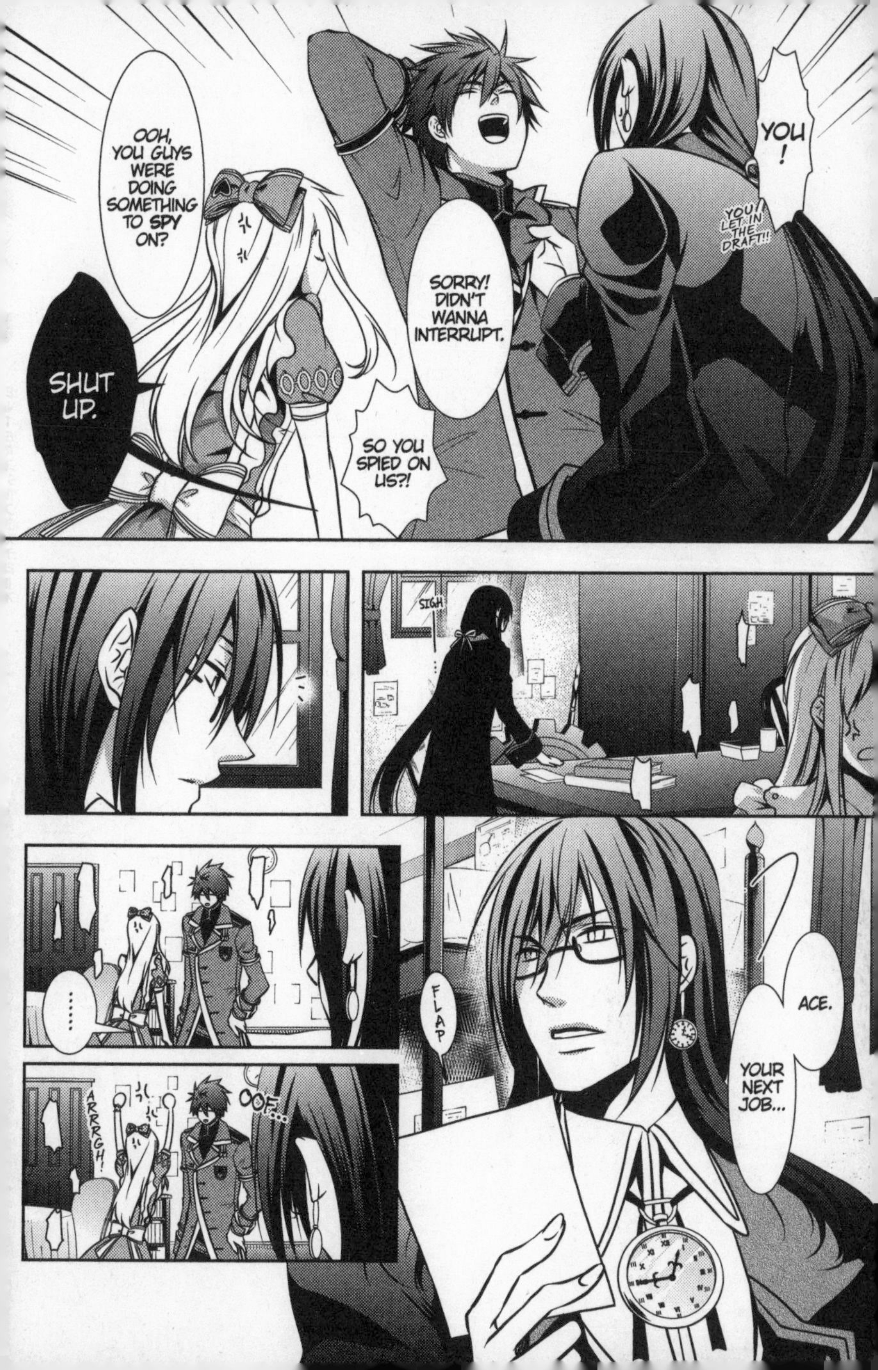
YOU!
YOU! LET IN THE DRAFT!!
SORRY! DIDN'T WANNA INTERRUPT.
SO YOU SPIED ON US?!
OOH, YOU GUYS WERE DOING SOMETHING TO SPY ON?
SHUT UP.
SIGH
...
ACE.
YOUR NEXT JOB...
FLAP
......
OOF...
ARRRGH!

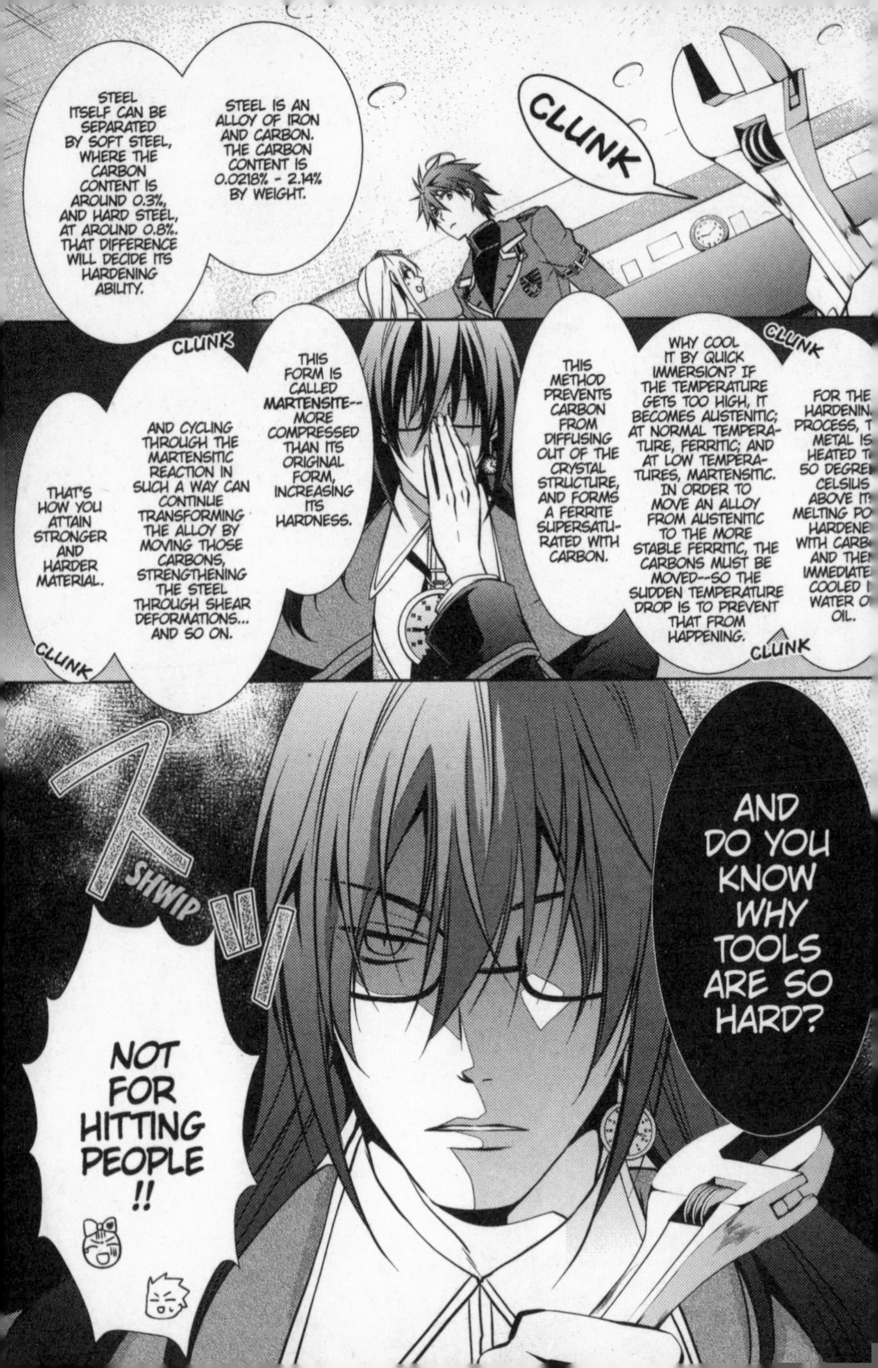
CLUNK
STEEL IS AN ALLOY OF IRON AND CARBON. THE CARBON CONTENT IS 0.0218% - 2.14% BY WEIGHT.
STEEL ITSELF CAN BE SEPARATED BY SOFT STEEL, WHERE THE CARBON CONTENT IS AROUND 0.3%, AND HARD STEEL, AT AROUND 0.8%. THAT DIFFERENCE WILL DECIDE ITS HARDENING ABILITY.
FOR THE HARDENIN PROCESS, T METAL IS HEATED T SO DEGRE CELSIUS ABOVE ITS MELTING PO HARDENE WITH CARBO AND THEN IMMEDIATE COOLED I WATER O OIL.
CLUNK
WHY COOL IT BY QUICK IMMERSION? IF THE TEMPERATURE GETS TOO HIGH, IT BECOMES AUSTENITIC; AT NORMAL TEMPERATURE, FERRITIC; AND AT LOW TEMPERATURES, MARTENSITIC. IN ORDER TO MOVE AN ALLOY FROM AUSTENITIC TO THE MORE STABLE FERRITIC, THE CARBONS MUST BE MOVED--SO THE SUDDEN TEMPERATURE DROP IS TO PREVENT THAT FROM HAPPENING.
CLUNK
THIS METHOD PREVENTS CARBON FROM DIFFUSING OUT OF THE CRYSTAL STRUCTURE, AND FORMS A FERRITE SUPERSATURATED WITH CARBON.
THIS FORM IS CALLED MARTENSITE--MORE COMPRESSED THAN ITS ORIGINAL FORM, INCREASING ITS HARDNESS.
CLUNK
AND CYCLING THROUGH THE MARTENSITIC REACTION IN SUCH A WAY CAN CONTINUE TRANSFORMING THE ALLOY BY MOVING THOSE CARBONS, STRENGTHENING THE STEEL THROUGH SHEAR DEFORMATIONS... AND SO ON.
THAT'S HOW YOU ATTAIN STRONGER AND HARDER MATERIAL.
CLUNK
AND DO YOU KNOW WHY TOOLS ARE SO HARD?
SHWIP
NOT FOR HITTING PEOPLE !!

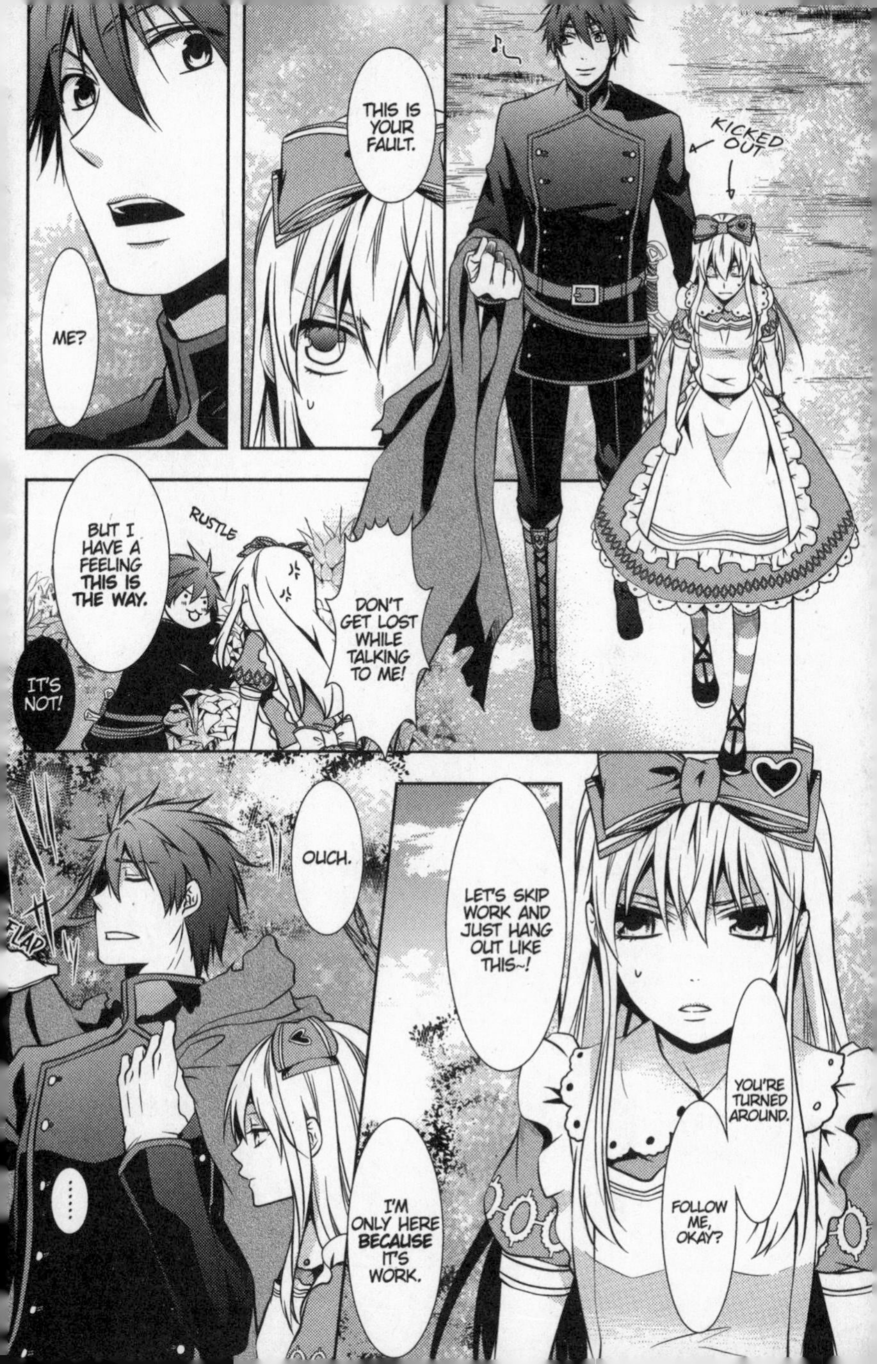
KICKED OUT
THIS IS YOUR FAULT.
ME?
BUT I HAVE A FEELING THIS IS THE WAY.
RUSTLE
IT'S NOT!
DON'T GET LOST WHILE TALKING TO ME!
YOU'RE TURNED AROUND.
FOLLOW ME, OKAY?
LET'S SKIP WORK AND JUST HANG OUT LIKE THIS~!
OUCH.
FLAP
I'M ONLY HERE BECAUSE IT'S WORK.
......

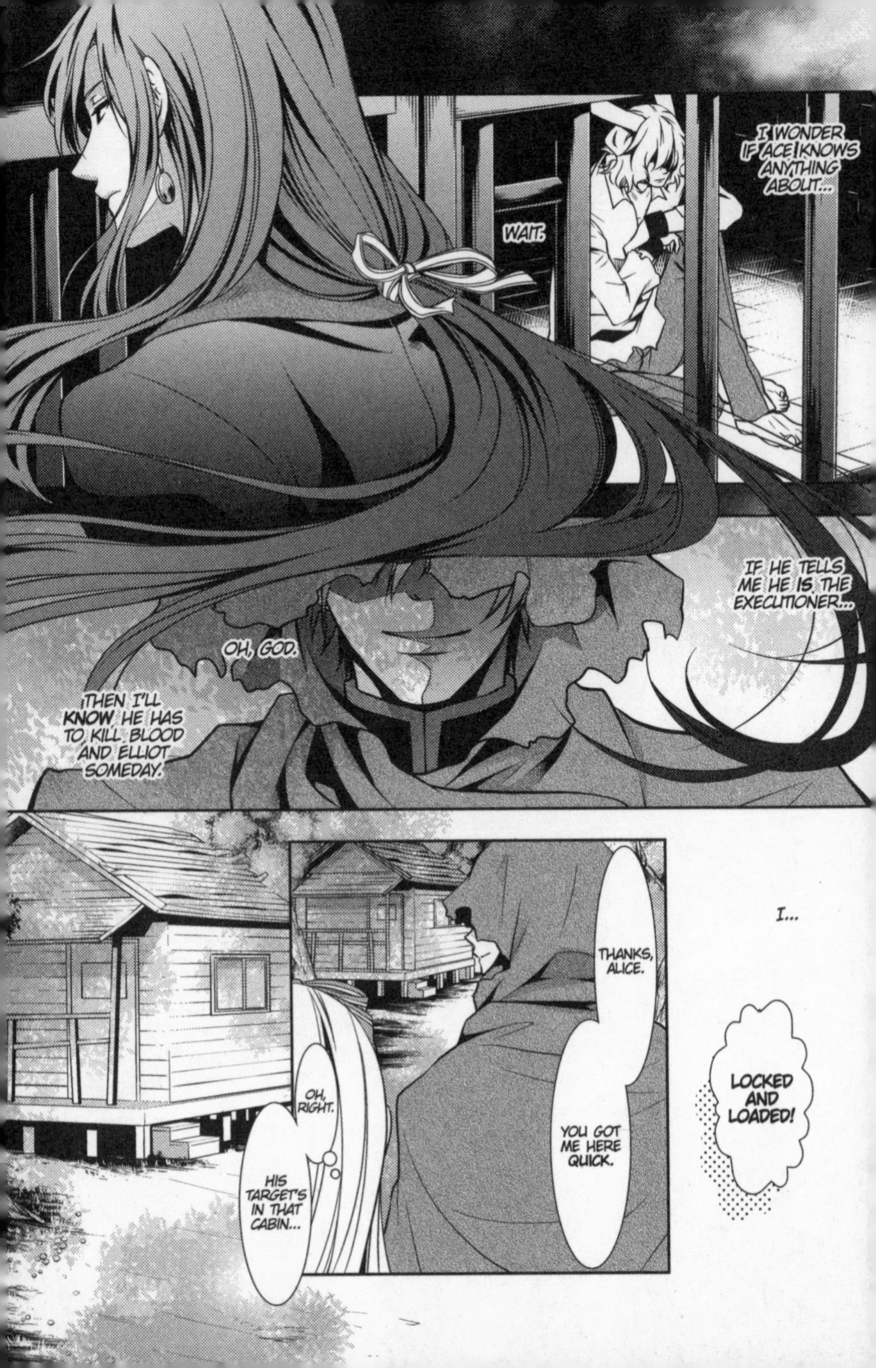
I WONDER IF ACE KNOWS ANYTHING ABOUT...
WAIT.
IF HE TELLS ME HE **IS** THE EXECUTIONER...
OH, GOD.
THEN I'LL **KNOW** HE HAS TO KILL BLOOD AND ELLIOT SOMEDAY.
I...
LOCKED AND LOADED!
THANKS, ALICE.
YOU GOT ME HERE QUICK.
OH, RIGHT.
HIS TARGET'S IN THAT CABIN...

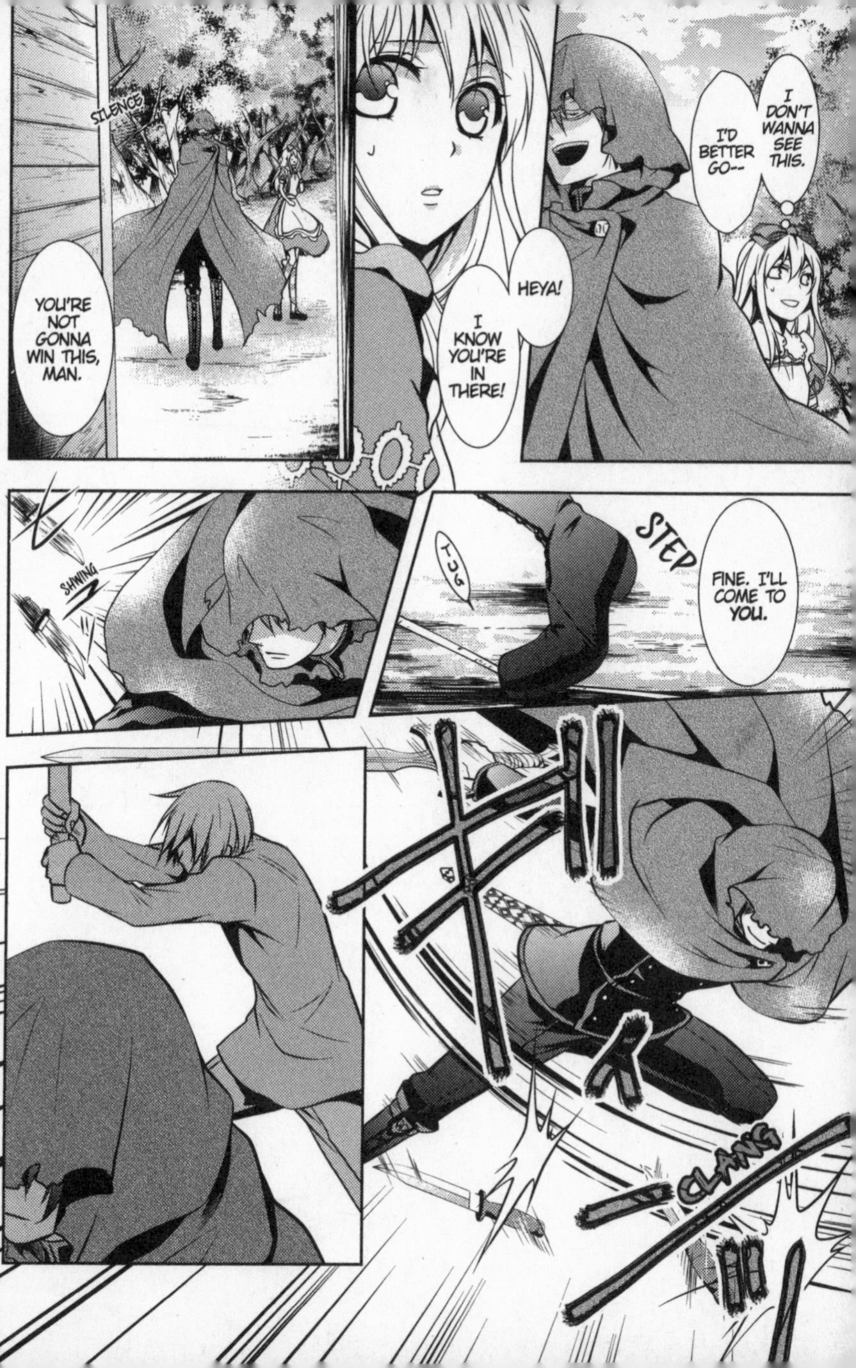
I DON'T WANNA SEE THIS.
I'D BETTER GO--
HEYA!
I KNOW YOU'RE IN THERE!
SILENCE
YOU'RE NOT GONNA WIN THIS, MAN.
FINE. I'LL COME TO YOU.
STEP
TUG
SHWING
CLANG

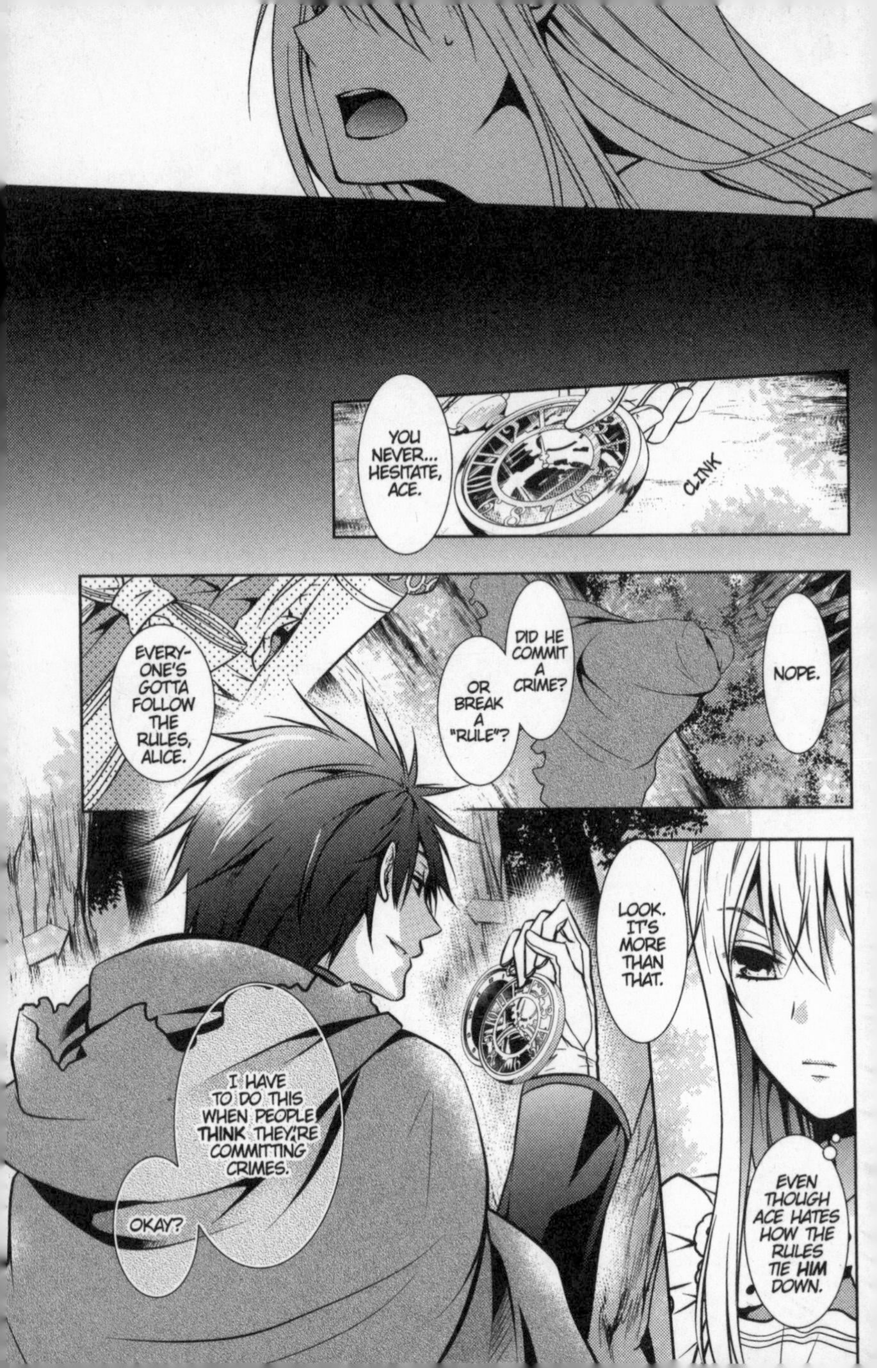
YOU NEVER... HESITATE, ACE.
CLINK
NOPE.
DID HE COMMIT A CRIME?
OR BREAK A "RULE"?
EVERY-ONE'S GOTTA FOLLOW THE RULES, ALICE.
LOOK. IT'S MORE THAN THAT.
I HAVE TO DO THIS WHEN PEOPLE **THINK** THEY'RE COMMITTING CRIMES.
OKAY?
EVEN THOUGH ACE HATES HOW THE RULES TIE **HIM** DOWN.

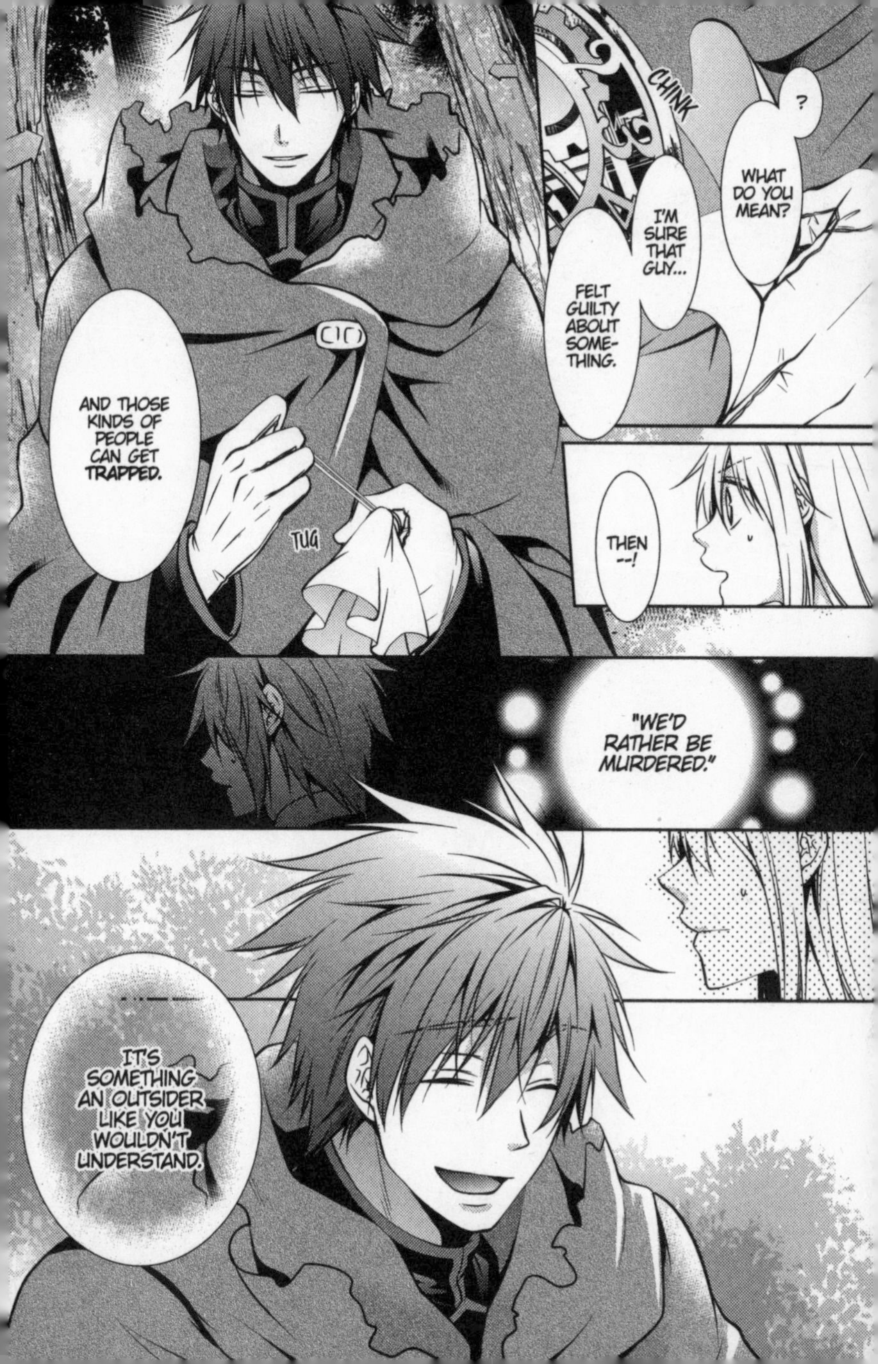
CHINK
?
WHAT DO YOU MEAN?
I'M SURE THAT GUY...
FELT GUILTY ABOUT SOME-THING.
THEN--!
AND THOSE KINDS OF PEOPLE CAN GET TRAPPED.
TUG
"WE'D RATHER BE MURDERED."
IT'S SOMETHING AN OUTSIDER LIKE YOU WOULDN'T UNDERSTAND.

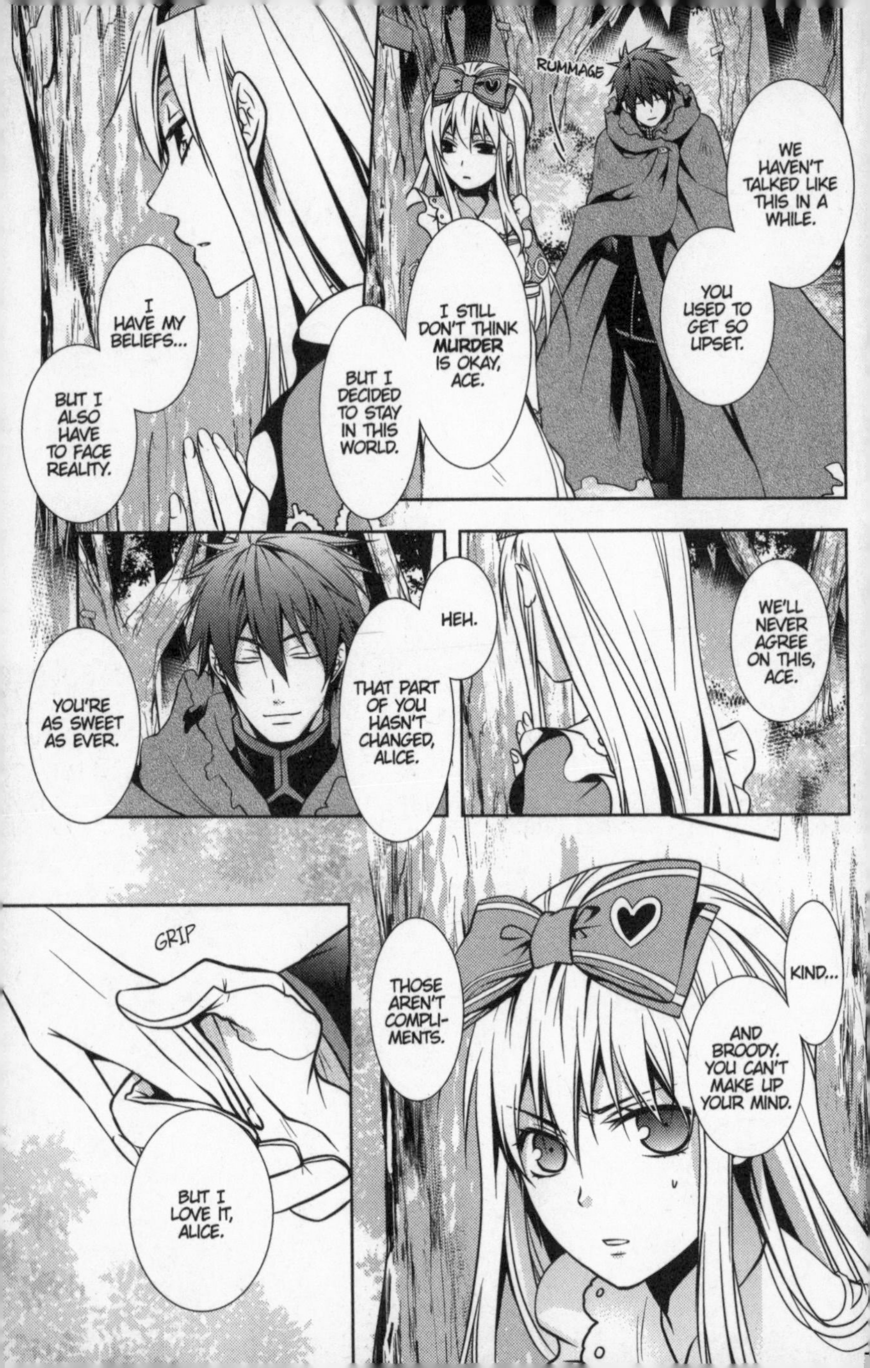
RUMMAGE
WE HAVEN'T TALKED LIKE THIS IN A WHILE.
YOU USED TO GET SO UPSET.
I STILL DON'T THINK **MURDER** IS OKAY, ACE.
BUT I DECIDED TO STAY IN THIS WORLD.
I HAVE MY BELIEFS...
BUT I ALSO HAVE TO FACE REALITY.
WE'LL NEVER AGREE ON THIS, ACE.
HEH.
THAT PART OF YOU HASN'T CHANGED, ALICE.
YOU'RE AS SWEET AS EVER.
KIND...
AND BROODY. YOU CAN'T MAKE UP YOUR MIND.
THOSE AREN'T COMPLI-MENTS.
GRIP
BUT I LOVE IT, ALICE.

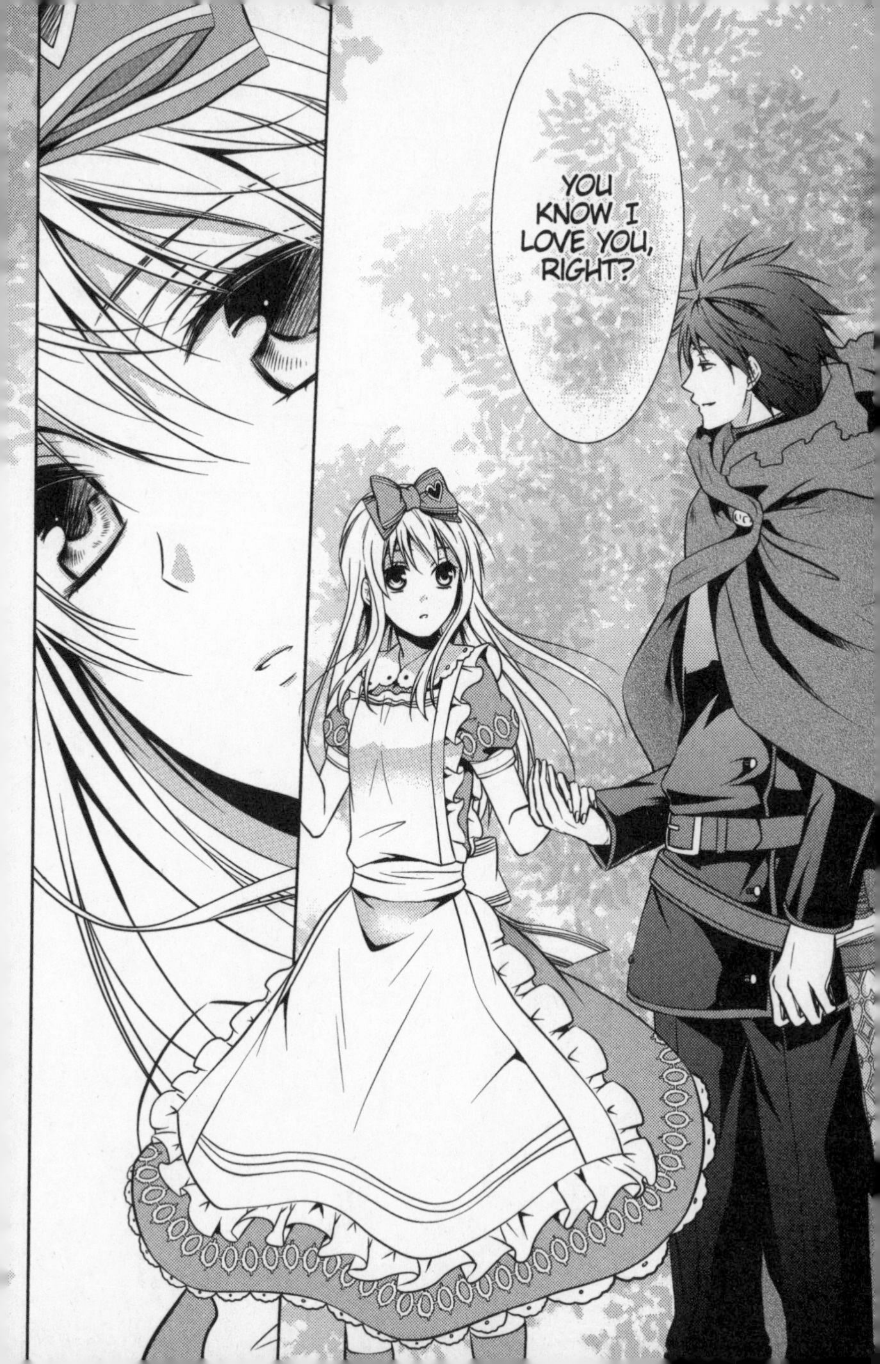
YOU KNOW I LOVE YOU, RIGHT?

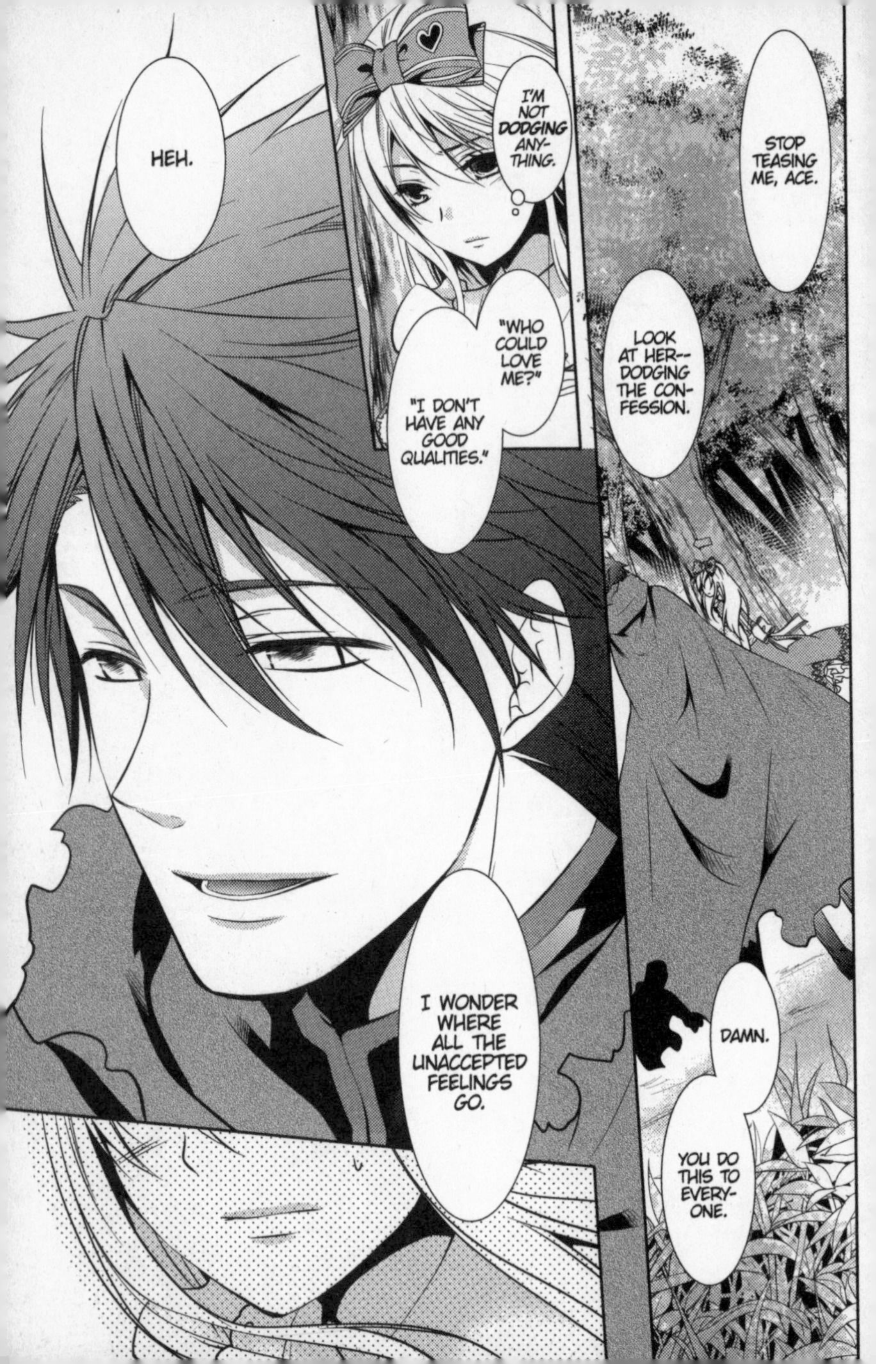
STOP TEASING ME, ACE.
LOOK AT HER-- DODGING THE CONFESSION.
DAMN.
YOU DO THIS TO EVERYONE.
I'M NOT DODGING ANYTHING.
"WHO COULD LOVE ME?"
"I DON'T HAVE ANY GOOD QUALITIES."
HEH.
I WONDER WHERE ALL THE UNACCEPTED FEELINGS GO.

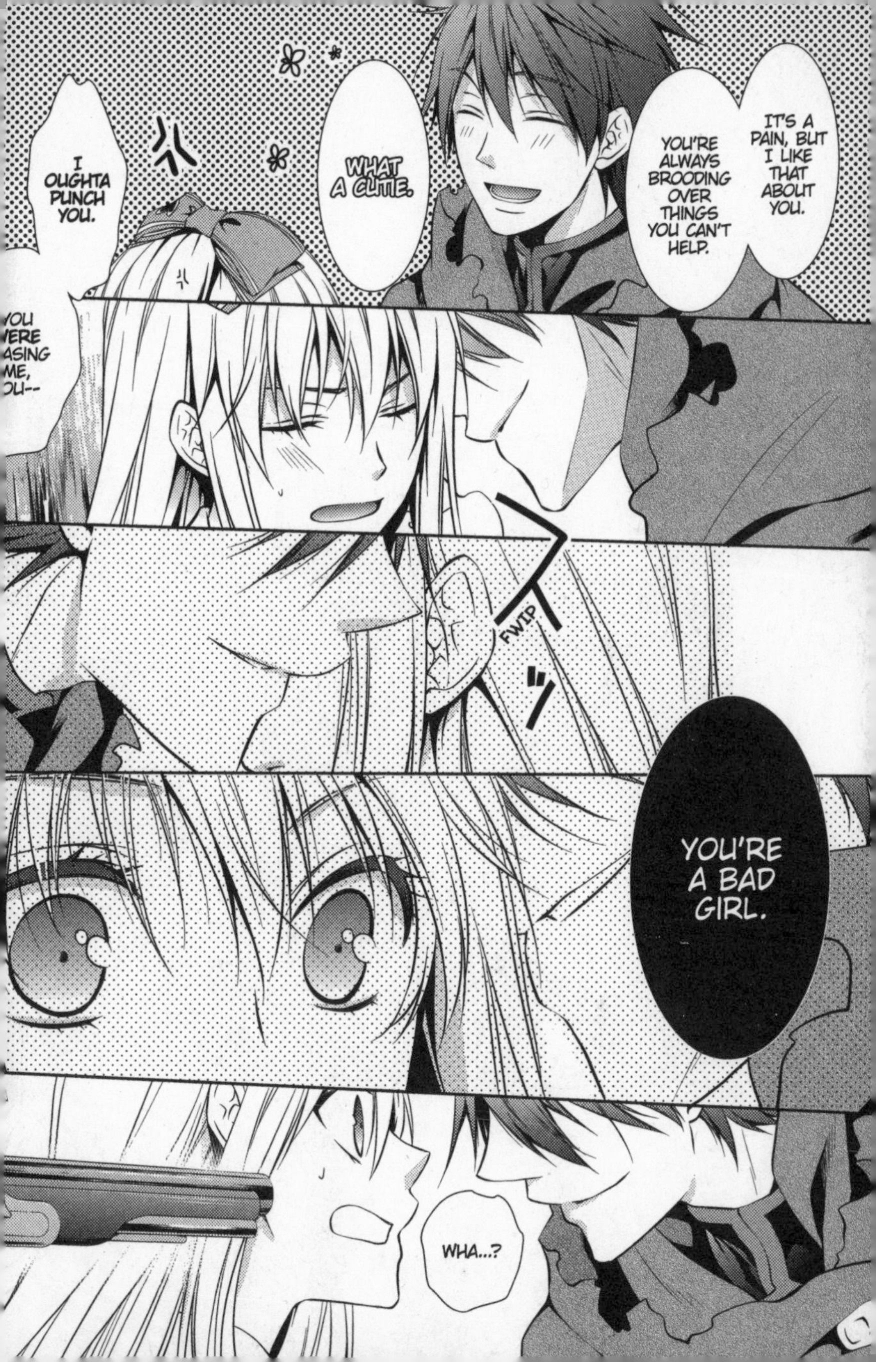
IT'S A PAIN, BUT I LIKE THAT ABOUT YOU.
YOU'RE ALWAYS BROODING OVER THINGS YOU CAN'T HELP.
WHAT A CUTIE.
I OUGHTA PUNCH YOU.
YOU VERE ASING ME, OU--
FWIP
YOU'RE A BAD GIRL.
WHA...?

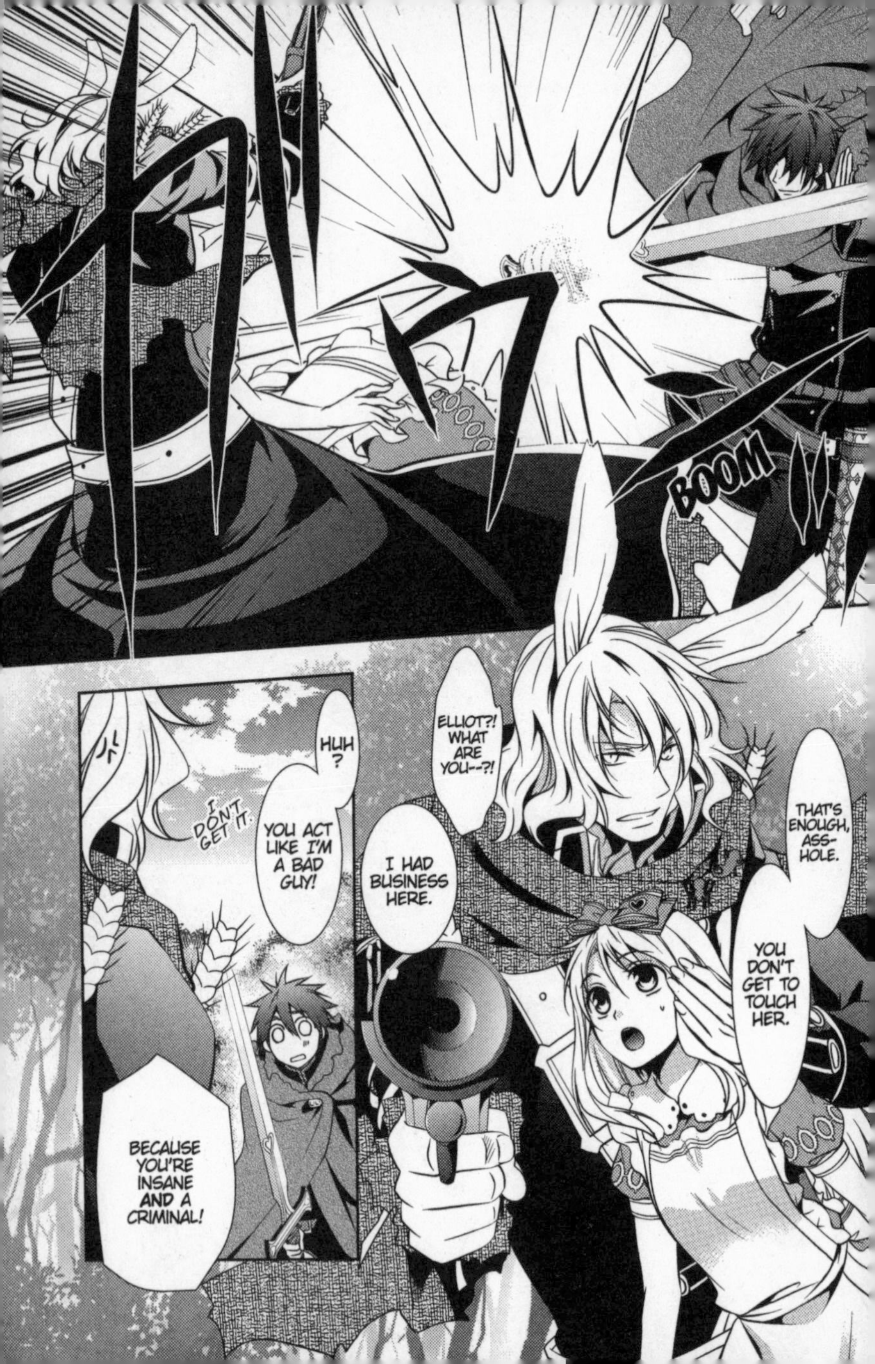
BOOM
ELLIOT?! WHAT ARE YOU--?!
THAT'S ENOUGH, ASS-HOLE.
YOU DON'T GET TO TOUCH HER.
I HAD BUSINESS HERE.
HUH?
YOU ACT LIKE I'M A BAD GUY!
I DON'T GET IT.
BECAUSE YOU'RE INSANE AND A CRIMINAL!

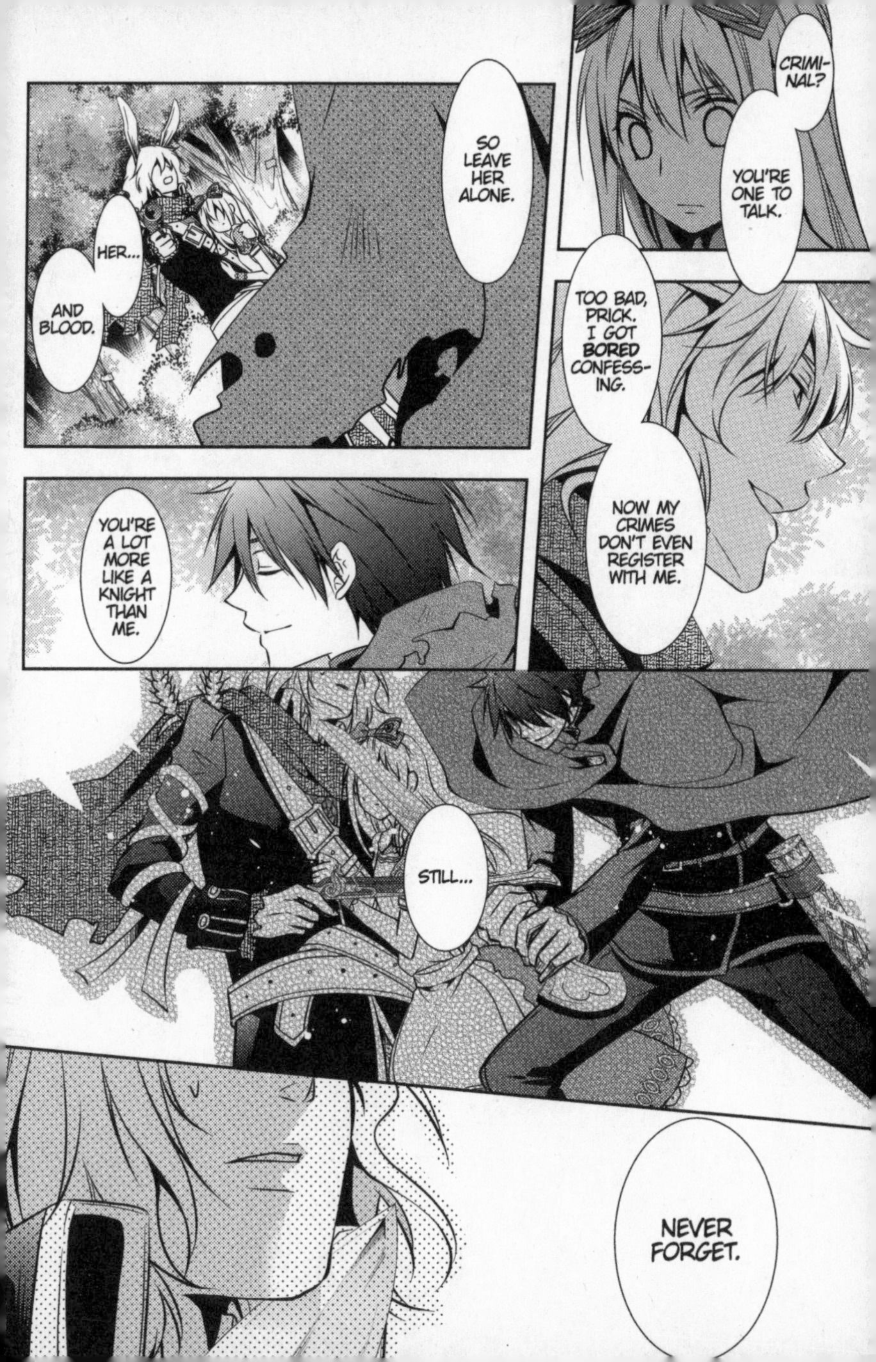
CRIMI-NAL?
YOU'RE ONE TO TALK.
SO LEAVE HER ALONE.
HER...
AND BLOOD.
TOO BAD, PRICK. I GOT BORED CONFESS-ING.
NOW MY CRIMES DON'T EVEN REGISTER WITH ME.
YOU'RE A LOT MORE LIKE A KNIGHT THAN ME.
STILL...
NEVER FORGET.

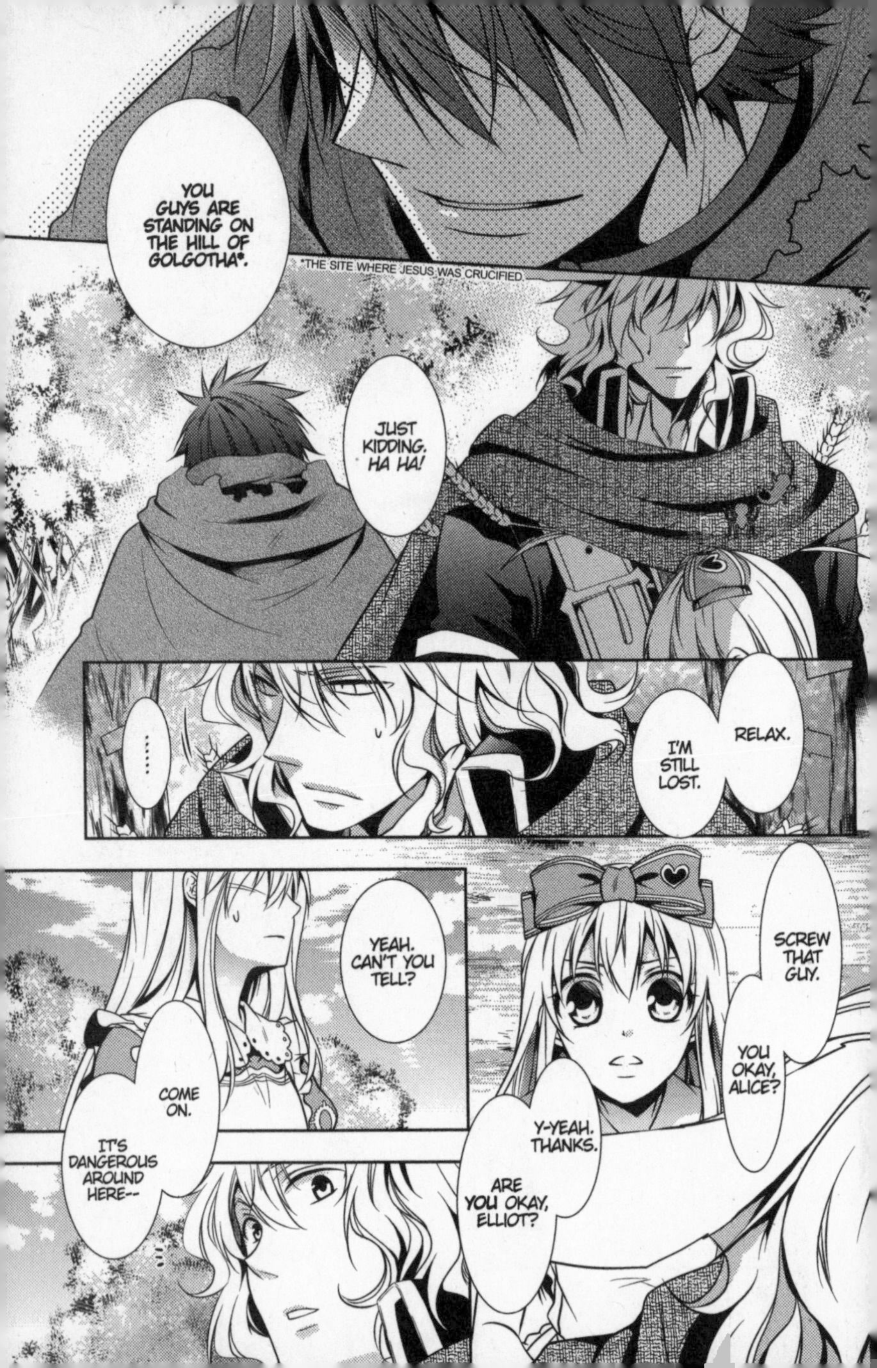
YOU GUYS ARE STANDING ON THE HILL OF GOLGOTHA*.
*THE SITE WHERE JESUS WAS CRUCIFIED.
JUST KIDDING. HA HA!
RELAX.
I'M STILL LOST.
......
SCREW THAT GUY.
YOU OKAY, ALICE?
Y-YEAH. THANKS.
ARE YOU OKAY, ELLIOT?
YEAH. CAN'T YOU TELL?
COME ON.
IT'S DANGEROUS AROUND HERE--

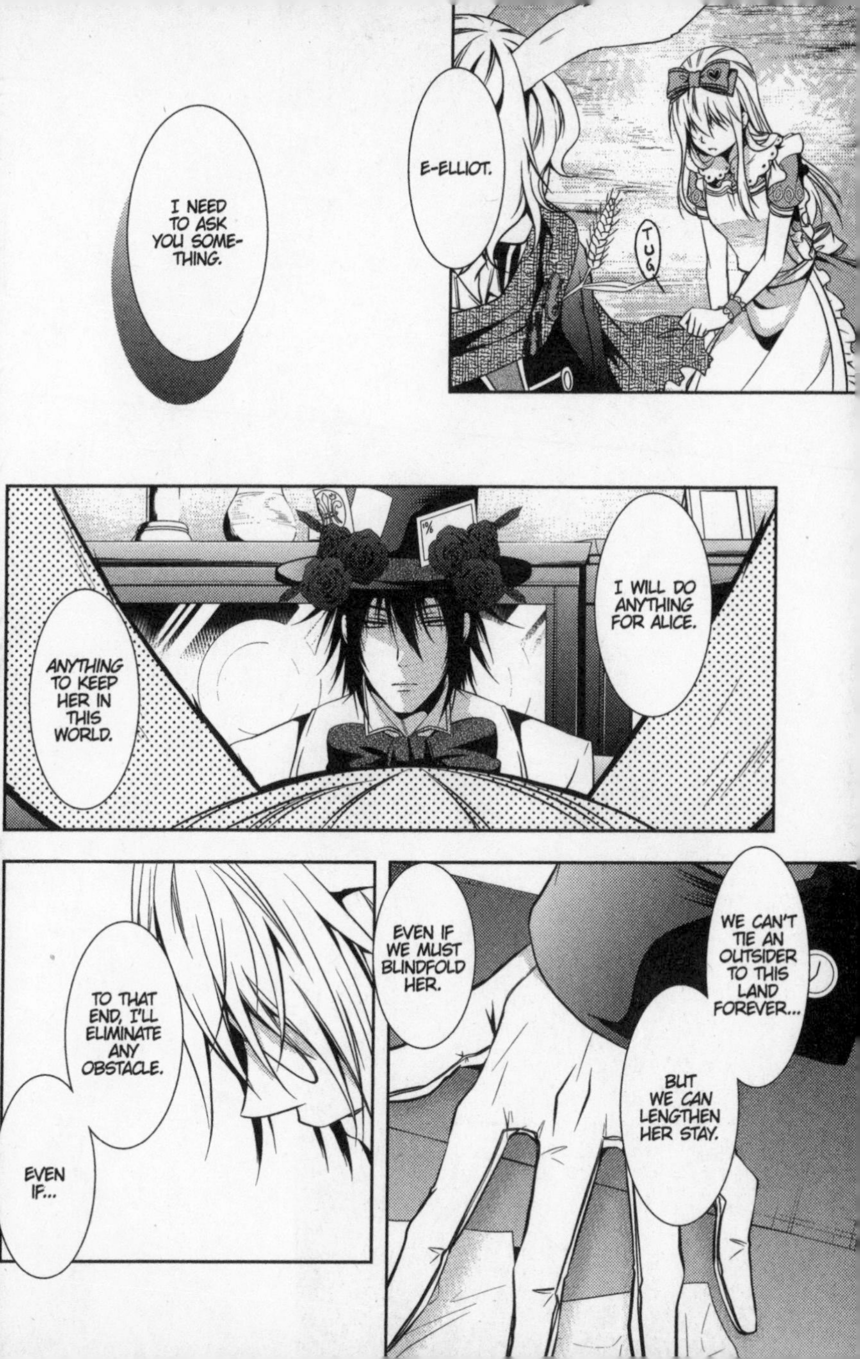
E-ELLIOT.
TUG
I NEED TO ASK YOU SOME-THING.
I WILL DO ANYTHING FOR ALICE.
ANYTHING TO KEEP HER IN THIS WORLD.
WE CAN'T TIE AN OUTSIDER TO THIS LAND FOREVER...
BUT WE CAN LENGTHEN HER STAY.
EVEN IF WE MUST BLINDFOLD HER.
TO THAT END, I'LL ELIMINATE ANY OBSTACLE.
EVEN IF...

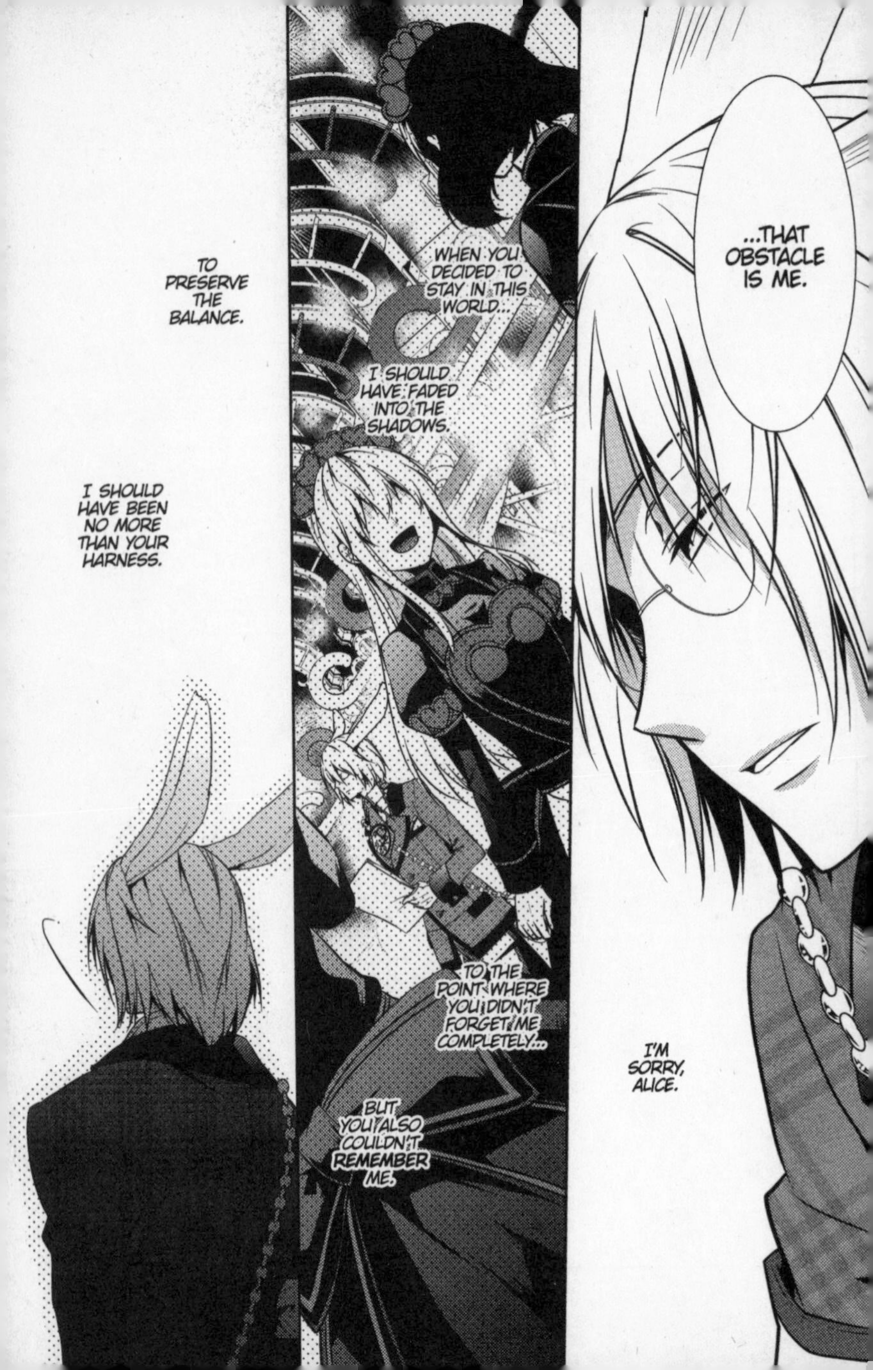
...THAT OBSTACLE IS ME.
I'M SORRY, ALICE.
WHEN YOU DECIDED TO STAY IN THIS WORLD...
I SHOULD HAVE FADED INTO THE SHADOWS.
TO THE POINT WHERE YOU DIDN'T FORGET ME COMPLETELY...
BUT YOU ALSO COULDN'T REMEMBER ME.
TO PRESERVE THE BALANCE.
I SHOULD HAVE BEEN NO MORE THAN YOUR HARNESS.

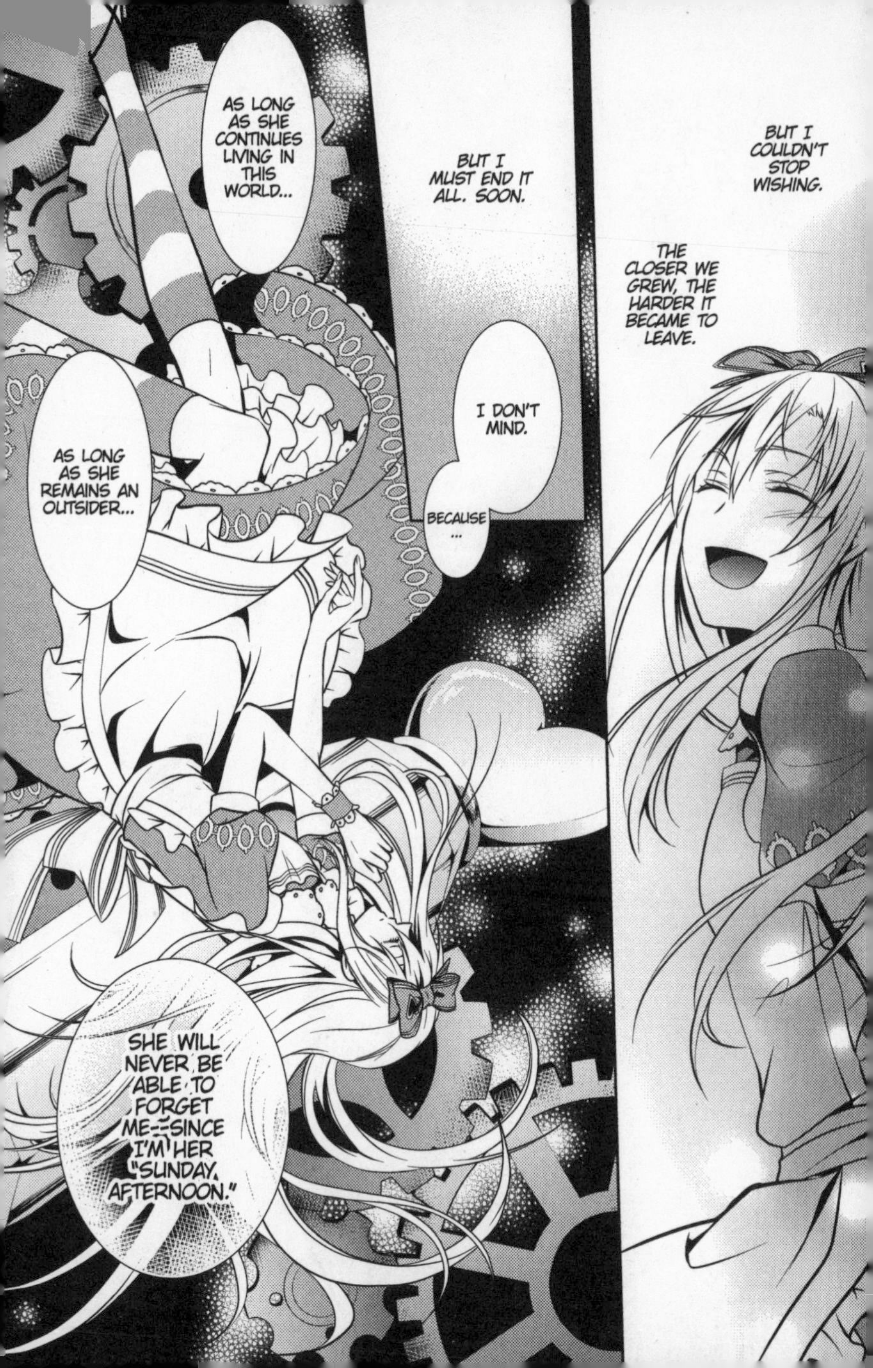
BUT I COULDN'T STOP WISHING.
THE CLOSER WE GREW, THE HARDER IT BECAME TO LEAVE.
BUT I MUST END IT ALL. SOON.
AS LONG AS SHE CONTINUES LIVING IN THIS WORLD...
I DON'T MIND.
BECAUSE...
AS LONG AS SHE REMAINS AN OUTSIDER...
SHE WILL NEVER BE ABLE TO FORGET ME--SINCE I'M HER "SUNDAY AFTERNOON."

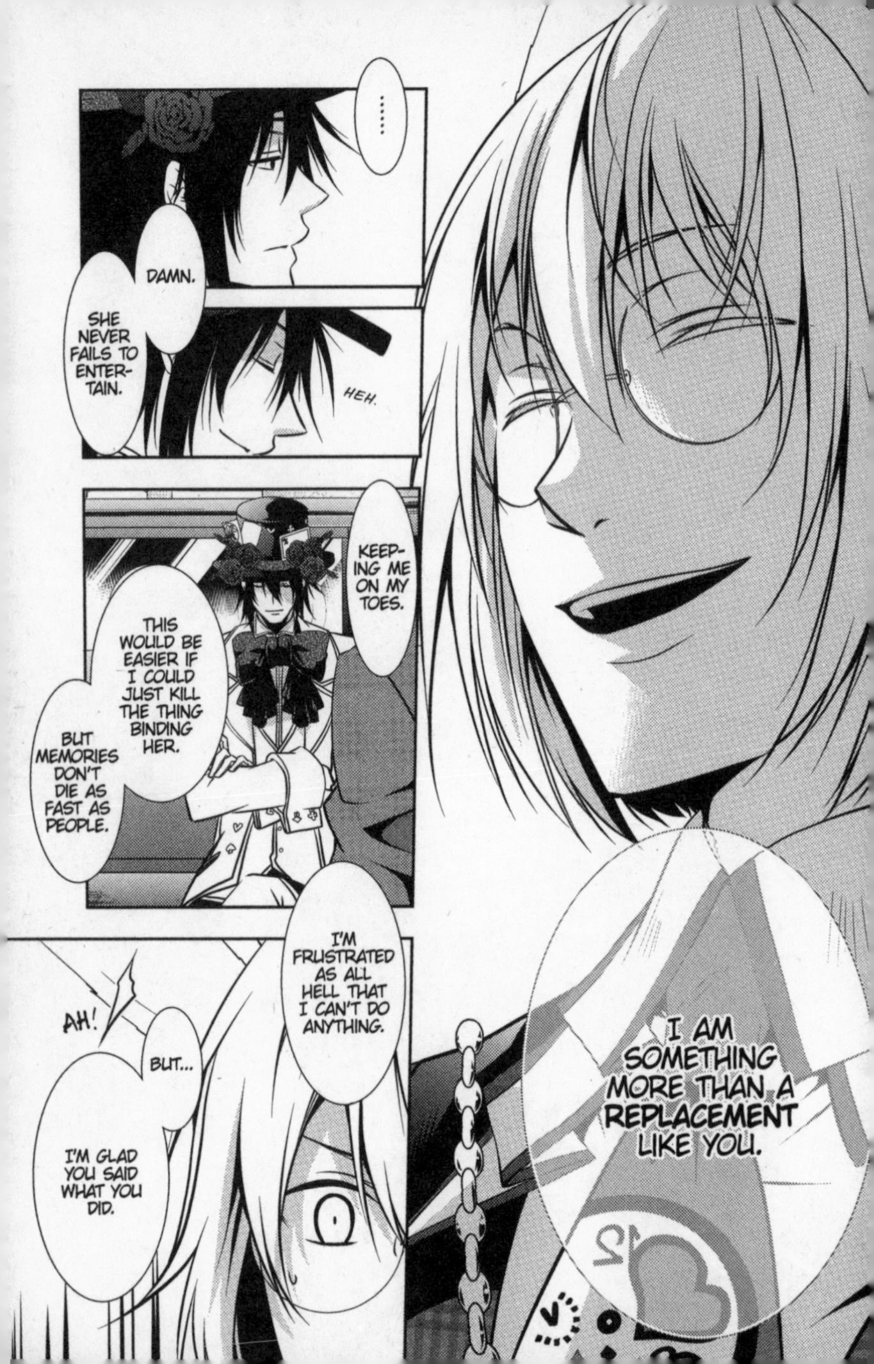

I AM SOMETHING MORE THAN A REPLACEMENT LIKE YOU.
......
DAMN.
SHE NEVER FAILS TO ENTERTAIN.
HEH.
KEEPING ME ON MY TOES.
THIS WOULD BE EASIER IF I COULD JUST KILL THE THING BINDING HER.
BUT MEMORIES DON'T DIE AS FAST AS PEOPLE.
I'M FRUSTRATED AS ALL HELL THAT I CAN'T DO ANYTHING.
AH!
BUT...
I'M GLAD YOU SAID WHAT YOU DID.

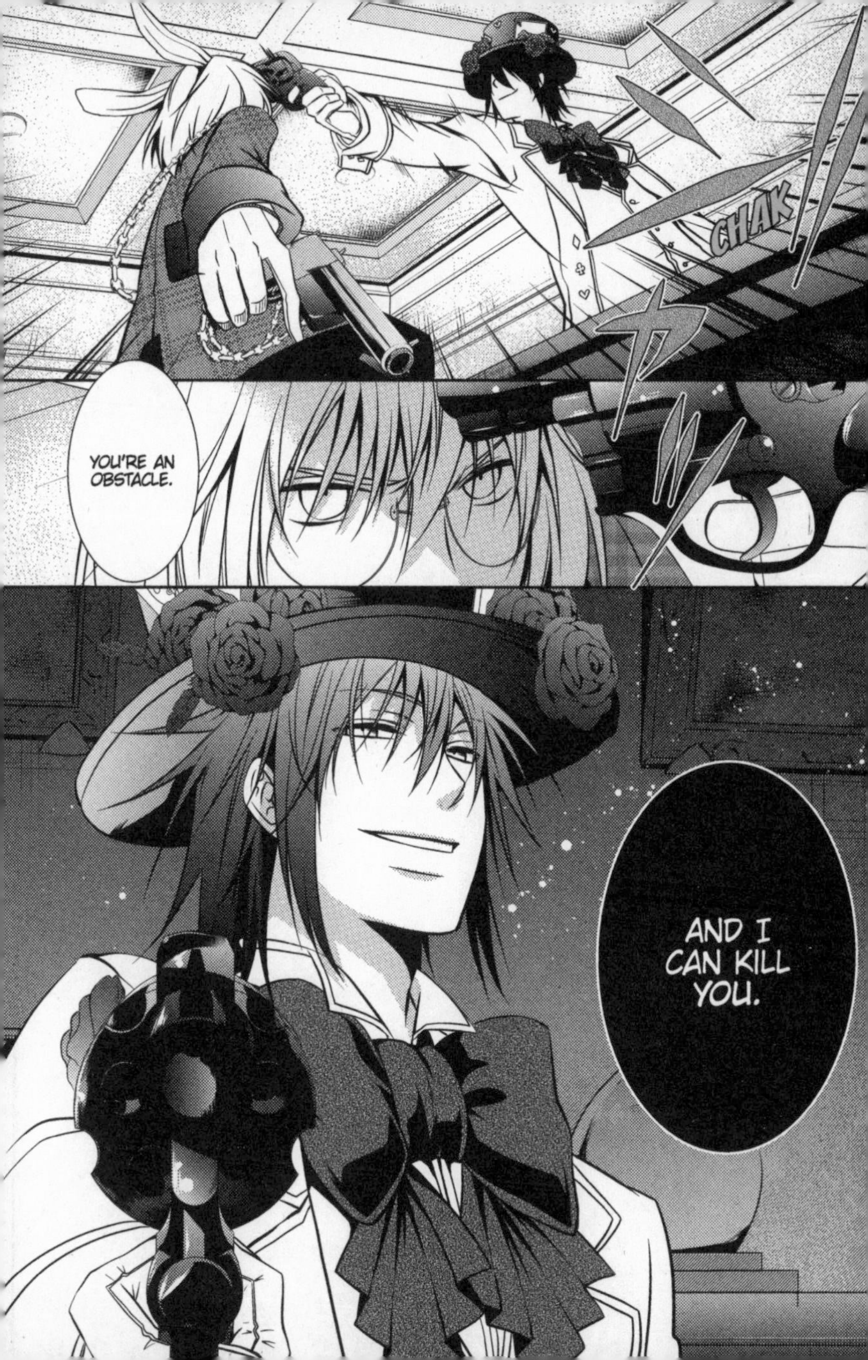
CHAK
ガッ
YOU'RE AN OBSTACLE.
AND I CAN KILL YOU.

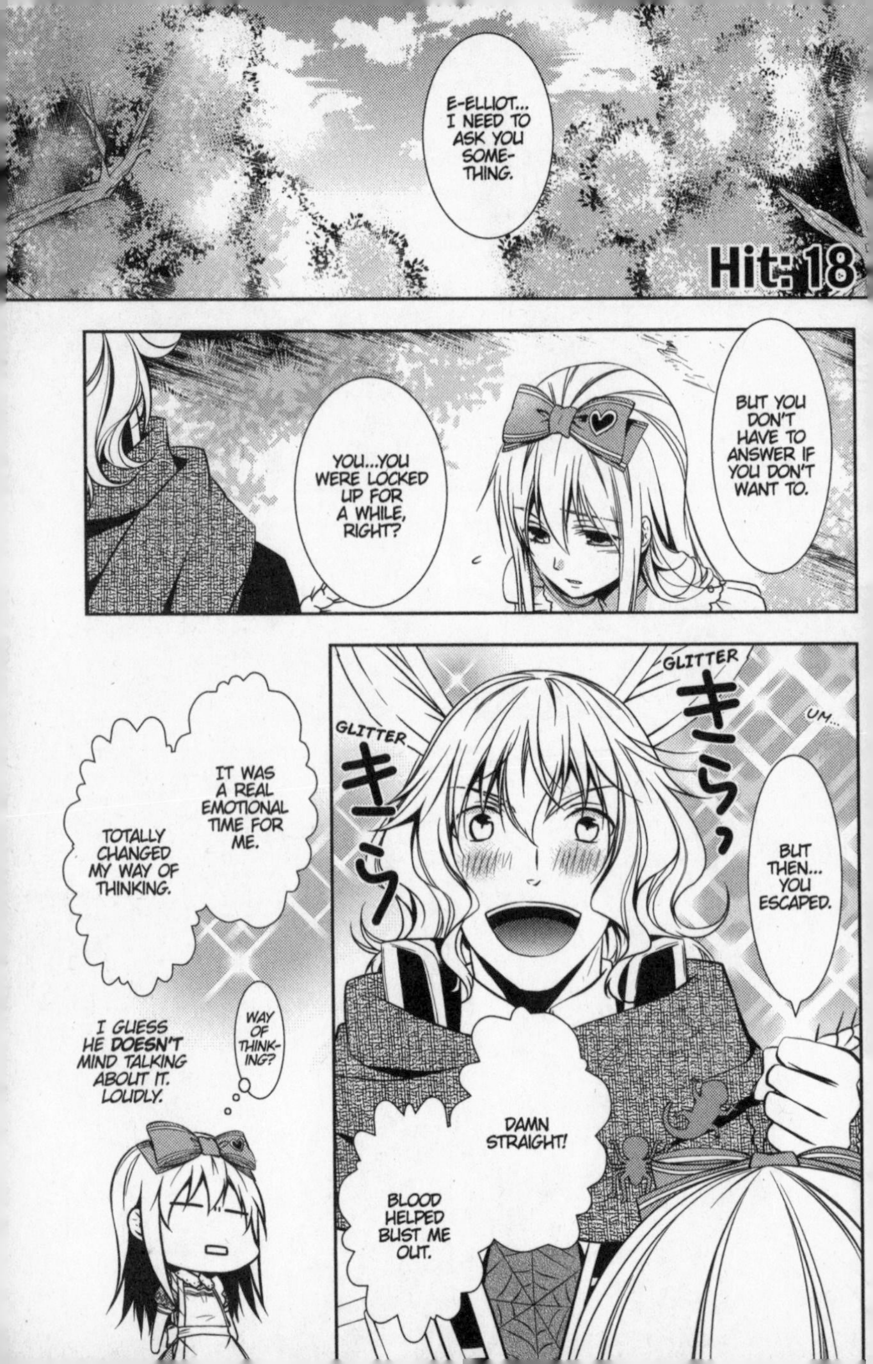
E-ELLIOT... I NEED TO ASK YOU SOME-THING.
Hit: 18
BUT YOU DON'T HAVE TO ANSWER IF YOU DON'T WANT TO.
YOU...YOU WERE LOCKED UP FOR A WHILE, RIGHT?
UM...
BUT THEN... YOU ESCAPED.
GLITTER
GLITTER
DAMN STRAIGHT!
BLOOD HELPED BUST ME OUT.
IT WAS A REAL EMOTIONAL TIME FOR ME.
TOTALLY CHANGED MY WAY OF THINKING.
WAY OF THINK-ING?
I GUESS HE DOESN'T MIND TALKING ABOUT IT. LOUDLY.

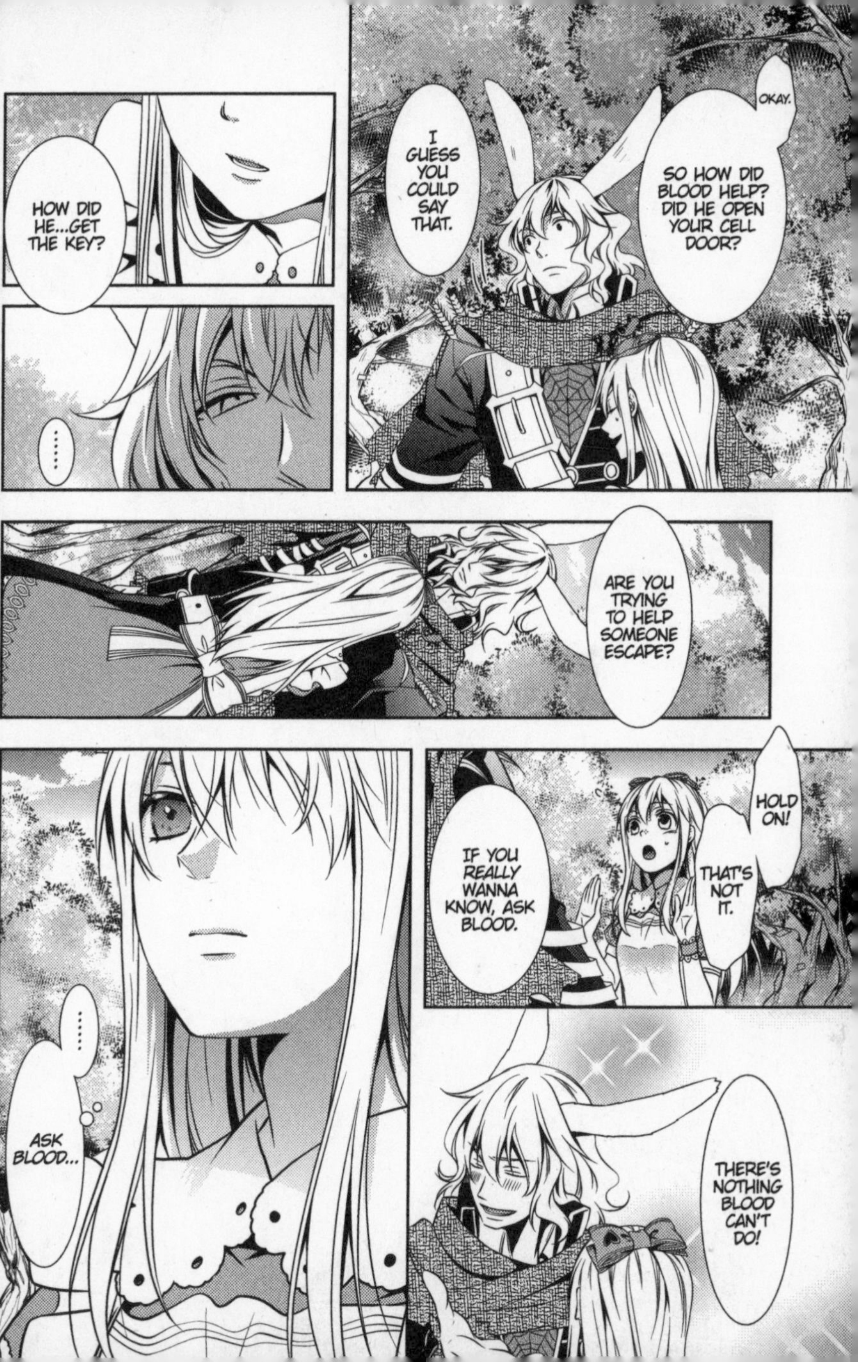
OKAY.
SO HOW DID BLOOD HELP? DID HE OPEN YOUR CELL DOOR?
I GUESS YOU COULD SAY THAT.
HOW DID HE...GET THE KEY?
......
ARE YOU TRYING TO HELP SOMEONE ESCAPE?
HOLD ON!
THAT'S NOT IT.
IF YOU REALLY WANNA KNOW, ASK BLOOD.
THERE'S NOTHING BLOOD CAN'T DO!
......
ASK BLOOD...

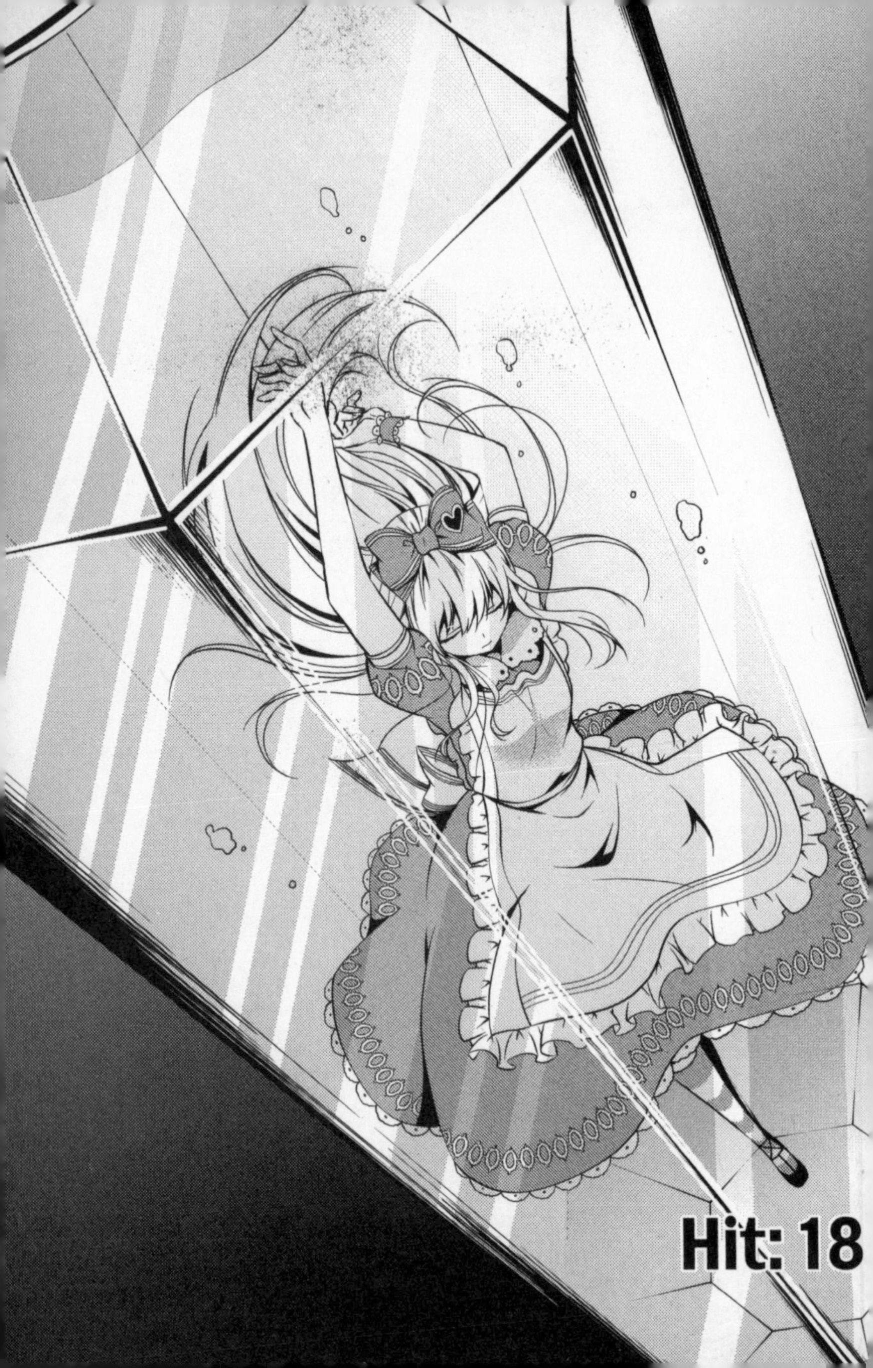
Hit: 18

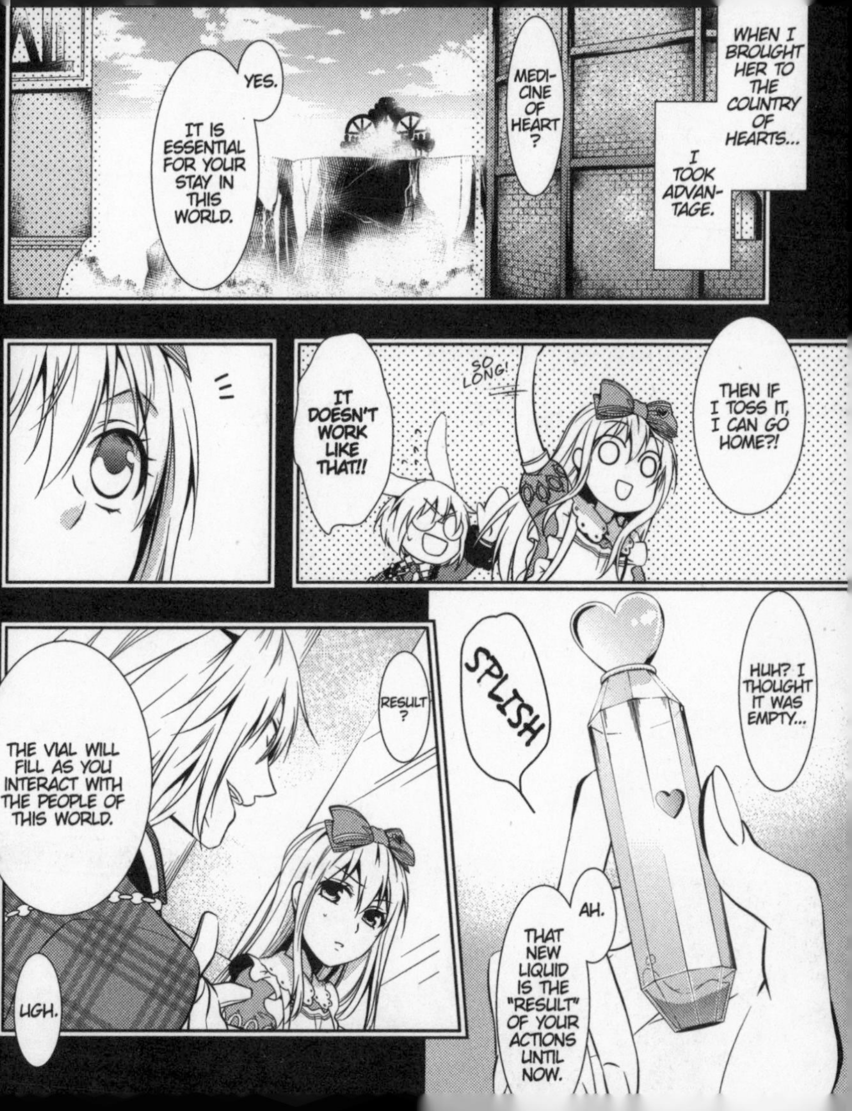
WHEN I BROUGHT HER TO THE COUNTRY OF HEARTS...
I TOOK ADVANTAGE.
MEDICINE OF HEART?
YES.
IT IS ESSENTIAL FOR YOUR STAY IN THIS WORLD.
THEN IF I TOSS IT, I CAN GO HOME?!
SO LONG!
IT DOESN'T WORK LIKE THAT!!
HUH? I THOUGHT IT WAS EMPTY...
SPLISH
AH.
THAT NEW LIQUID IS THE "RESULT" OF YOUR ACTIONS UNTIL NOW.
RESULT?
THE VIAL WILL FILL AS YOU INTERACT WITH THE PEOPLE OF THIS WORLD.
UGH.

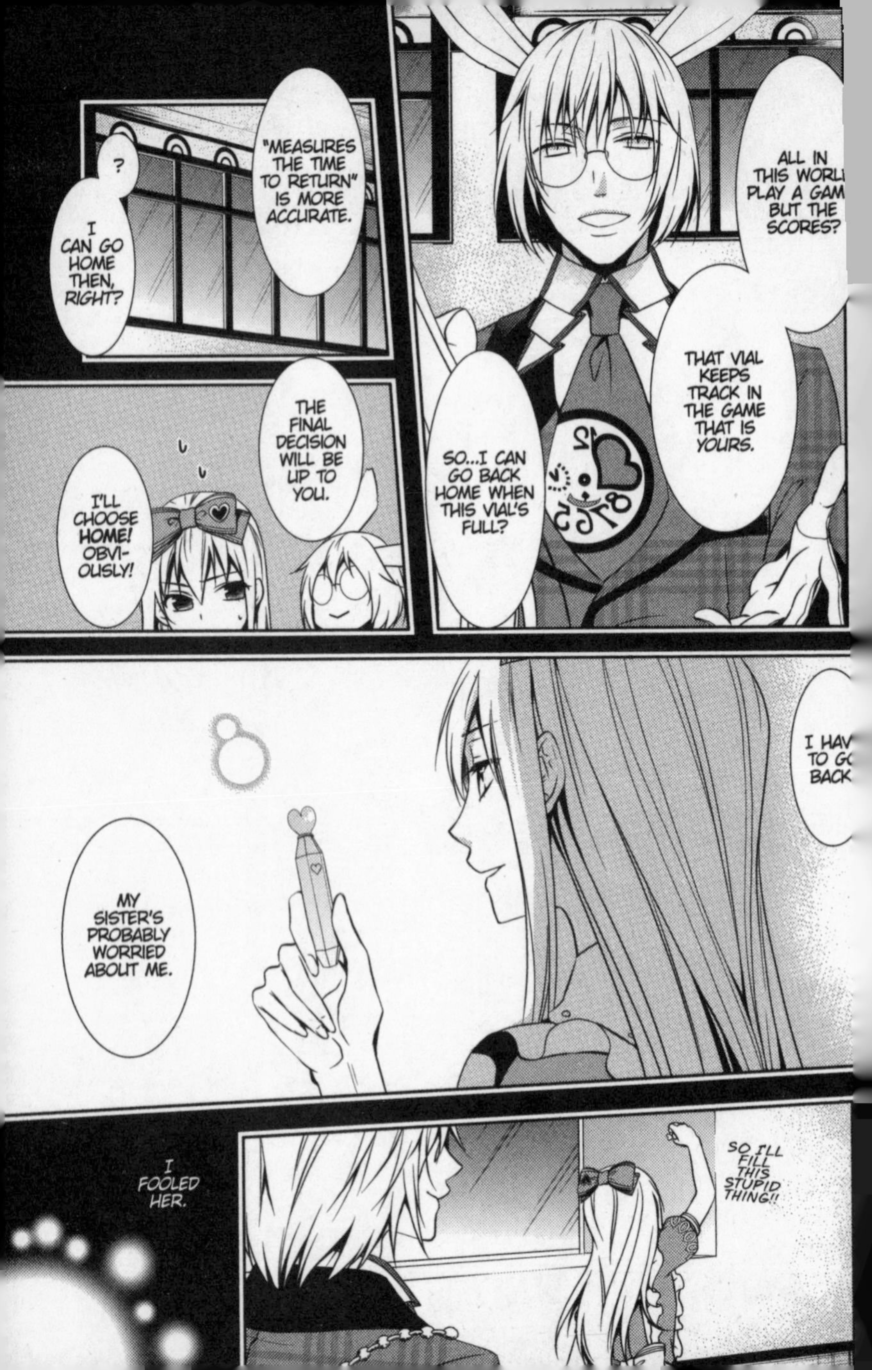
ALL IN THIS WORL PLAY A GAM BUT THE SCORES?
THAT VIAL KEEPS TRACK IN THE GAME THAT IS YOURS.
SO...I CAN GO BACK HOME WHEN THIS VIAL'S FULL?
"MEASURES THE TIME TO RETURN" IS MORE ACCURATE.
?
I CAN GO HOME THEN, RIGHT?
THE FINAL DECISION WILL BE UP TO YOU.
I'LL CHOOSE HOME! OBVI-OUSLY!
I HAV TO GO BACK
MY SISTER'S PROBABLY WORRIED ABOUT ME.
SO I'LL FILL THIS STUPID THING!!
I FOOLED HER.

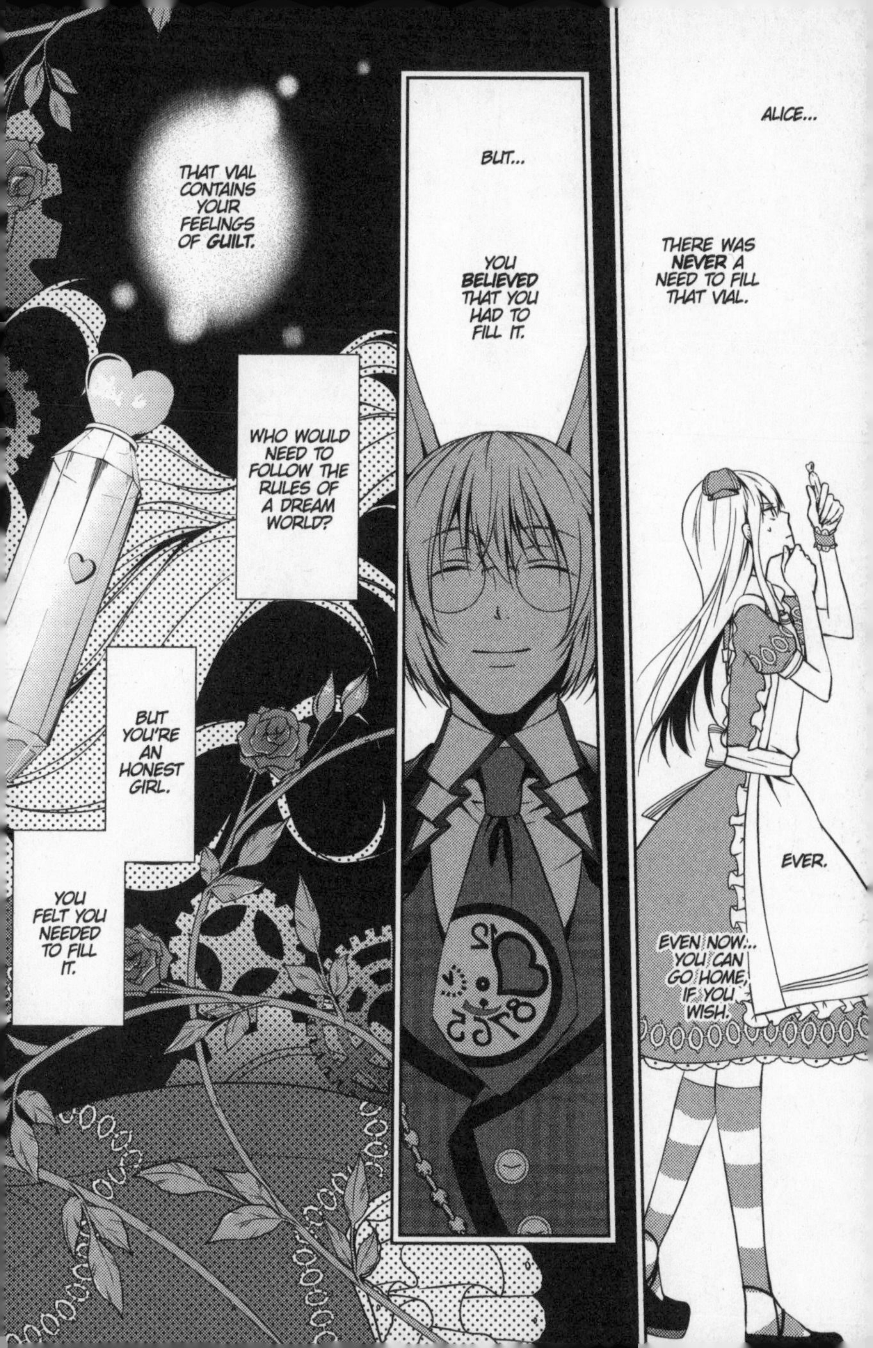
ALICE...
THERE WAS NEVER A NEED TO FILL THAT VIAL.
EVER.
EVEN NOW... YOU CAN GO HOME, IF YOU WISH.
BUT...
YOU BELIEVED THAT YOU HAD TO FILL IT.
THAT VIAL CONTAINS YOUR FEELINGS OF GUILT.
WHO WOULD NEED TO FOLLOW THE RULES OF A DREAM WORLD?
BUT YOU'RE AN HONEST GIRL.
YOU FELT YOU NEEDED TO FILL IT.

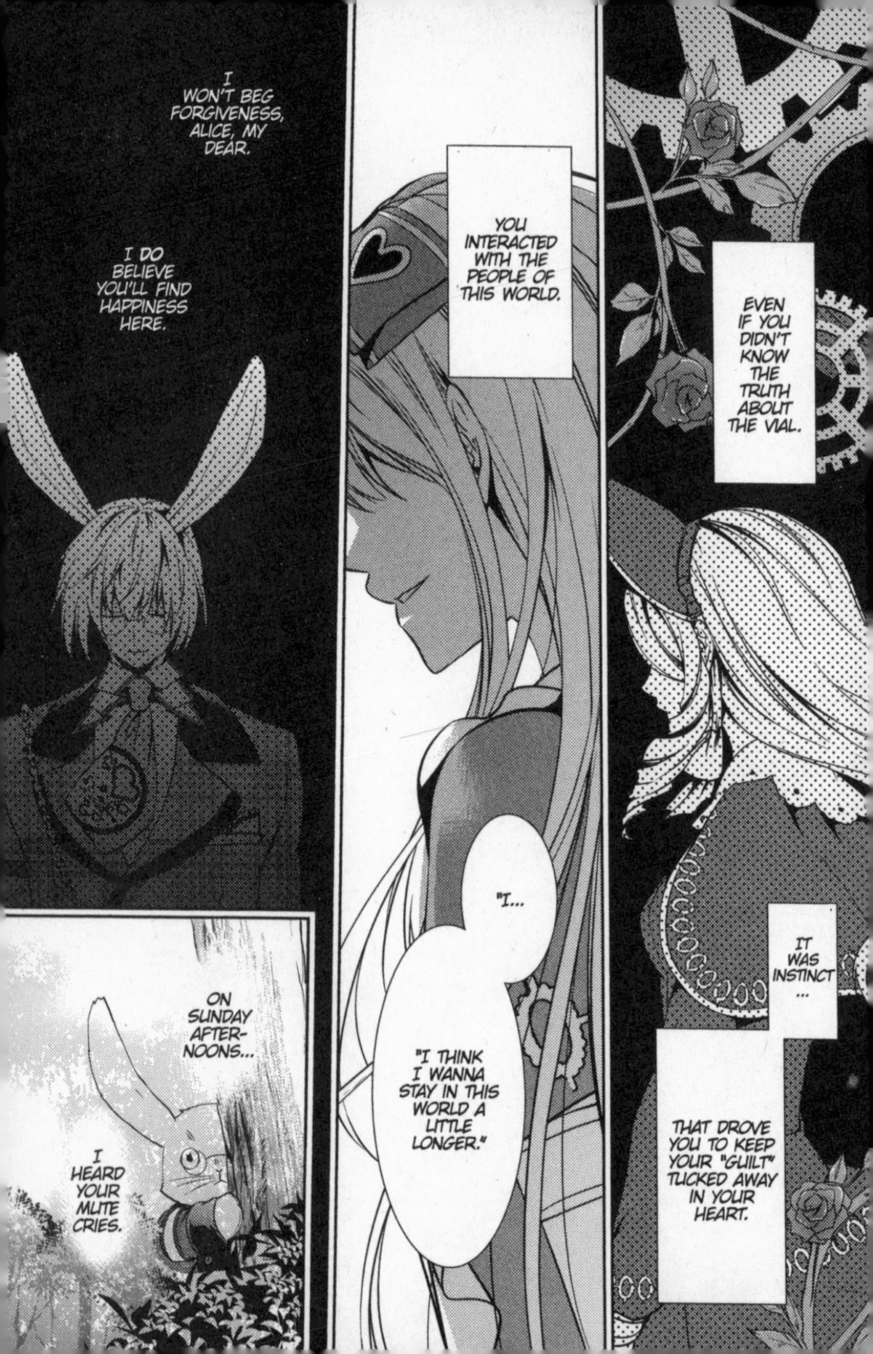
EVEN IF YOU DIDN'T KNOW THE TRUTH ABOUT THE VIAL.
IT WAS INSTINCT...
THAT DROVE YOU TO KEEP YOUR "GUILT" TUCKED AWAY IN YOUR HEART.
YOU INTERACTED WITH THE PEOPLE OF THIS WORLD.
"I...
"I THINK I WANNA STAY IN THIS WORLD A LITTLE LONGER."
I WON'T BEG FORGIVENESS, ALICE, MY DEAR.
I DO BELIEVE YOU'LL FIND HAPPINESS HERE.
ON SUNDAY AFTERNOONS...
I HEARD YOUR MUTE CRIES.

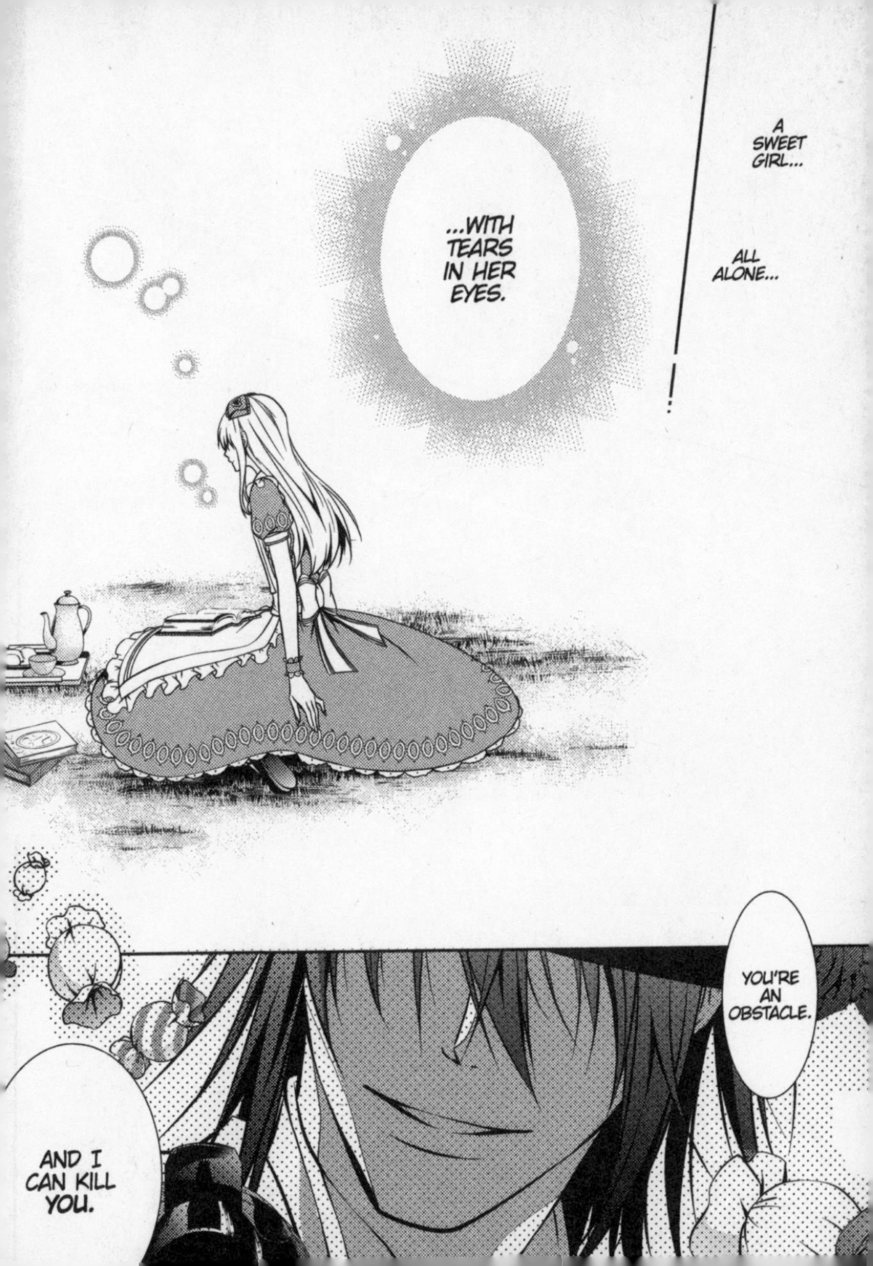
A SWEET GIRL...
ALL ALONE...
...WITH TEARS IN HER EYES.
YOU'RE AN OBSTACLE.
AND I CAN KILL YOU.

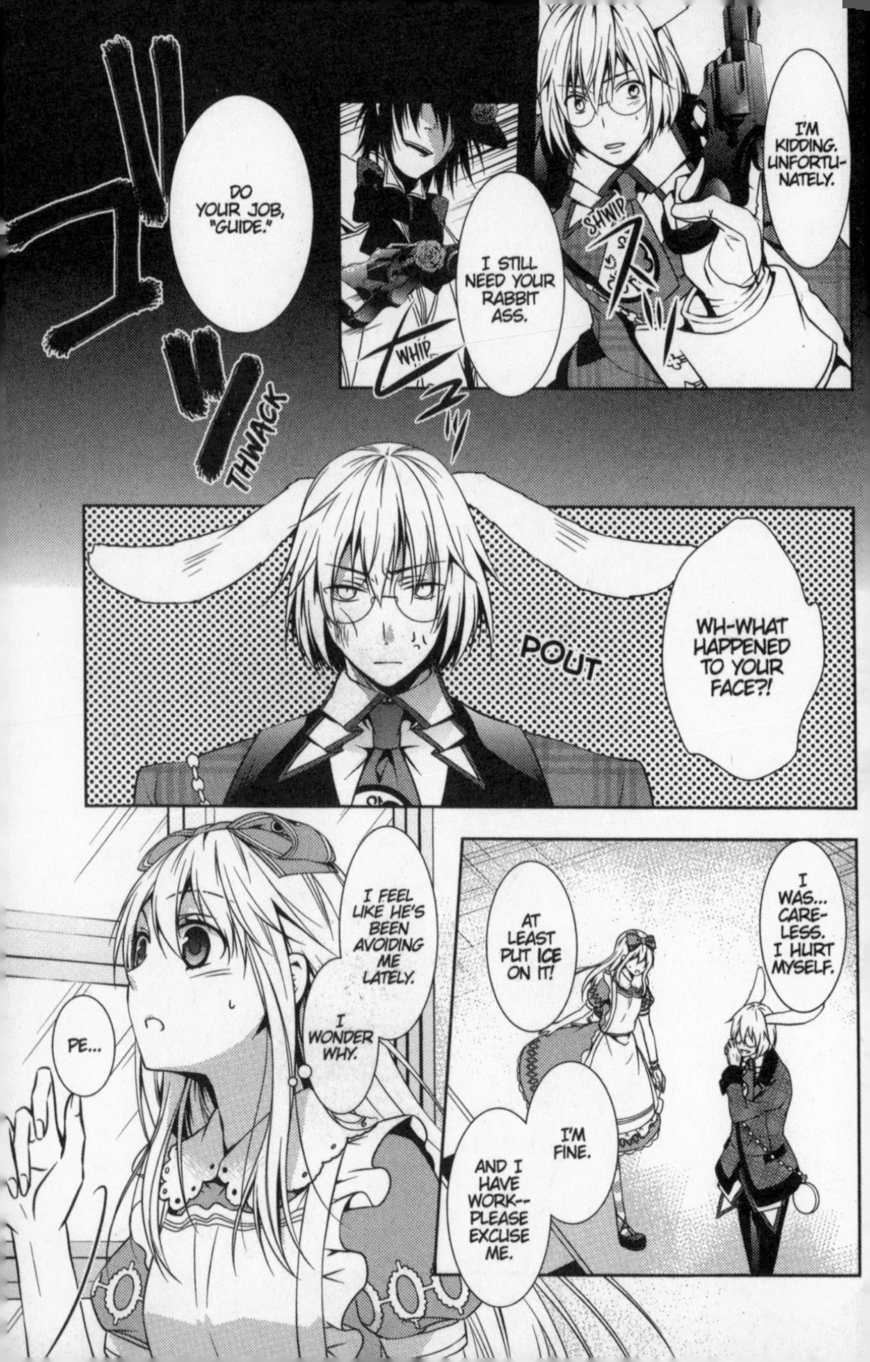
I'M KIDDING. UNFORTUNATELY.
SHWIP
I STILL NEED YOUR RABBIT ASS.
WHIP
DO YOUR JOB, "GUIDE."
THWACK
WH-WHAT HAPPENED TO YOUR FACE?!
POUT
I WAS... CARELESS. I HURT MYSELF.
AT LEAST PUT ICE ON IT!
I'M FINE.
AND I HAVE WORK--PLEASE EXCUSE ME.
I FEEL LIKE HE'S BEEN AVOIDING ME LATELY.
I WONDER WHY.
PE...

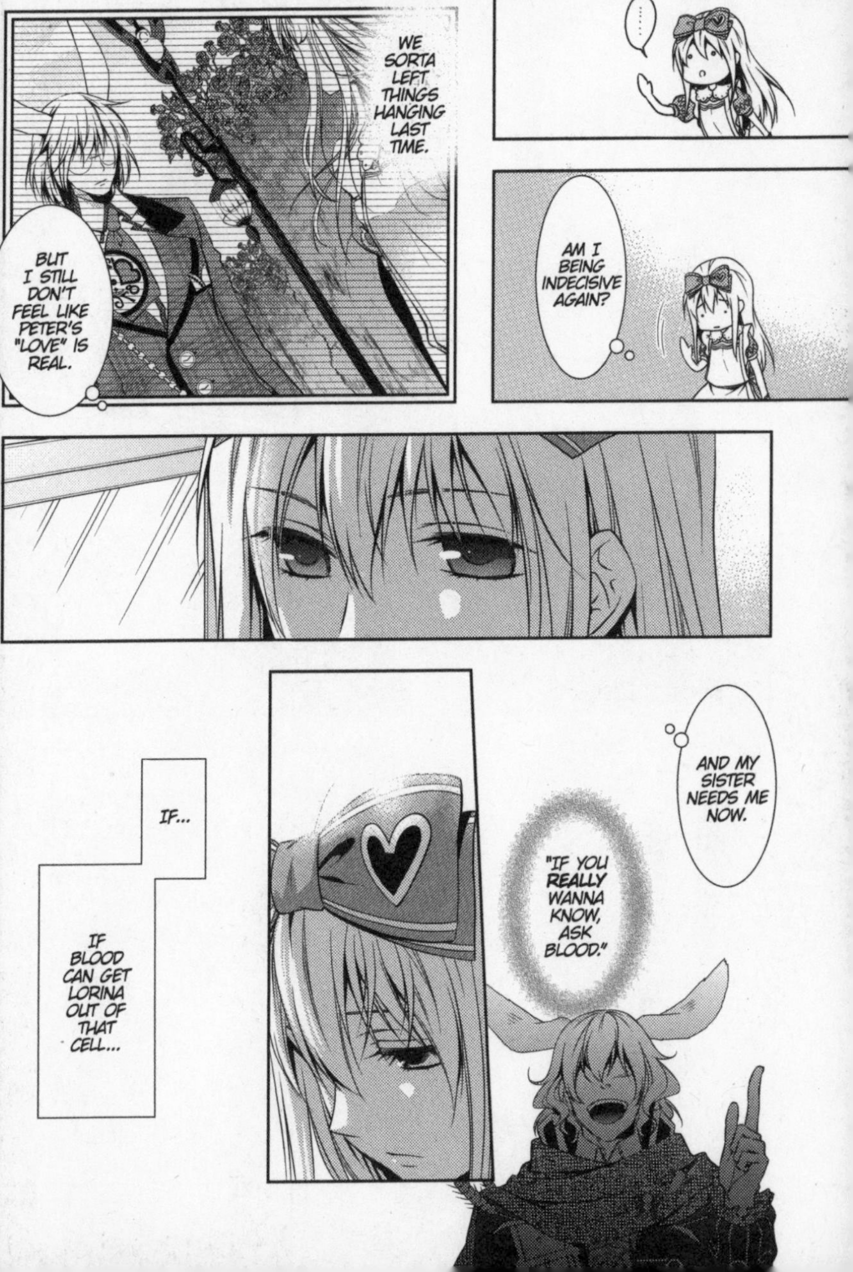
......
AM I BEING INDECISIVE AGAIN?
WE SORTA LEFT THINGS HANGING LAST TIME.
BUT I STILL DON'T FEEL LIKE PETER'S "LOVE" IS REAL.
AND MY SISTER NEEDS ME NOW.
"IF YOU REALLY WANNA KNOW, ASK BLOOD."
IF...
IF BLOOD CAN GET LORINA OUT OF THAT CELL...

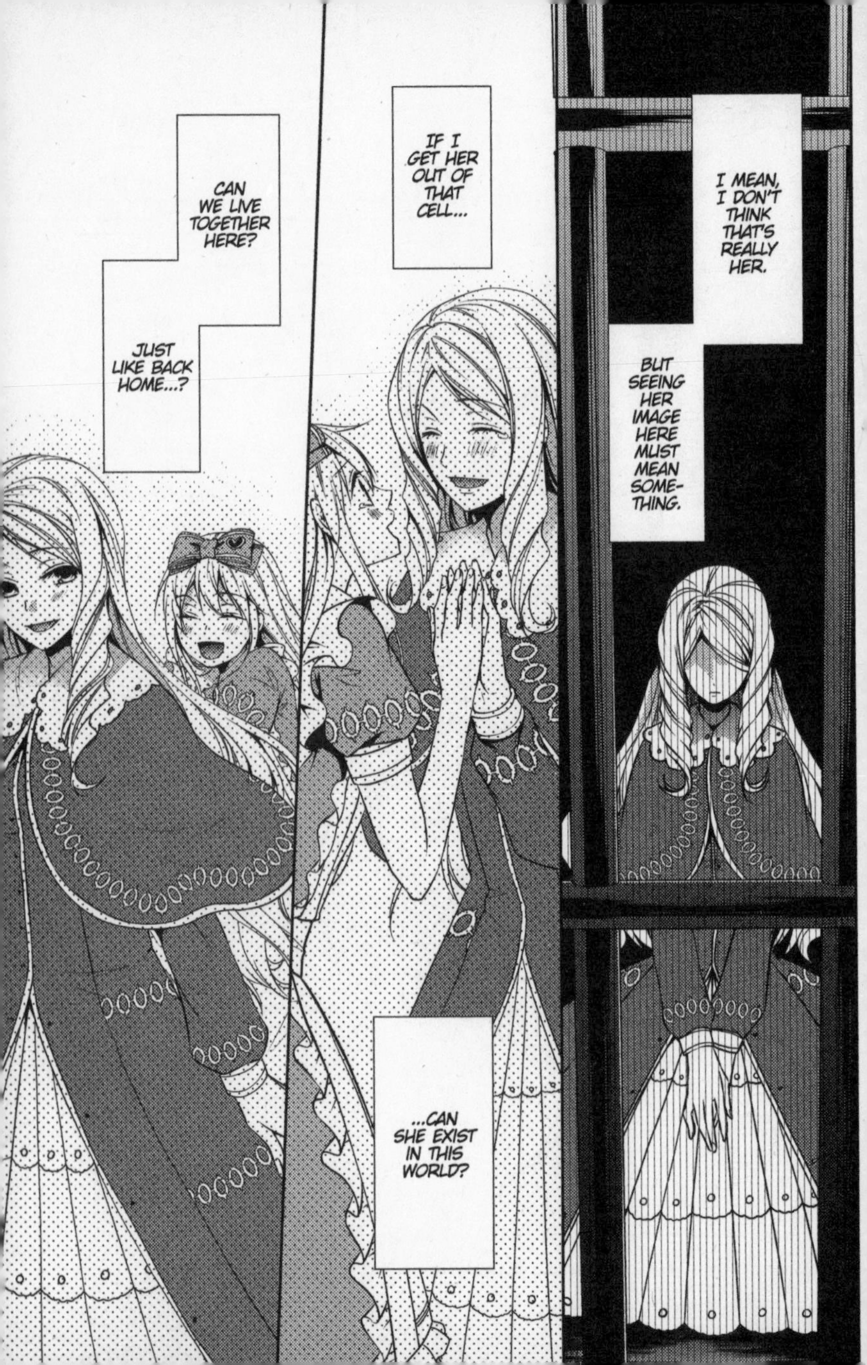
I MEAN, I DON'T THINK THAT'S REALLY HER.
BUT SEEING HER IMAGE HERE MUST MEAN SOME-THING.
IF I GET HER OUT OF THAT CELL...
...CAN SHE EXIST IN THIS WORLD?
CAN WE LIVE TOGETHER HERE?
JUST LIKE BACK HOME...?

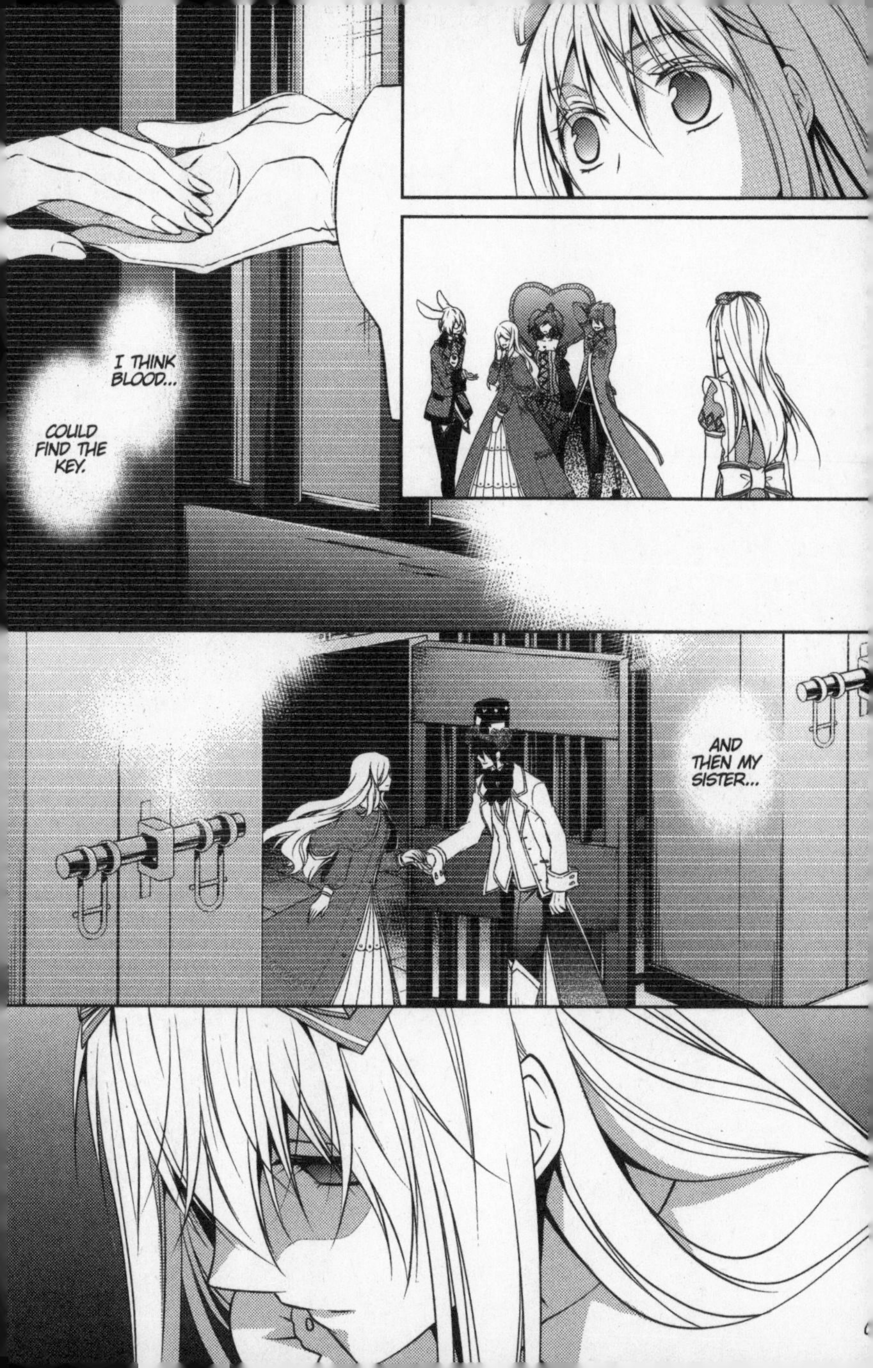
I THINK BLOOD...
COULD FIND THE KEY.
AND THEN MY SISTER...

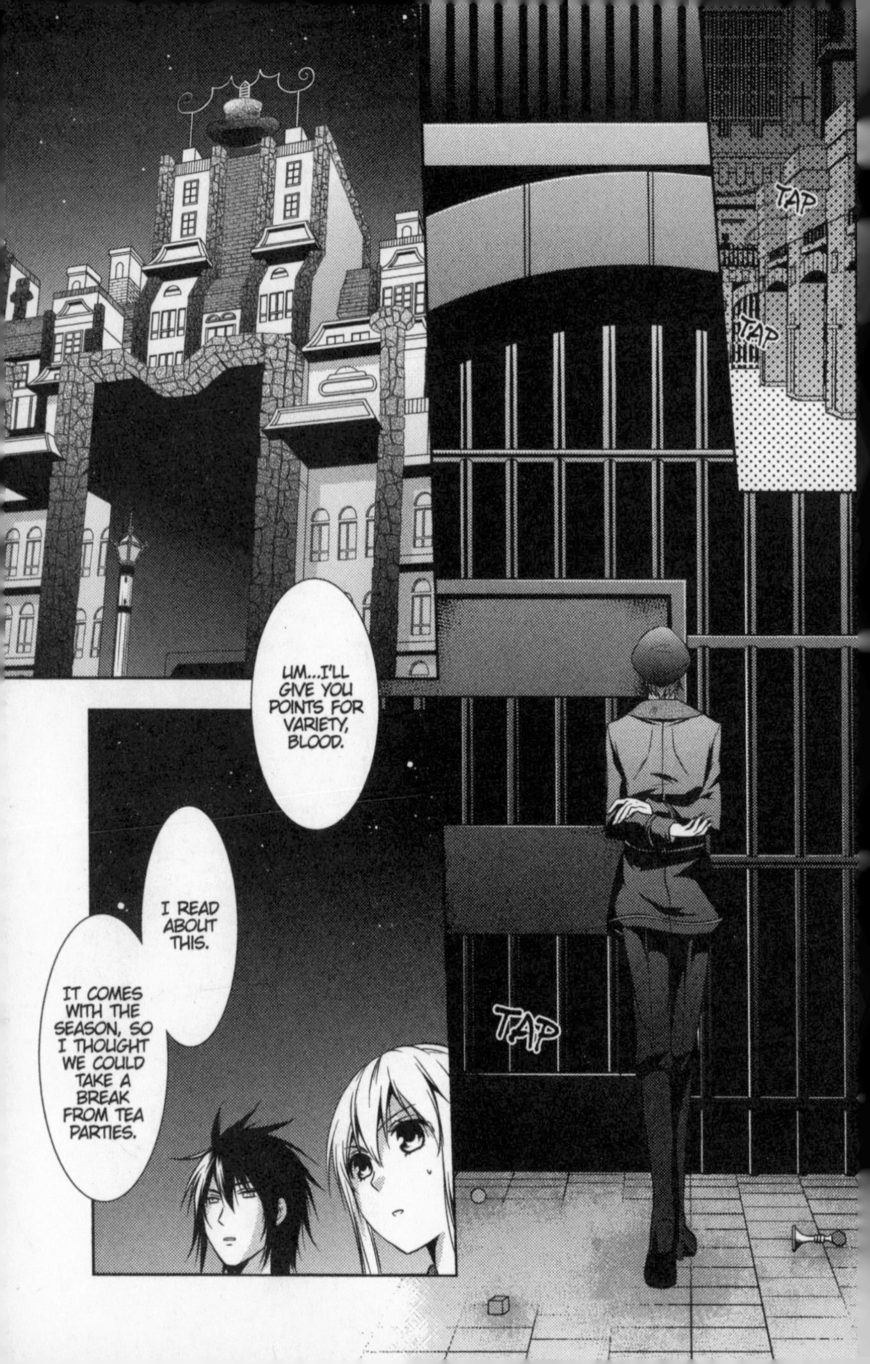
TAP
TAP
TAP
UM...I'LL GIVE YOU POINTS FOR VARIETY, BLOOD.
I READ ABOUT THIS.
IT COMES WITH THE SEASON, SO I THOUGHT WE COULD TAKE A BREAK FROM TEA PARTIES.

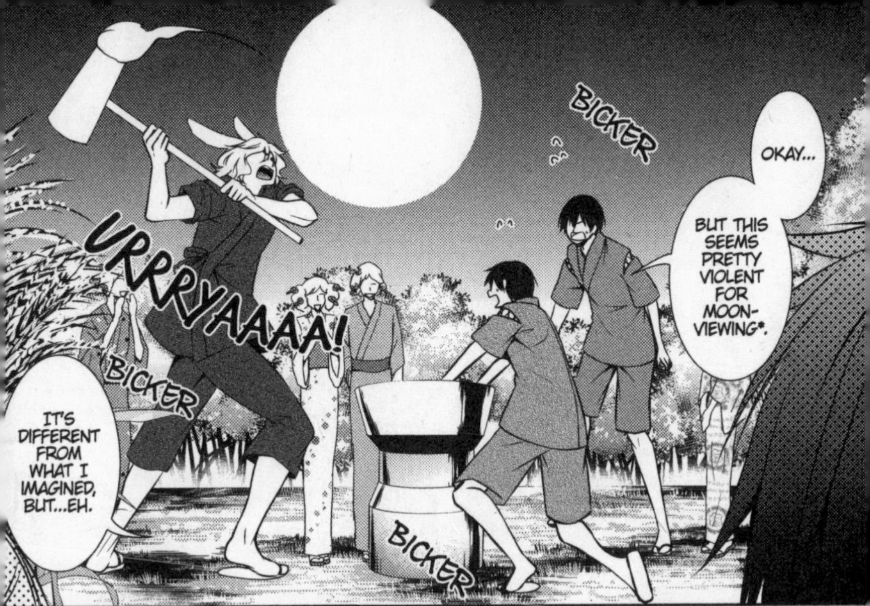
BICKER
OKAY...
BUT THIS SEEMS PRETTY VIOLENT FOR MOON-VIEWING*.
URRRYAAAA!
BICKER
IT'S DIFFERENT FROM WHAT I IMAGINED, BUT...EH.
BICKER

*A JAPANESE PARTY WHERE GUESTS WATCH THE FULL MOON, DRINK BOOZE, AND MAKE AND EAT MOCHI (LIKE THE "RABBITS ON THE MOON").

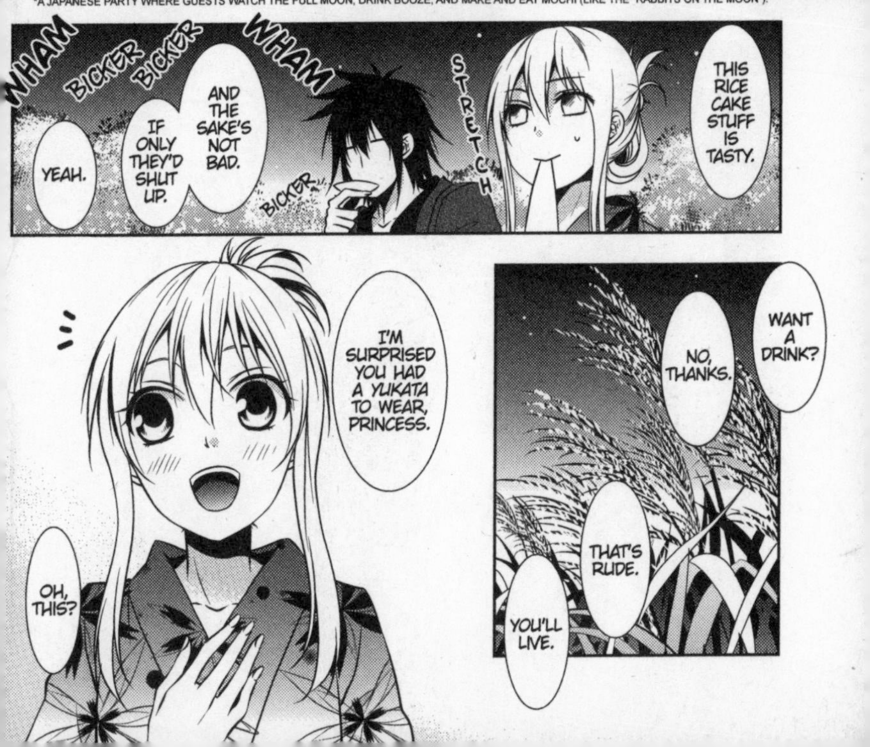
THIS RICE CAKE STUFF IS TASTY.
STRETCH
WHAM
AND THE SAKE'S NOT BAD.
BICKER BICKER
IF ONLY THEY'D SHUT UP.
BICKER
YEAH.
WHAM
WANT A DRINK?
NO, THANKS.
THAT'S RUDE.
YOU'LL LIVE.
I'M SURPRISED YOU HAD A YUKATA TO WEAR, PRINCESS.
OH, THIS?

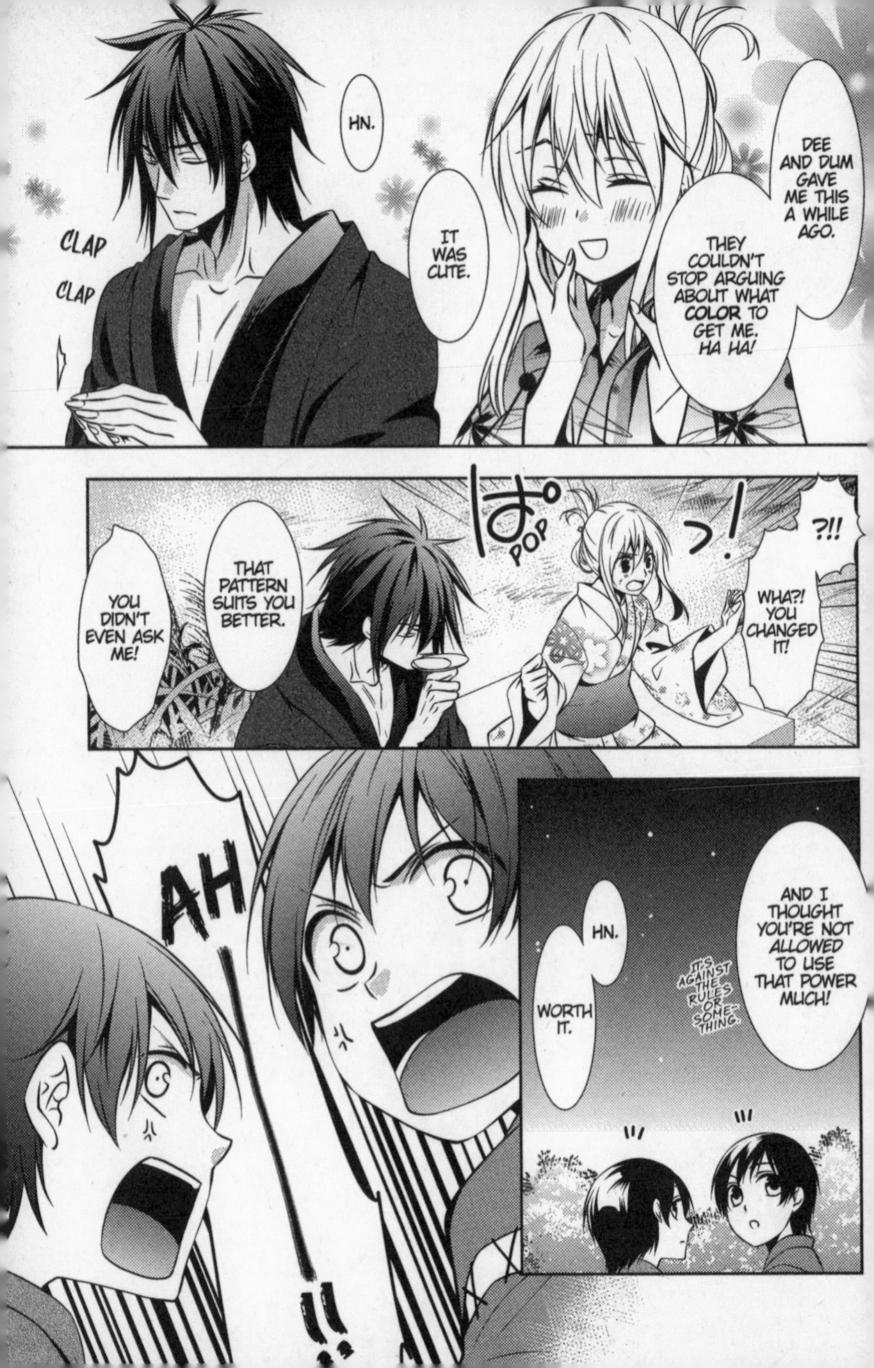
DEE AND DUM GAVE ME THIS A WHILE AGO.
THEY COULDN'T STOP ARGUING ABOUT WHAT **COLOR** TO GET ME. HA HA!
IT WAS CUTE.
HN.
CLAP
CLAP
?!!
WHA?! YOU CHANGED IT!
POP
THAT PATTERN SUITS YOU BETTER.
YOU DIDN'T EVEN ASK ME!
AND I THOUGHT YOU'RE NOT ALLOWED TO USE THAT POWER MUCH!
IT'S AGAINST THE RULES OR SOMETHING.
HN.
WORTH IT.
AH

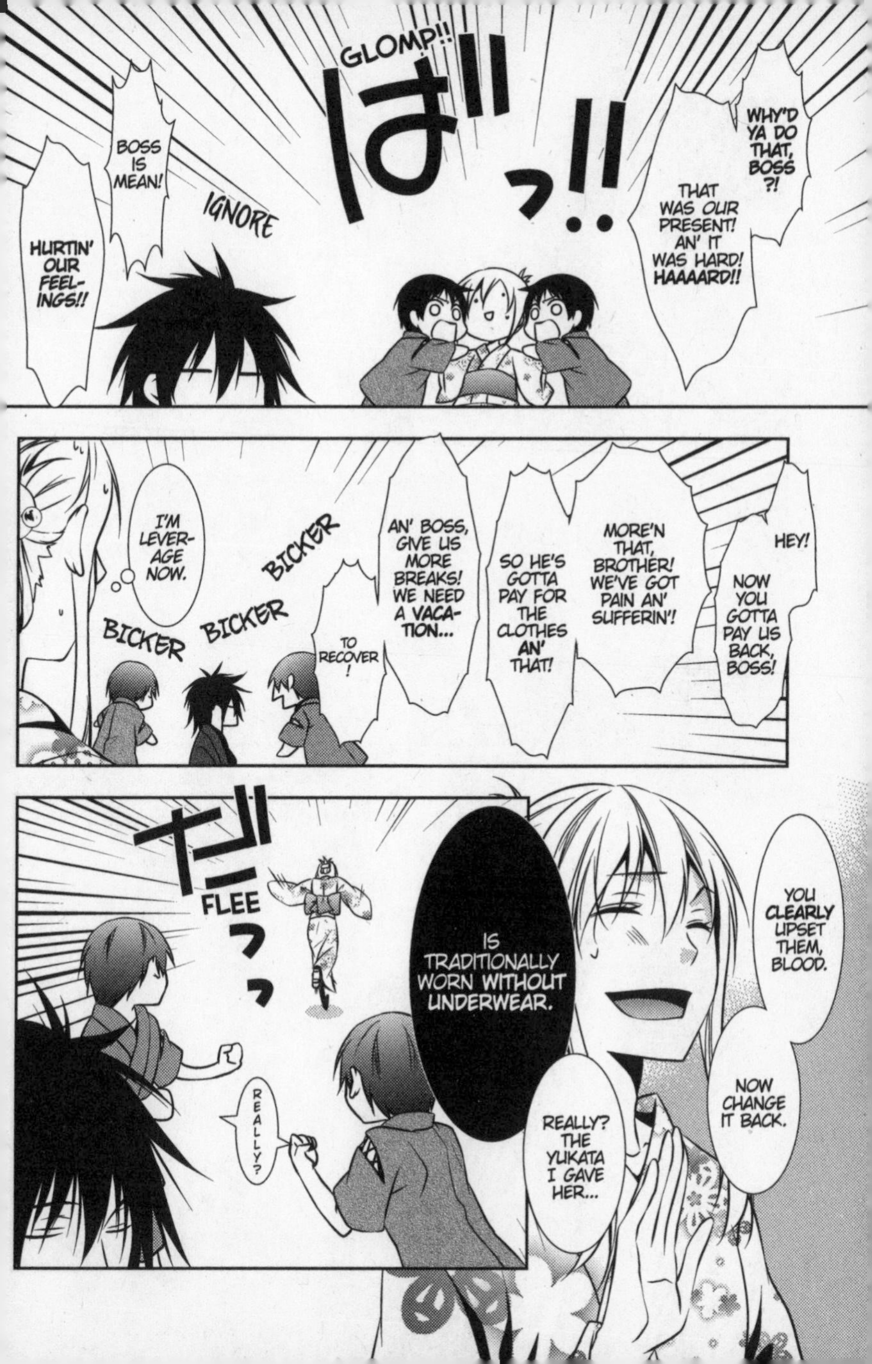
WHY'D YA DO THAT, BOSS?!
THAT WAS OUR PRESENT! AN' IT WAS HARD! HAAAARD!!
ぱっ!!
GLOMP!!
IGNORE
BOSS IS MEAN!
HURTIN' OUR FEEL-INGS!!
HEY!
NOW YOU GOTTA PAY US BACK, BOSS!
MORE'N THAT, BROTHER! WE'VE GOT PAIN AN' SUFFERIN'!
SO HE'S GOTTA PAY FOR THE CLOTHES AN' THAT!
AN' BOSS, GIVE US MORE BREAKS! WE NEED A VACA-TION...
TO RECOVER!
BICKER
BICKER
BICKER
I'M LEVER-AGE NOW.
YOU CLEARLY UPSET THEM, BLOOD.
NOW CHANGE IT BACK.
REALLY? THE YUKATA I GAVE HER...
IS TRADITIONALLY WORN WITHOUT UNDERWEAR.
REALLY?
FLEE

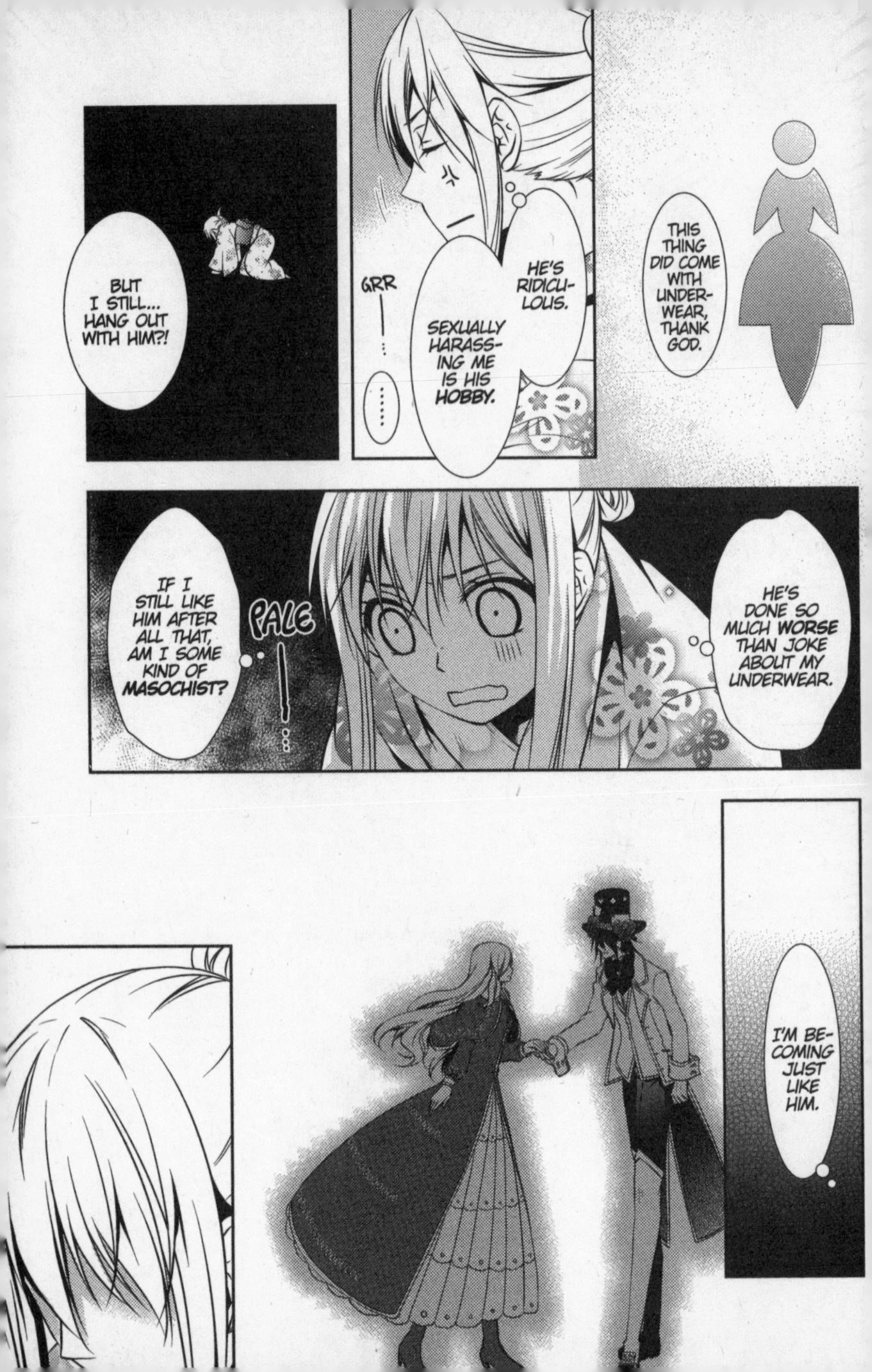
THIS THING DID COME WITH UNDERWEAR, THANK GOD.
HE'S RIDICULOUS.
SEXUALLY HARASSING ME IS HIS HOBBY.
GRR
......
BUT I STILL... HANG OUT WITH HIM?!
HE'S DONE SO MUCH WORSE THAN JOKE ABOUT MY UNDERWEAR.
PALE
IF I STILL LIKE HIM AFTER ALL THAT, AM I SOME KIND OF MASOCHIST?
I'M BECOMING JUST LIKE HIM.

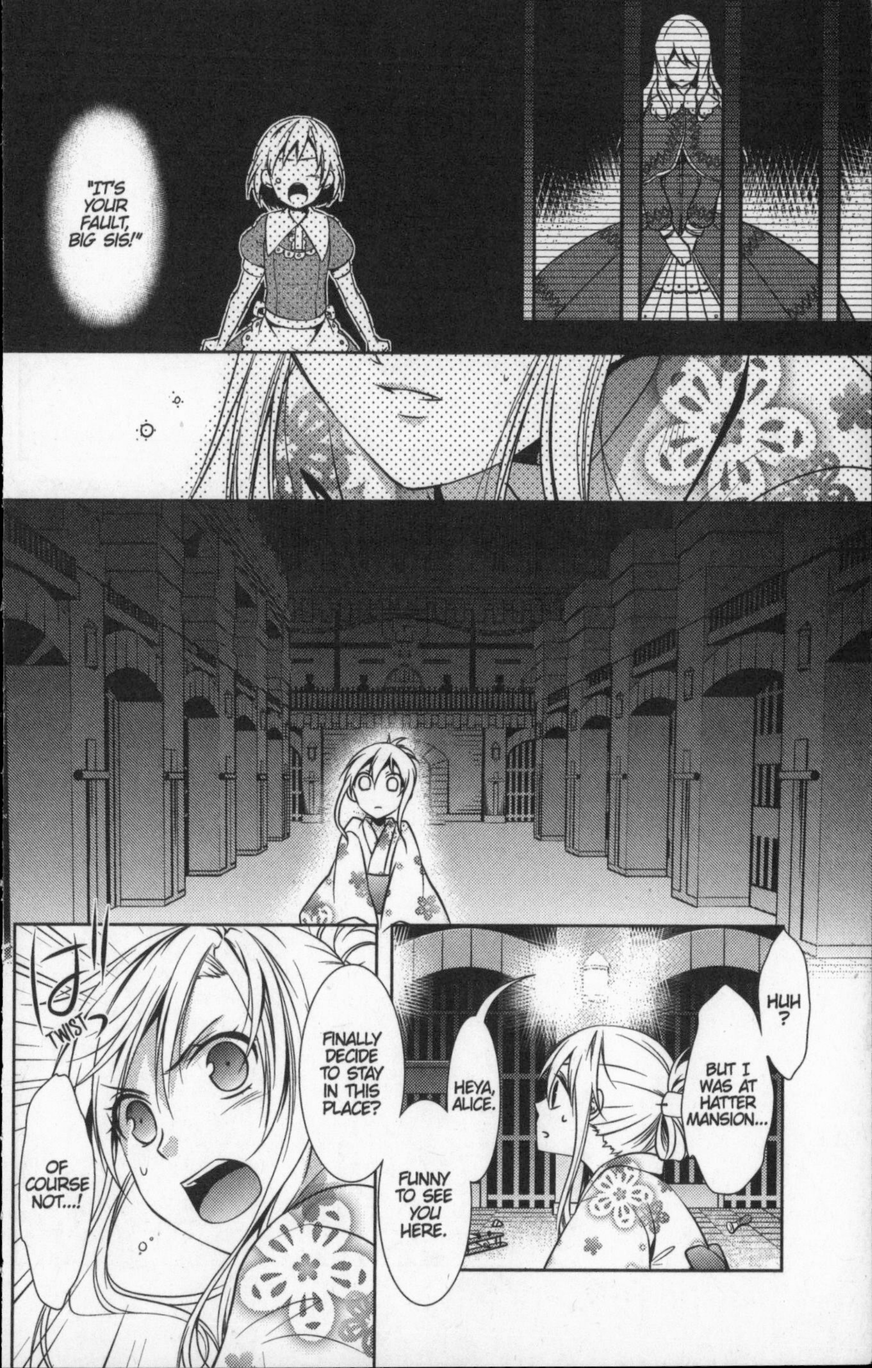
"IT'S YOUR FAULT, BIG SIS!"
HUH?
BUT I WAS AT HATTER MANSION...
HEYA, ALICE.
FINALLY DECIDE TO STAY IN THIS PLACE?
FUNNY TO SEE YOU HERE.
TWIST
OF COURSE NOT...!

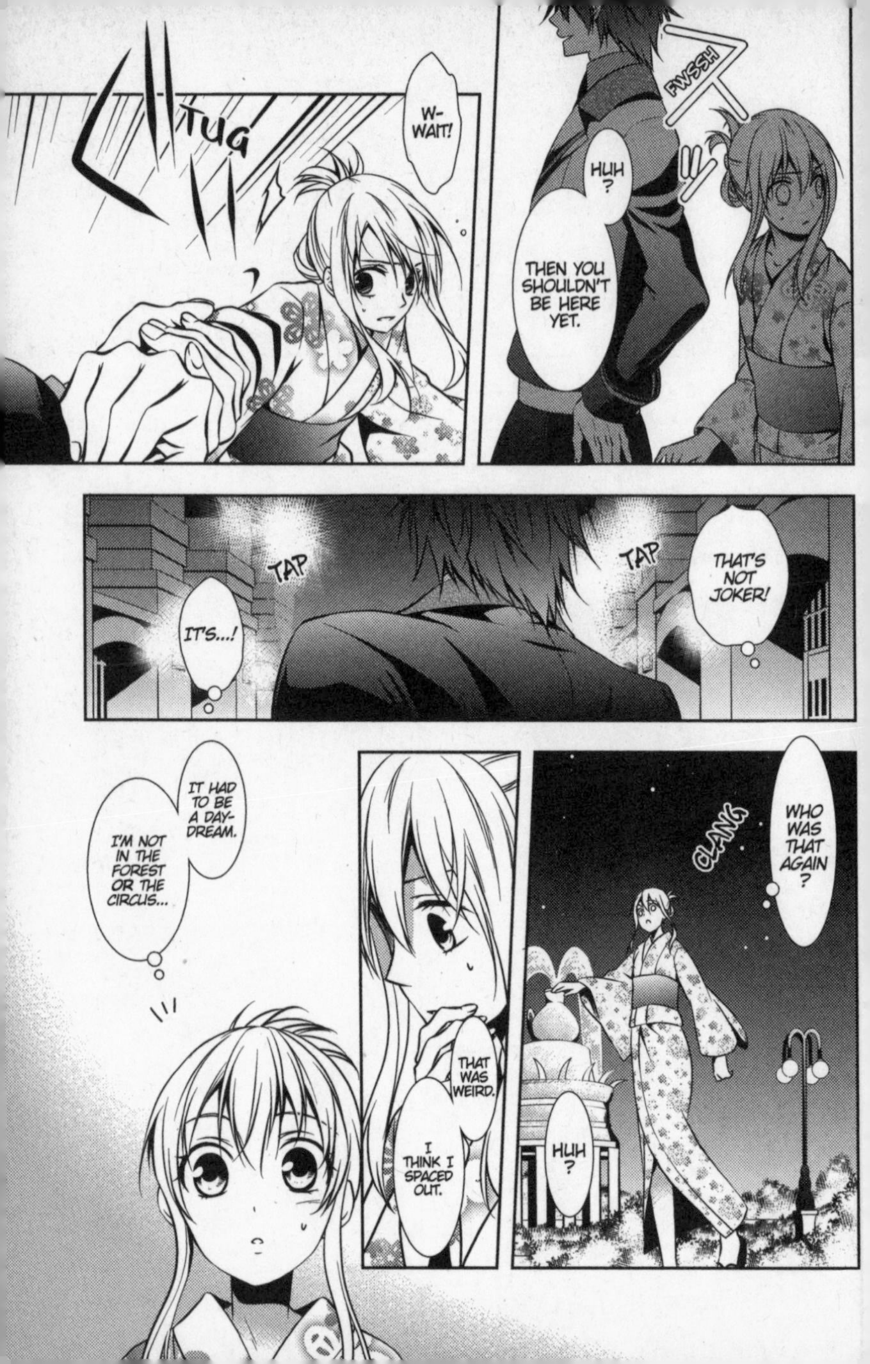
FWSSH
HUH?
THEN YOU SHOULDN'T BE HERE YET.
W-WAIT!
TUG
THAT'S NOT JOKER!
TAP
TAP
IT'S...!
WHO WAS THAT AGAIN?
CLANG
HUH?
THAT WAS WEIRD.
I THINK I SPACED OUT.
IT HAD TO BE A DAY-DREAM.
I'M NOT IN THE FOREST OR THE CIRCUS...

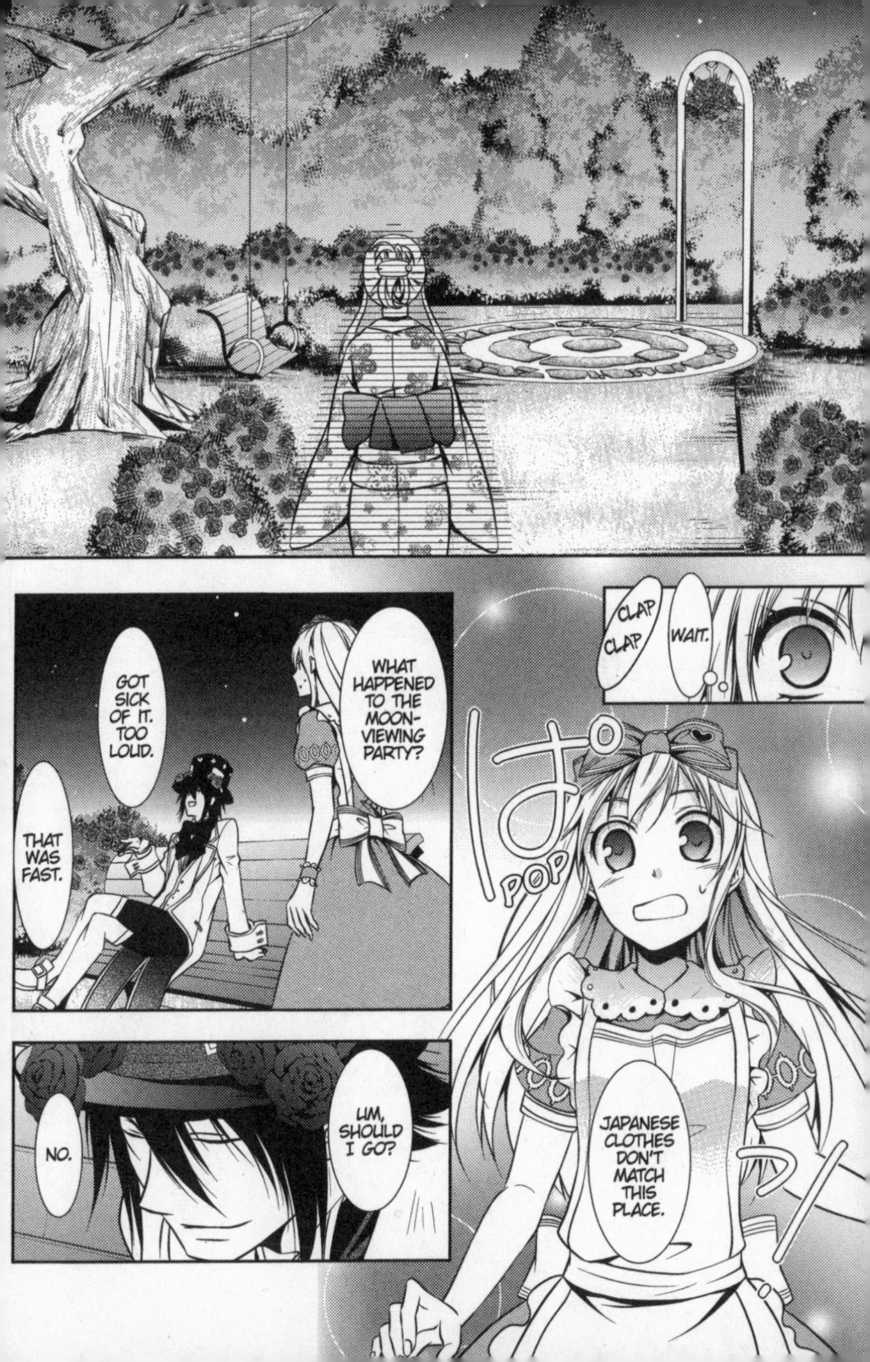
CLAP CLAP
WAIT.
ぽ
POP
JAPANESE CLOTHES DON'T MATCH THIS PLACE.
WHAT HAPPENED TO THE MOON-VIEWING PARTY?
GOT SICK OF IT. TOO LOUD.
THAT WAS FAST.
UM, SHOULD I GO?
NO.

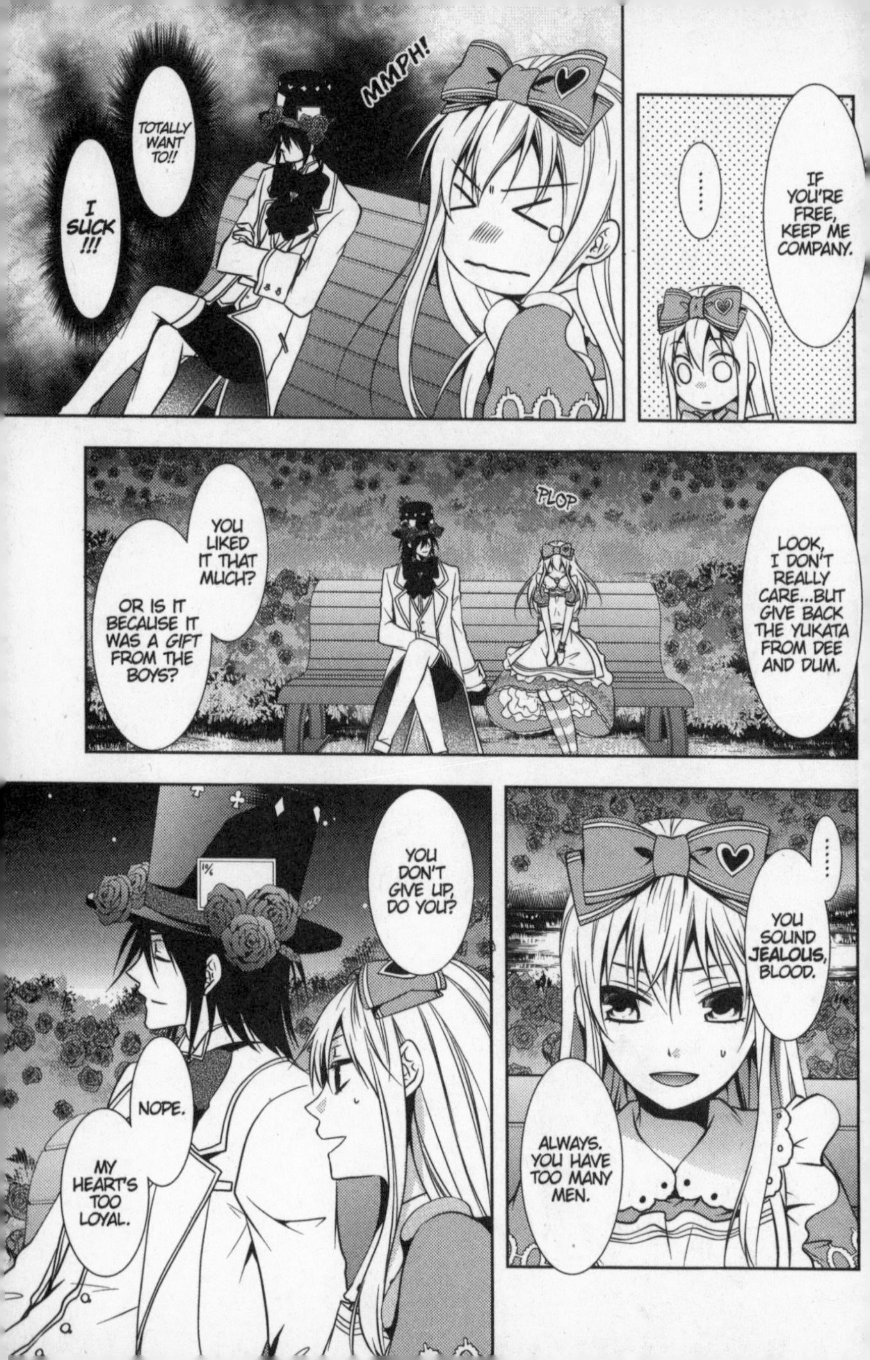
IF YOU'RE FREE, KEEP ME COMPANY.
......
MMPH!
TOTALLY WANT TO!!
I SUCK!!!
LOOK, I DON'T REALLY CARE...BUT GIVE BACK THE YUKATA FROM DEE AND DUM.
PLOP
YOU LIKED IT THAT MUCH?
OR IS IT BECAUSE IT WAS A GIFT FROM THE BOYS?
......
YOU SOUND JEALOUS, BLOOD.
ALWAYS. YOU HAVE TOO MANY MEN.
YOU DON'T GIVE UP, DO YOU?
NOPE.
MY HEART'S TOO LOYAL.

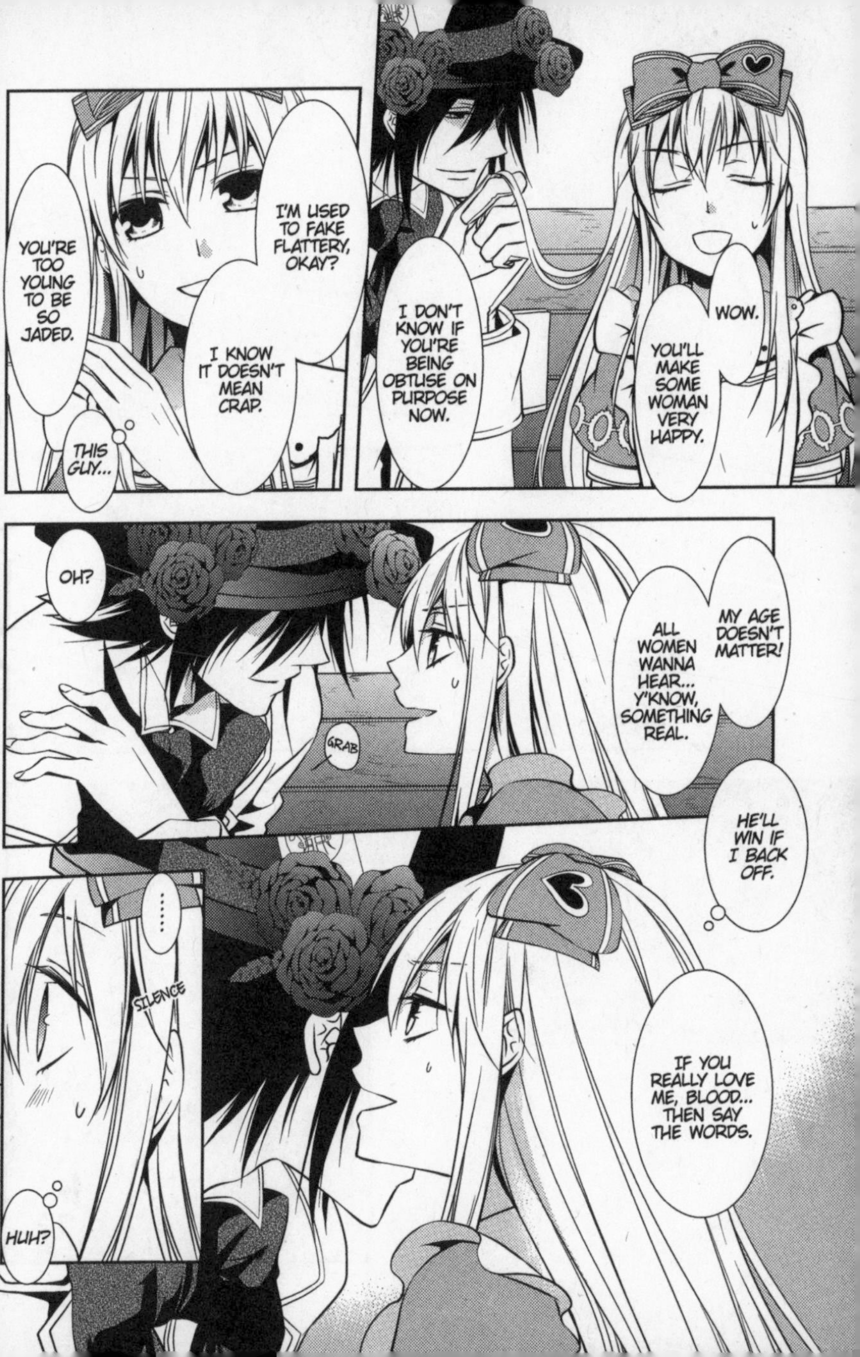
WOW.
YOU'LL MAKE SOME WOMAN VERY HAPPY.
I DON'T KNOW IF YOU'RE BEING OBTUSE ON PURPOSE NOW.
I'M USED TO FAKE FLATTERY, OKAY?
I KNOW IT DOESN'T MEAN CRAP.
YOU'RE TOO YOUNG TO BE SO JADED.
THIS GUY...
MY AGE DOESN'T MATTER!
ALL WOMEN WANNA HEAR... Y'KNOW, SOMETHING REAL.
GRAB
OH?
HE'LL WIN IF I BACK OFF.
IF YOU REALLY LOVE ME, BLOOD... THEN SAY THE WORDS.
......
SILENCE
HUH?

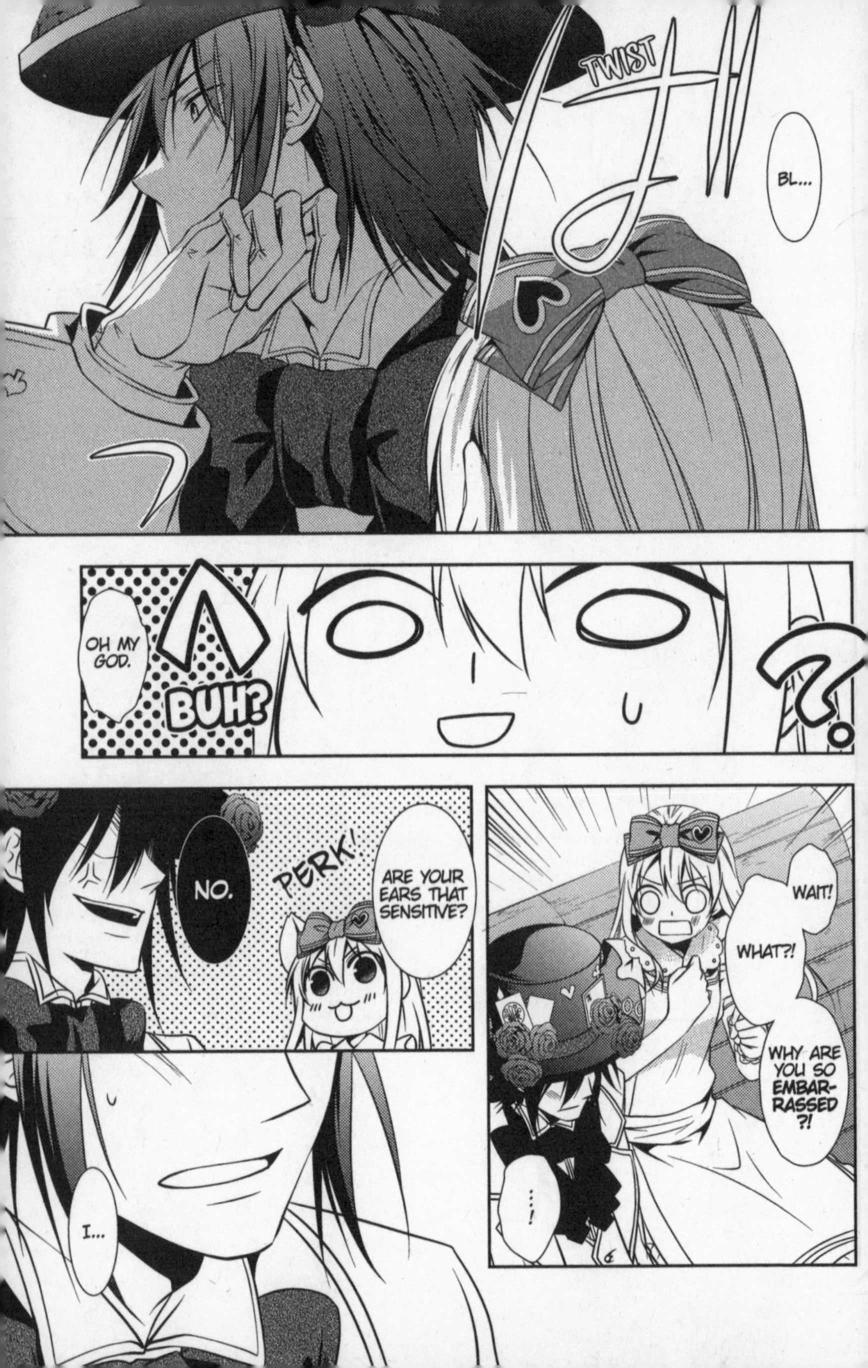
TWIST
BL...
?
BUH?
OH MY GOD.
WAIT!
WHAT?!
WHY ARE YOU SO EMBARRASSED?!
...!
ARE YOUR EARS THAT SENSITIVE?
PERK!
NO.
I...

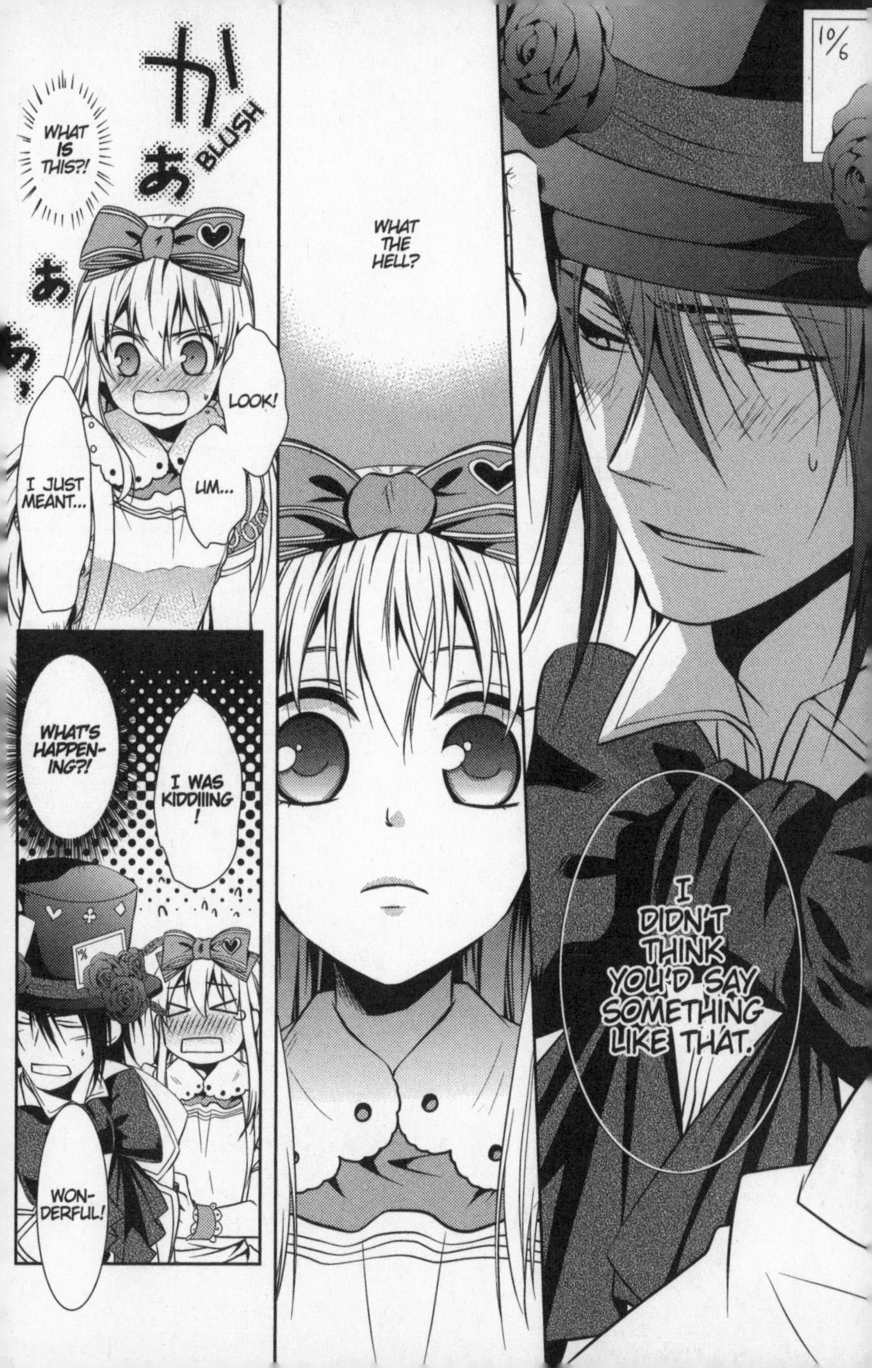
I DIDN'T THINK YOU'D SAY SOMETHING LIKE THAT.
WHAT THE HELL?
かあああ
BLUSH
WHAT IS THIS?!
LOOK!
UM...
I JUST MEANT...
I WAS KIDDIIING!
WHAT'S HAPPEN-ING?!
WON-DERFUL!

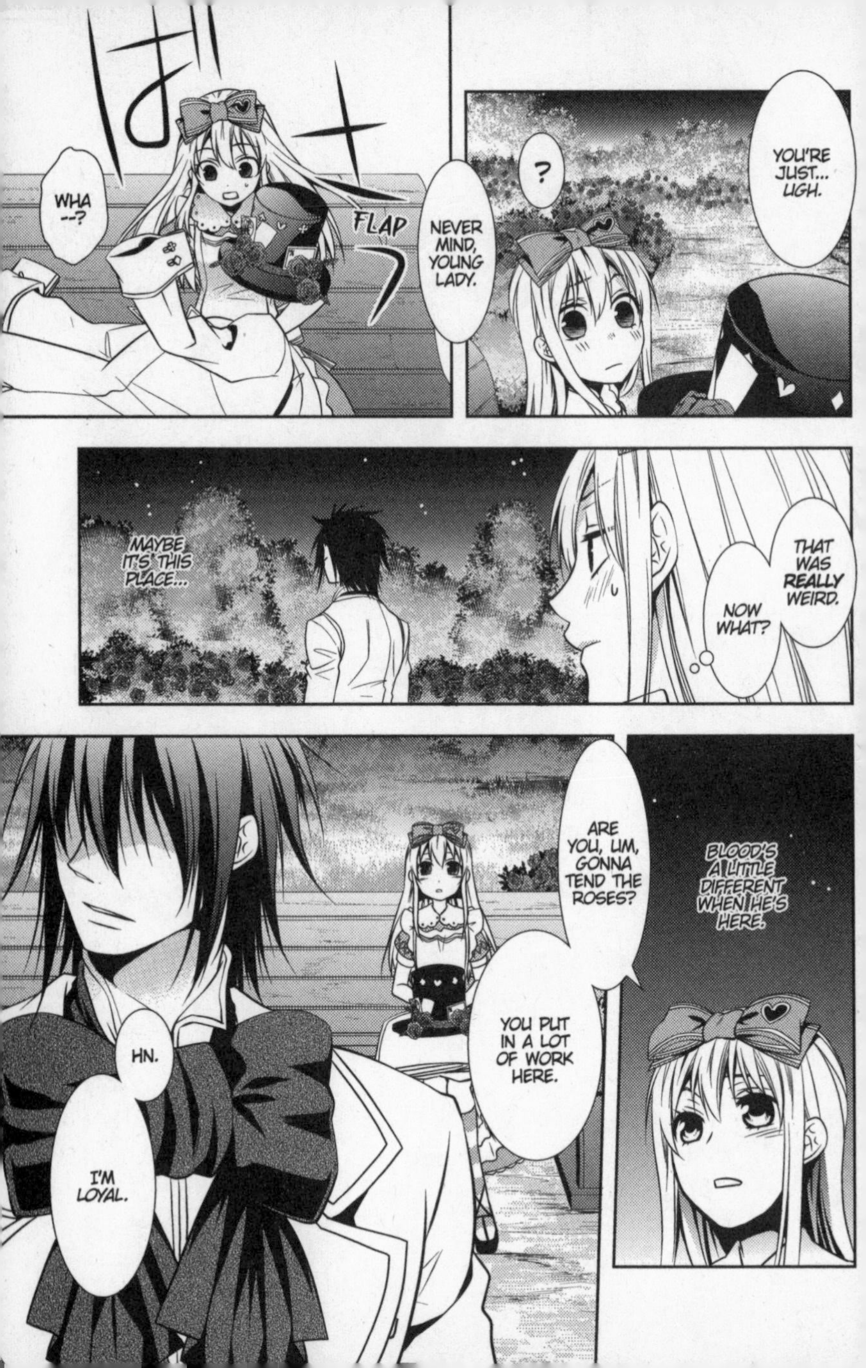
YOU'RE JUST... UGH.
?
NEVER MIND, YOUNG LADY.
WHA --?
FLAP
THAT WAS REALLY WEIRD.
NOW WHAT?
MAYBE IT'S THIS PLACE...
BLOOD'S A LITTLE DIFFERENT WHEN HE'S HERE.
ARE YOU, UM, GONNA TEND THE ROSES?
YOU PUT IN A LOT OF WORK HERE.
HN.
I'M LOYAL.

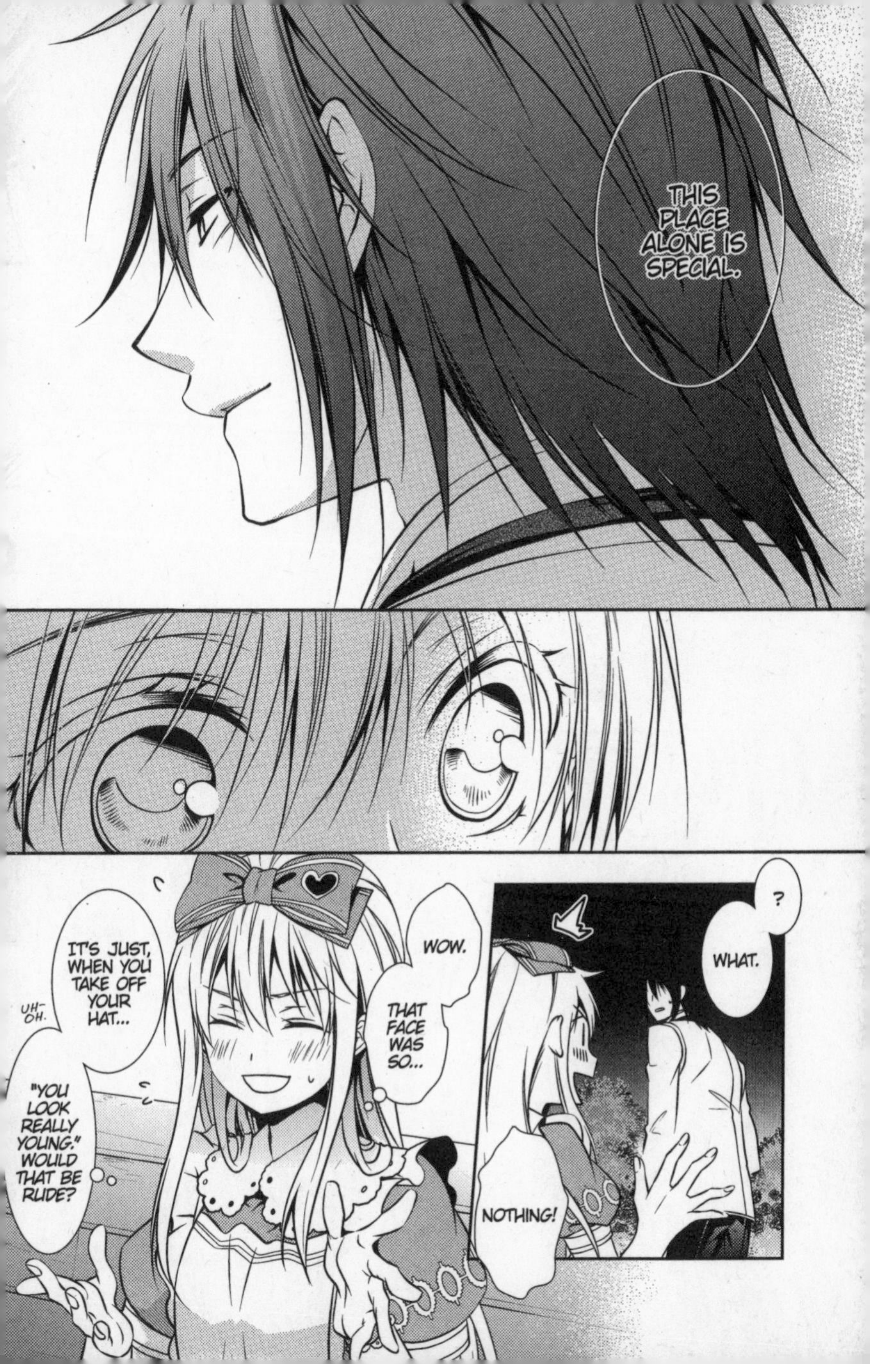
THIS PLACE ALONE IS SPECIAL.
?
WHAT.
NOTHING!
WOW.
THAT FACE WAS SO...
IT'S JUST, WHEN YOU TAKE OFF YOUR HAT...
UH-OH.
"YOU LOOK REALLY YOUNG." WOULD THAT BE RUDE?

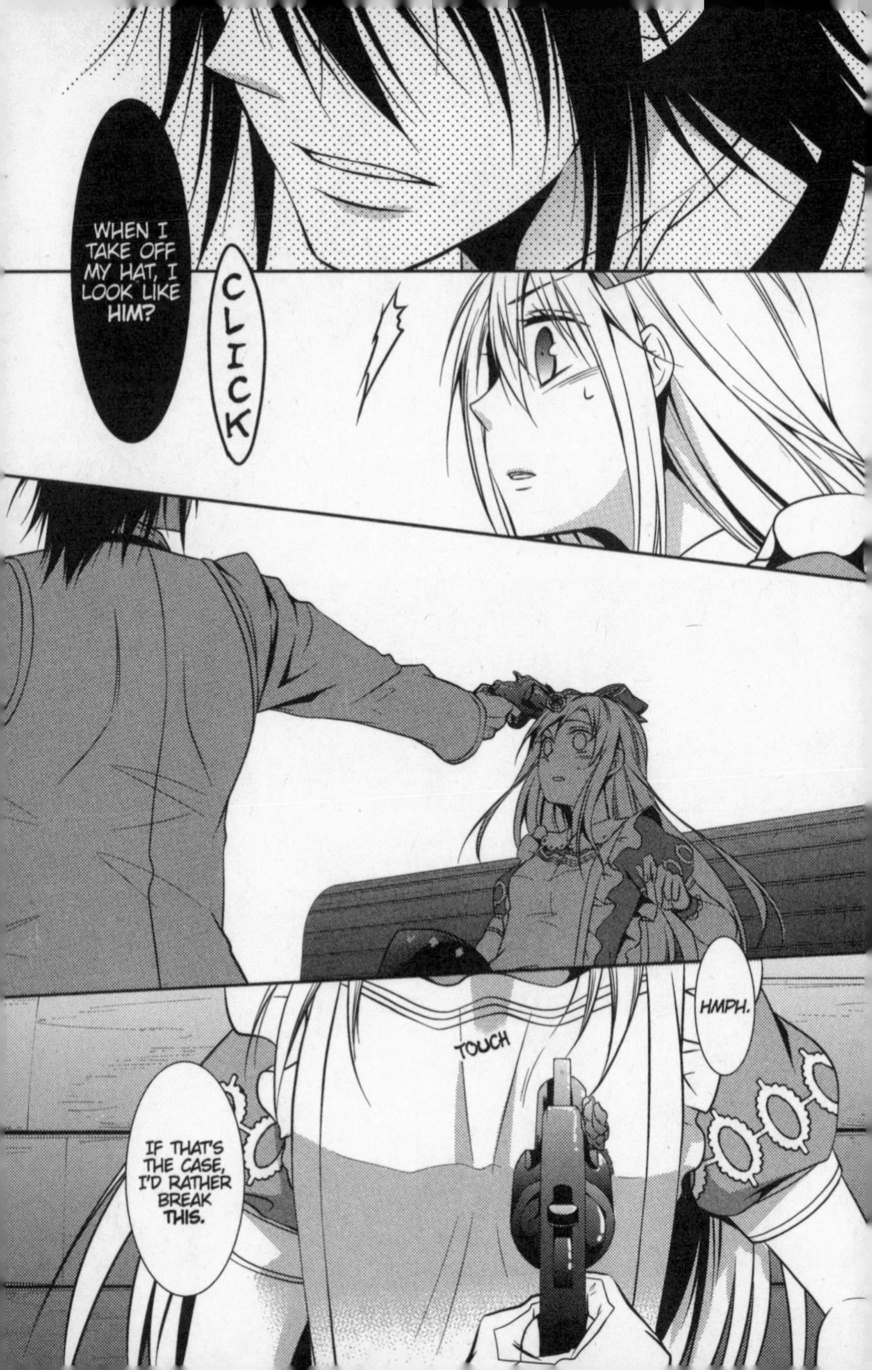
WHEN I TAKE OFF MY HAT, I LOOK LIKE HIM?
CLICK
HMPH.
TOUCH
IF THAT'S THE CASE, I'D RATHER BREAK THIS.

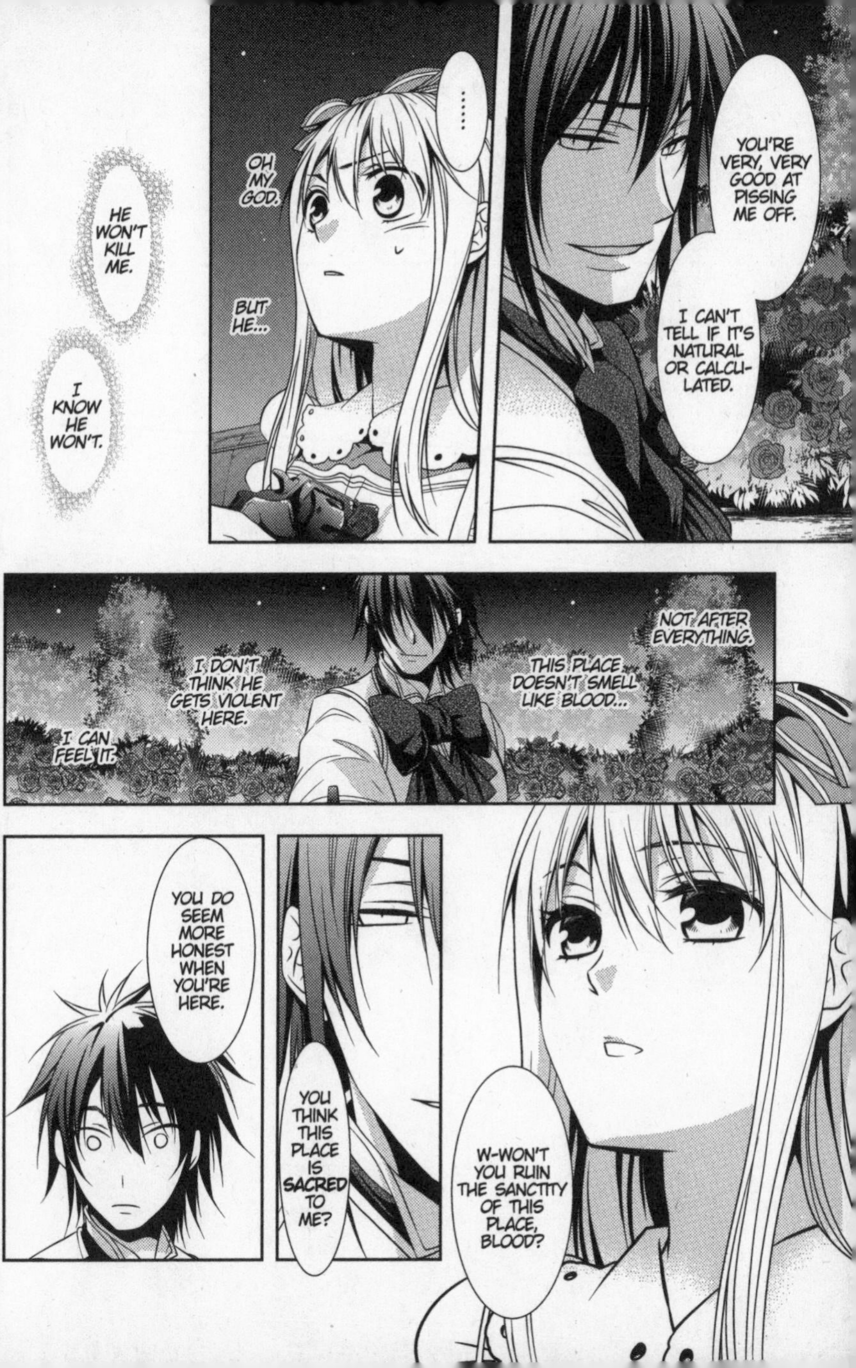
YOU'RE VERY, VERY GOOD AT PISSING ME OFF.
I CAN'T TELL IF IT'S NATURAL OR CALCU-LATED.
......
OH MY GOD.
BUT HE...
HE WON'T KILL ME.
I KNOW HE WON'T.
NOT AFTER EVERYTHING.
THIS PLACE DOESN'T SMELL LIKE BLOOD...
I DON'T THINK HE GETS VIOLENT HERE.
I CAN FEEL IT.
W-WON'T YOU RUIN THE SANCTITY OF THIS PLACE, BLOOD?
YOU THINK THIS PLACE IS SACRED TO ME?
YOU DO SEEM MORE HONEST WHEN YOU'RE HERE.

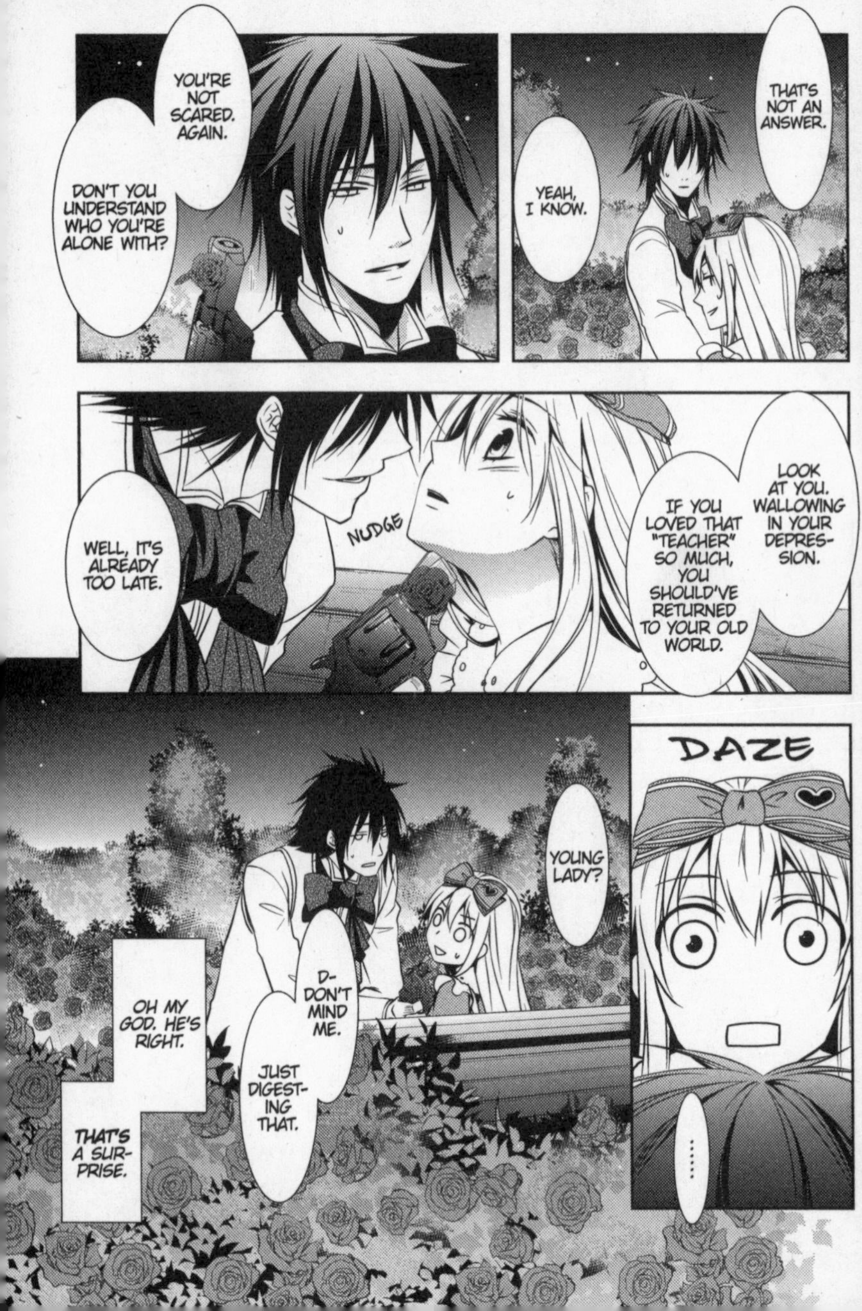
THAT'S NOT AN ANSWER.
YEAH, I KNOW.
YOU'RE NOT SCARED. AGAIN.
DON'T YOU UNDERSTAND WHO YOU'RE ALONE WITH?
LOOK AT YOU. WALLOWING IN YOUR DEPRES-SION.
IF YOU LOVED THAT "TEACHER" SO MUCH, YOU SHOULD'VE RETURNED TO YOUR OLD WORLD.
NUDGE
WELL, IT'S ALREADY TOO LATE.
DAZE
……
YOUNG LADY?
D-DON'T MIND ME.
JUST DIGEST-ING THAT.
OH MY GOD. HE'S RIGHT.
THAT'S A SUR-PRISE.

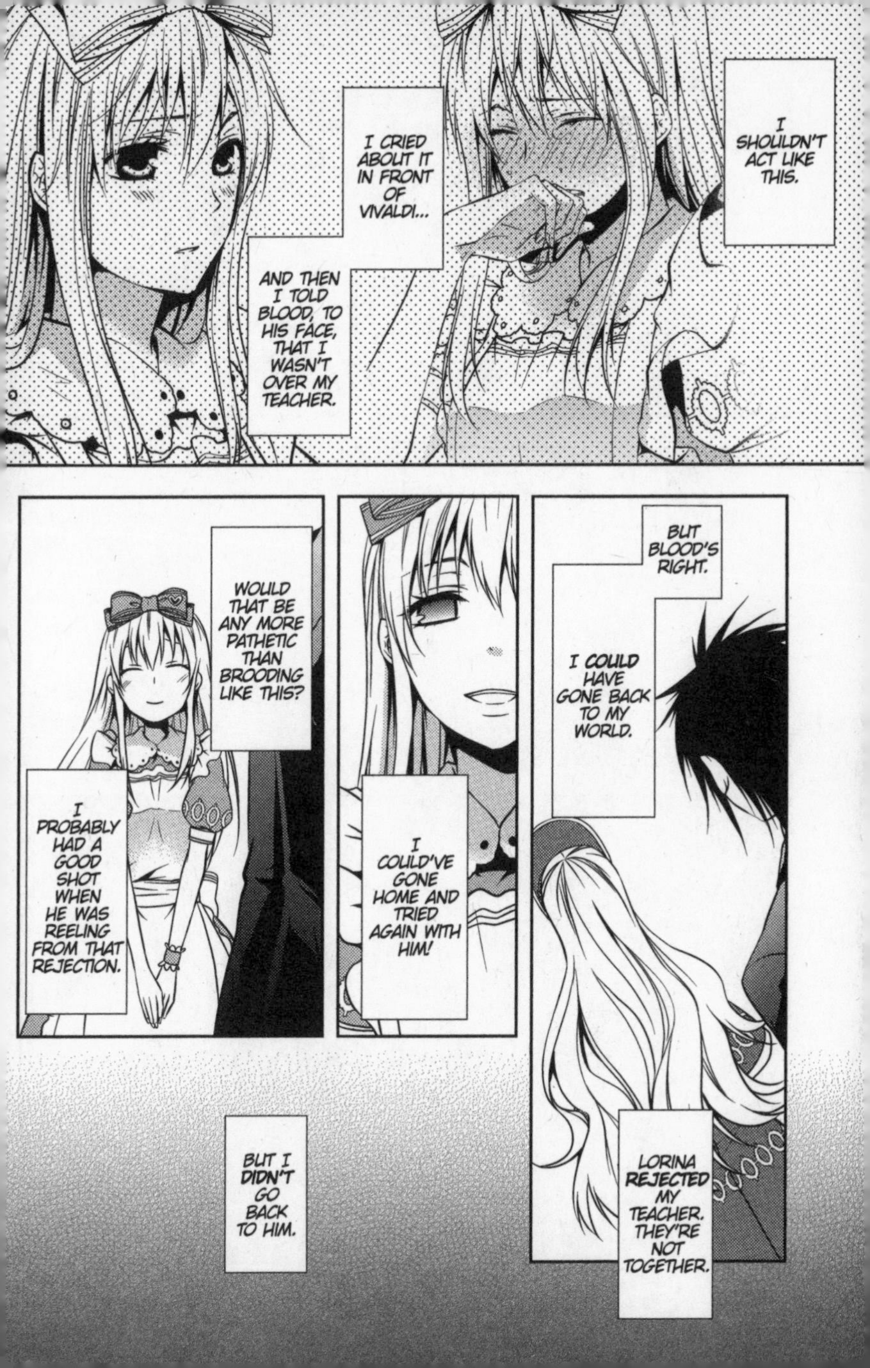
I SHOULDN'T ACT LIKE THIS.
I CRIED ABOUT IT IN FRONT OF VIVALDI...
AND THEN I TOLD BLOOD, TO HIS FACE, THAT I WASN'T OVER MY TEACHER.
BUT BLOOD'S RIGHT.
I COULD HAVE GONE BACK TO MY WORLD.
LORINA REJECTED MY TEACHER. THEY'RE NOT TOGETHER.
I COULD'VE GONE HOME AND TRIED AGAIN WITH HIM!
WOULD THAT BE ANY MORE PATHETIC THAN BROODING LIKE THIS?
I PROBABLY HAD A GOOD SHOT WHEN HE WAS REELING FROM THAT REJECTION.
BUT I DIDN'T GO BACK TO HIM.

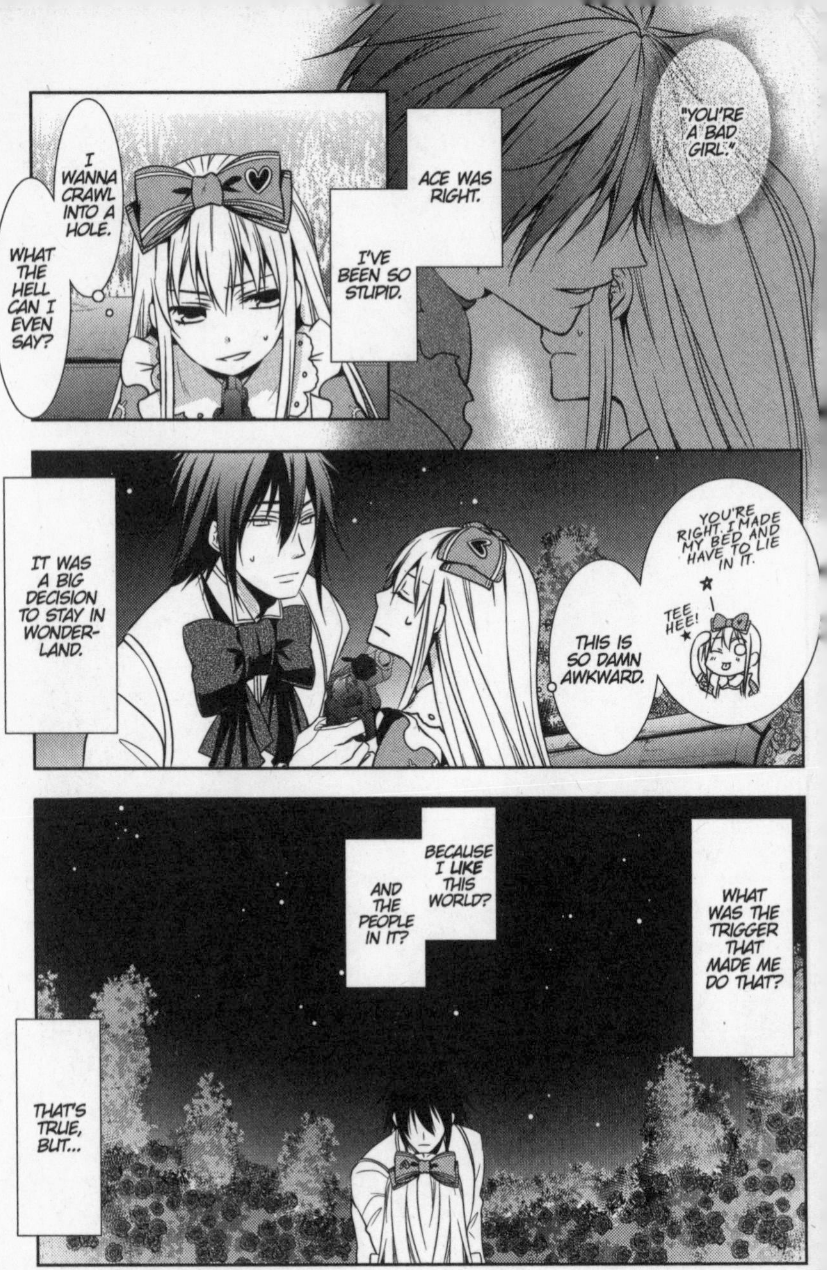
"YOU'RE A BAD GIRL."
ACE WAS RIGHT.
I'VE BEEN SO STUPID.
I WANNA CRAWL INTO A HOLE.
WHAT THE HELL CAN I EVEN SAY?
YOU'RE RIGHT. I MADE MY BED AND HAVE TO LIE IN IT.
TEE HEE!
THIS IS SO DAMN AWKWARD.
IT WAS A BIG DECISION TO STAY IN WONDERLAND.
WHAT WAS THE TRIGGER THAT MADE ME DO THAT?
BECAUSE I LIKE THIS WORLD?
AND THE PEOPLE IN IT?
THAT'S TRUE, BUT...

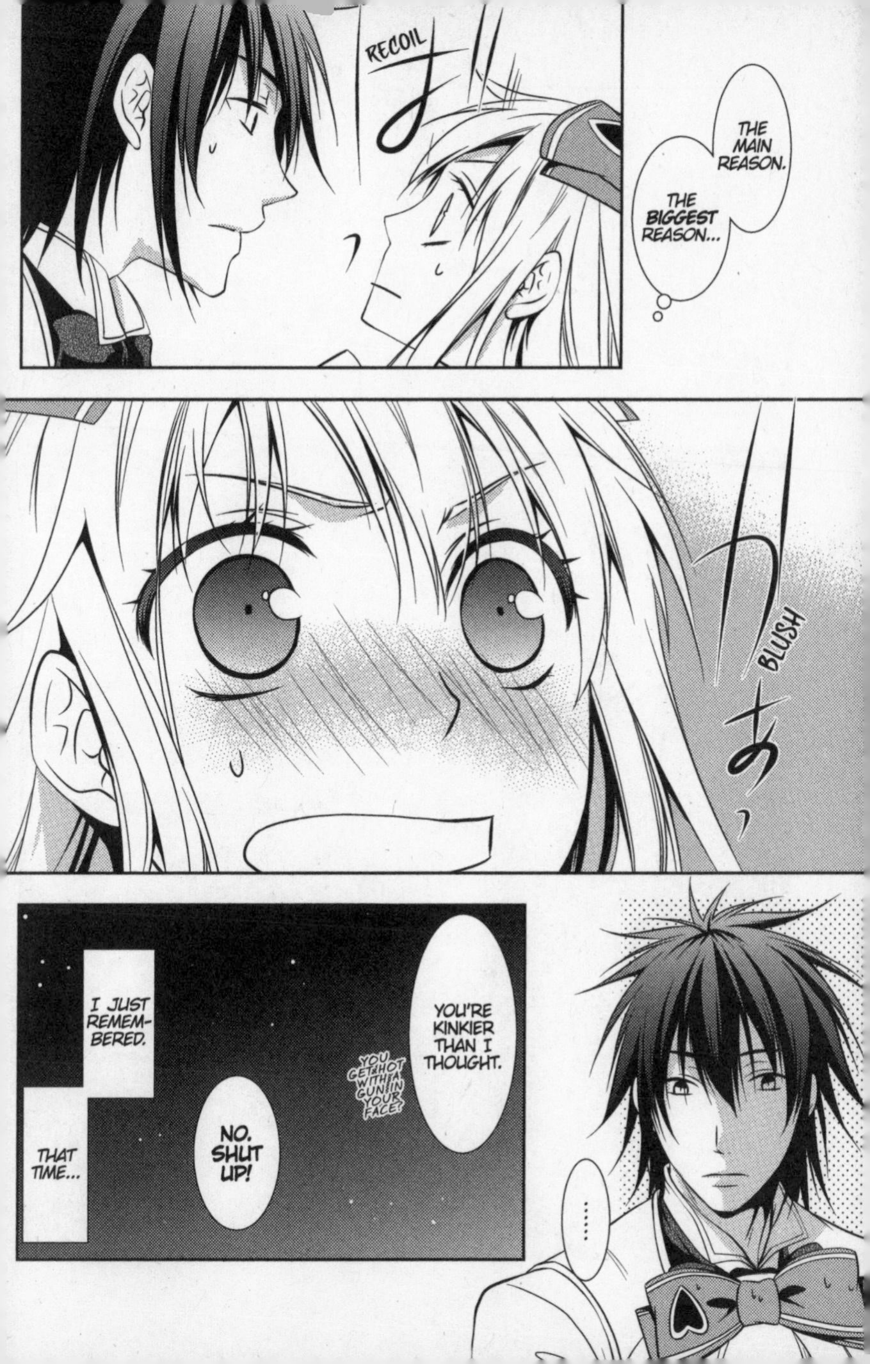
THE MAIN REASON.
THE BIGGEST REASON...
RECOIL
BLUSH
あっ
......
YOU'RE KINKIER THAN I THOUGHT.
YOU GET HOT WITH A GUN IN YOUR FACE?
NO. SHUT UP!
I JUST REMEMBERED.
THAT TIME...

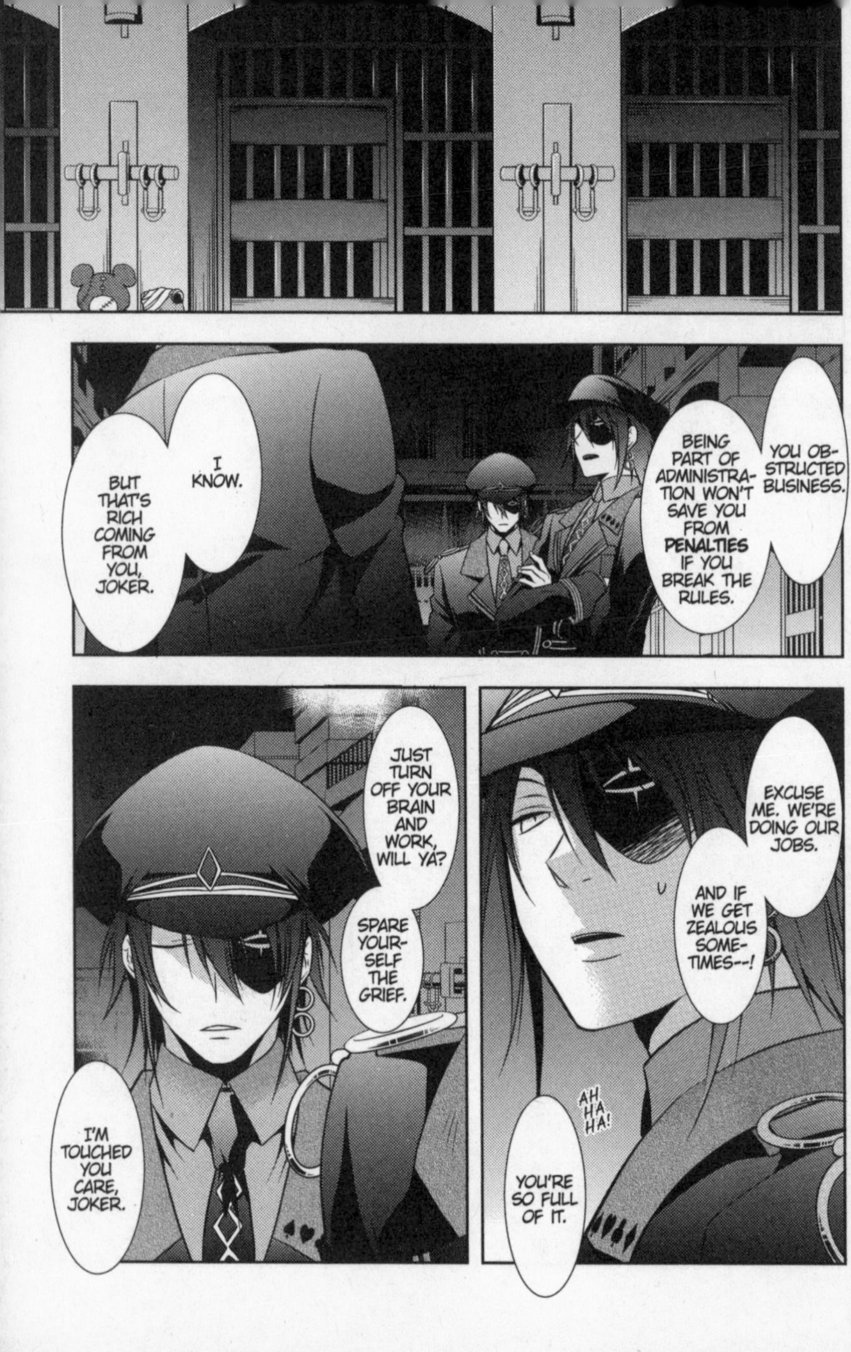
YOU OBSTRUCTED BUSINESS.
BEING PART OF ADMINISTRATION WON'T SAVE YOU FROM PENALTIES IF YOU BREAK THE RULES.
I KNOW.
BUT THAT'S RICH COMING FROM YOU, JOKER.
EXCUSE ME. WE'RE DOING OUR JOBS.
AND IF WE GET ZEALOUS SOMETIMES--!
AH HA HA!
YOU'RE SO FULL OF IT.
JUST TURN OFF YOUR BRAIN AND WORK, WILL YA?
SPARE YOURSELF THE GRIEF.
I'M TOUCHED YOU CARE, JOKER.

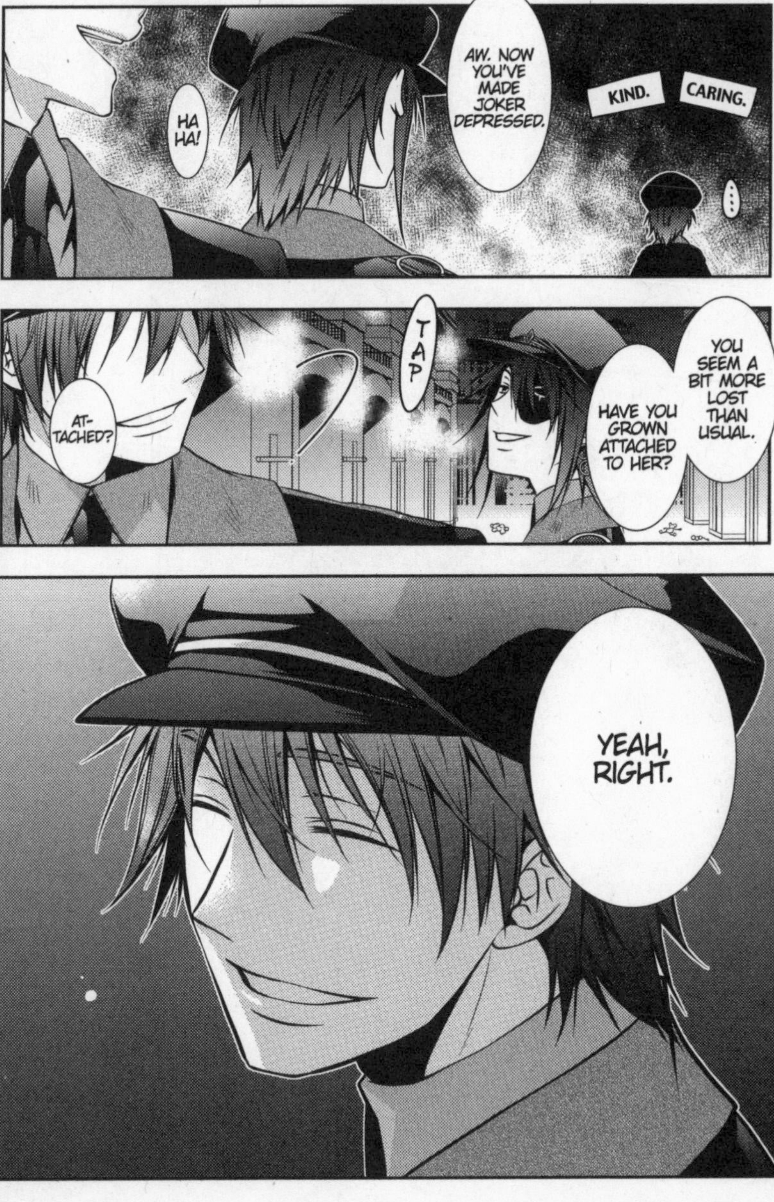
CARING.
KIND.
...
AW. NOW YOU'VE MADE JOKER DEPRESSED.
HA HA!
YOU SEEM A BIT MORE LOST THAN USUAL.
HAVE YOU GROWN ATTACHED TO HER?
TAP
AT-TACHED?
YEAH, RIGHT.

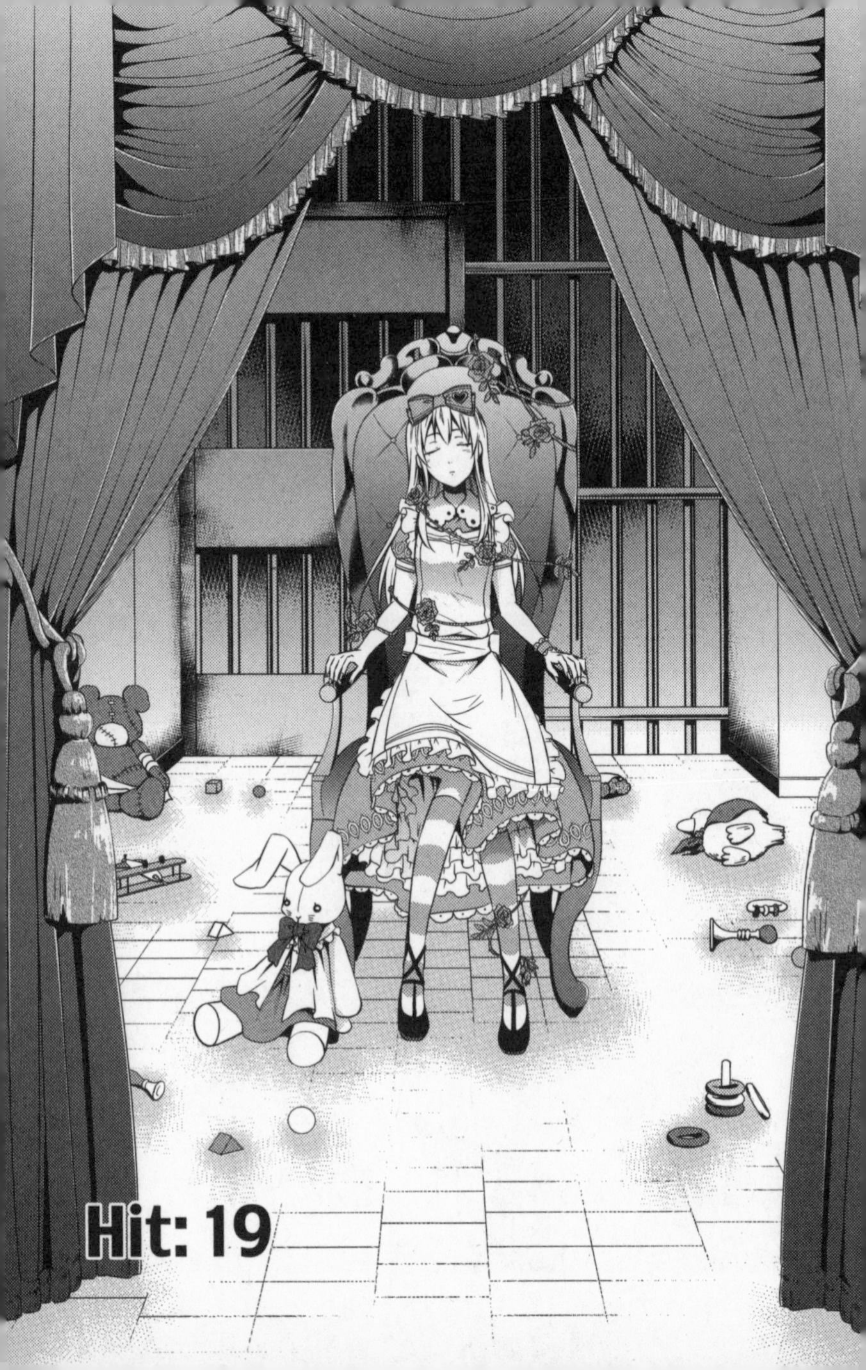
Hit: 19

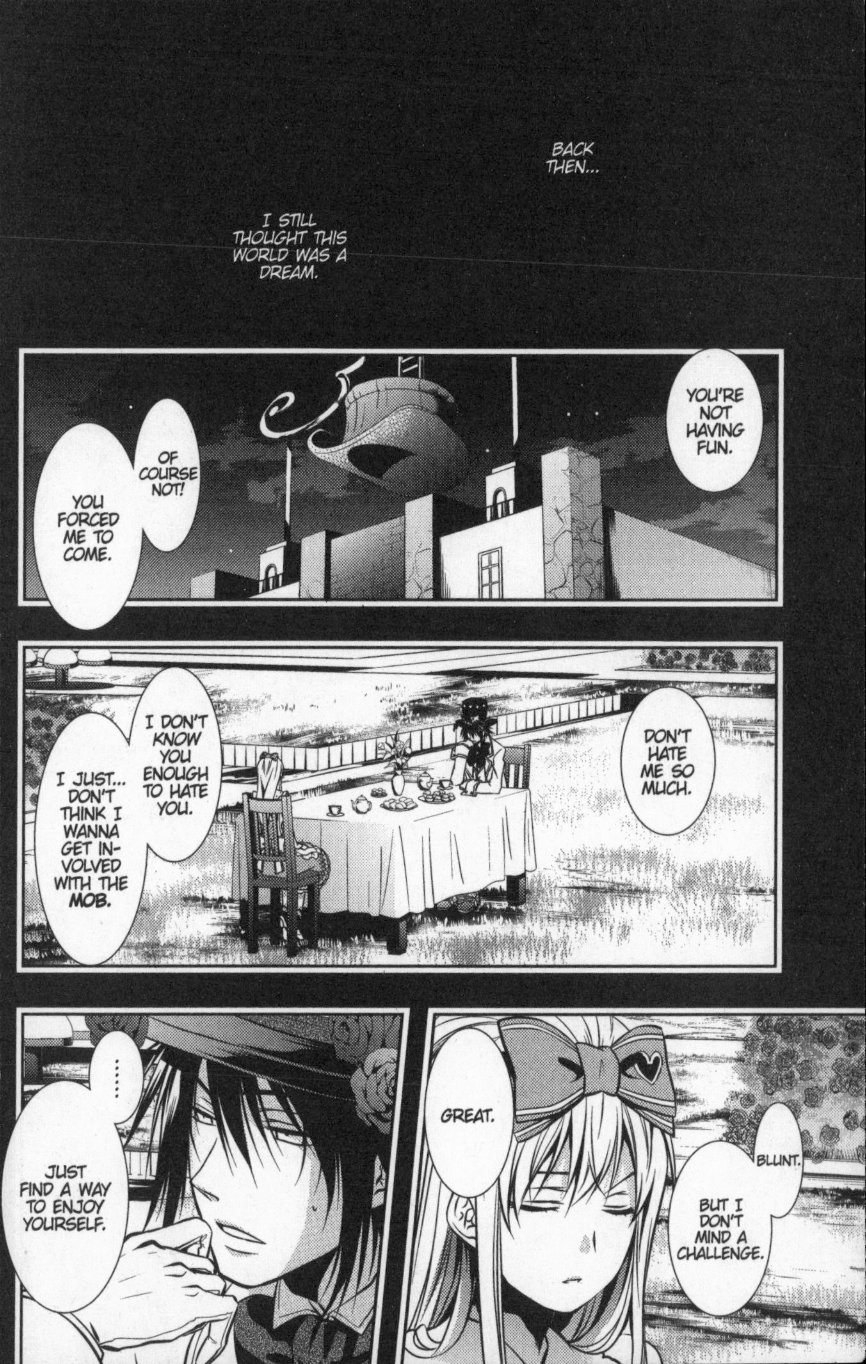

BACK THEN...
I STILL THOUGHT THIS WORLD WAS A DREAM.
YOU'RE NOT HAVING FUN.
OF COURSE NOT!
YOU FORCED ME TO COME.
DON'T HATE ME SO MUCH.
I DON'T KNOW YOU ENOUGH TO HATE YOU.
I JUST... DON'T THINK I WANNA GET IN-VOLVED WITH THE MOB.
BLUNT.
BUT I DON'T MIND A CHALLENGE.
GREAT.
......
JUST FIND A WAY TO ENJOY YOURSELF.

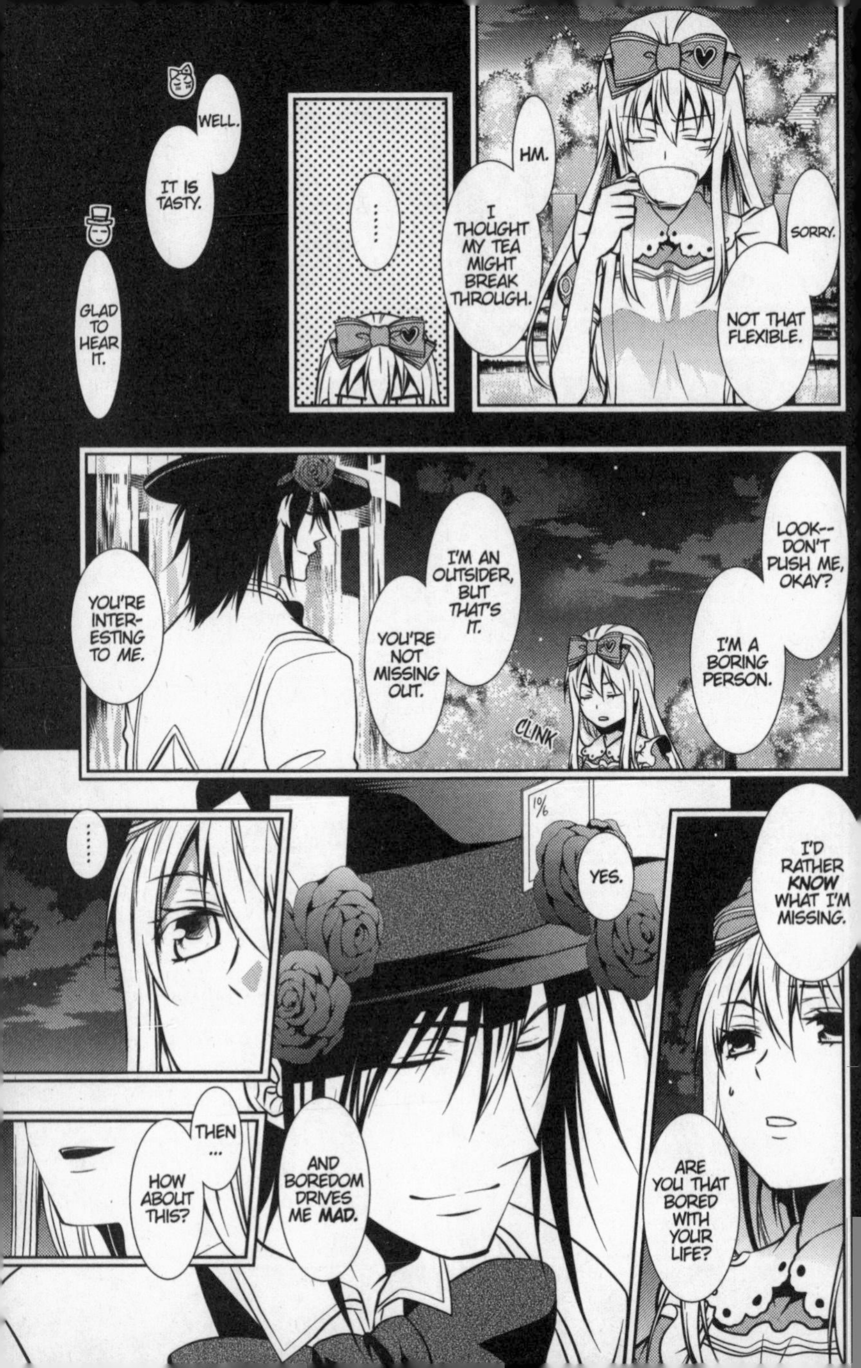
HM.
I THOUGHT MY TEA MIGHT BREAK THROUGH.
SORRY.
NOT THAT FLEXIBLE.
......
WELL.
IT IS TASTY.
GLAD TO HEAR IT.
LOOK-- DON'T PUSH ME, OKAY?
I'M A BORING PERSON.
CLINK
I'M AN OUTSIDER, BUT THAT'S IT.
YOU'RE NOT MISSING OUT.
YOU'RE INTERESTING TO ME.
I'D RATHER KNOW WHAT I'M MISSING.
YES.
......
ARE YOU THAT BORED WITH YOUR LIFE?
AND BOREDOM DRIVES ME MAD.
THEN ...
HOW ABOUT THIS?

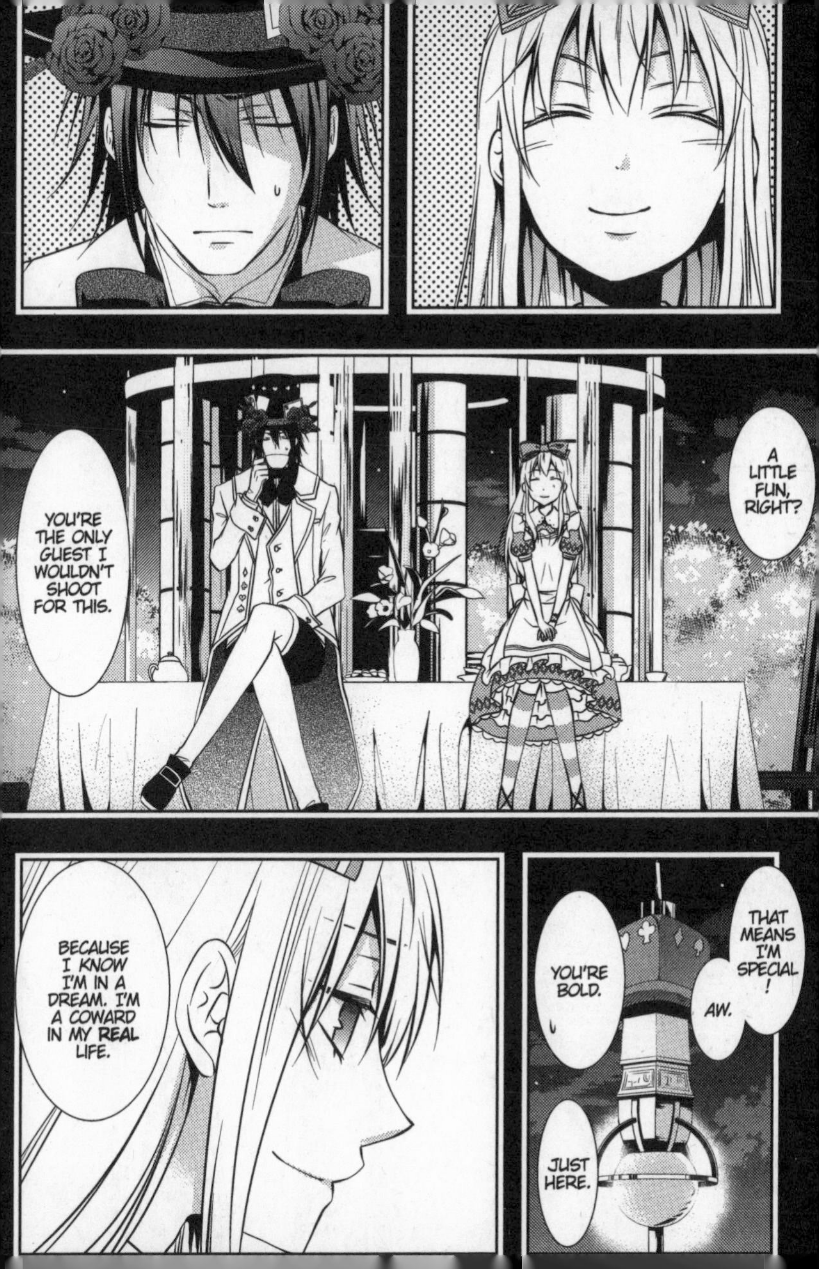
A LITTLE FUN, RIGHT?
YOU'RE THE ONLY GUEST I WOULDN'T SHOOT FOR THIS.
THAT MEANS I'M SPECIAL!
AW.
YOU'RE BOLD.
JUST HERE.
BECAUSE I KNOW I'M IN A DREAM. I'M A COWARD IN MY REAL LIFE.

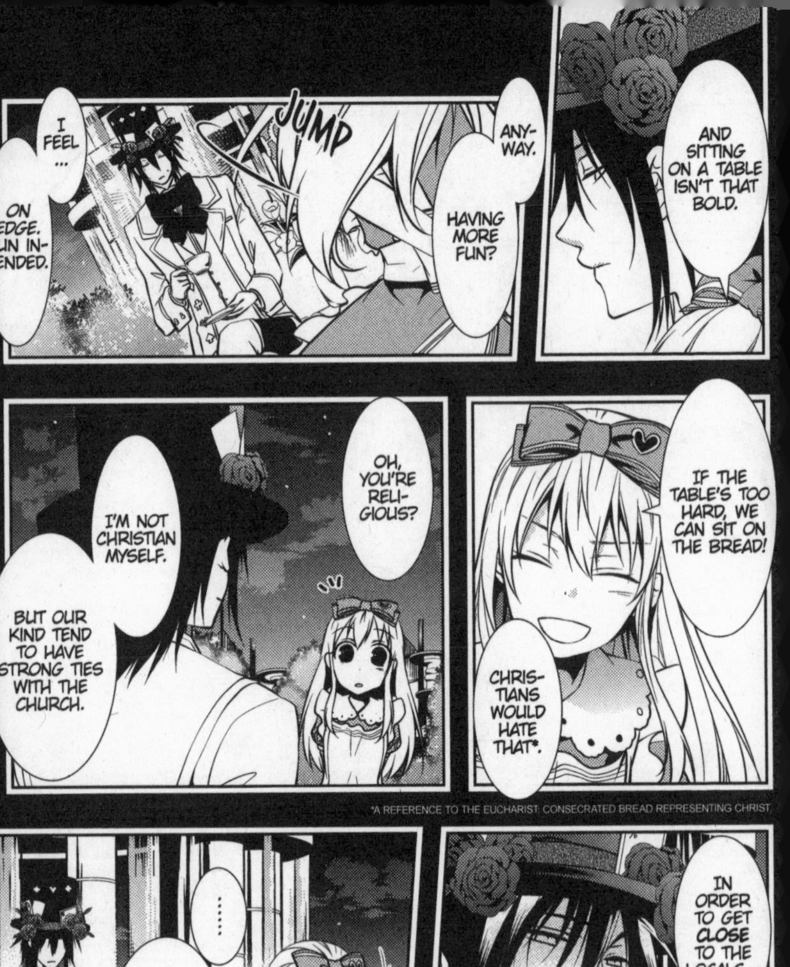
AND SITTING ON A TABLE ISN'T THAT BOLD.
ANY-WAY.
HAVING MORE FUN?
JUMP
I FEEL ...
ON EDGE. PUN IN-TENDED.
IF THE TABLE'S TOO HARD, WE CAN SIT ON THE BREAD!
CHRIS-TIANS WOULD HATE THAT*.
OH, YOU'RE RELI-GIOUS?
I'M NOT CHRISTIAN MYSELF.
BUT OUR KIND TEND TO HAVE STRONG TIES WITH THE CHURCH.

*A REFERENCE TO THE EUCHARIST: CONSECRATED BREAD REPRESENTING CHRIST.

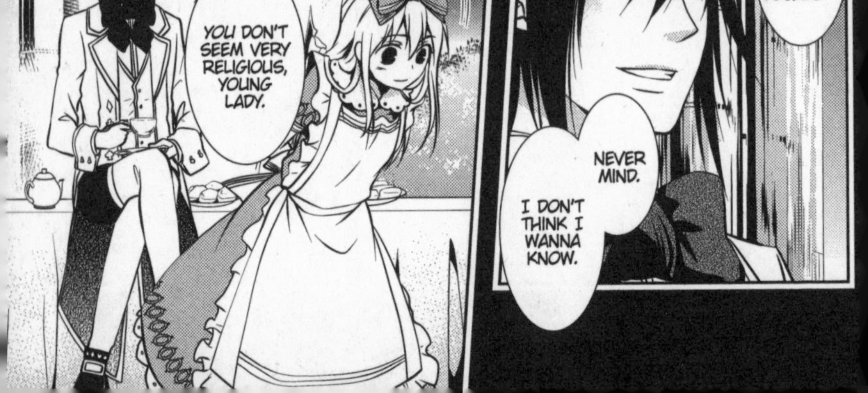
IN ORDER TO GET CLOSE TO THE LOCALS--
NEVER MIND.
I DON'T THINK I WANNA KNOW.
......
YOU DON'T SEEM VERY RELIGIOUS, YOUNG LADY.

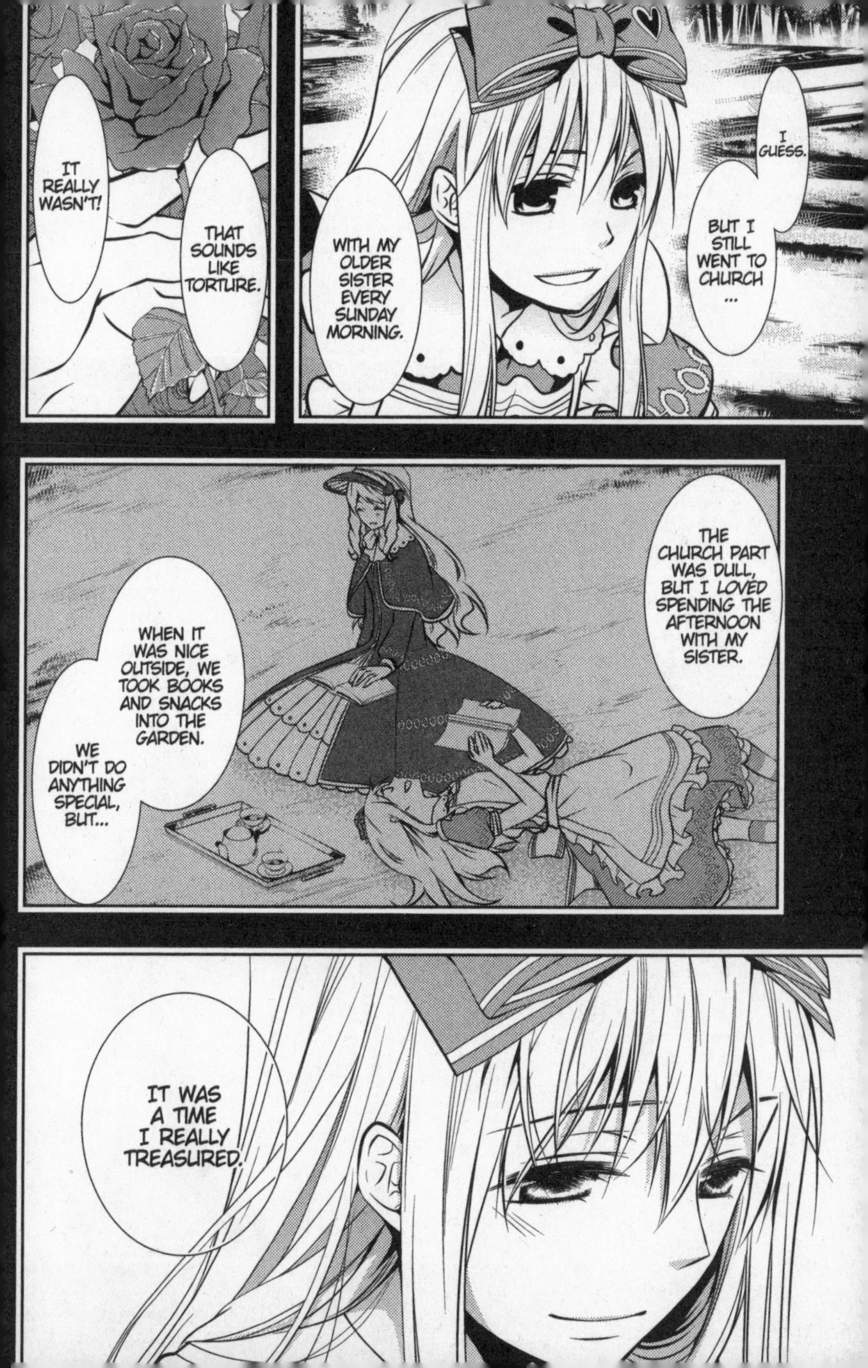
I GUESS.
BUT I STILL WENT TO CHURCH ...
WITH MY OLDER SISTER EVERY SUNDAY MORNING.
THAT SOUNDS LIKE TORTURE.
IT REALLY WASN'T!
THE CHURCH PART WAS DULL, BUT I LOVED SPENDING THE AFTERNOON WITH MY SISTER.
WHEN IT WAS NICE OUTSIDE, WE TOOK BOOKS AND SNACKS INTO THE GARDEN.
WE DIDN'T DO ANYTHING SPECIAL, BUT...
IT WAS A TIME I REALLY TREASURED.

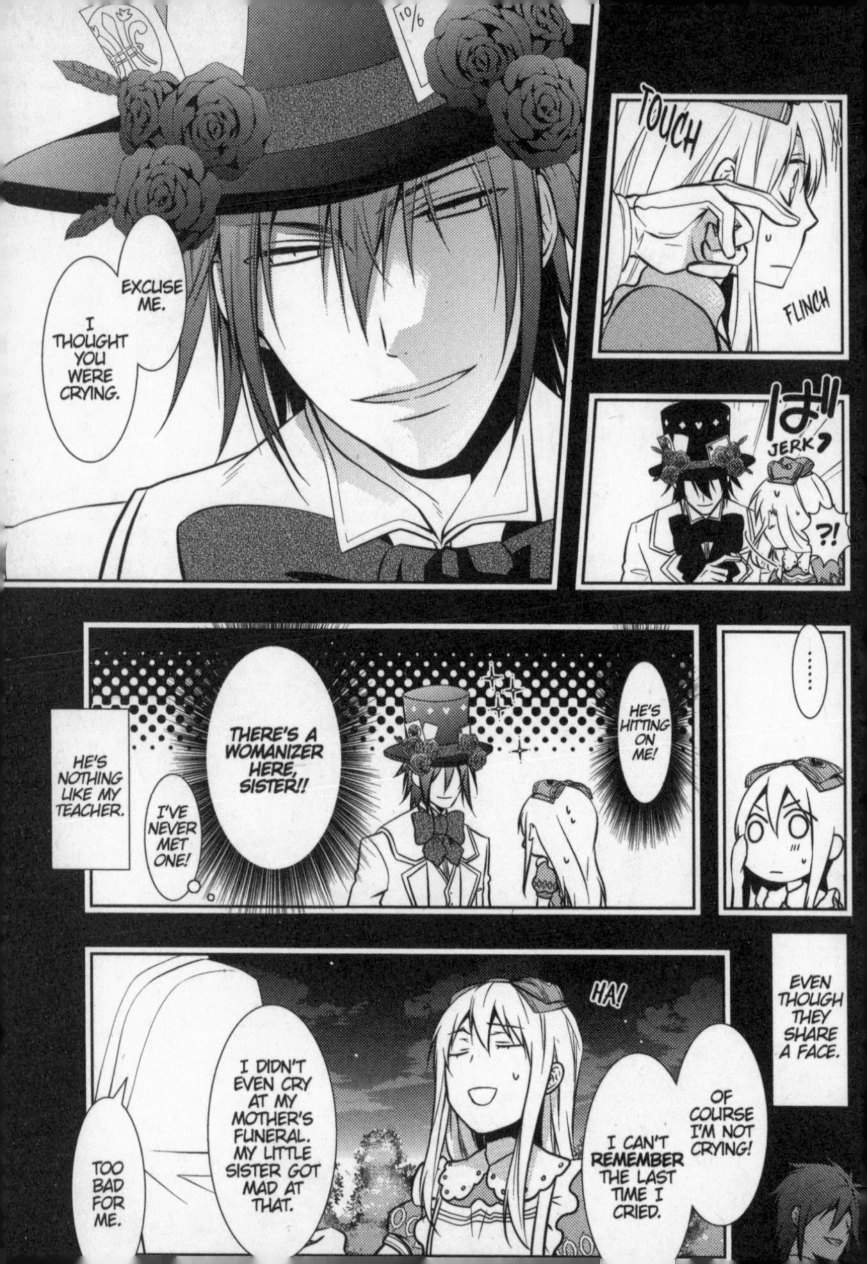
TOUCH
FLINCH
ばっ
JERK
?!
EXCUSE ME.
I THOUGHT YOU WERE CRYING.
......
HE'S HITTING ON ME!
THERE'S A WOMANIZER HERE, SISTER!!
HE'S NOTHING LIKE MY TEACHER.
I'VE NEVER MET ONE!
EVEN THOUGH THEY SHARE A FACE.
HA!
OF COURSE I'M NOT CRYING!
I CAN'T REMEMBER THE LAST TIME I CRIED.
I DIDN'T EVEN CRY AT MY MOTHER'S FUNERAL. MY LITTLE SISTER GOT MAD AT THAT.
TOO BAD FOR ME.

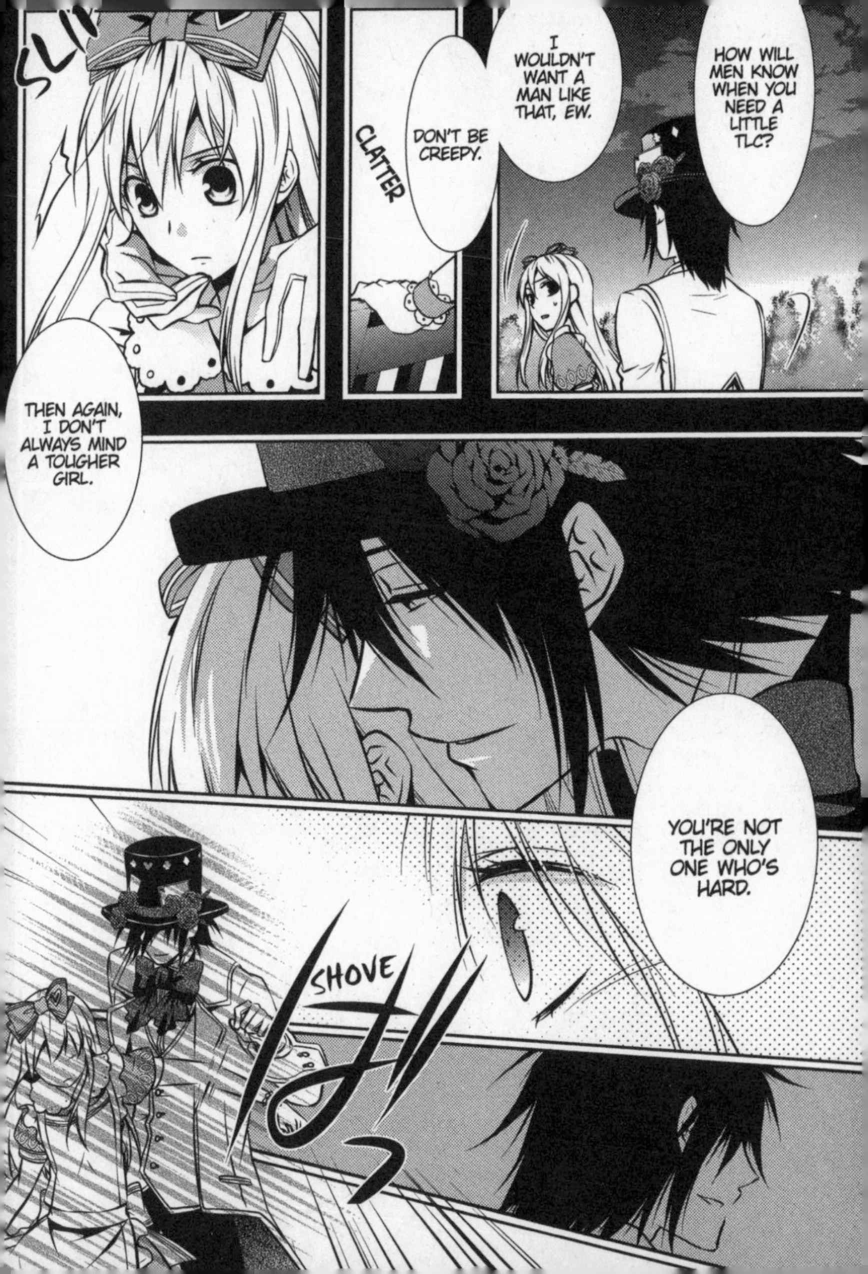
HOW WILL MEN KNOW WHEN YOU NEED A LITTLE TLC?
I WOULDN'T WANT A MAN LIKE THAT, EW.
DON'T BE CREEPY.
CLATTER
THEN AGAIN, I DON'T ALWAYS MIND A TOUGHER GIRL.
YOU'RE NOT THE ONLY ONE WHO'S HARD.
SHOVE

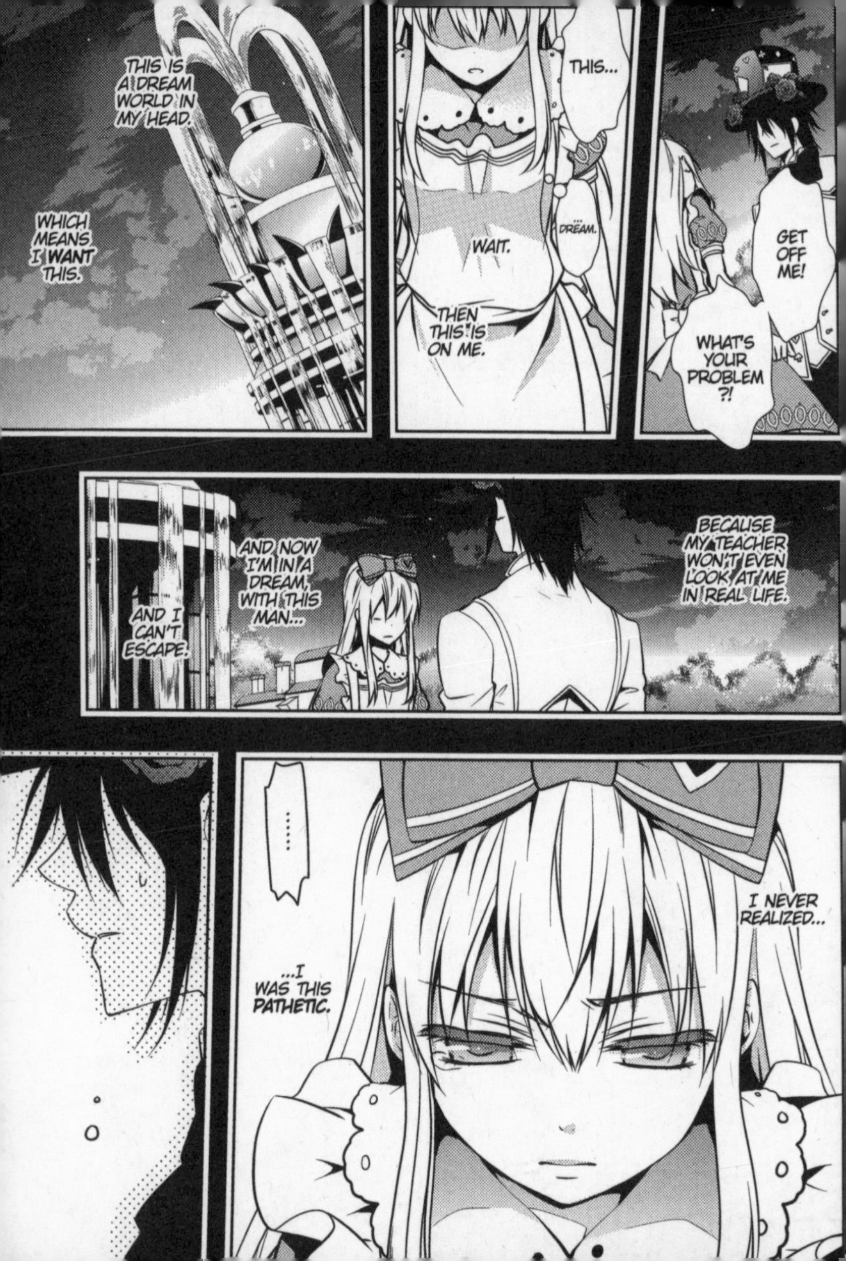
GET OFF ME!
WHAT'S YOUR PROBLEM?!
THIS...
...DREAM.
WAIT.
THEN THIS IS ON ME.
THIS IS A DREAM WORLD IN MY HEAD.
WHICH MEANS I WANT THIS.
BECAUSE MY TEACHER WON'T EVEN LOOK AT ME IN REAL LIFE.
AND NOW I'M IN A DREAM, WITH THIS MAN...
AND I CAN'T ESCAPE.
......
I NEVER REALIZED...
...I WAS THIS PATHETIC.

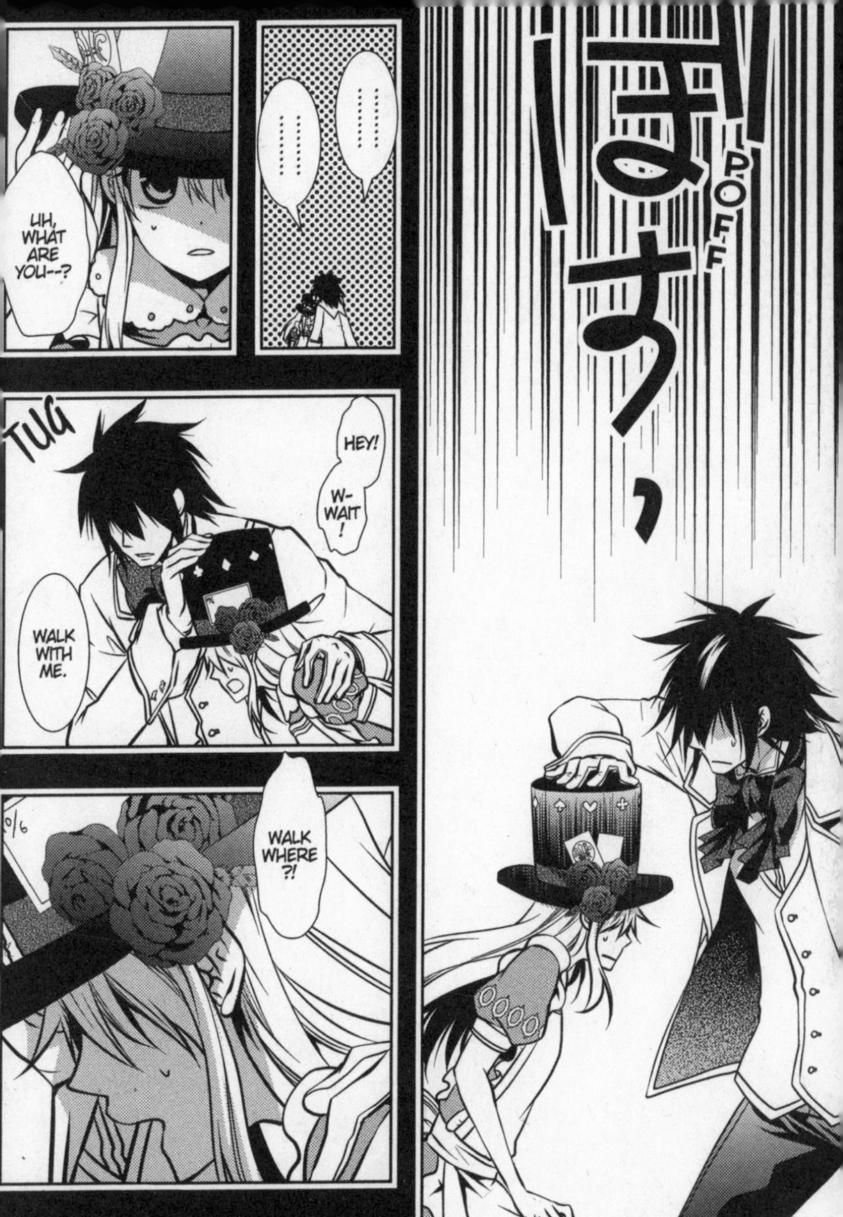
ぽすっ
POFF
......
......
UH, WHAT ARE YOU--?
HEY!
W-WAIT!
TUG
WALK WITH ME.
WALK WHERE?!

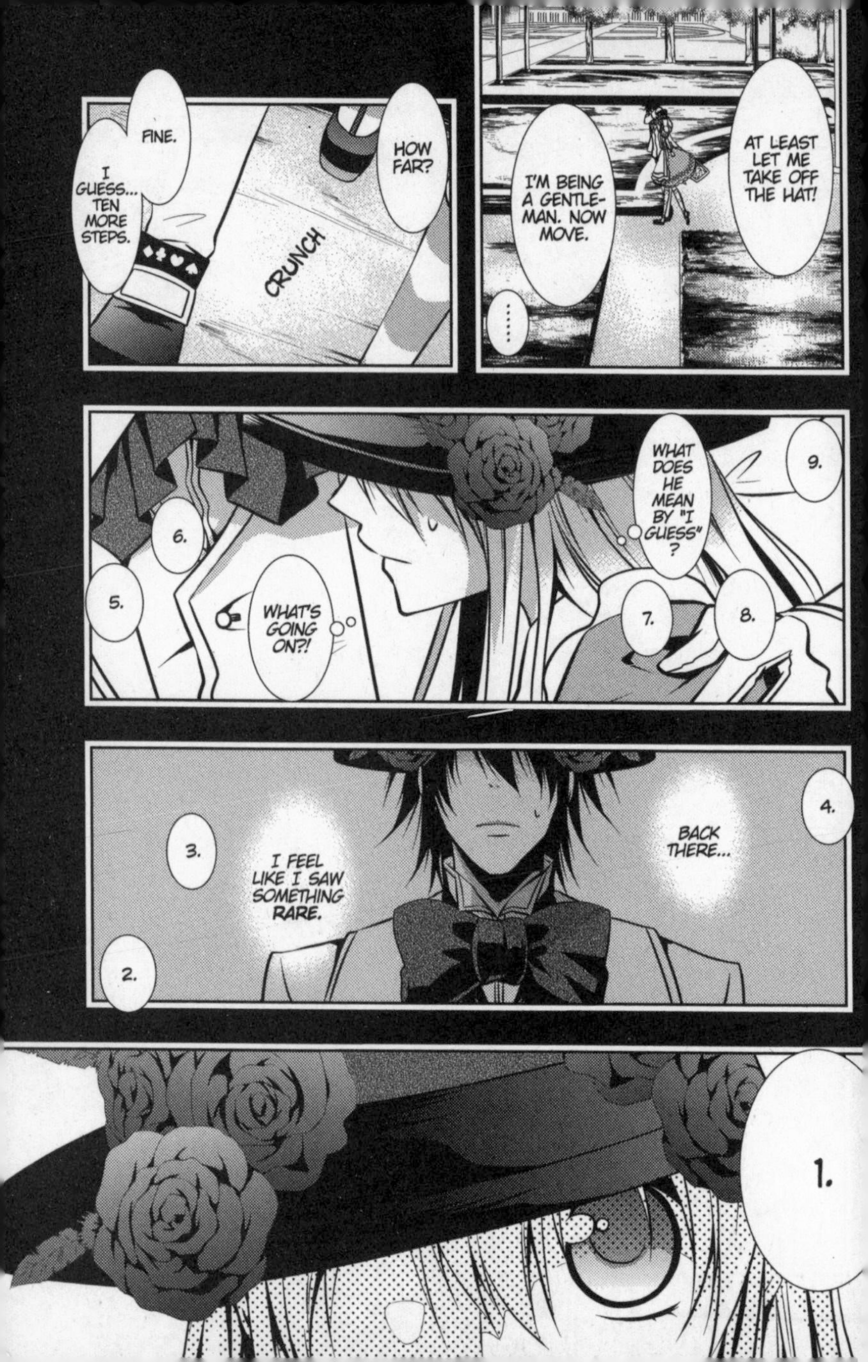
AT LEAST LET ME TAKE OFF THE HAT!
I'M BEING A GENTLE-MAN. NOW MOVE.
......
HOW FAR?
FINE.
I GUESS... TEN MORE STEPS.
CRUNCH
9.
WHAT DOES HE MEAN BY "I GUESS"?
8.
7.
WHAT'S GOING ON?!
6.
5.
4.
BACK THERE...
I FEEL LIKE I SAW SOMETHING RARE.
3.
2.
1.

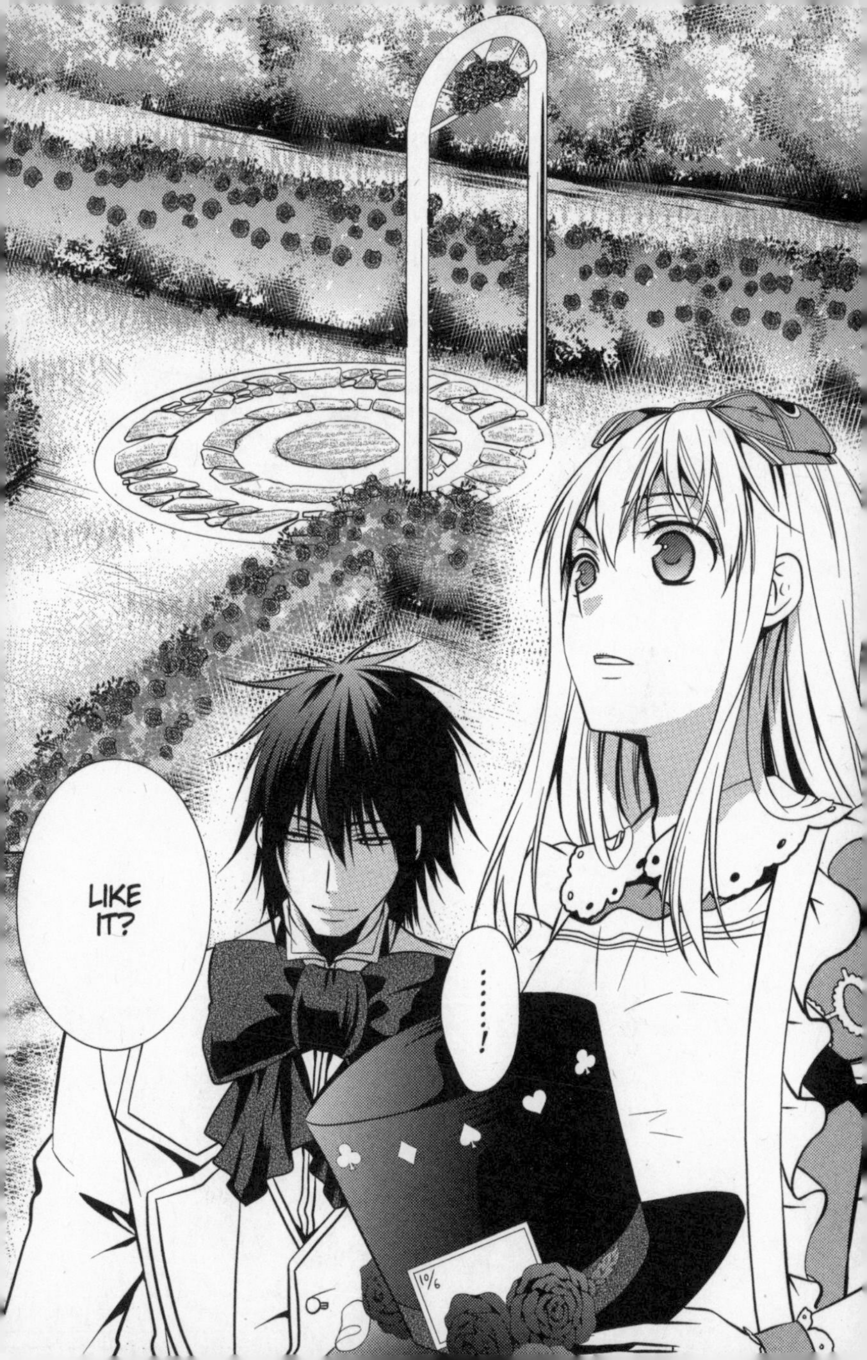
......!
LIKE IT?

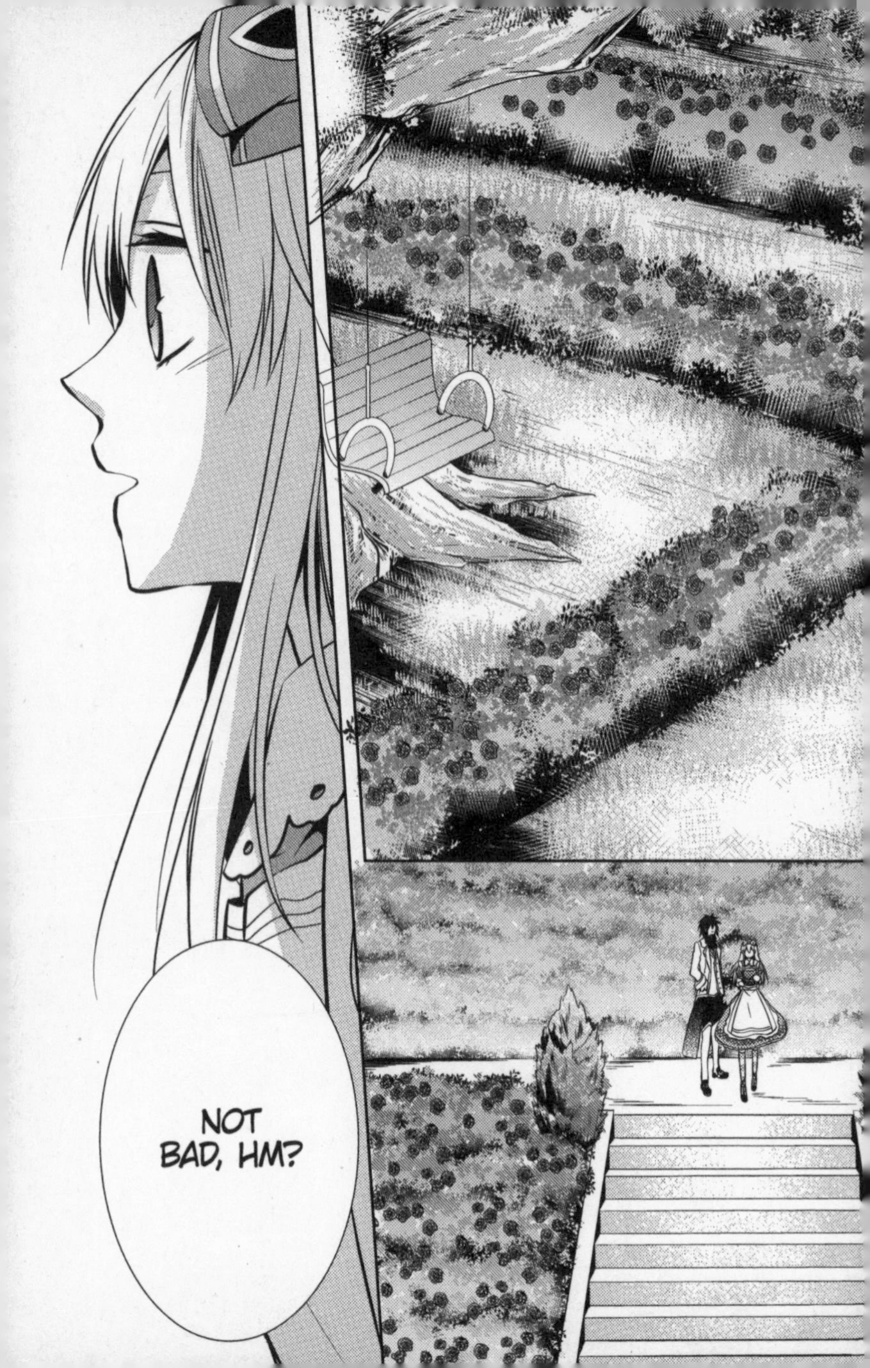
NOT BAD, HM?

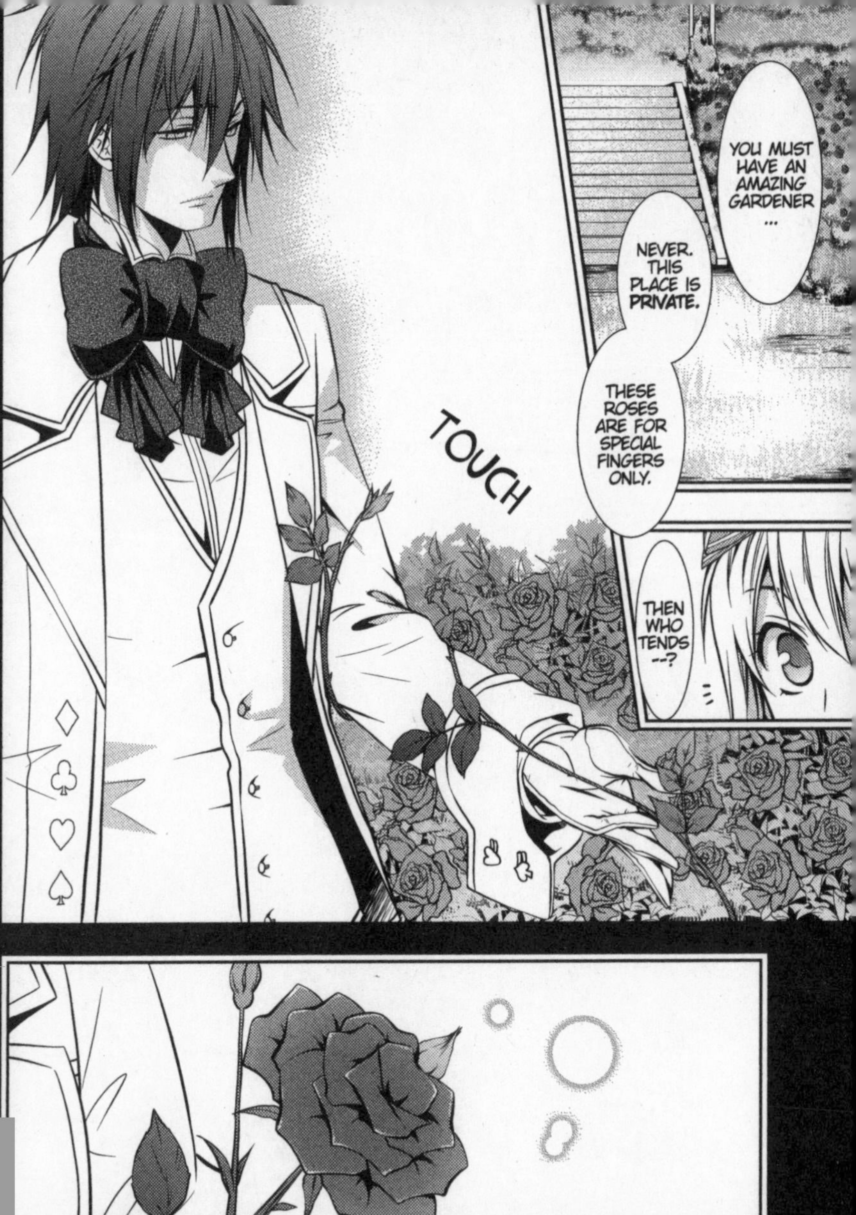
YOU MUST HAVE AN AMAZING GARDENER ...
NEVER. THIS PLACE IS PRIVATE.
THESE ROSES ARE FOR SPECIAL FINGERS ONLY.
THEN WHO TENDS --?
TOUCH

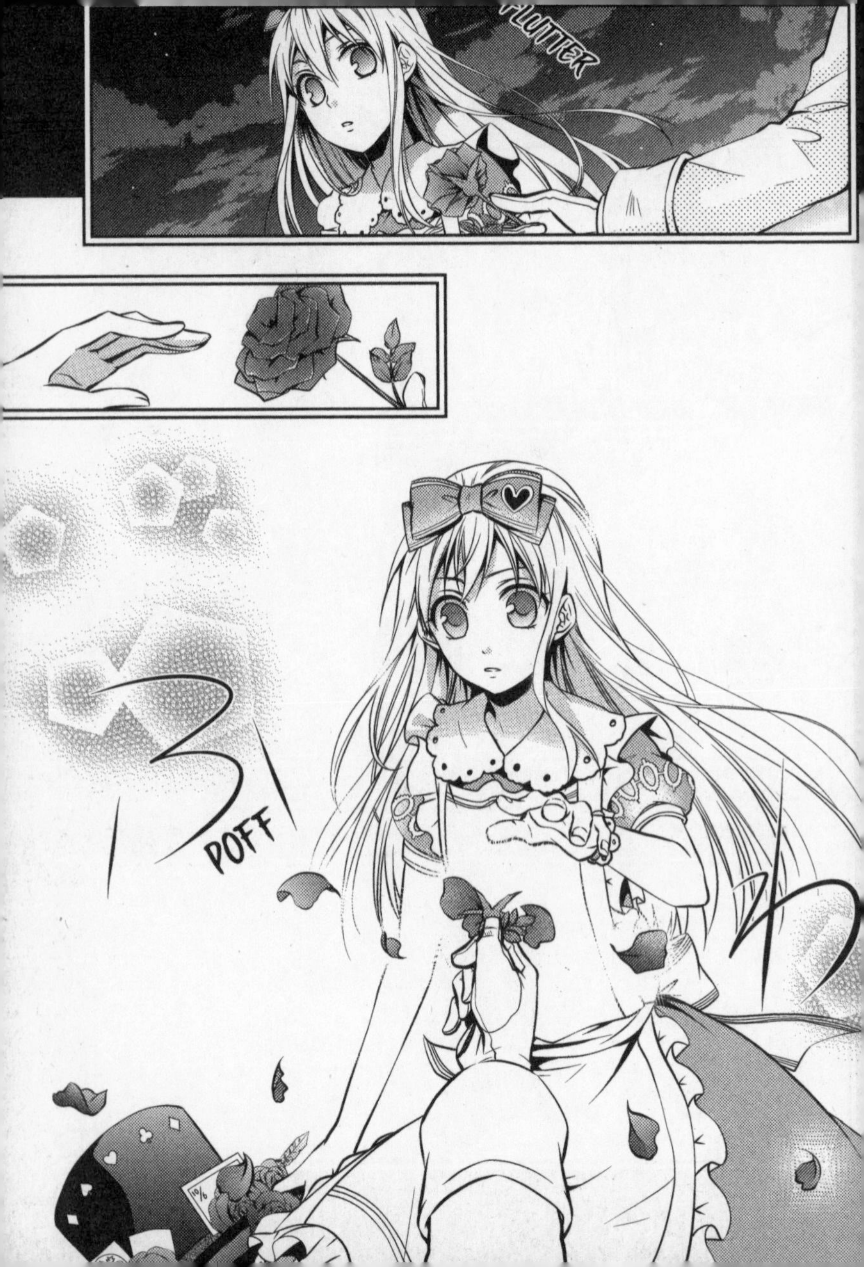
FLUTTER
POFF

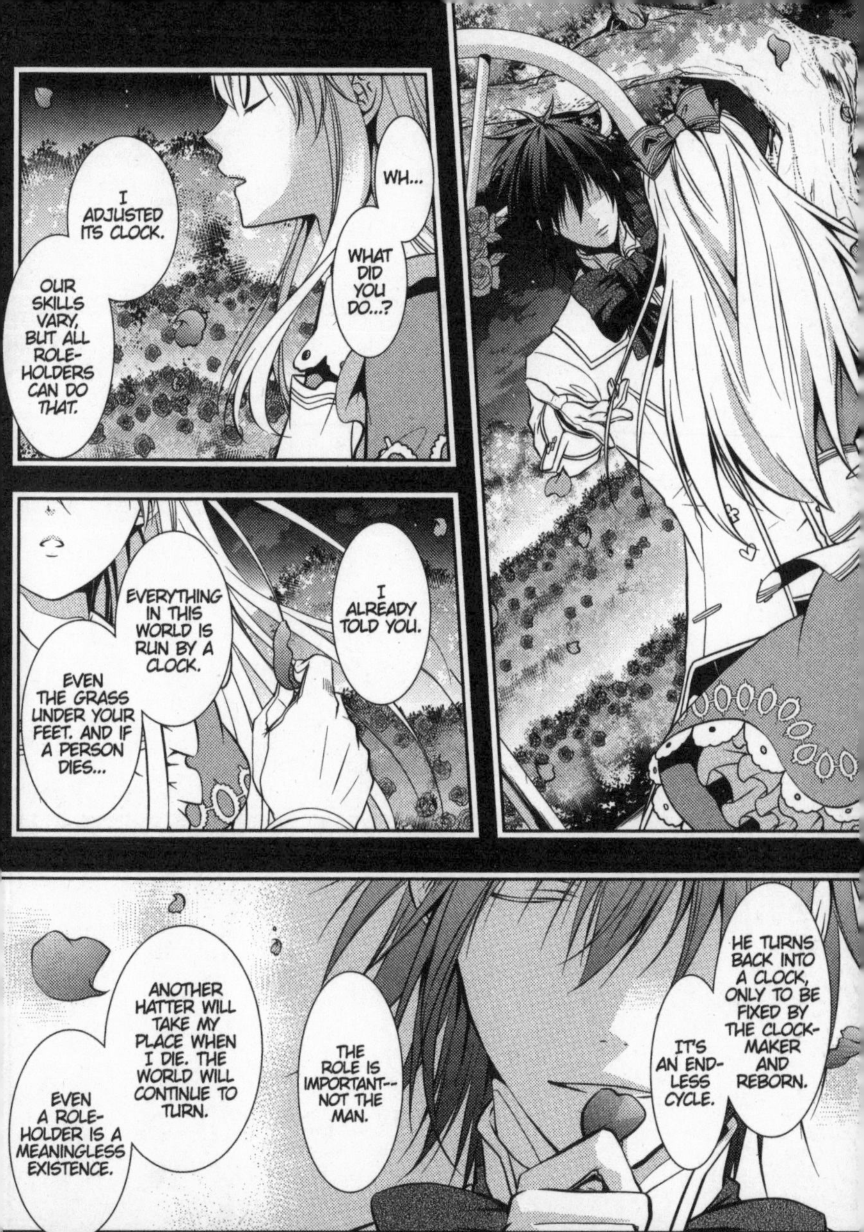
WH...
WHAT DID YOU DO...?
I ADJUSTED ITS CLOCK.
OUR SKILLS VARY, BUT ALL ROLE-HOLDERS CAN DO THAT.
I ALREADY TOLD YOU.
EVERYTHING IN THIS WORLD IS RUN BY A CLOCK.
EVEN THE GRASS UNDER YOUR FEET. AND IF A PERSON DIES...
HE TURNS BACK INTO A CLOCK, ONLY TO BE FIXED BY THE CLOCKMAKER AND REBORN.
IT'S AN ENDLESS CYCLE.
THE ROLE IS IMPORTANT--NOT THE MAN.
ANOTHER HATTER WILL TAKE MY PLACE WHEN I DIE. THE WORLD WILL CONTINUE TO TURN.
EVEN A ROLE-HOLDER IS A MEANINGLESS EXISTENCE.

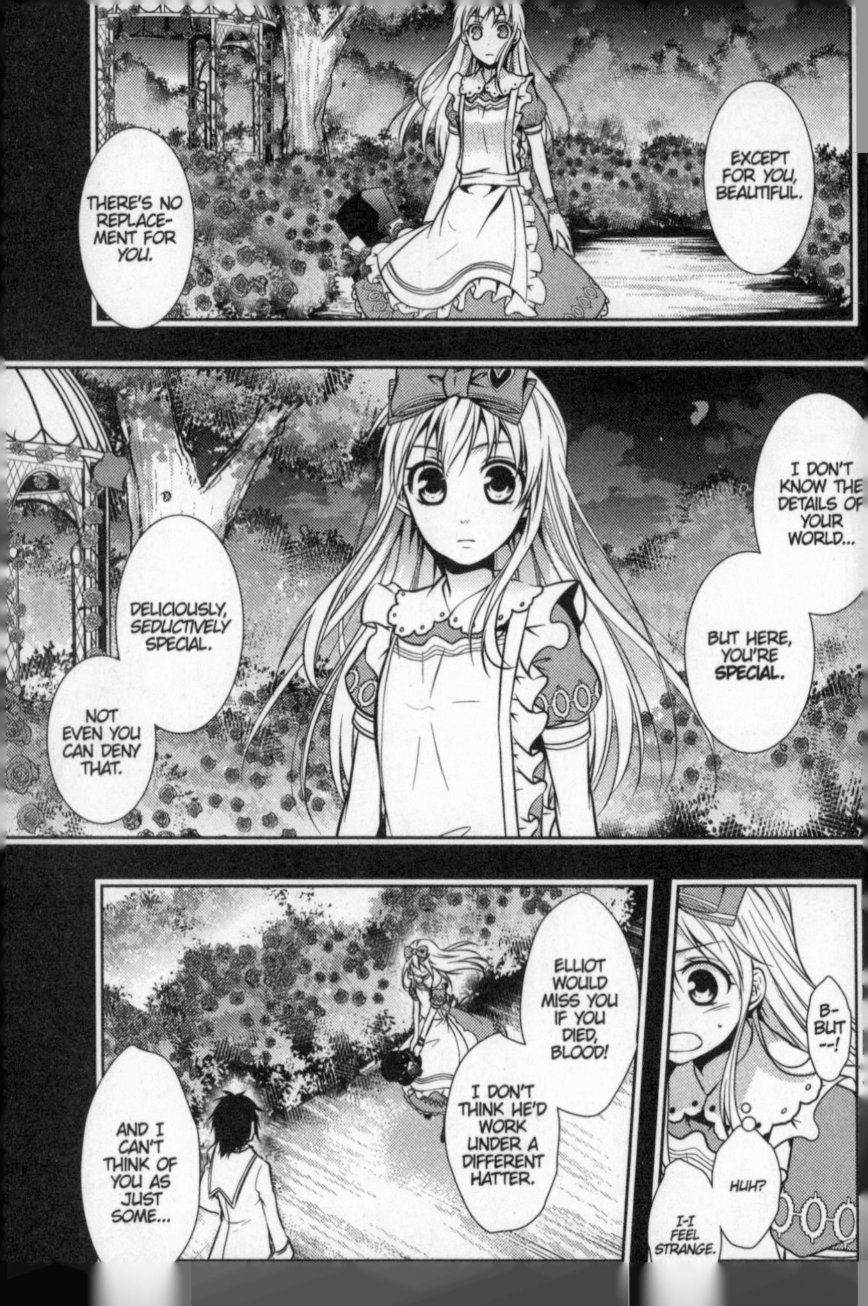
EXCEPT FOR YOU, BEAUTIFUL.
THERE'S NO REPLACEMENT FOR YOU.
I DON'T KNOW THE DETAILS OF YOUR WORLD...
BUT HERE, YOU'RE SPECIAL.
DELICIOUSLY, SEDUCTIVELY SPECIAL.
NOT EVEN YOU CAN DENY THAT.
B-BUT--!
HUH?
I-I FEEL STRANGE.
ELLIOT WOULD MISS YOU IF YOU DIED, BLOOD!
I DON'T THINK HE'D WORK UNDER A DIFFERENT HATTER.
AND I CAN'T THINK OF YOU AS JUST SOME...

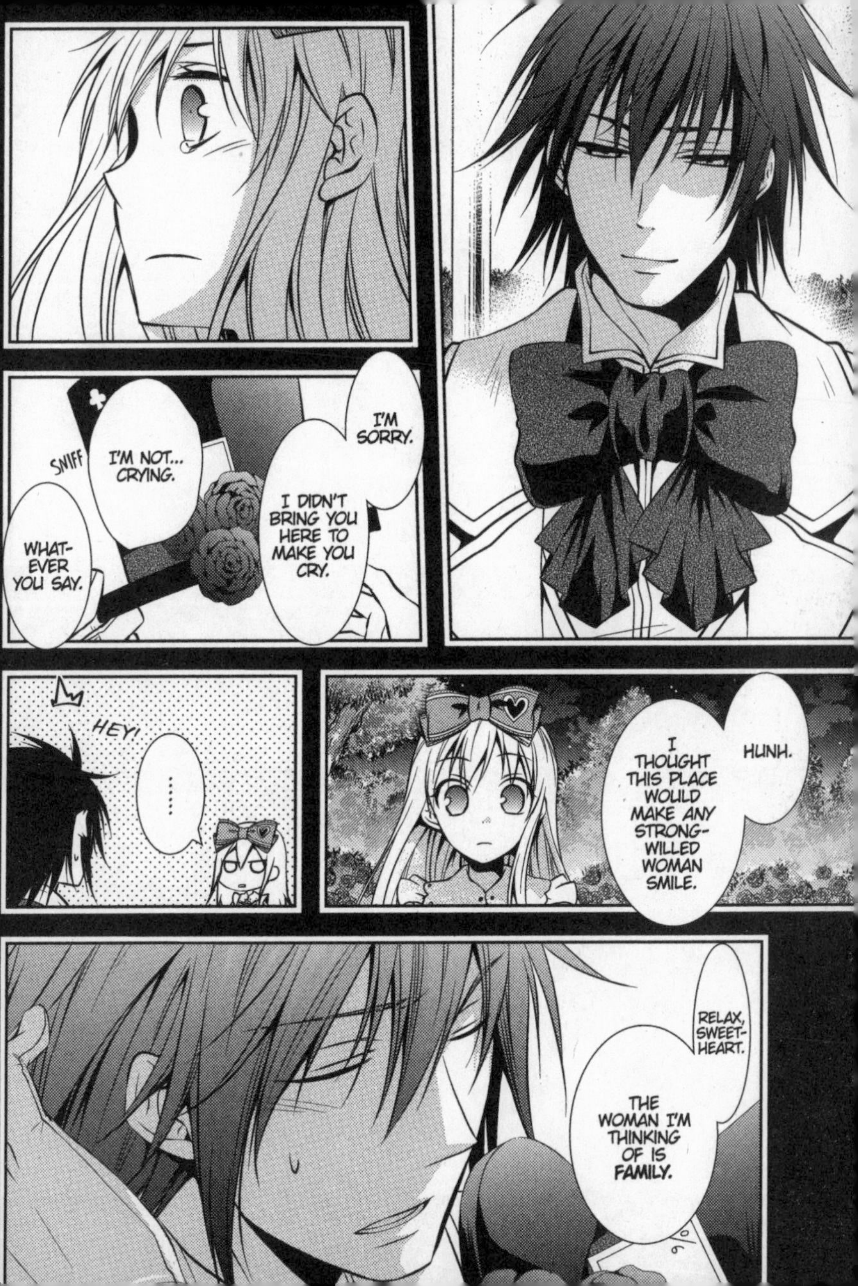
I'M SORRY.
I DIDN'T BRING YOU HERE TO MAKE YOU CRY.
I'M NOT... CRYING.
SNIFF
WHAT-EVER YOU SAY.
HUNH.
I THOUGHT THIS PLACE WOULD MAKE ANY STRONG-WILLED WOMAN SMILE.
HEY!
......
RELAX, SWEET-HEART.
THE WOMAN I'M THINKING OF IS FAMILY.

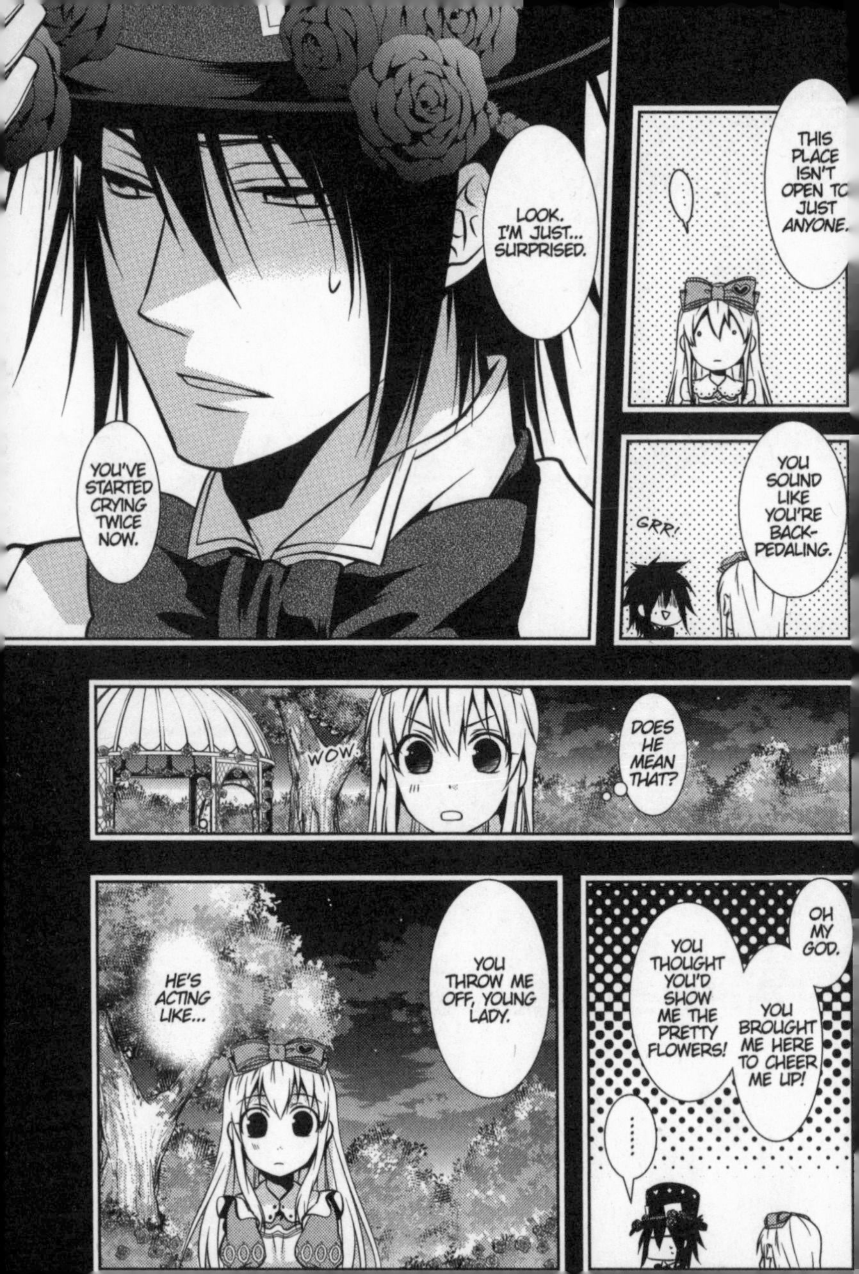
THIS PLACE ISN'T OPEN TO JUST ANYONE.
YOU SOUND LIKE YOU'RE BACK-PEDALING.
GRR!
LOOK. I'M JUST... SURPRISED.
YOU'VE STARTED CRYING TWICE NOW.
DOES HE MEAN THAT?
WOW.
OH MY GOD.
YOU BROUGHT ME HERE TO CHEER ME UP!
YOU THOUGHT YOU'D SHOW ME THE PRETTY FLOWERS!
......
YOU THROW ME OFF, YOUNG LADY.
HE'S ACTING LIKE...

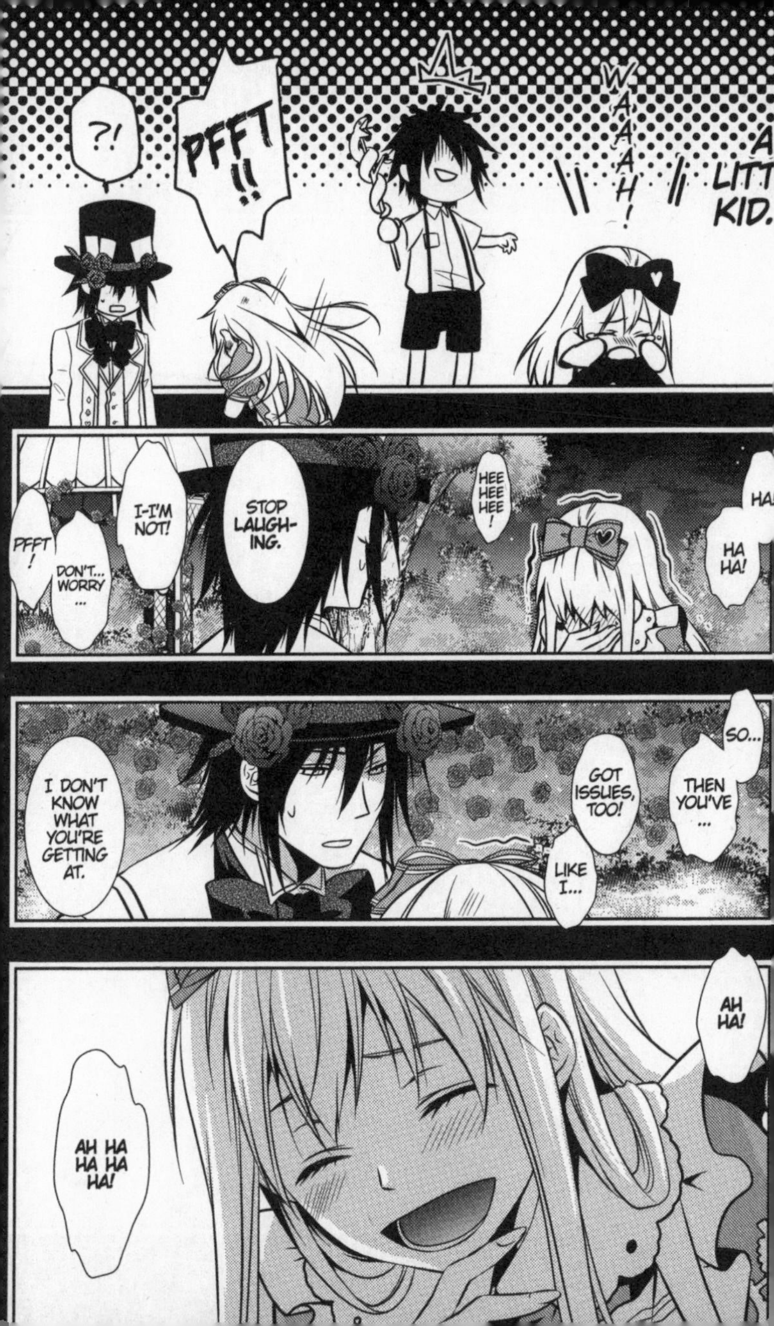
A LITT KID.
WAAAH!
PFFT!!
?!
HA!
HA HA!
HEE HEE HEE!
STOP LAUGHING.
I-I'M NOT!
PFFT!
DON'T... WORRY...
SO...
THEN YOU'VE...
GOT ISSUES, TOO!
LIKE I...
I DON'T KNOW WHAT YOU'RE GETTING AT.
AH HA!
AH HA HA HA HA!

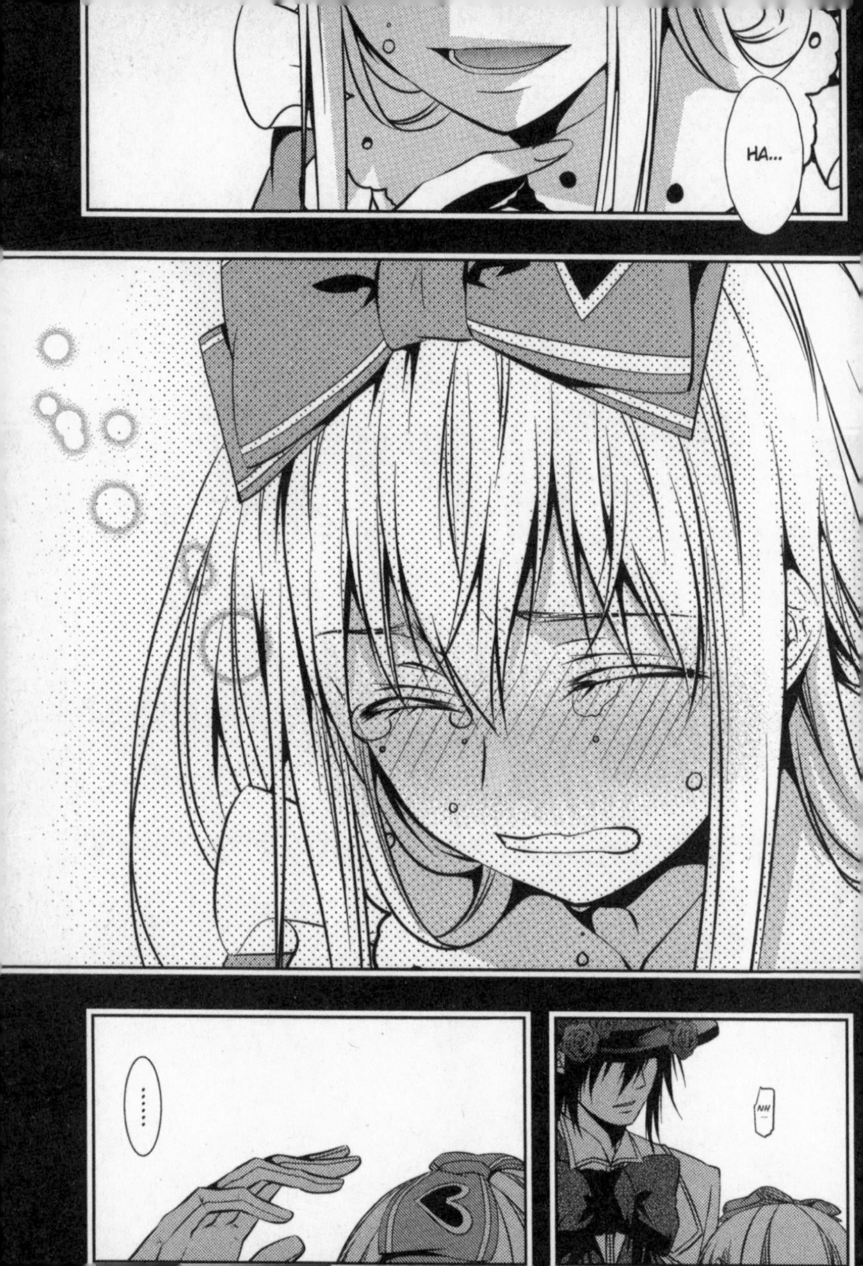
HA...
NH...
......

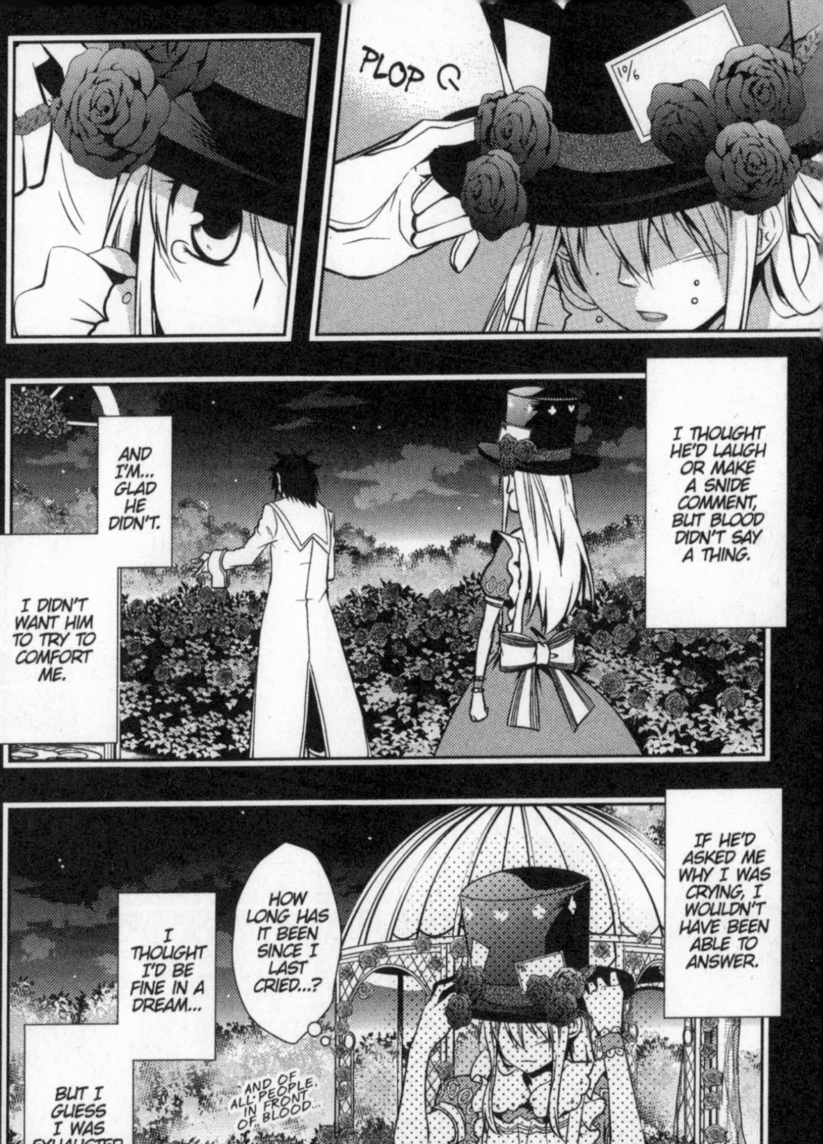
PLOP
10/6
I THOUGHT HE'D LAUGH OR MAKE A SNIDE COMMENT, BUT BLOOD DIDN'T SAY A THING.
AND I'M... GLAD HE DIDN'T.
I DIDN'T WANT HIM TO TRY TO COMFORT ME.
IF HE'D ASKED ME WHY I WAS CRYING, I WOULDN'T HAVE BEEN ABLE TO ANSWER.
HOW LONG HAS IT BEEN SINCE I LAST CRIED...?
I THOUGHT I'D BE FINE IN A DREAM...
AND OF ALL PEOPLE, IN FRONT OF BLOOD...
BUT I GUESS I WAS EXHAUSTED.

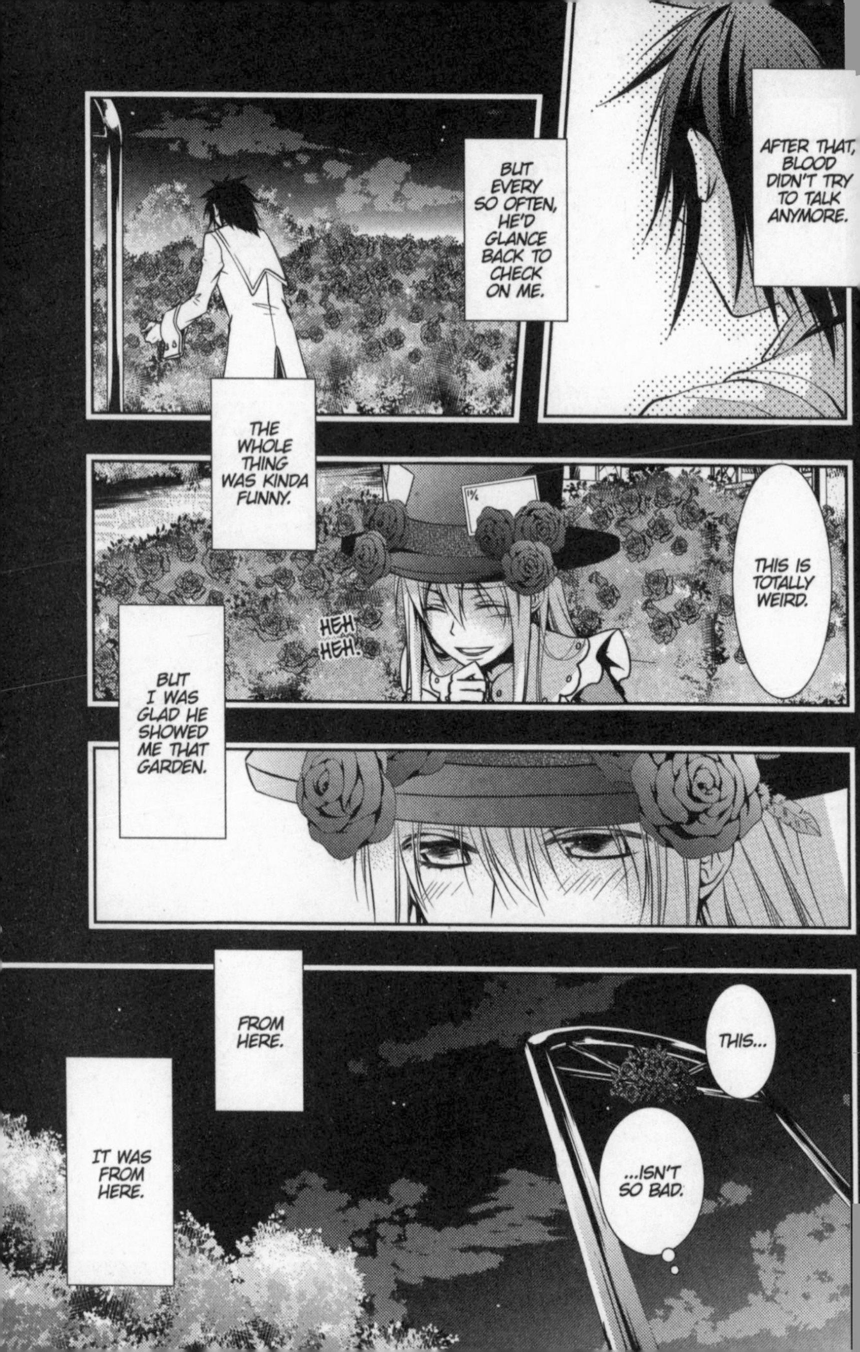
AFTER THAT, BLOOD DIDN'T TRY TO TALK ANYMORE.
BUT EVERY SO OFTEN, HE'D GLANCE BACK TO CHECK ON ME.
THE WHOLE THING WAS KINDA FUNNY.
THIS IS TOTALLY WEIRD.
HEH HEH.
BUT I WAS GLAD HE SHOWED ME THAT GARDEN.
THIS...
...ISN'T SO BAD.
FROM HERE.
IT WAS FROM HERE.

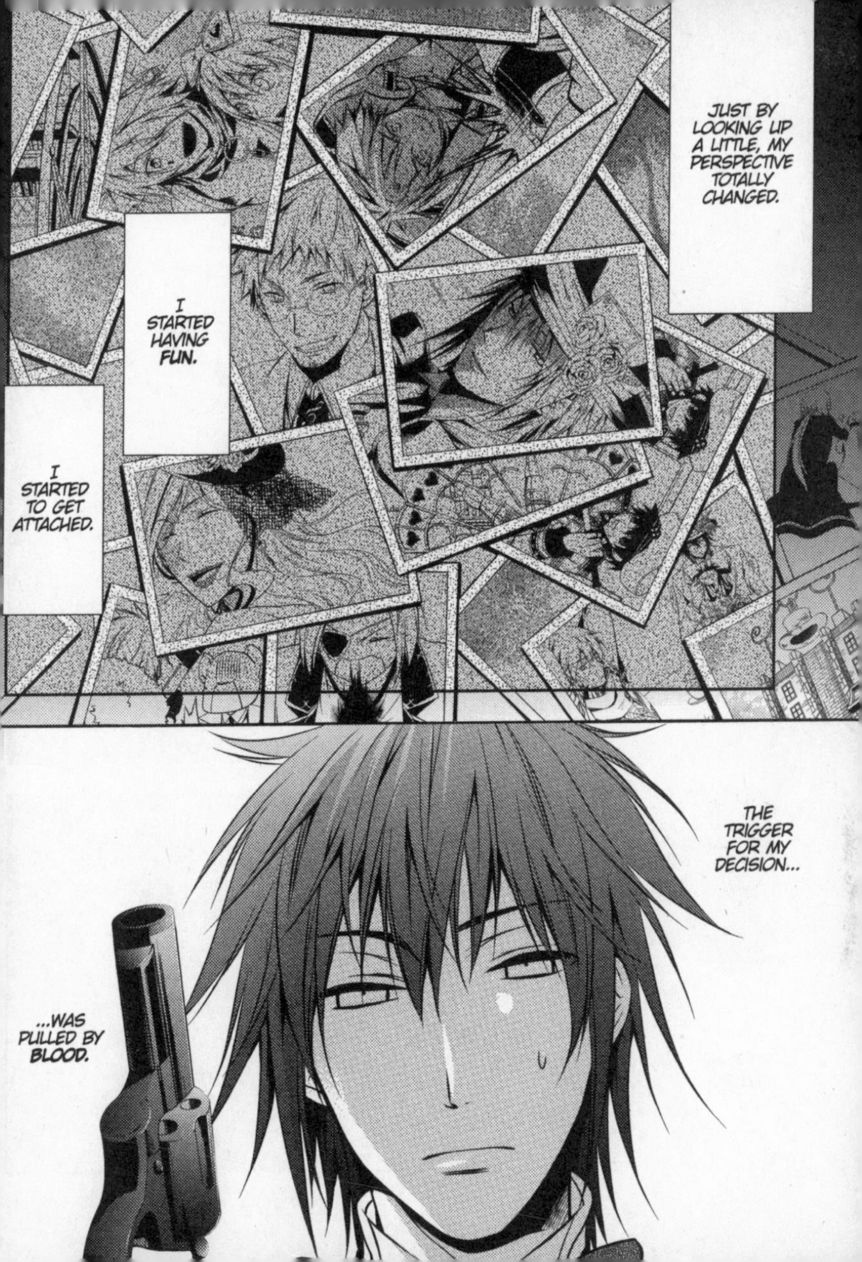
JUST BY LOOKING UP A LITTLE, MY PERSPECTIVE TOTALLY CHANGED.
I STARTED HAVING FUN.
I STARTED TO GET ATTACHED.
THE TRIGGER FOR MY DECISION...
...WAS PULLED BY BLOOD.

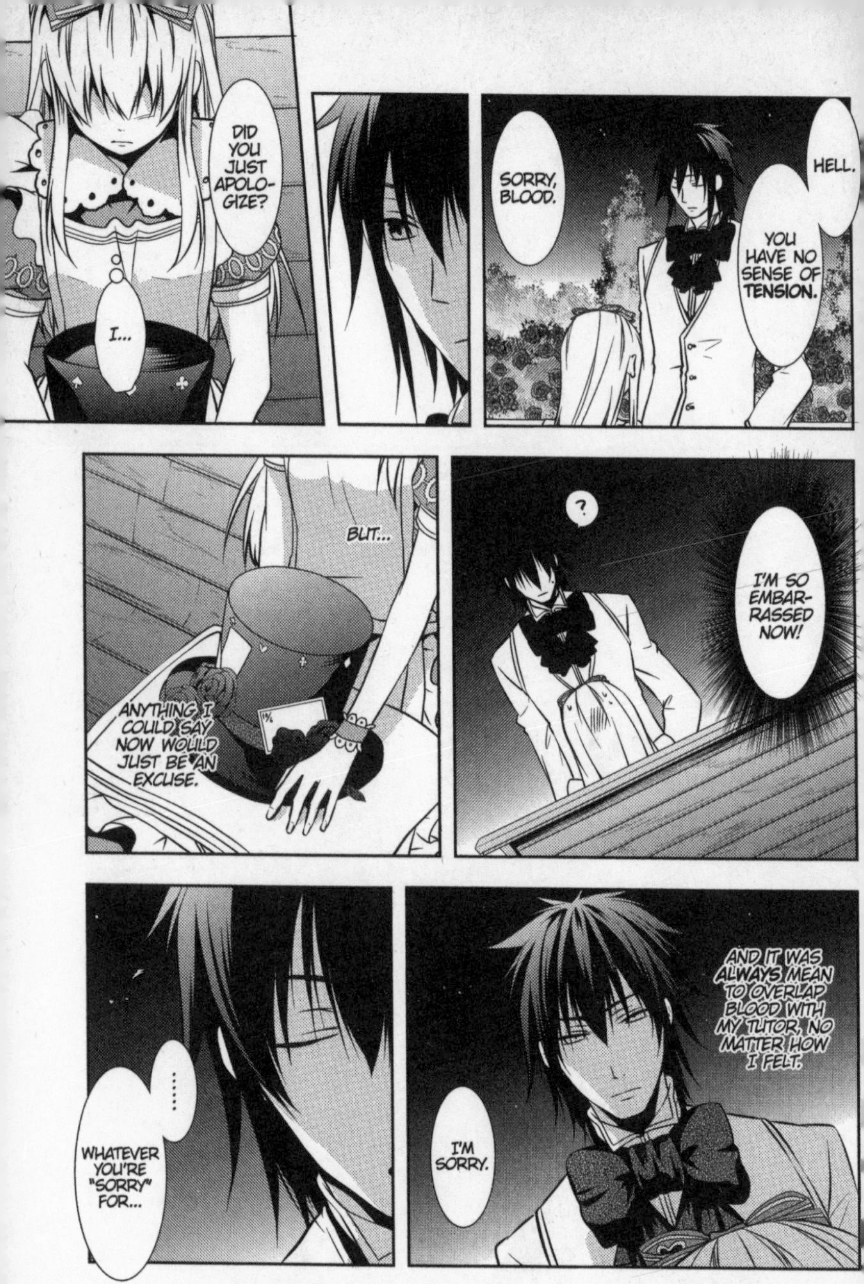
HELL.
YOU HAVE NO SENSE OF TENSION.
SORRY, BLOOD.
DID YOU JUST APOLOGIZE?
I...
?
I'M SO EMBARRASSED NOW!
BUT...
ANYTHING I COULD SAY NOW WOULD JUST BE AN EXCUSE.
AND IT WAS ALWAYS MEAN TO OVERLAP BLOOD WITH MY TUTOR, NO MATTER HOW I FELT.
I'M SORRY.
......
WHATEVER YOU'RE "SORRY" FOR...

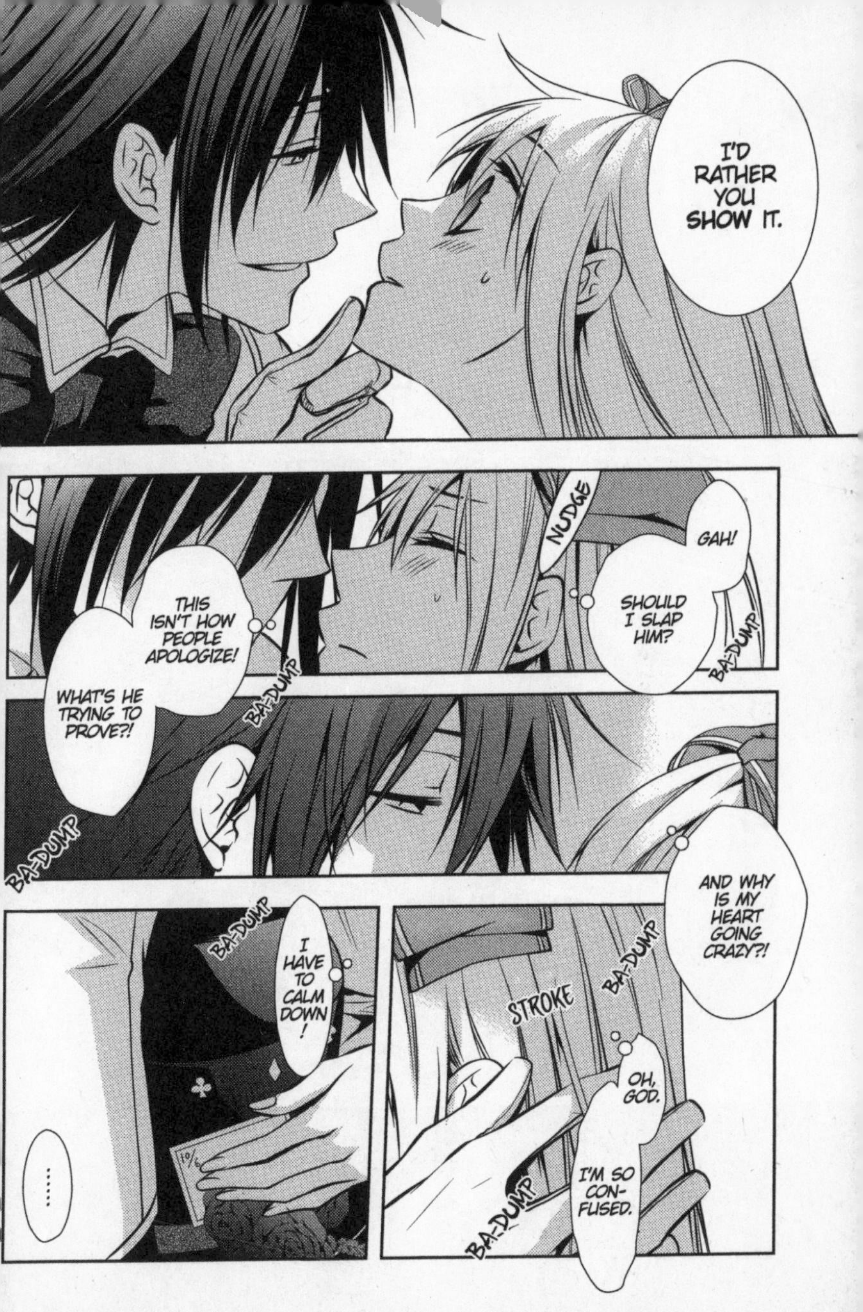
I'D RATHER YOU SHOW IT.
NUDGE
GAH!
SHOULD I SLAP HIM?
BA-DUMP
THIS ISN'T HOW PEOPLE APOLOGIZE!
WHAT'S HE TRYING TO PROVE?!
BA-DUMP
AND WHY IS MY HEART GOING CRAZY?!
BA-DUMP
BA-DUMP
STROKE
OH, GOD.
I'M SO CON-FUSED.
BA-DUMP
BA-DUMP
I HAVE TO CALM DOWN!
......

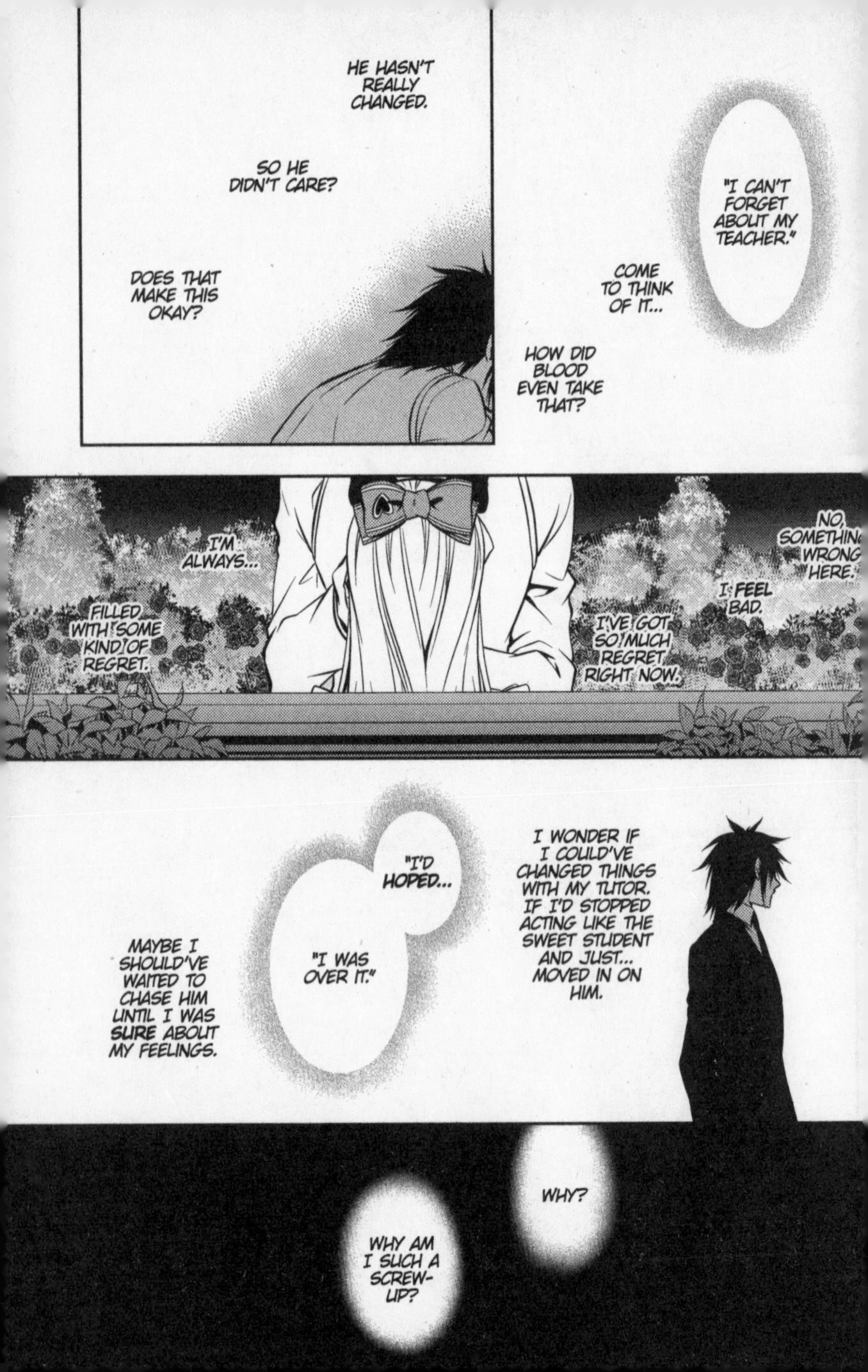
"I CAN'T FORGET ABOUT MY TEACHER."
COME TO THINK OF IT...
HOW DID BLOOD EVEN TAKE THAT?
HE HASN'T REALLY CHANGED.
SO HE DIDN'T CARE?
DOES THAT MAKE THIS OKAY?
NO, SOMETHIN WRONG HERE.
I FEEL BAD.
I'VE GOT SO MUCH REGRET RIGHT NOW.
I'M ALWAYS...
FILLED WITH SOME KIND OF REGRET.
I WONDER IF I COULD'VE CHANGED THINGS WITH MY TUTOR. IF I'D STOPPED ACTING LIKE THE SWEET STUDENT AND JUST... MOVED IN ON HIM.
"I'D HOPED...
"I WAS OVER IT."
MAYBE I SHOULD'VE WAITED TO CHASE HIM UNTIL I WAS SURE ABOUT MY FEELINGS.
WHY?
WHY AM I SUCH A SCREW-UP?

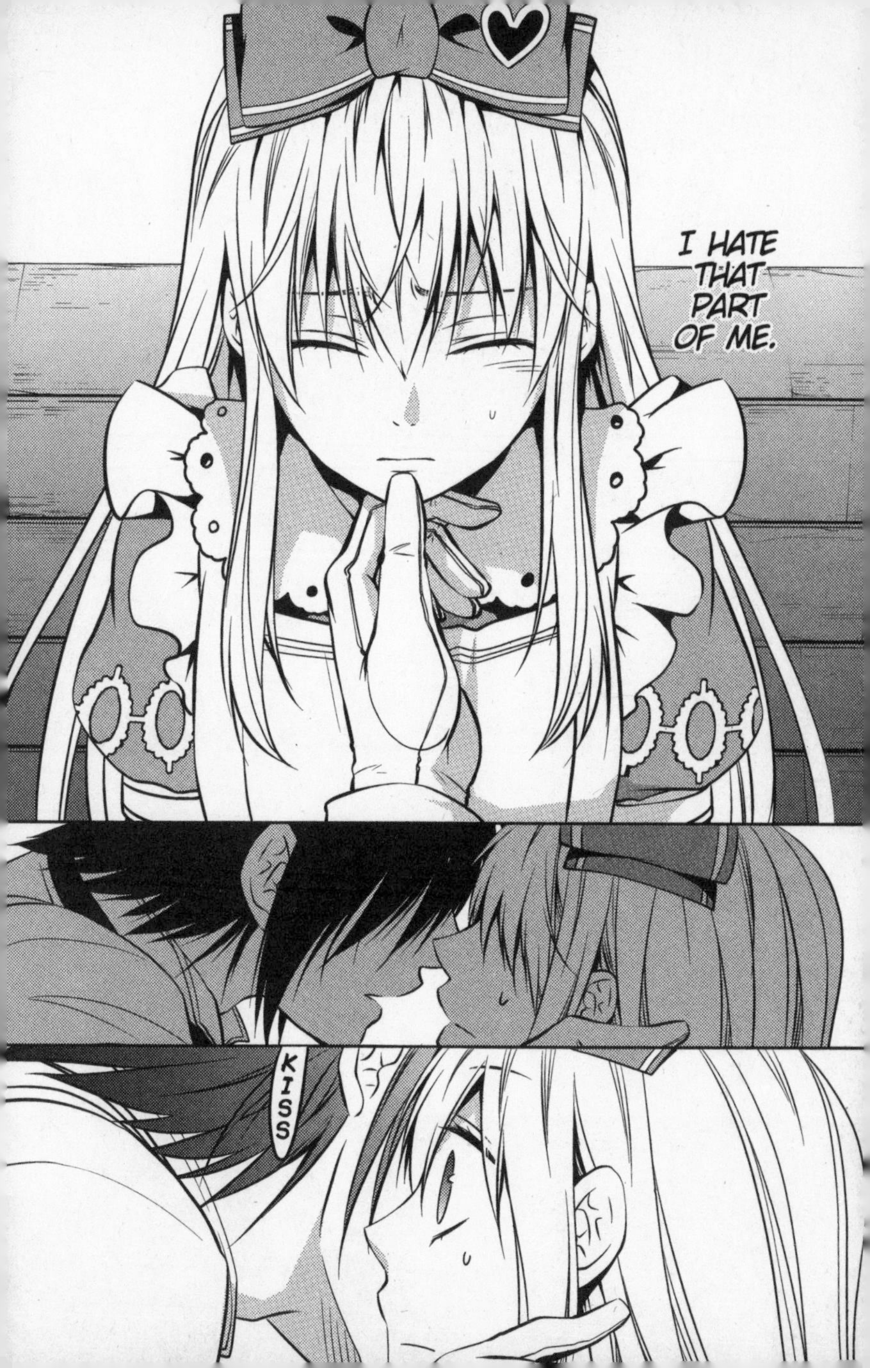
I HATE THAT PART OF ME.
KISS

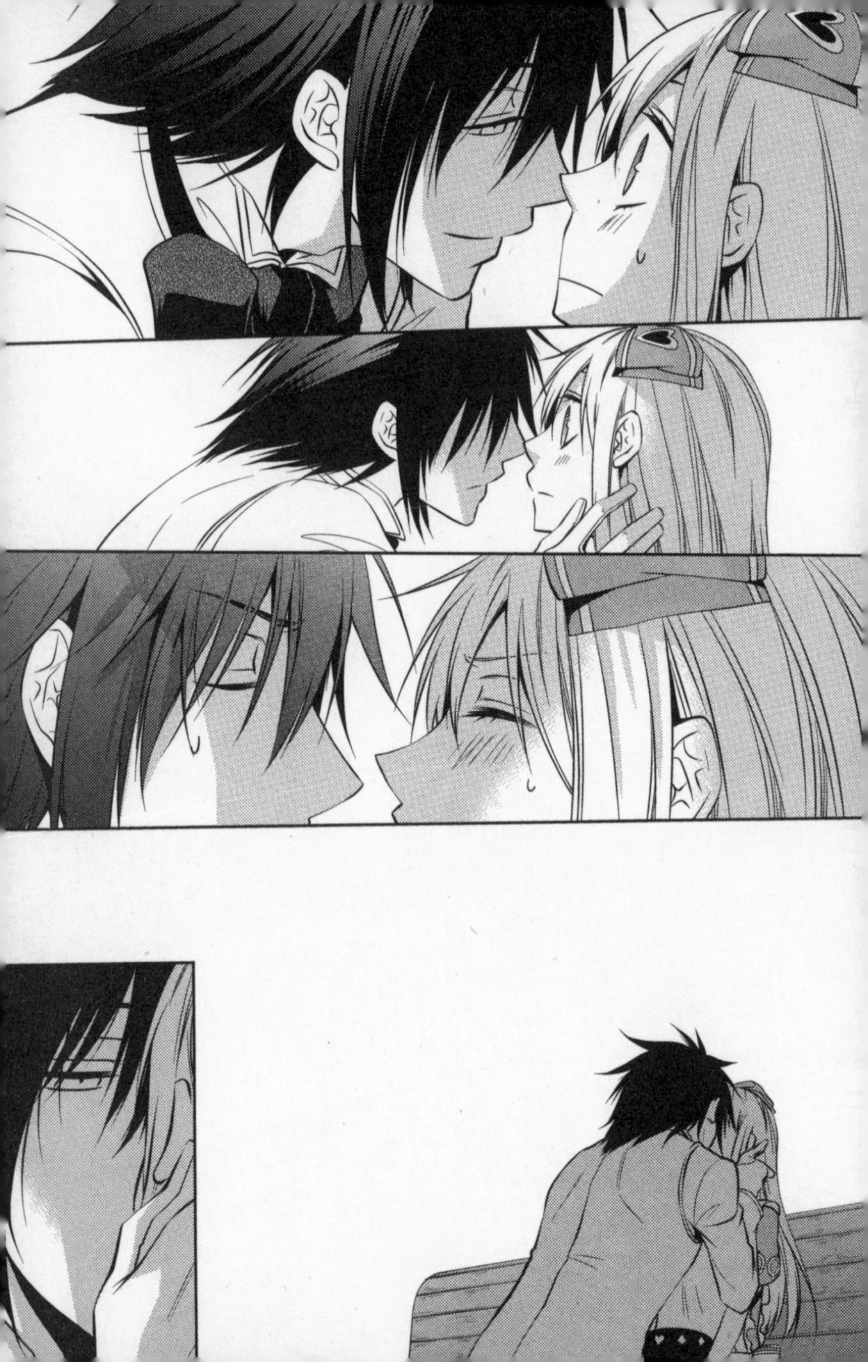

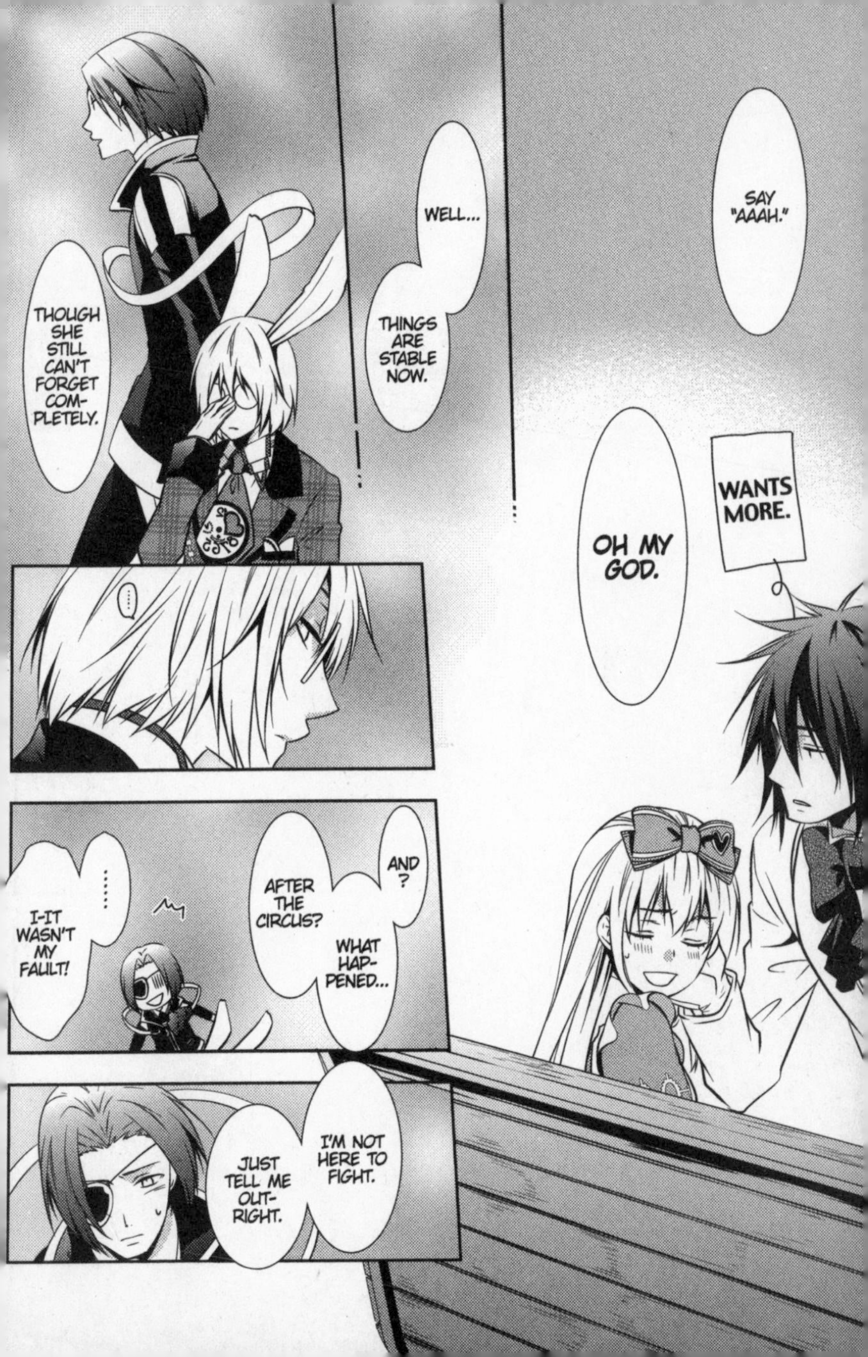
SAY "AAAH."
WANTS MORE.
OH MY GOD.
WELL...
THINGS ARE STABLE NOW.
THOUGH SHE STILL CAN'T FORGET COM-PLETELY.
......
AND?
AFTER THE CIRCUS?
WHAT HAP-PENED...
......
I-IT WASN'T MY FAULT!
I'M NOT HERE TO FIGHT.
JUST TELL ME OUT-RIGHT.

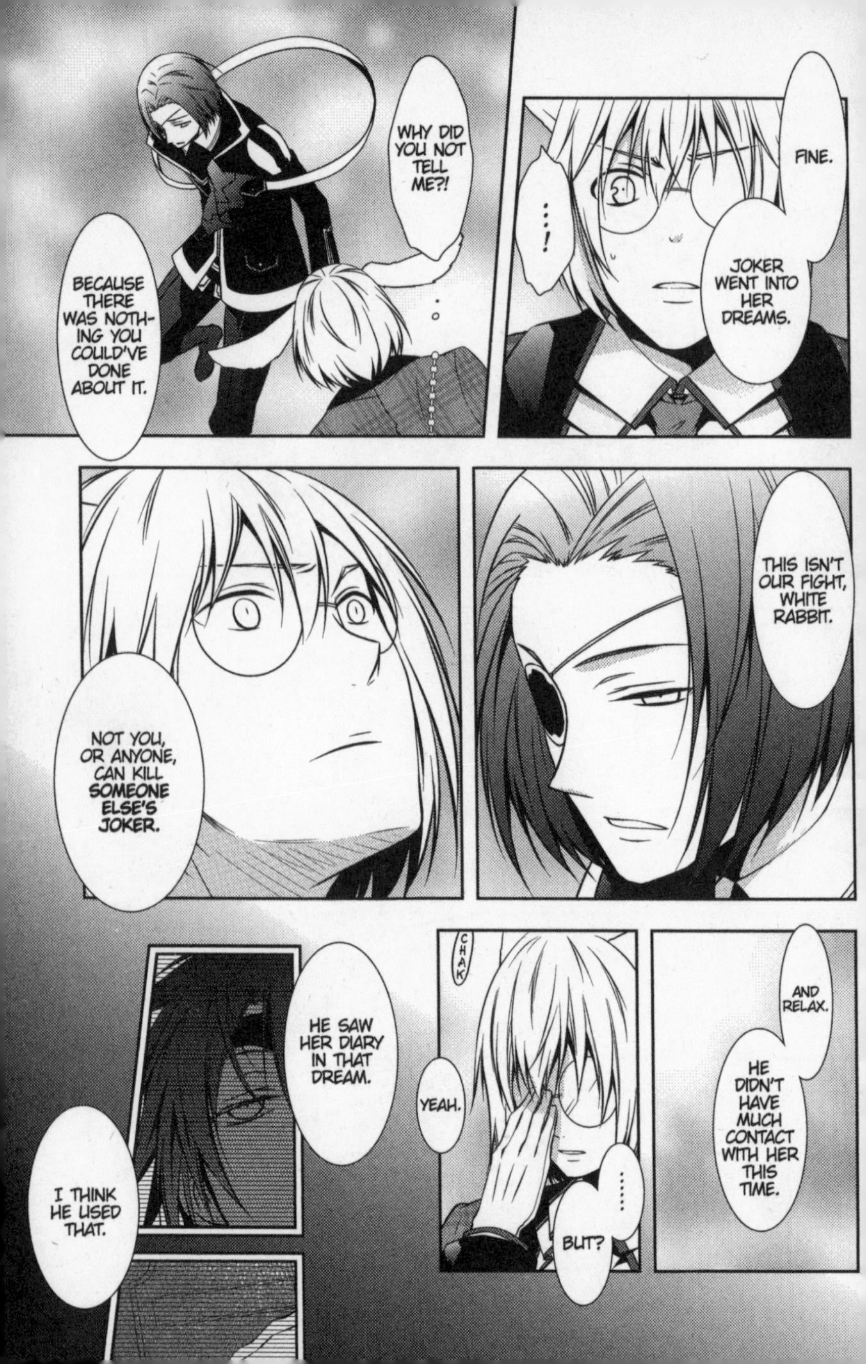
FINE.
JOKER WENT INTO HER DREAMS.
...!
WHY DID YOU NOT TELL ME?!
BECAUSE THERE WAS NOTHING YOU COULD'VE DONE ABOUT IT.
THIS ISN'T OUR FIGHT, WHITE RABBIT.
NOT YOU, OR ANYONE, CAN KILL SOMEONE ELSE'S JOKER.
AND RELAX.
HE DIDN'T HAVE MUCH CONTACT WITH HER THIS TIME.
CHAK
YEAH.
......
BUT?
HE SAW HER DIARY IN THAT DREAM.
I THINK HE USED THAT.

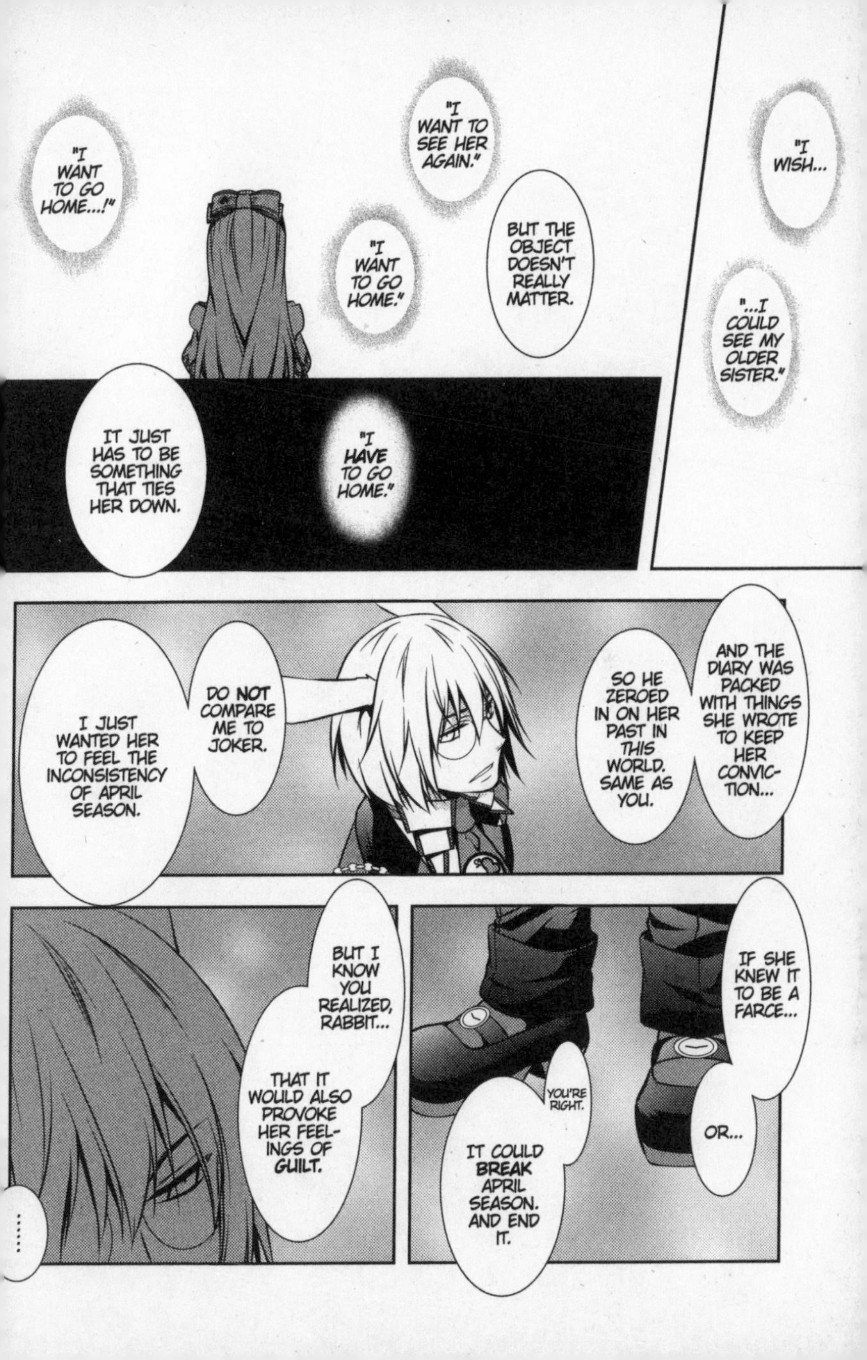
"I WISH...
"...I COULD SEE MY OLDER SISTER."
"I WANT TO SEE HER AGAIN."
"I WANT TO GO HOME...!"
BUT THE OBJECT DOESN'T REALLY MATTER.
"I WANT TO GO HOME."
"I HAVE TO GO HOME."
IT JUST HAS TO BE SOMETHING THAT TIES HER DOWN.
AND THE DIARY WAS PACKED WITH THINGS SHE WROTE TO KEEP HER CONVIC-TION...
SO HE ZEROED IN ON HER PAST IN THIS WORLD. SAME AS YOU.
DO NOT COMPARE ME TO JOKER.
I JUST WANTED HER TO FEEL THE INCONSISTENCY OF APRIL SEASON.
IF SHE KNEW IT TO BE A FARCE...
OR...
YOU'RE RIGHT.
IT COULD BREAK APRIL SEASON. AND END IT.
BUT I KNOW YOU REALIZED, RABBIT...
THAT IT WOULD ALSO PROVOKE HER FEEL-INGS OF GUILT.
......

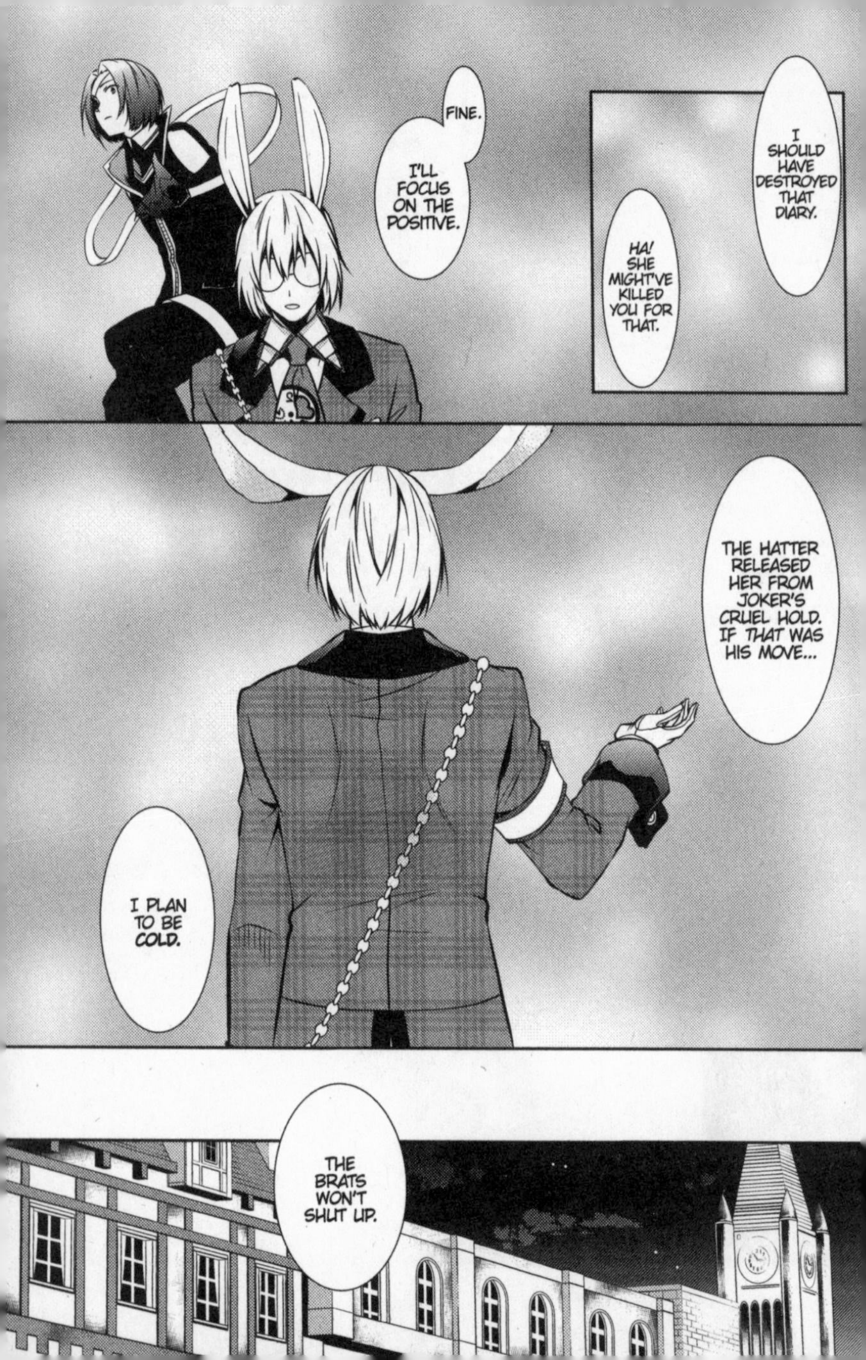
I SHOULD HAVE DESTROYED THAT DIARY.
HA! SHE MIGHT'VE KILLED YOU FOR THAT.
FINE.
I'LL FOCUS ON THE POSITIVE.
THE HATTER RELEASED HER FROM JOKER'S CRUEL HOLD. IF *THAT* WAS HIS MOVE...
I PLAN TO BE COLD.
THE BRATS WON'T SHUT UP.

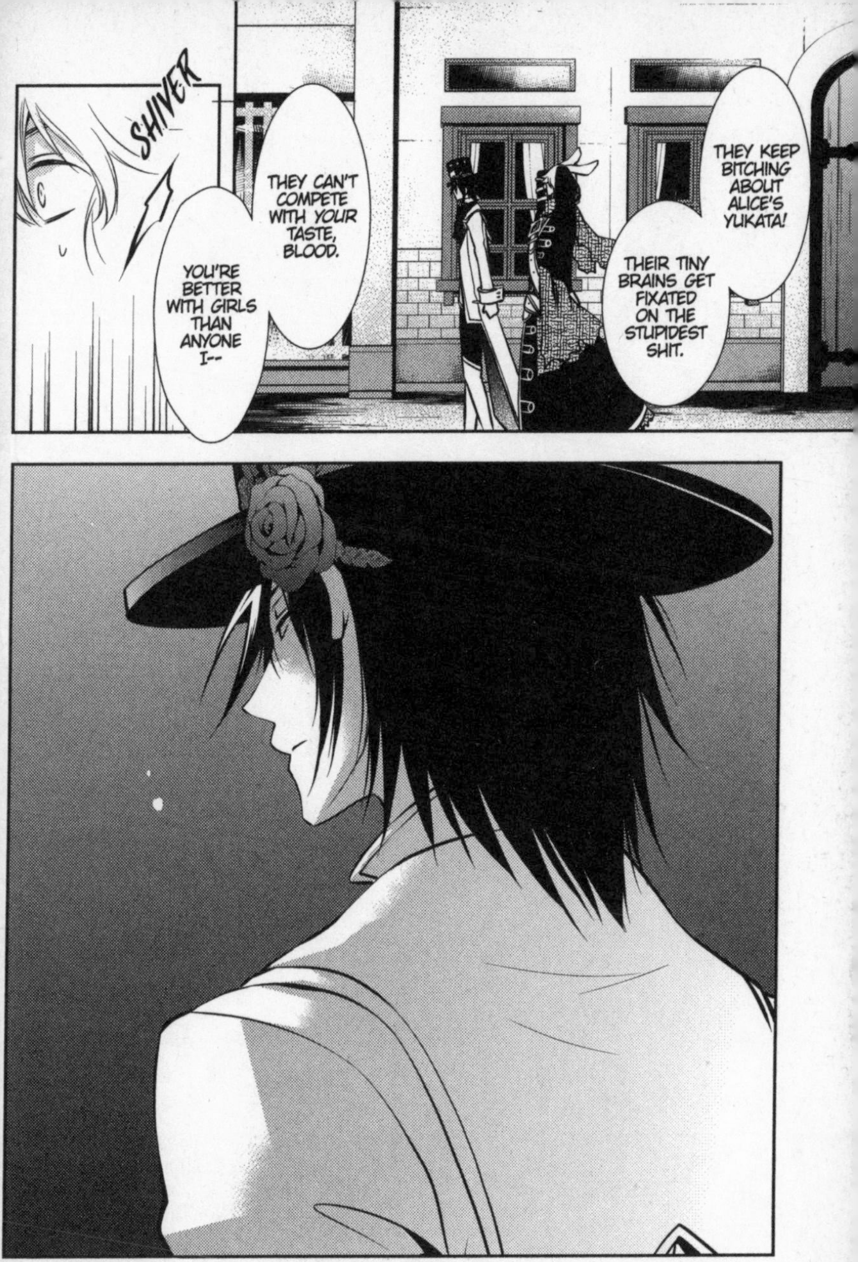
THEY KEEP BITCHING ABOUT ALICE'S YUKATA!
THEIR TINY BRAINS GET FIXATED ON THE STUPIDEST SHIT.
THEY CAN'T COMPETE WITH YOUR TASTE, BLOOD.
YOU'RE BETTER WITH GIRLS THAN ANYONE I--
SHIVER

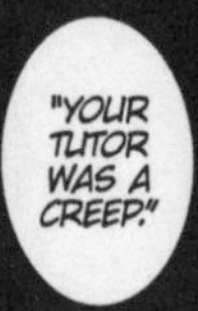
"YOUR TUTOR WAS A CREEP."

Hit: 20

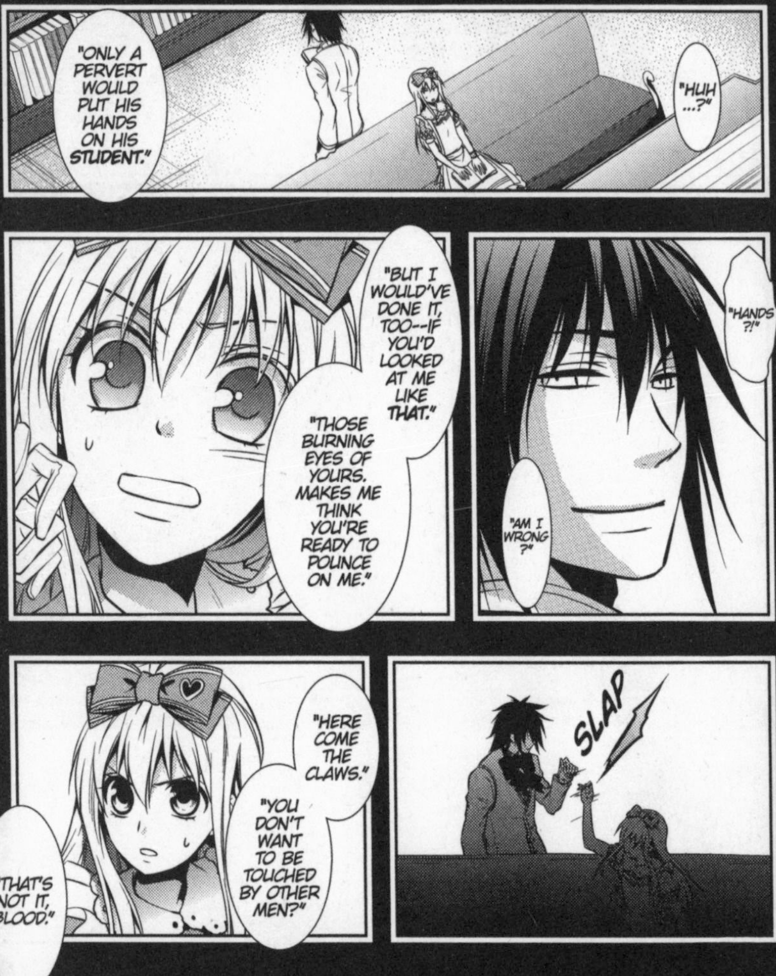
"HUH ...?"
"ONLY A PERVERT WOULD PUT HIS HANDS ON HIS STUDENT."
"HANDS ?!"
"AM I WRONG ?"
"BUT I WOULD'VE DONE IT, TOO--IF YOU'D LOOKED AT ME LIKE THAT."
"THOSE BURNING EYES OF YOURS. MAKES ME THINK YOU'RE READY TO POUNCE ON ME."
SLAP
"HERE COME THE CLAWS."
"YOU DON'T WANT TO BE TOUCHED BY OTHER MEN?"
"THAT'S NOT IT, BLOOD."

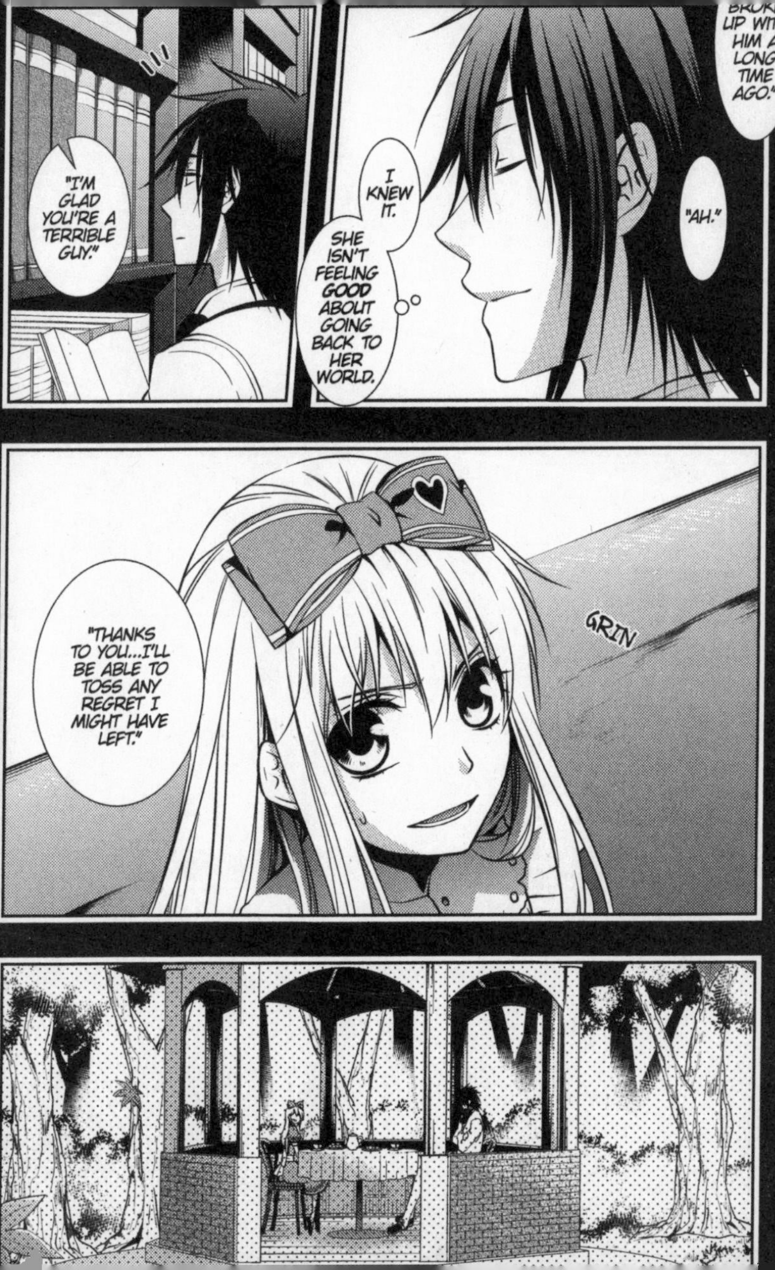
BROKE UP WITH HIM A LONG TIME AGO."
"AH."
I KNEW IT.
SHE ISN'T FEELING GOOD ABOUT GOING BACK TO HER WORLD.
"I'M GLAD YOU'RE A TERRIBLE GUY."
GRIN
"THANKS TO YOU...I'LL BE ABLE TO TOSS ANY REGRET I MIGHT HAVE LEFT."

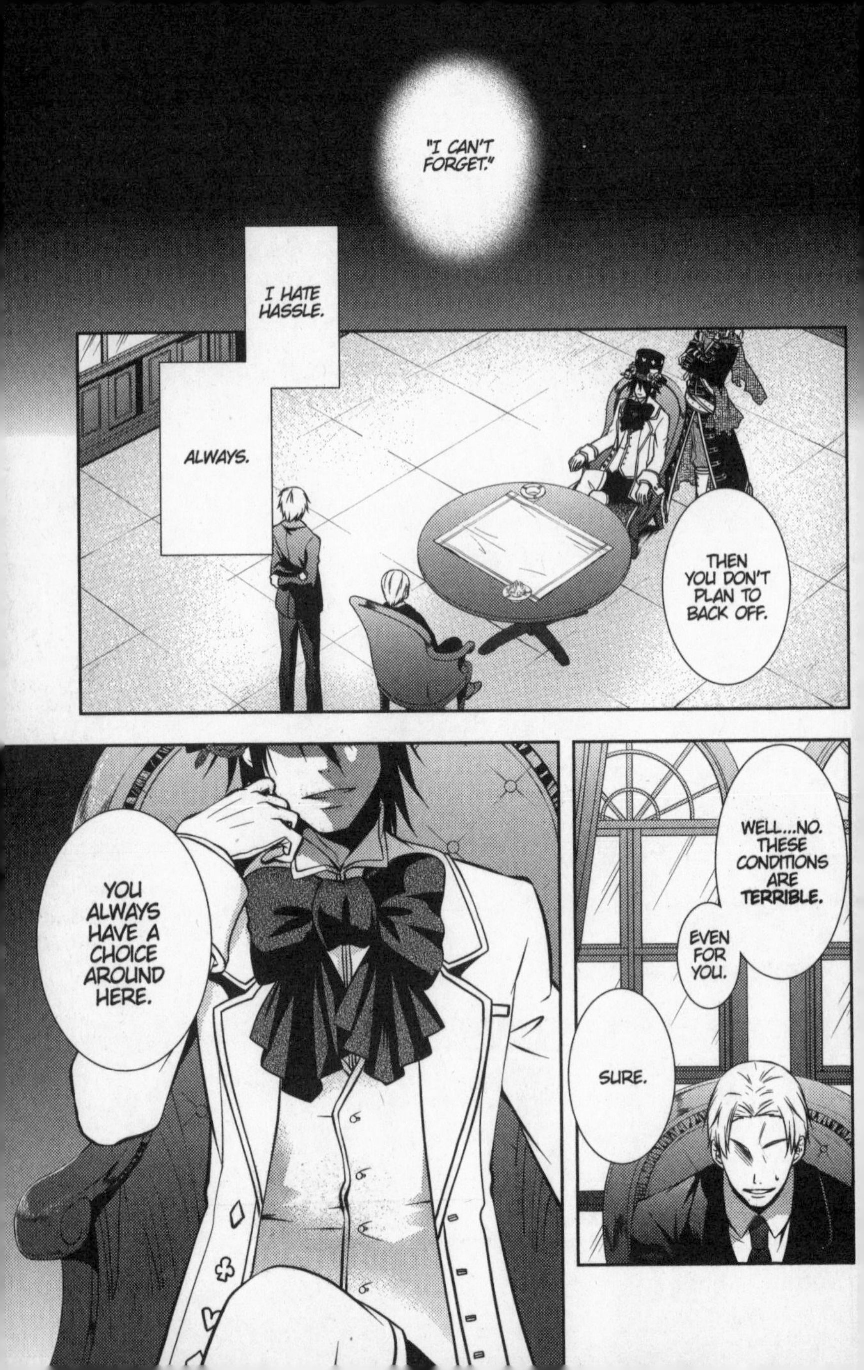
"I CAN'T FORGET."
I HATE HASSLE.
ALWAYS.
THEN YOU DON'T PLAN TO BACK OFF.
WELL...NO. THESE CONDITIONS ARE TERRIBLE.
EVEN FOR YOU.
SURE.
YOU ALWAYS HAVE A CHOICE AROUND HERE.

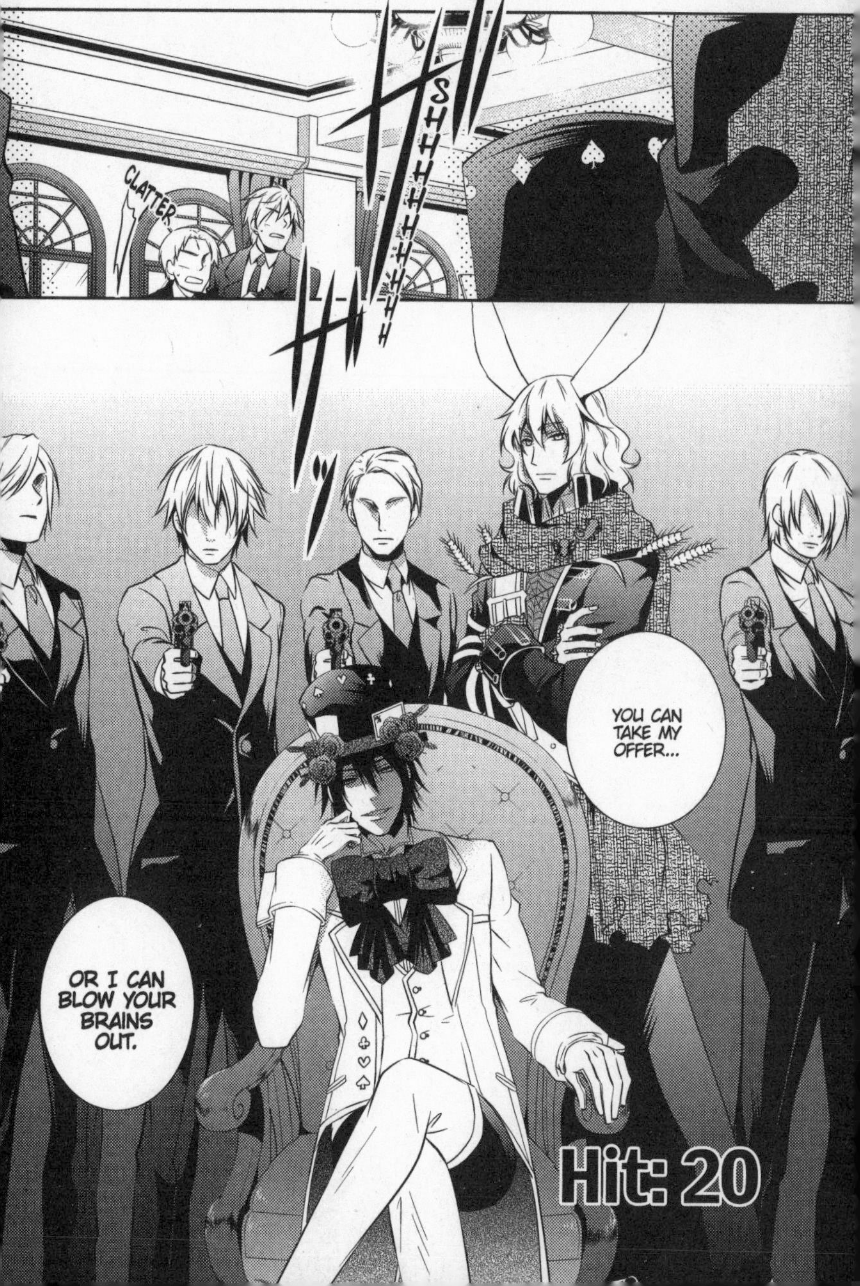
SHHHHHHHHHHH
CLATTER
YOU CAN TAKE MY OFFER...
OR I CAN BLOW YOUR BRAINS OUT.

Hit: 20

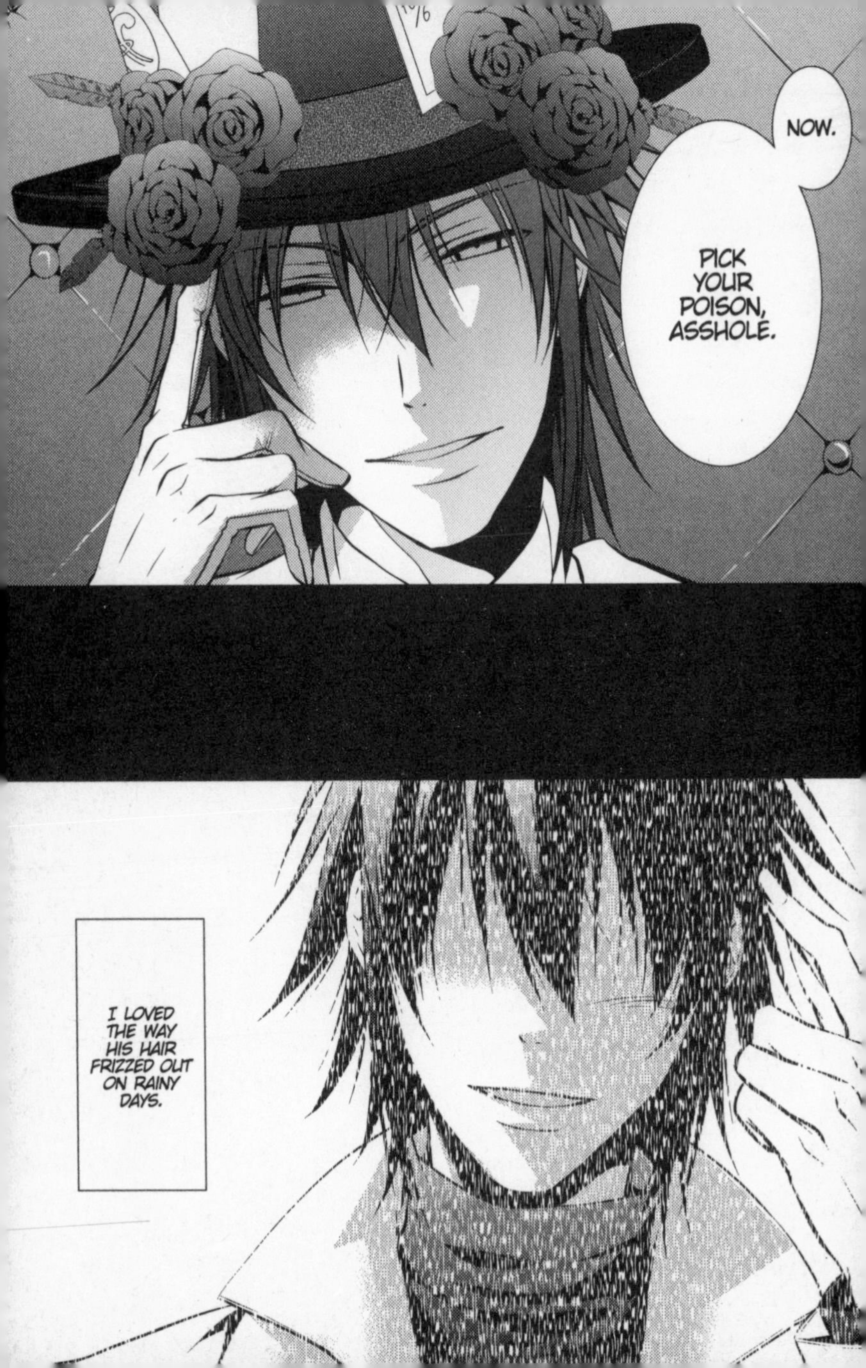
NOW.
PICK YOUR POISON, ASSHOLE.
I LOVED THE WAY HIS HAIR FRIZZED OUT ON RAINY DAYS.

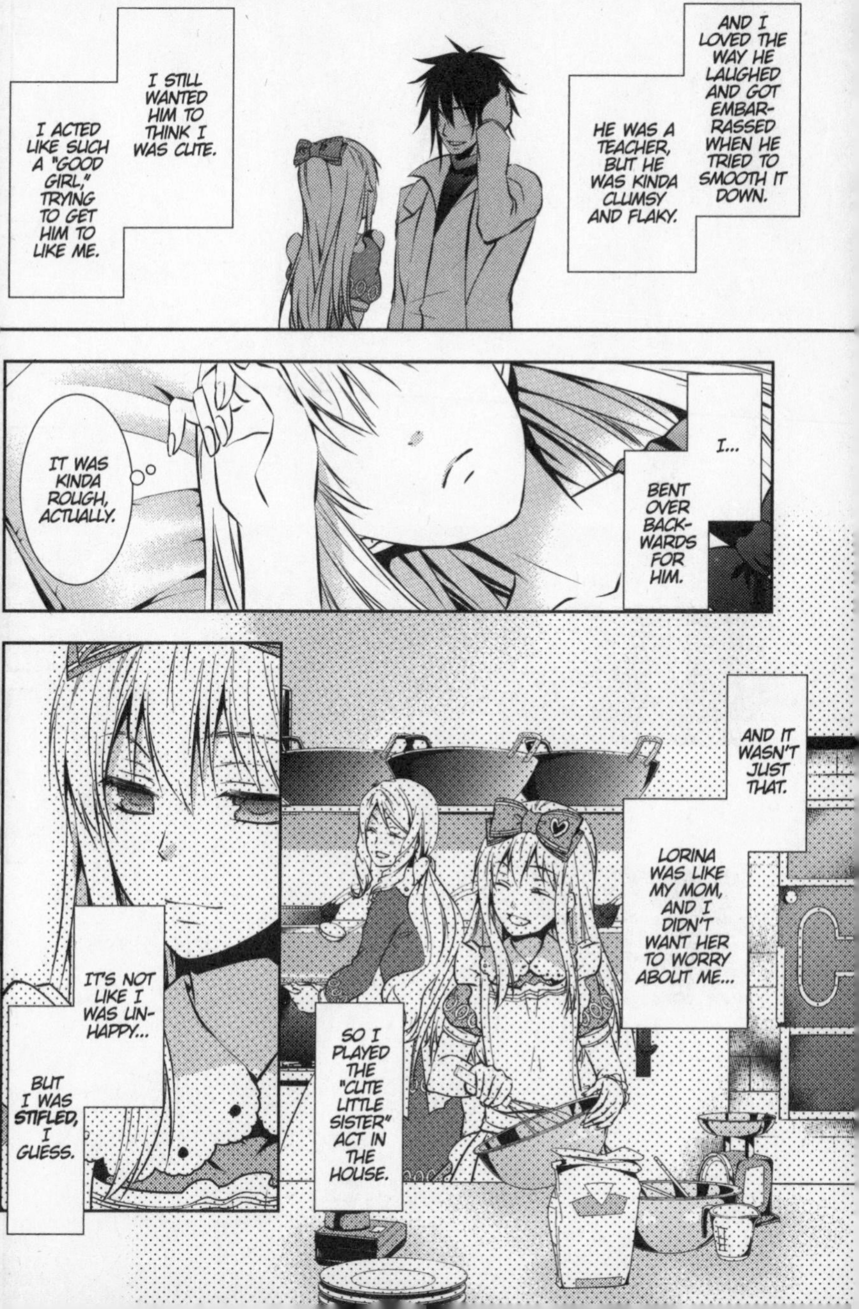
AND I LOVED THE WAY HE LAUGHED AND GOT EMBAR-RASSED WHEN HE TRIED TO SMOOTH IT DOWN.
HE WAS A TEACHER, BUT HE WAS KINDA CLUMSY AND FLAKY.
I STILL WANTED HIM TO THINK I WAS CUTE.
I ACTED LIKE SUCH A "GOOD GIRL," TRYING TO GET HIM TO LIKE ME.
I...
BENT OVER BACK-WARDS FOR HIM.
IT WAS KINDA ROUGH, ACTUALLY.
AND IT WASN'T JUST THAT.
LORINA WAS LIKE MY MOM, AND I DIDN'T WANT HER TO WORRY ABOUT ME...
SO I PLAYED THE "CUTE LITTLE SISTER" ACT IN THE HOUSE.
IT'S NOT LIKE I WAS UN-HAPPY...
BUT I WAS STIFLED, I GUESS.

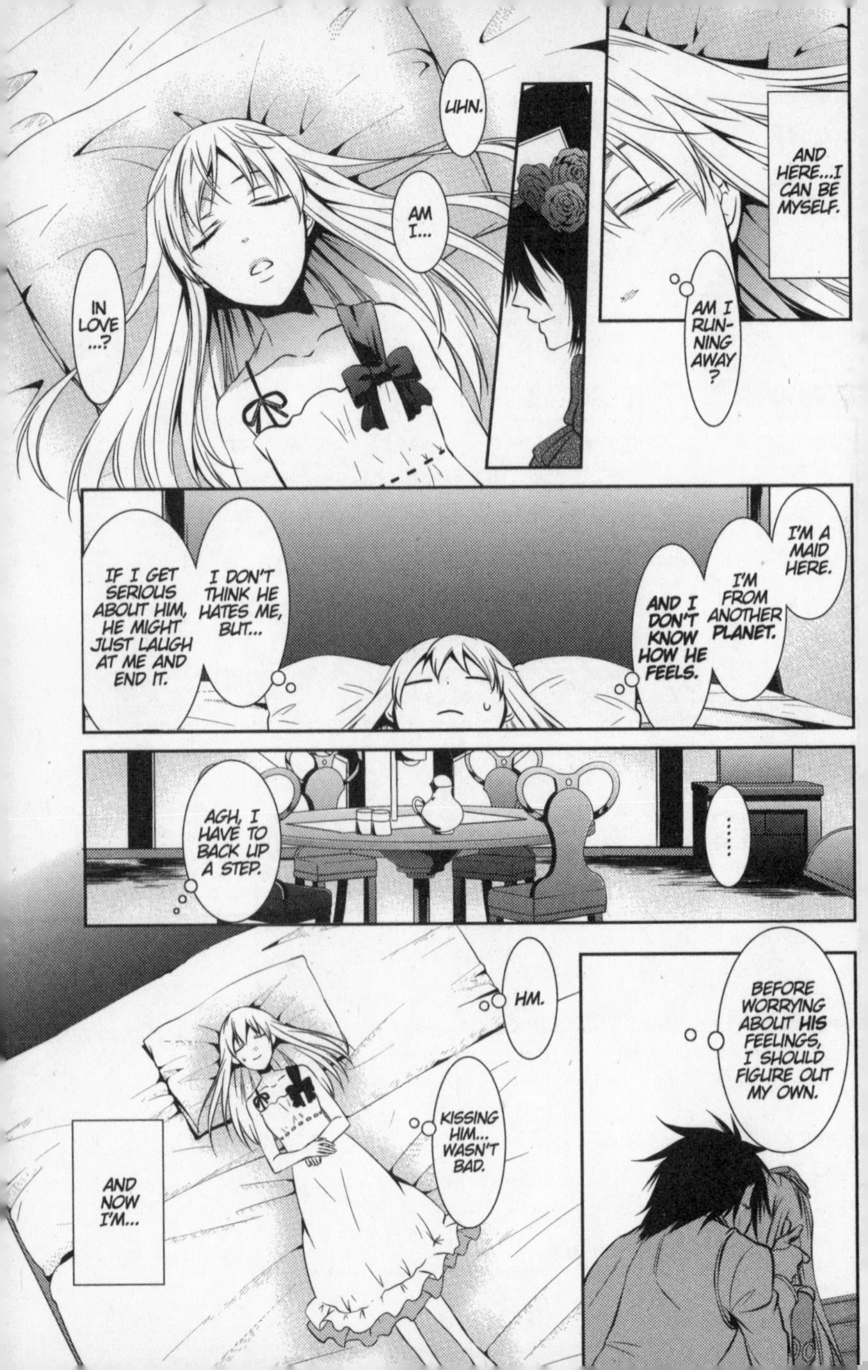
AND HERE...I CAN BE MYSELF.
AM I RUNNING AWAY?
UHN.
AM I...
IN LOVE ...?
I'M A MAID HERE.
I'M FROM ANOTHER PLANET.
AND I DON'T KNOW HOW HE FEELS.
I DON'T THINK HE HATES ME, BUT...
IF I GET SERIOUS ABOUT HIM, HE MIGHT JUST LAUGH AT ME AND END IT.
......
AGH, I HAVE TO BACK UP A STEP.
BEFORE WORRYING ABOUT HIS FEELINGS, I SHOULD FIGURE OUT MY OWN.
HM.
KISSING HIM... WASN'T BAD.
AND NOW I'M...

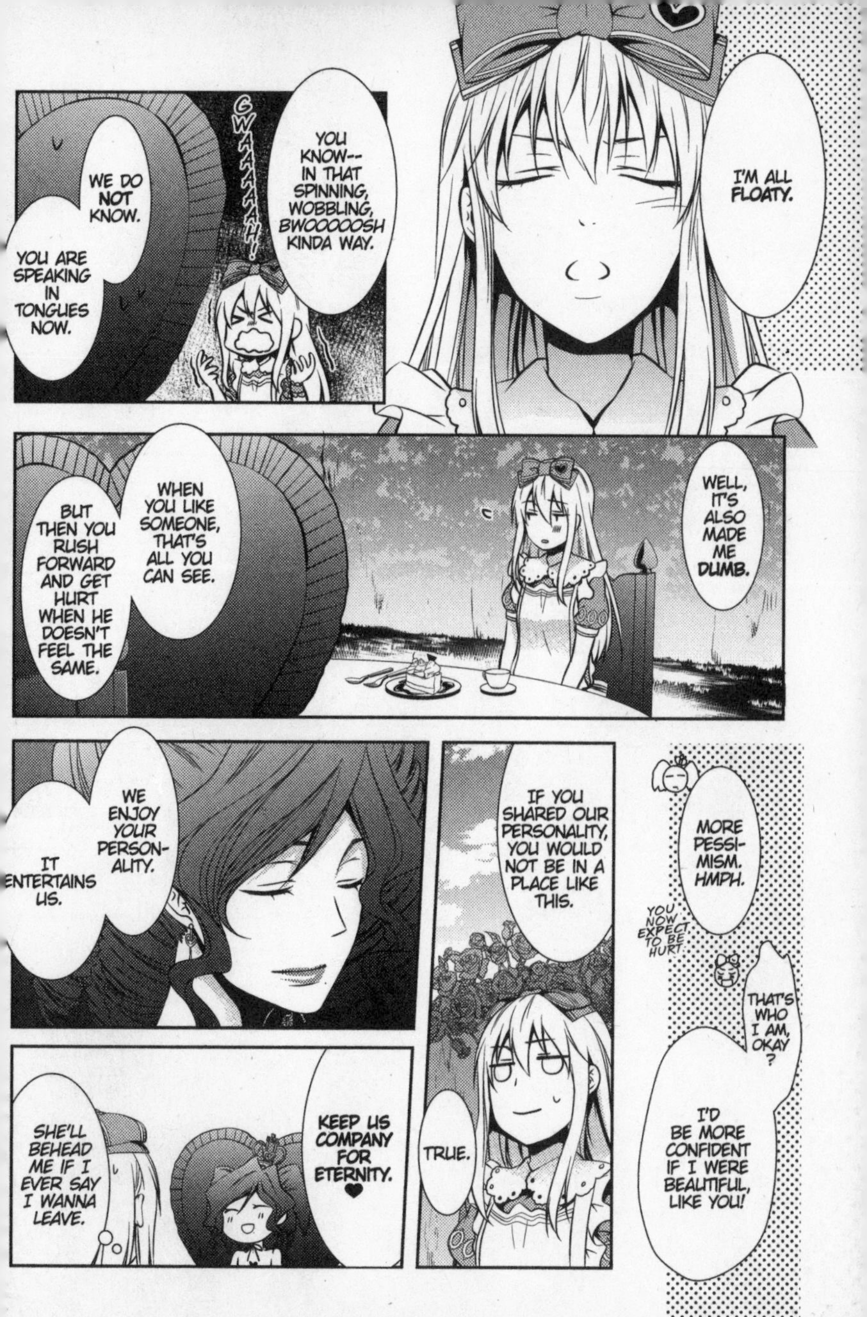
I'M ALL FLOATY.
YOU KNOW-- IN THAT SPINNING, WOBBLING, BWOOOOOSH KINDA WAY.
GWAAAAAAAH!
WE DO NOT KNOW.
YOU ARE SPEAKING IN TONGUES NOW.
WELL, IT'S ALSO MADE ME DUMB.
WHEN YOU LIKE SOMEONE, THAT'S ALL YOU CAN SEE.
BUT THEN YOU RUSH FORWARD AND GET HURT WHEN HE DOESN'T FEEL THE SAME.
MORE PESSIMISM. HMPH.
YOU NOW EXPECT TO BE HURT.
THAT'S WHO I AM, OKAY?
I'D BE MORE CONFIDENT IF I WERE BEAUTIFUL, LIKE YOU!
IF YOU SHARED OUR PERSONALITY, YOU WOULD NOT BE IN A PLACE LIKE THIS.
TRUE.
WE ENJOY YOUR PERSONALITY.
IT ENTERTAINS US.
KEEP US COMPANY FOR ETERNITY. ♥
SHE'LL BEHEAD ME IF I EVER SAY I WANNA LEAVE.

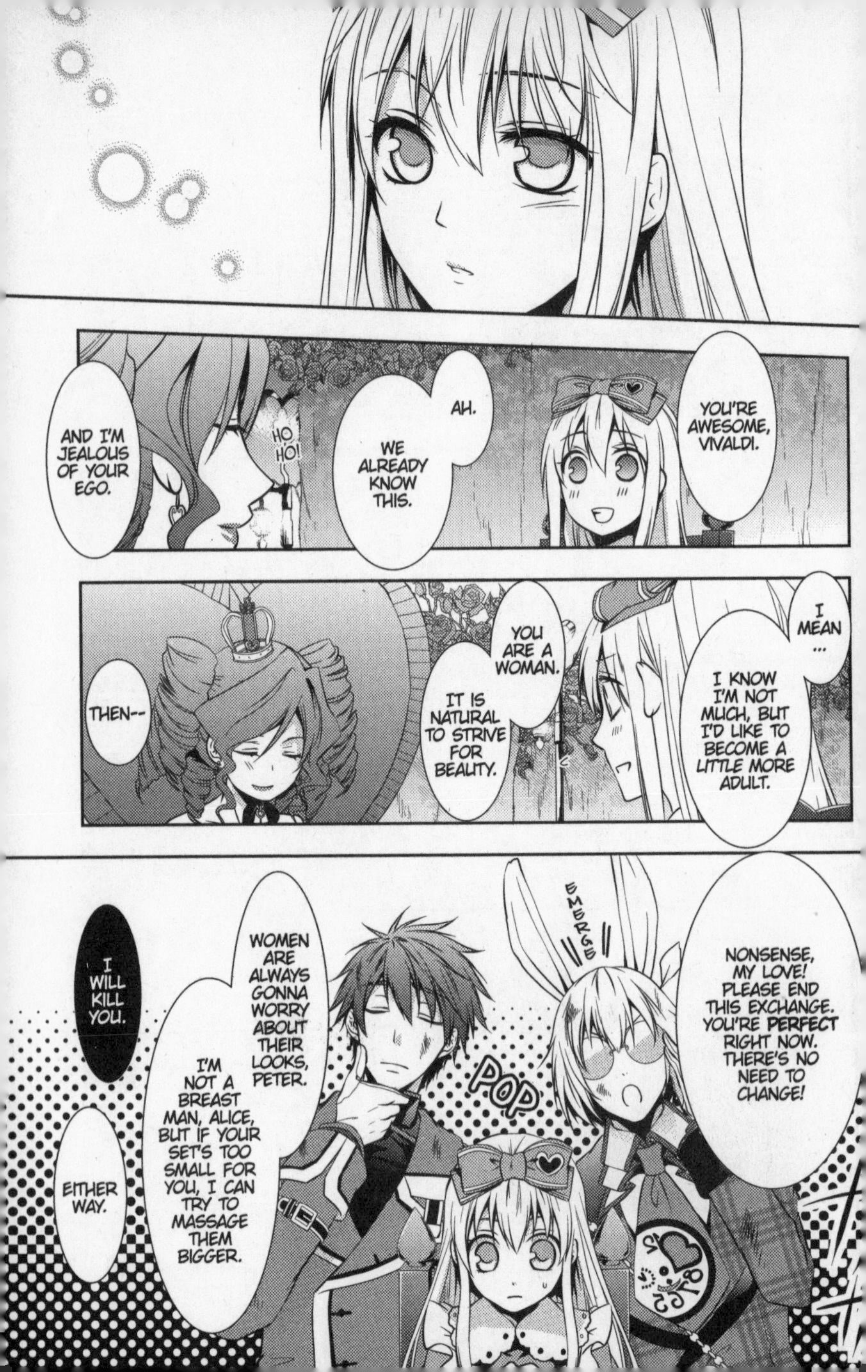
YOU'RE AWESOME, VIVALDI.
AH.
WE ALREADY KNOW THIS.
HO HO!
AND I'M JEALOUS OF YOUR EGO.
I MEAN ...
I KNOW I'M NOT MUCH, BUT I'D LIKE TO BECOME A LITTLE MORE ADULT.
YOU ARE A WOMAN.
IT IS NATURAL TO STRIVE FOR BEAUTY.
THEN--
NONSENSE, MY LOVE! PLEASE END THIS EXCHANGE. YOU'RE PERFECT RIGHT NOW. THERE'S NO NEED TO CHANGE!
EMERGE
POP
WOMEN ARE ALWAYS GONNA WORRY ABOUT THEIR LOOKS, PETER.
I'M NOT A BREAST MAN, ALICE, BUT IF YOUR SET'S TOO SMALL FOR YOU, I CAN TRY TO MASSAGE THEM BIGGER.
I WILL KILL YOU.
EITHER WAY.

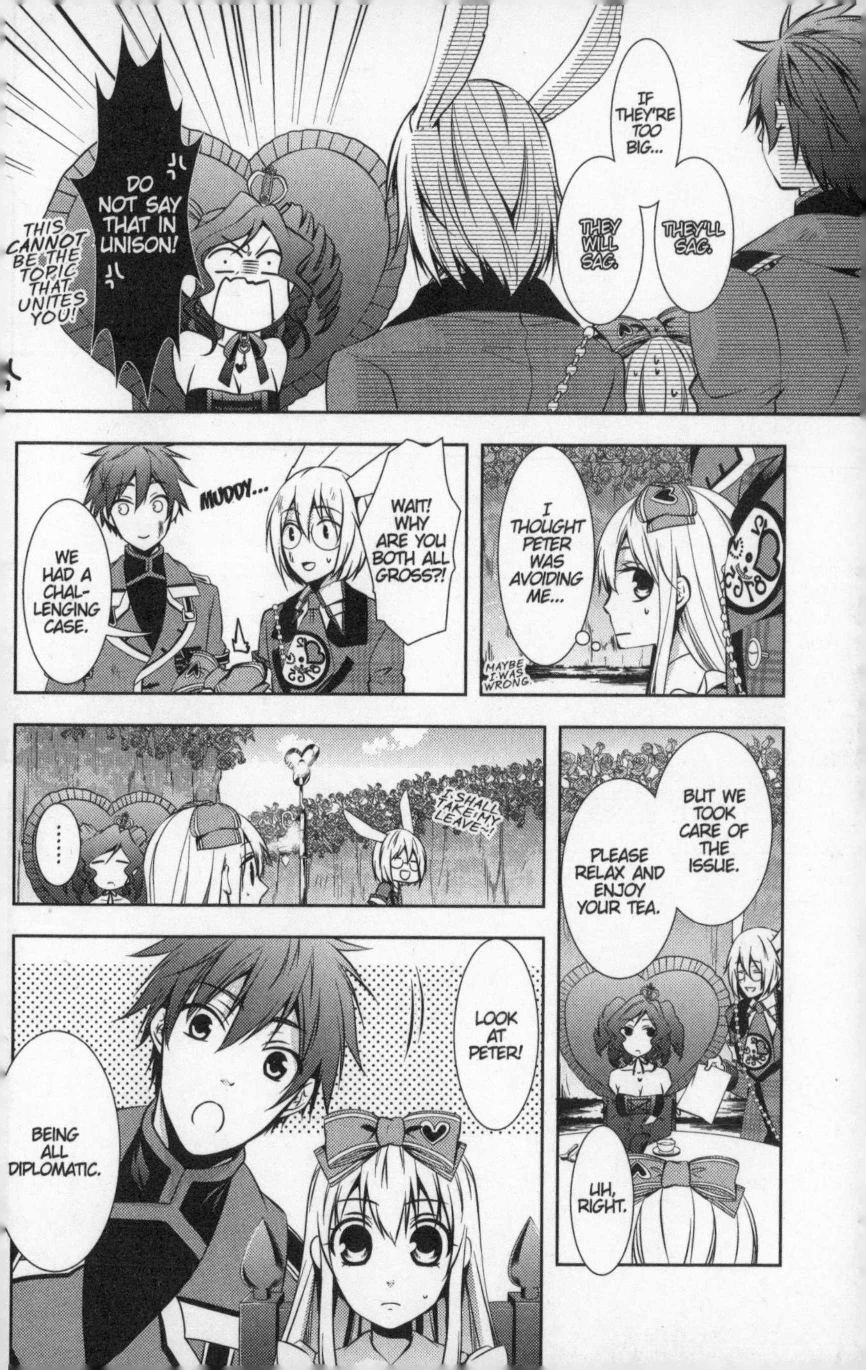
IF THEY'RE TOO BIG...
THEY'LL SAG.
THEY WILL SAG.
DO NOT SAY THAT IN UNISON!
THIS CANNOT BE THE TOPIC THAT UNITES YOU!
I THOUGHT PETER WAS AVOIDING ME...
MAYBE I WAS WRONG.
WAIT! WHY ARE YOU BOTH ALL GROSS?!
MUDDY...
WE HAD A CHAL-LENGING CASE.
BUT WE TOOK CARE OF THE ISSUE.
PLEASE RELAX AND ENJOY YOUR TEA.
UH, RIGHT.
I SHALL TAKE MY LEAVE~!
......
LOOK AT PETER!
BEING ALL DIPLOMATIC.

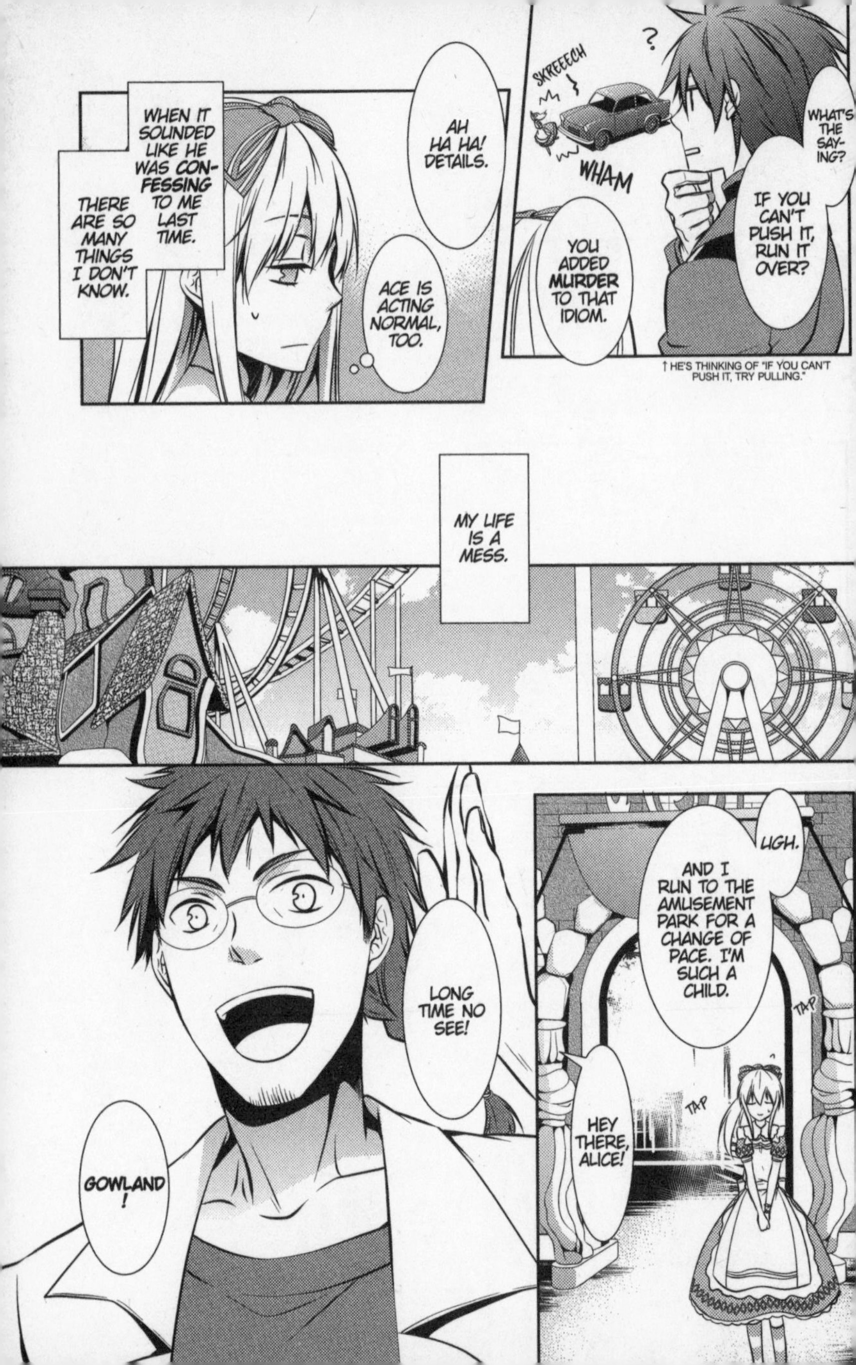
?
SKREEECH
WHAM
WHAT'S THE SAYING?
IF YOU CAN'T PUSH IT, RUN IT OVER?
YOU ADDED MURDER TO THAT IDIOM.
↑ HE'S THINKING OF "IF YOU CAN'T PUSH IT, TRY PULLING."
AH HA HA! DETAILS.
ACE IS ACTING NORMAL, TOO.
WHEN IT SOUNDED LIKE HE WAS CONFESSING TO ME LAST TIME.
THERE ARE SO MANY THINGS I DON'T KNOW.
MY LIFE IS A MESS.
UGH.
AND I RUN TO THE AMUSEMENT PARK FOR A CHANGE OF PACE. I'M SUCH A CHILD.
TAP
TAP
HEY THERE, ALICE!
LONG TIME NO SEE!
GOWLAND!

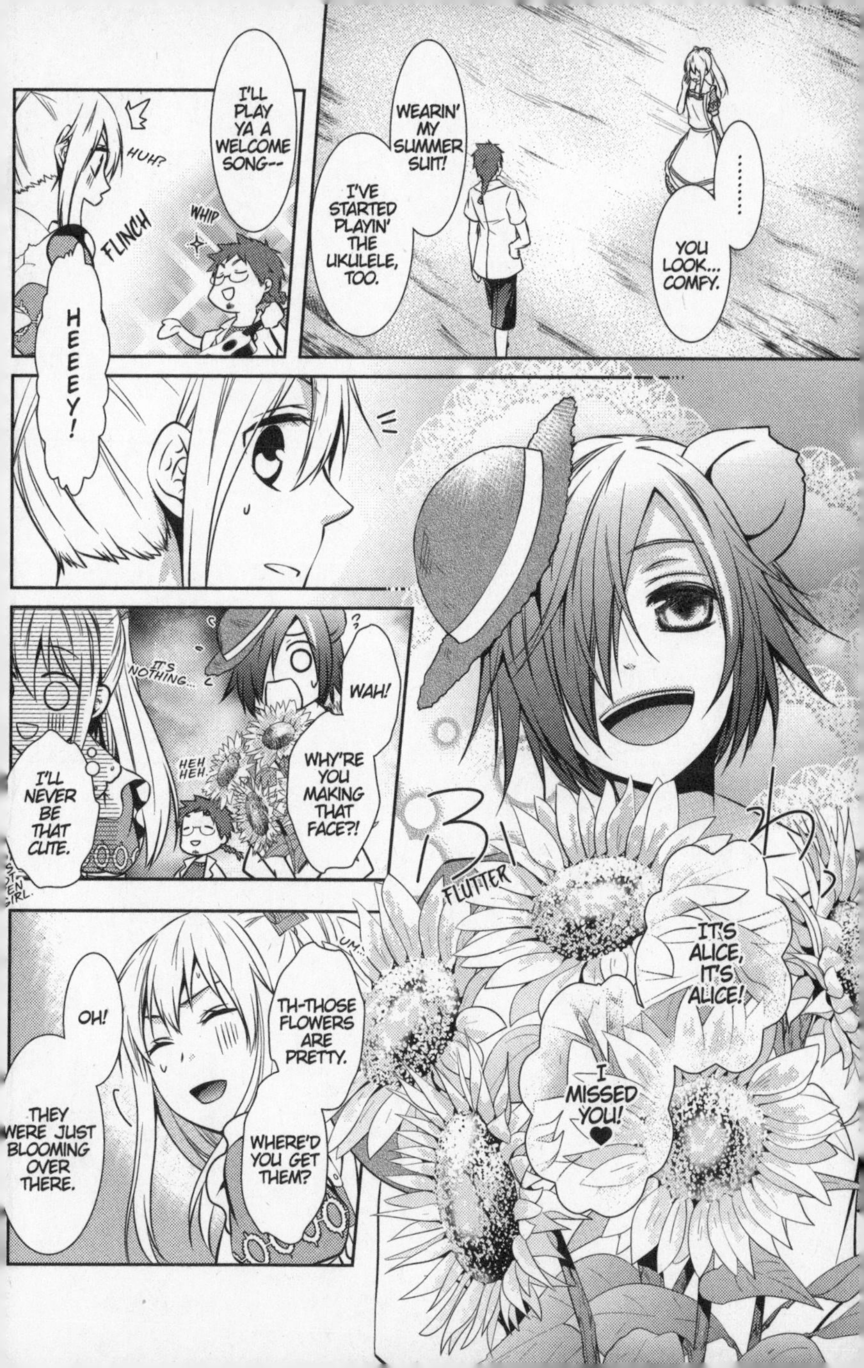
......
YOU LOOK... COMFY.
WEARIN' MY SUMMER SUIT!
I'VE STARTED PLAYIN' THE UKULELE, TOO.
I'LL PLAY YA A WELCOME SONG--
HUH?
WHIP
FLINCH
HEEEEY!
FLUTTER
IT'S ALICE, IT'S ALICE!
I MISSED YOU! ♥
WAH!
WHY'RE YOU MAKING THAT FACE?!
IT'S NOTHING...
HEH HEH.
I'LL NEVER BE THAT CUTE.
UM...
TH-THOSE FLOWERS ARE PRETTY.
WHERE'D YOU GET THEM?
OH!
THEY WERE JUST BLOOMING OVER THERE.

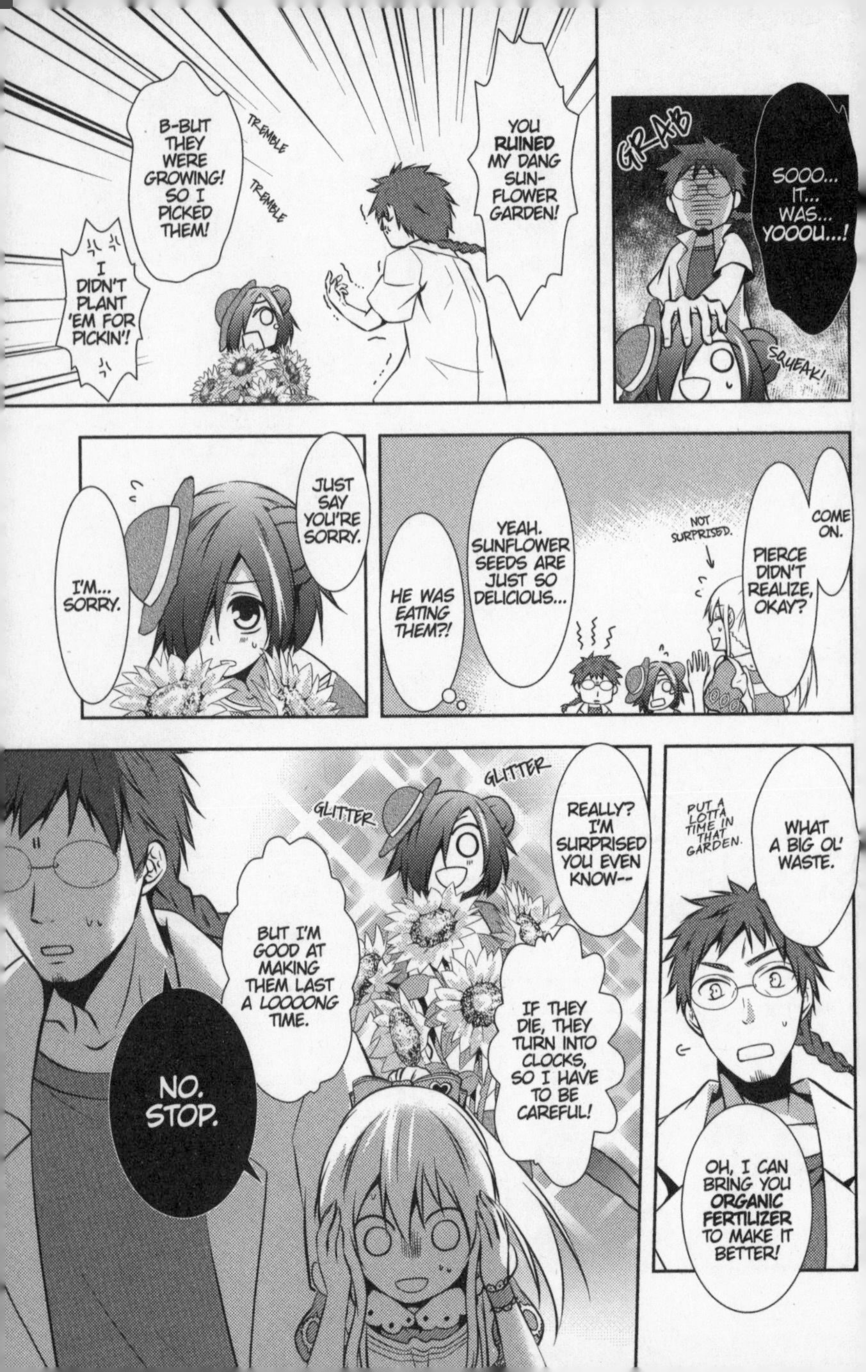
GRAB
SOOO... IT... WAS... YOOOU...!
SQUEAK!
YOU RUINED MY DANG SUN-FLOWER GARDEN!
TREMBLE
TREMBLE
B-BUT THEY WERE GROWING! SO I PICKED THEM!
I DIDN'T PLANT 'EM FOR PICKIN'!
COME ON.
PIERCE DIDN'T REALIZE, OKAY?
NOT SURPRISED.
YEAH. SUNFLOWER SEEDS ARE JUST SO DELICIOUS...
HE WAS EATING THEM?!
JUST SAY YOU'RE SORRY.
I'M... SORRY.
WHAT A BIG OL' WASTE.
PUT A LOTTA TIME IN THAT GARDEN.
OH, I CAN BRING YOU ORGANIC FERTILIZER TO MAKE IT BETTER!
REALLY? I'M SURPRISED YOU EVEN KNOW--
GLITTER
GLITTER
BUT I'M GOOD AT MAKING THEM LAST A LOOOONG TIME.
IF THEY DIE, THEY TURN INTO CLOCKS, SO I HAVE TO BE CAREFUL!
NO. STOP.

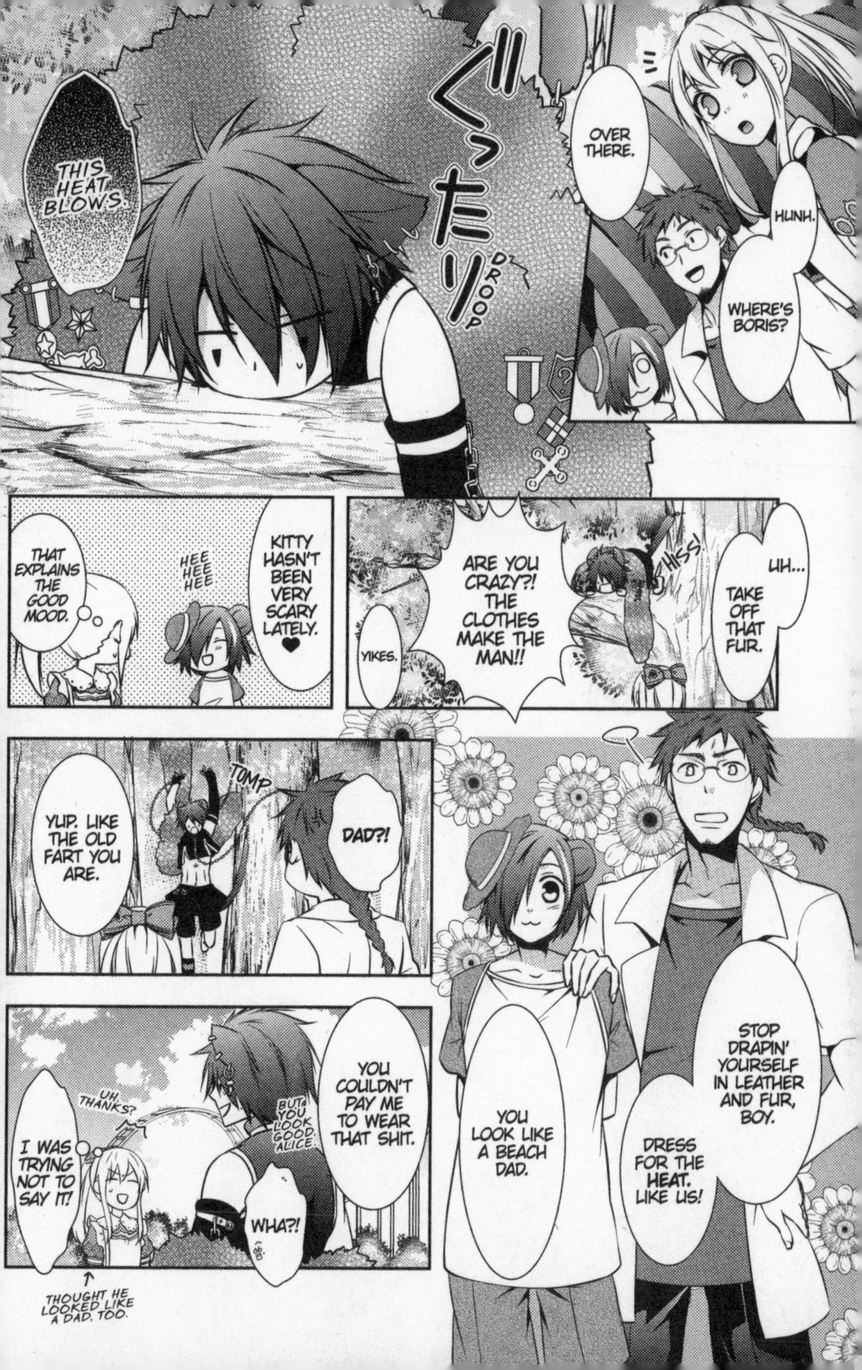
HUNH.
WHERE'S BORIS?
OVER THERE.
ぐったり
DROOP
THIS HEAT BLOWS.
UH... TAKE OFF THAT FUR.
HISS!
ARE YOU CRAZY?! THE CLOTHES MAKE THE MAN!!
YIKES.
KITTY HASN'T BEEN VERY SCARY LATELY. ♥
HEE HEE HEE
THAT EXPLAINS THE GOOD MOOD.
STOP DRAPIN' YOURSELF IN LEATHER AND FUR, BOY.
DRESS FOR THE HEAT. LIKE US!
YOU LOOK LIKE A BEACH DAD.
TOMP
DAD?!
YUP. LIKE THE OLD FART YOU ARE.
YOU COULDN'T PAY ME TO WEAR THAT SHIT.
BUT YOU LOOK GOOD, ALICE.
WHA?!
UH, THANKS?
I WAS TRYING NOT TO SAY IT!
THOUGHT HE LOOKED LIKE A DAD, TOO.

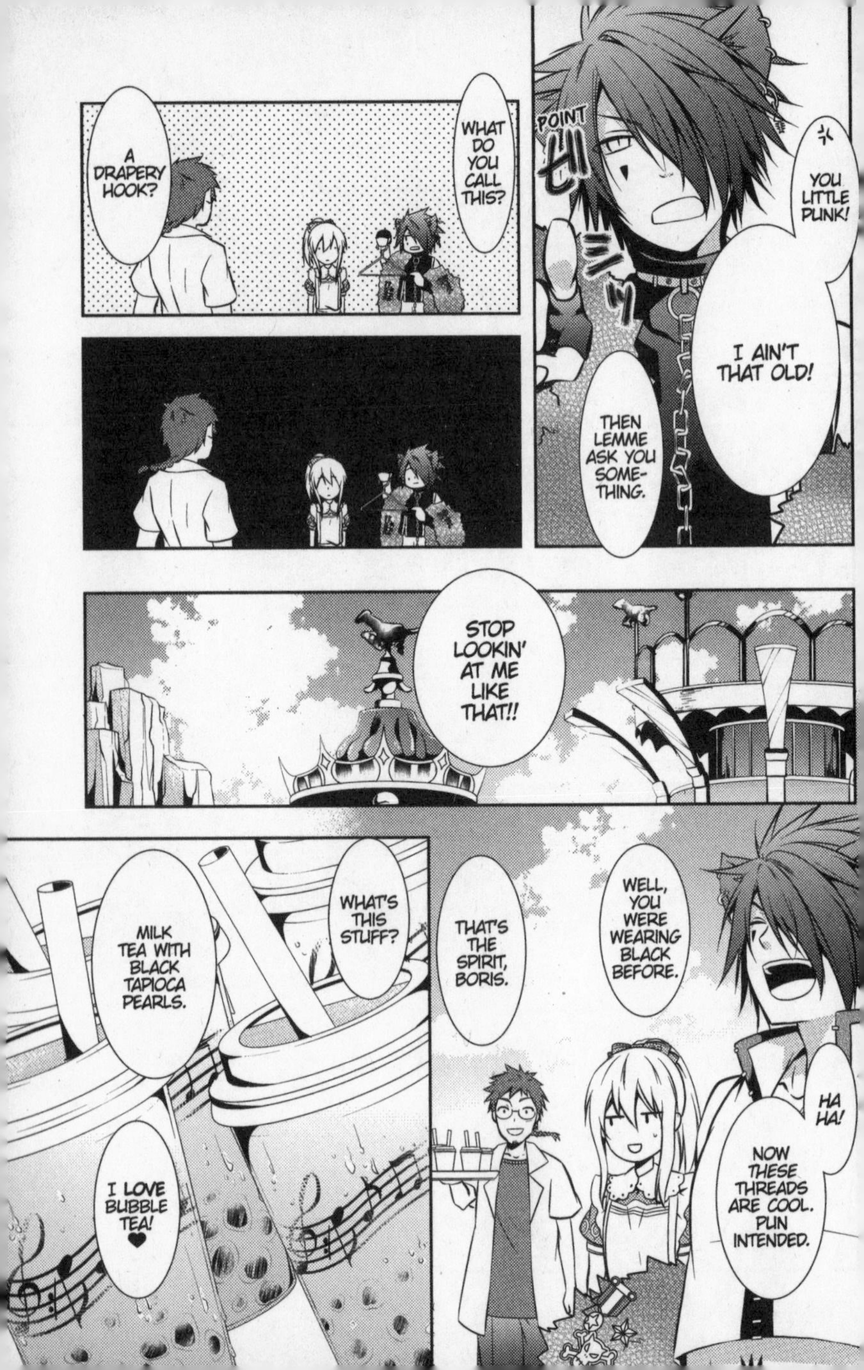
POINT
YOU LITTLE PUNK!
I AIN'T THAT OLD!
THEN LEMME ASK YOU SOME-THING.
WHAT DO YOU CALL THIS?
A DRAPERY HOOK?
STOP LOOKIN' AT ME LIKE THAT!!
WELL, YOU WERE WEARING BLACK BEFORE.
THAT'S THE SPIRIT, BORIS.
HA HA!
NOW THESE THREADS ARE COOL. PUN INTENDED.
WHAT'S THIS STUFF?
MILK TEA WITH BLACK TAPIOCA PEARLS.
I LOVE BUBBLE TEA! ♥

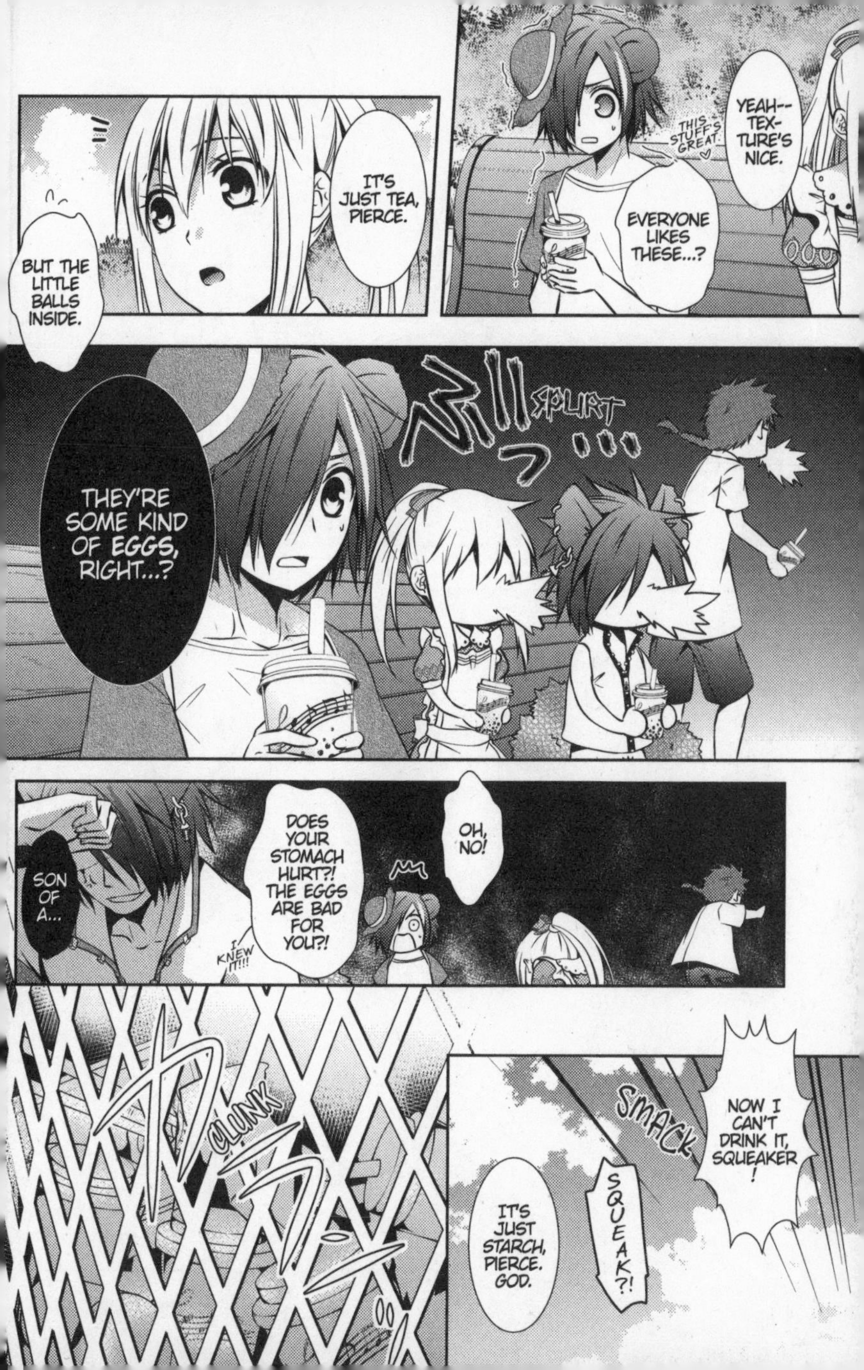
YEAH-- TEX-TURE'S NICE.
THIS STUFF'S GREAT ♥
EVERYONE LIKES THESE...?
IT'S JUST TEA, PIERCE.
BUT THE LITTLE BALLS INSIDE.
SPLURT
THEY'RE SOME KIND OF EGGS, RIGHT...?
OH, NO!
DOES YOUR STOMACH HURT?! THE EGGS ARE BAD FOR YOU?!
I KNEW IT!!!
SON OF A...
NOW I CAN'T DRINK IT, SQUEAKER!
SMACK
SQUEAK?!
IT'S JUST STARCH, PIERCE. GOD.
CLUNK

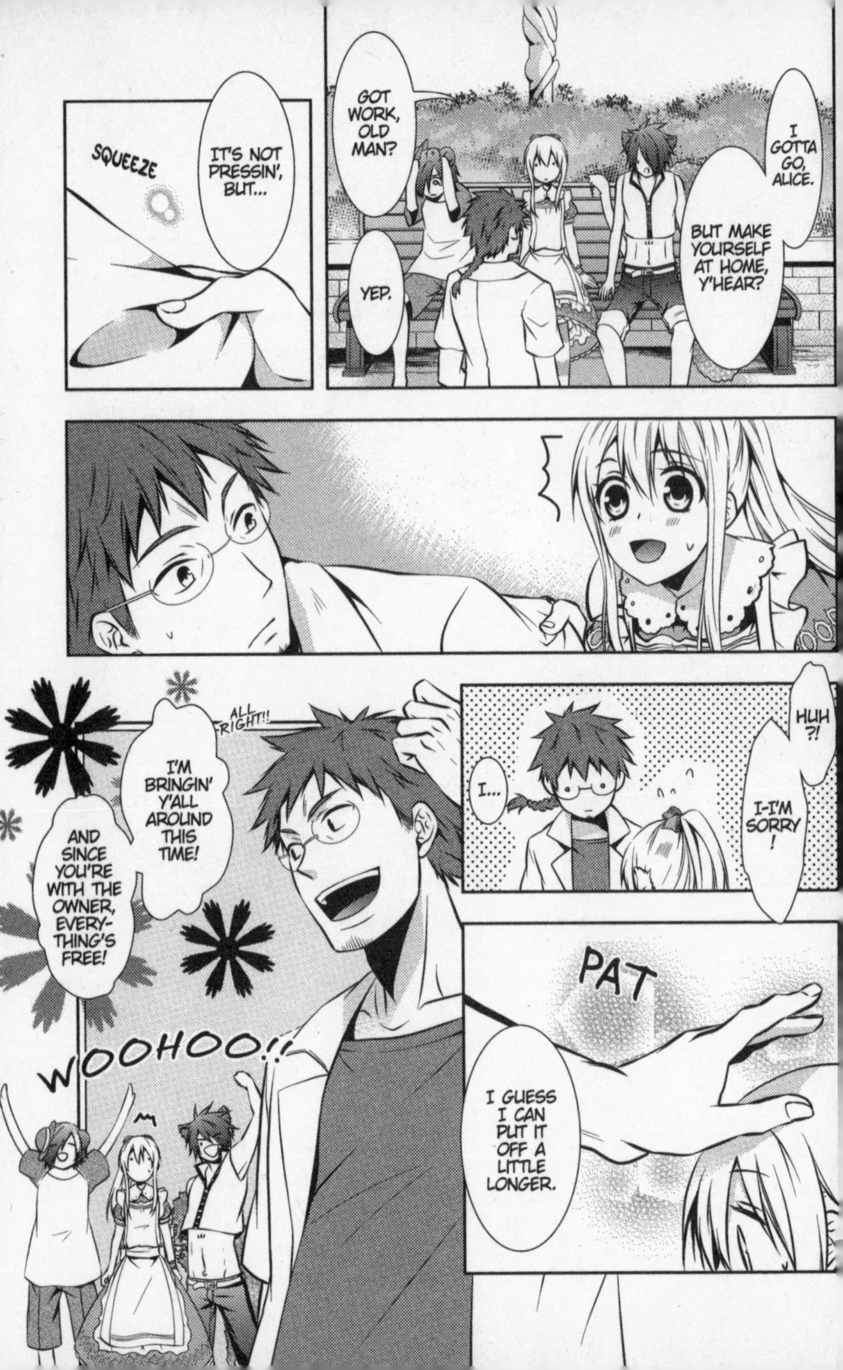
I GOTTA GO, ALICE.
BUT MAKE YOURSELF AT HOME, Y'HEAR?
GOT WORK, OLD MAN?
YEP.
IT'S NOT PRESSIN', BUT...
SQUEEZE
HUH?!
I-I'M SORRY!
I...
PAT
I GUESS I CAN PUT IT OFF A LITTLE LONGER.
ALL RIGHT!!
I'M BRINGIN' Y'ALL AROUND THIS TIME!
AND SINCE YOU'RE WITH THE OWNER, EVERY-THING'S FREE!
WOOHOO!!

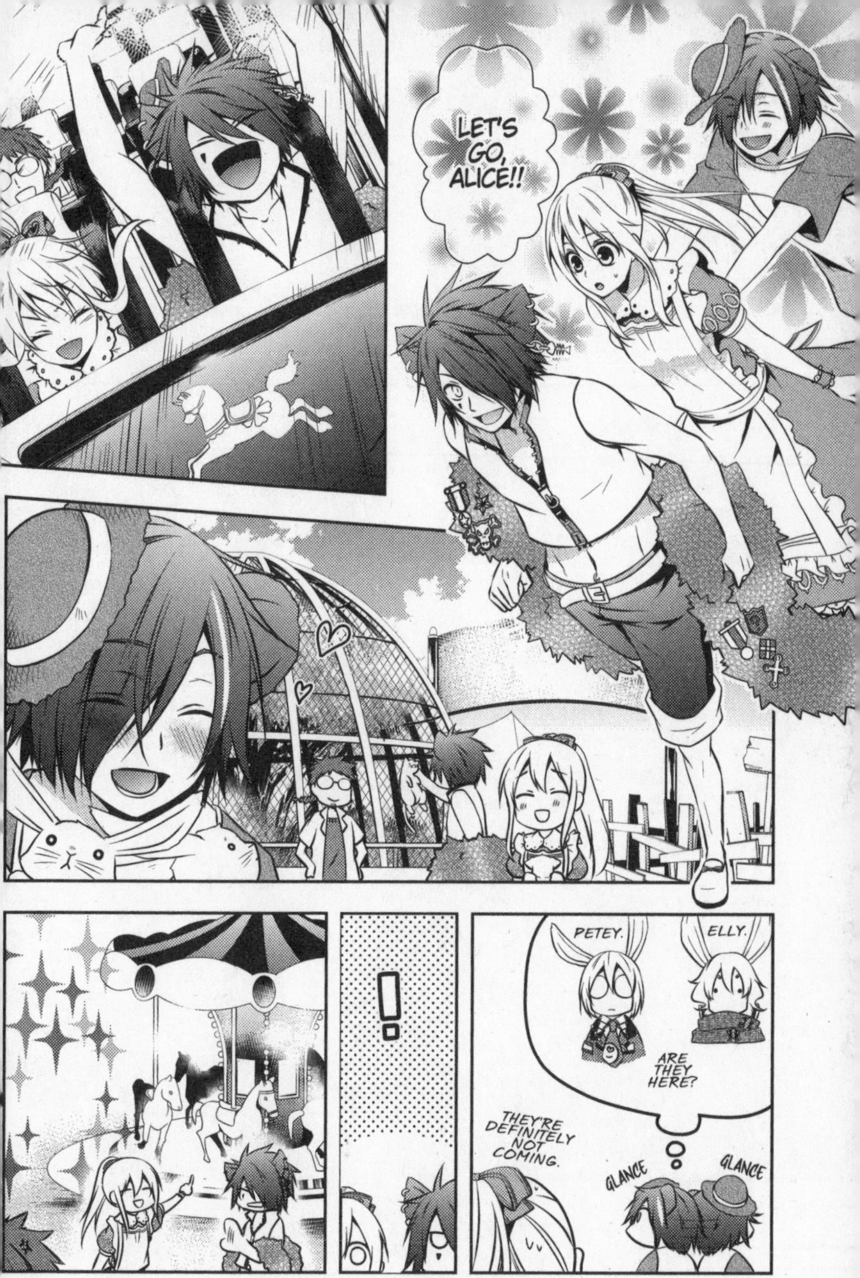
LET'S GO, ALICE!!
PETEY.
ELLY.
ARE THEY HERE?
GLANCE
GLANCE
THEY'RE DEFINITELY NOT COMING.
!

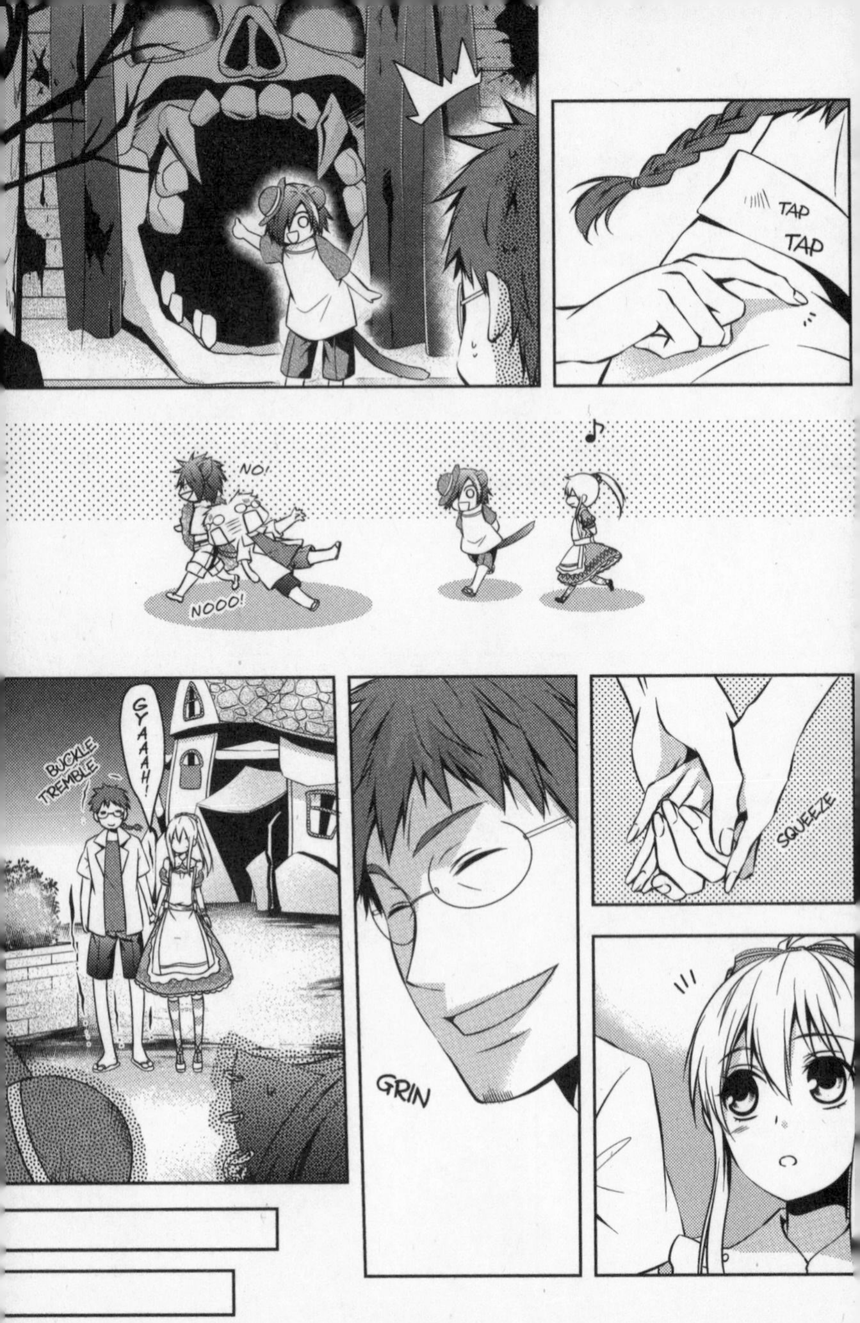
TAP
TAP
NO!
NOOO!
SQUEEZE
GRIN
GYAAAH!
BUCKLE TREMBLE

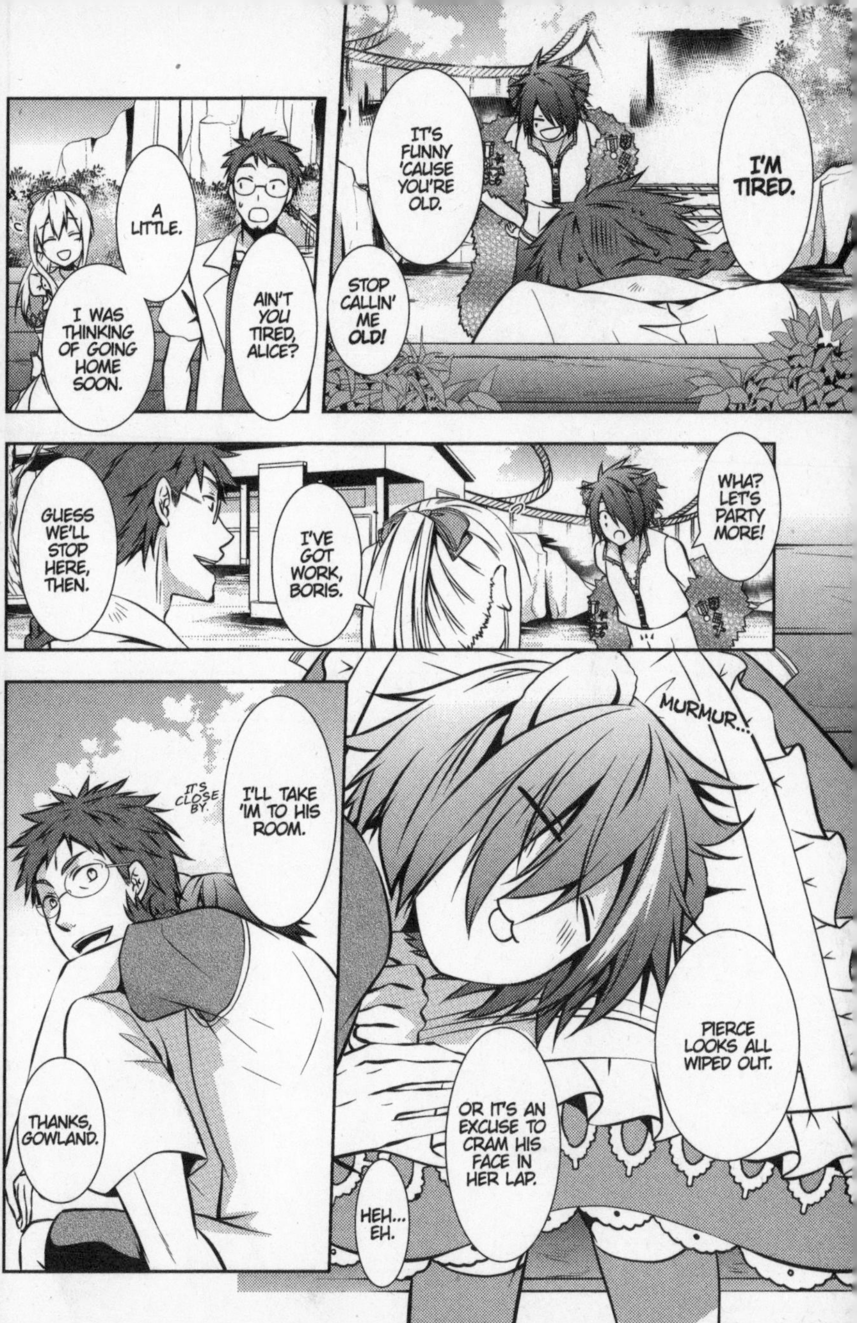
I'M TIRED.
IT'S FUNNY 'CAUSE YOU'RE OLD.
STOP CALLIN' ME OLD!
AIN'T YOU TIRED, ALICE?
A LITTLE.
I WAS THINKING OF GOING HOME SOON.
WHA? LET'S PARTY MORE!
I'VE GOT WORK, BORIS.
GUESS WE'LL STOP HERE, THEN.
MURMUR...
PIERCE LOOKS ALL WIPED OUT.
OR IT'S AN EXCUSE TO CRAM HIS FACE IN HER LAP.
HEH... EH.
I'LL TAKE 'IM TO HIS ROOM.
IT'S CLOSE BY.
THANKS, GOWLAND.

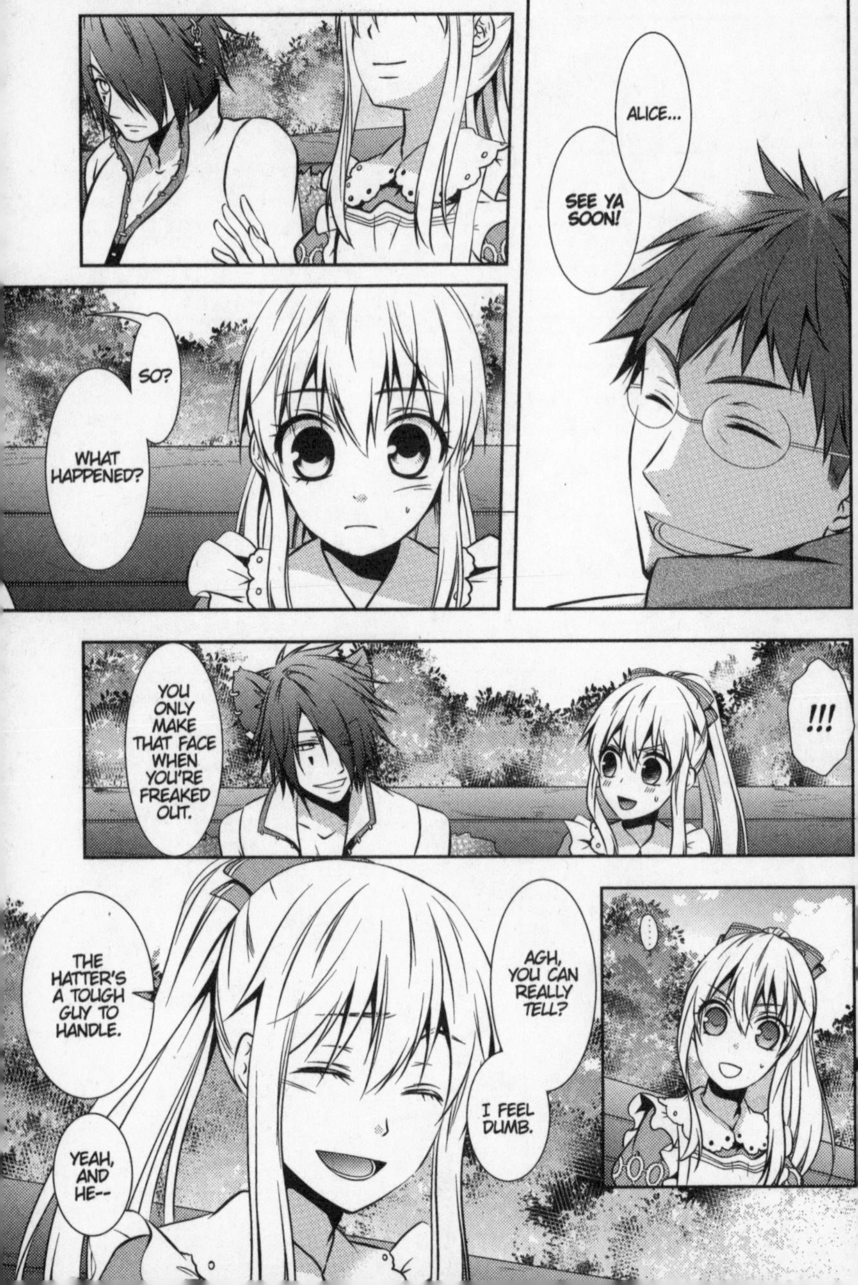
ALICE...
SEE YA SOON!
SO?
WHAT HAPPENED?
!!!
YOU ONLY MAKE THAT FACE WHEN YOU'RE FREAKED OUT.
...
AGH, YOU CAN REALLY TELL?
I FEEL DUMB.
THE HATTER'S A TOUGH GUY TO HANDLE.
YEAH, AND HE--

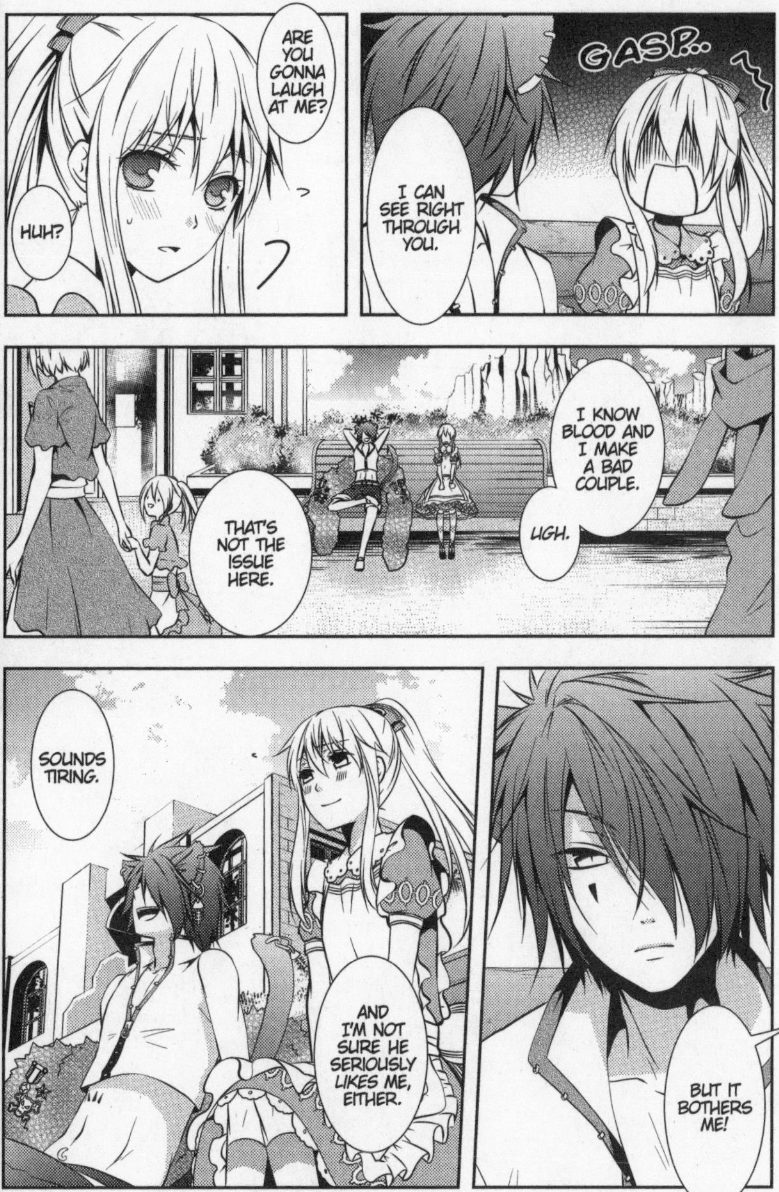
GASP...
I CAN SEE RIGHT THROUGH YOU.
ARE YOU GONNA LAUGH AT ME?
HUH?
I KNOW BLOOD AND I MAKE A BAD COUPLE.
UGH.
THAT'S NOT THE ISSUE HERE.
BUT IT BOTHERS ME!
SOUNDS TIRING.
AND I'M NOT SURE HE SERIOUSLY LIKES ME, EITHER.

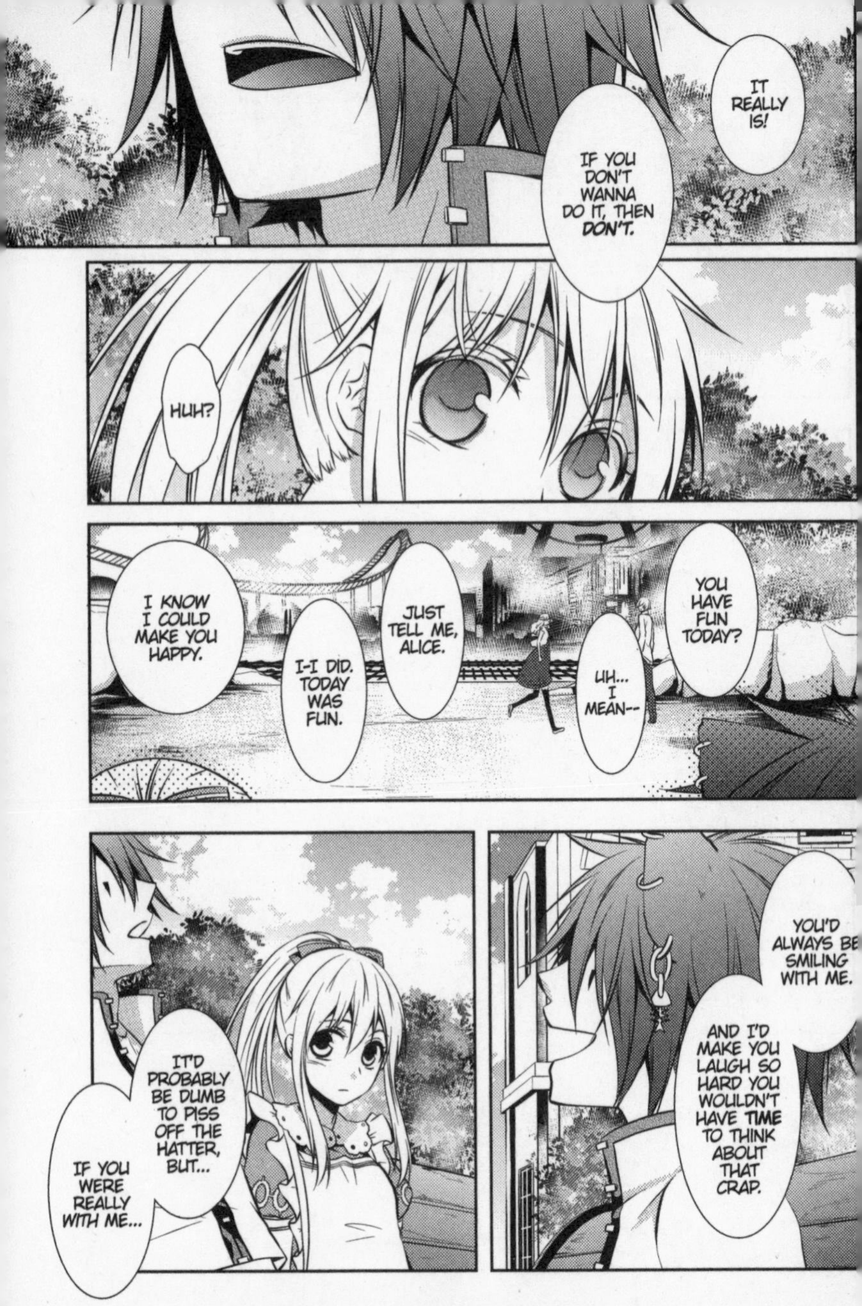
IT REALLY IS!
IF YOU DON'T WANNA DO IT, THEN DON'T.
HUH?
YOU HAVE FUN TODAY?
UH... I MEAN--
JUST TELL ME, ALICE.
I-I DID. TODAY WAS FUN.
I KNOW I COULD MAKE YOU HAPPY.
YOU'D ALWAYS BE SMILING WITH ME.
AND I'D MAKE YOU LAUGH SO HARD YOU WOULDN'T HAVE TIME TO THINK ABOUT THAT CRAP.
IT'D PROBABLY BE DUMB TO PISS OFF THE HATTER, BUT...
IF YOU WERE REALLY WITH ME...

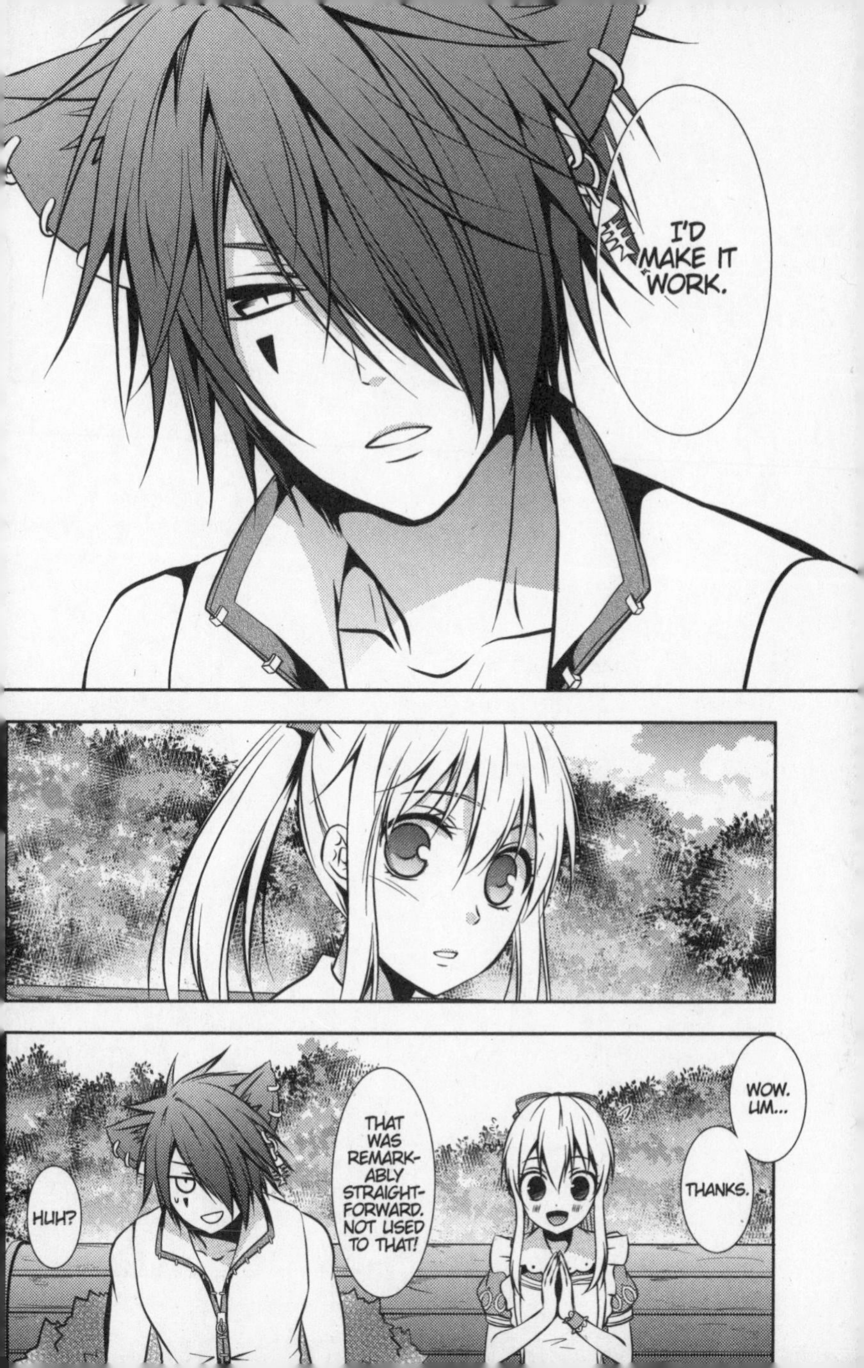
I'D MAKE IT WORK.
WOW. UM...
THANKS.
THAT WAS REMARKABLY STRAIGHTFORWARD. NOT USED TO THAT!
HUH?

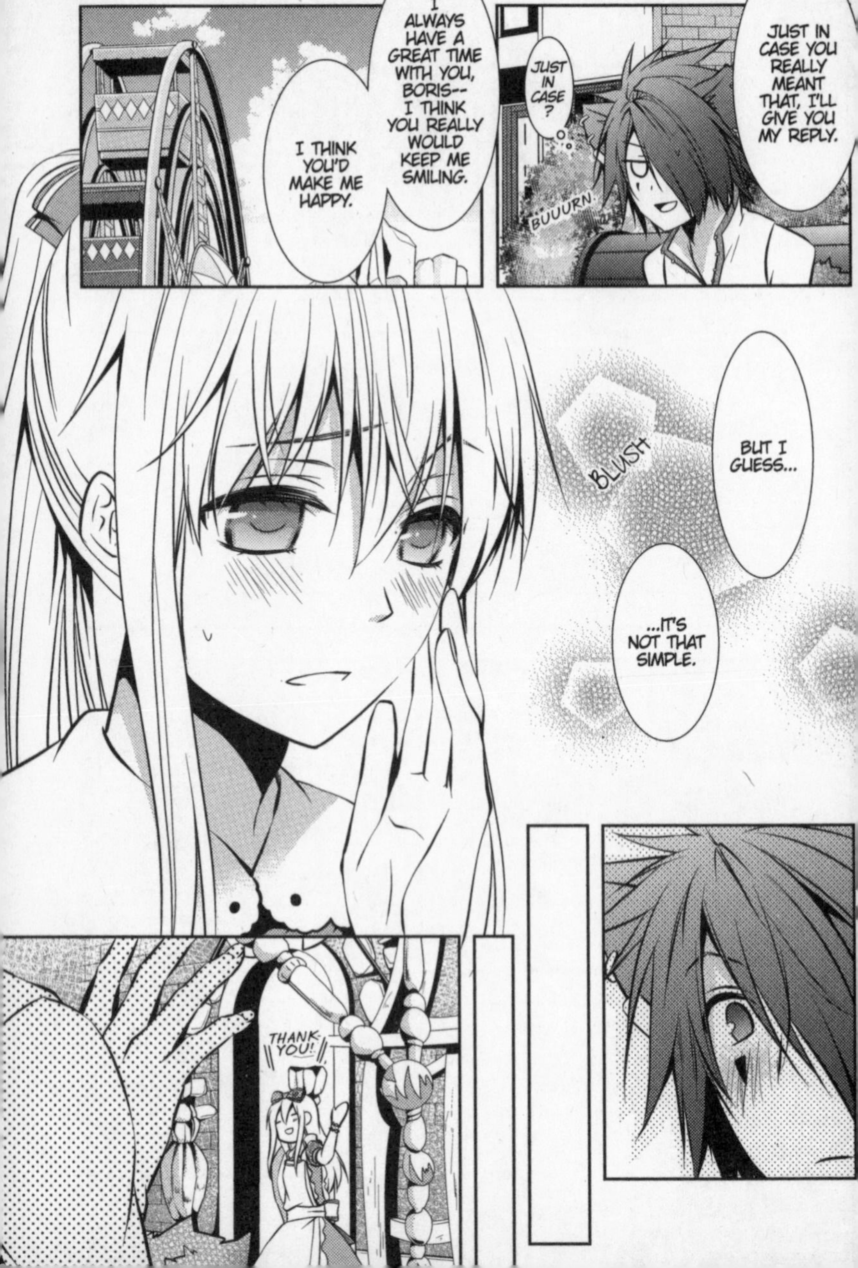
JUST IN CASE YOU REALLY MEANT THAT, I'LL GIVE YOU MY REPLY.
JUST IN CASE?
BUUURN.
I ALWAYS HAVE A GREAT TIME WITH YOU, BORIS-- I THINK YOU REALLY WOULD KEEP ME SMILING.
I THINK YOU'D MAKE ME HAPPY.
BUT I GUESS...
...IT'S NOT THAT SIMPLE.
BLUSH
THANK YOU!

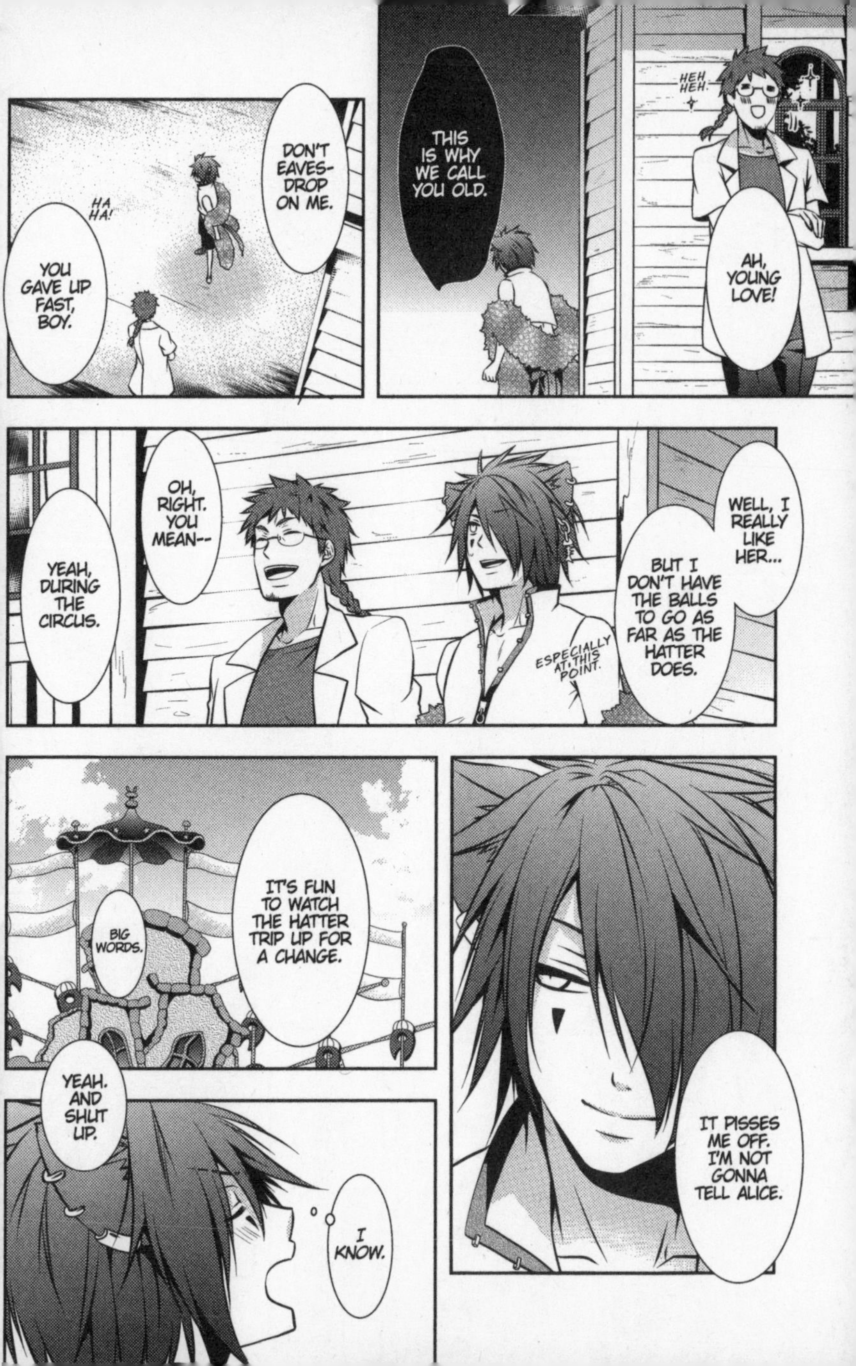
HEH HEH.
AH, YOUNG LOVE!
THIS IS WHY WE CALL YOU OLD.
DON'T EAVES-DROP ON ME.
HA HA!
YOU GAVE UP FAST, BOY.
WELL, I REALLY LIKE HER...
BUT I DON'T HAVE THE BALLS TO GO AS FAR AS THE HATTER DOES.
ESPECIALLY AT THIS POINT.
OH, RIGHT. YOU MEAN--
YEAH, DURING THE CIRCUS.
IT PISSES ME OFF. I'M NOT GONNA TELL ALICE.
IT'S FUN TO WATCH THE HATTER TRIP UP FOR A CHANGE.
BIG WORDS.
YEAH. AND SHUT UP.
I KNOW.

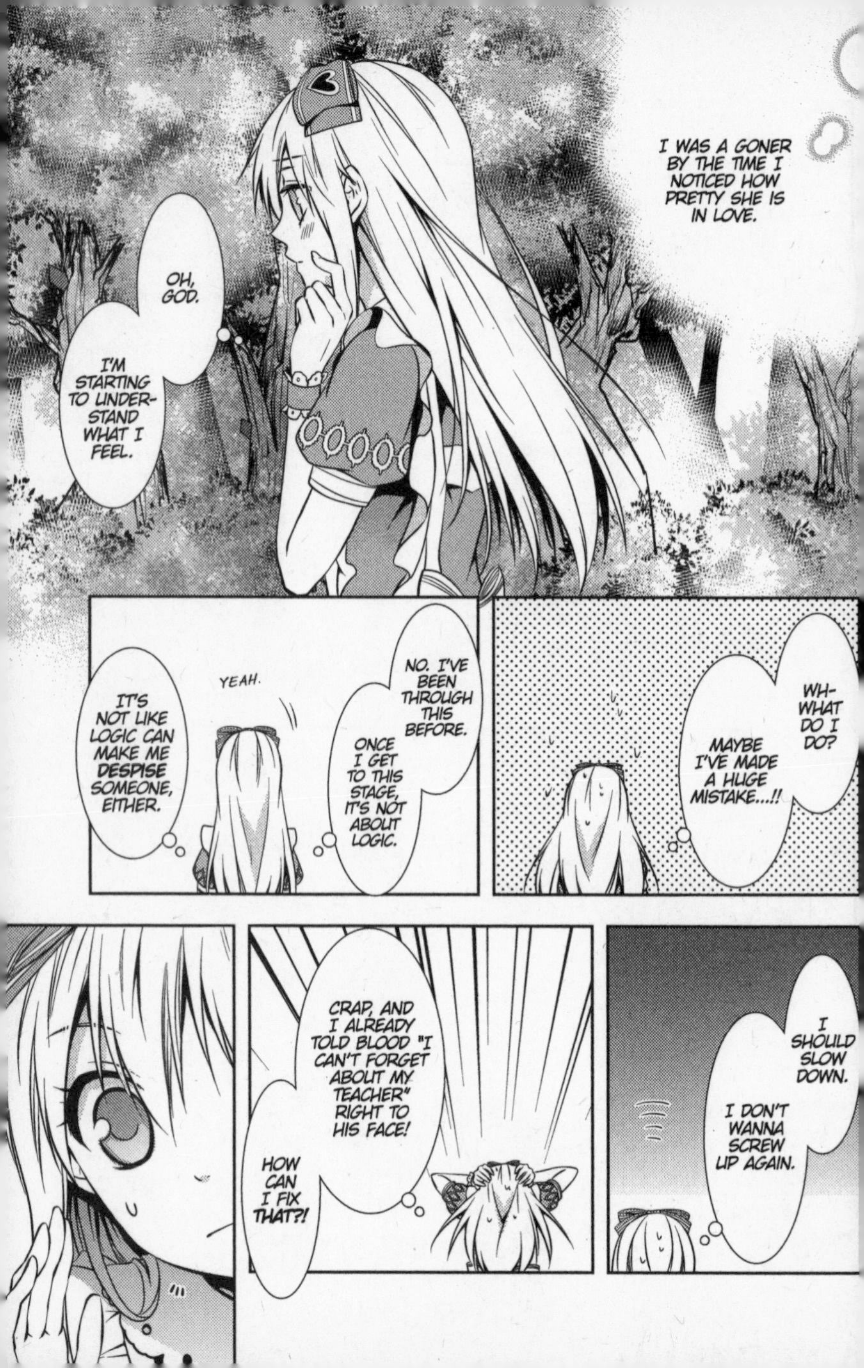
I WAS A GONER BY THE TIME I NOTICED HOW PRETTY SHE IS IN LOVE.
OH, GOD.
I'M STARTING TO UNDERSTAND WHAT I FEEL.
WH-WHAT DO I DO?
MAYBE I'VE MADE A HUGE MISTAKE...!!
NO. I'VE BEEN THROUGH THIS BEFORE.
ONCE I GET TO THIS STAGE, IT'S NOT ABOUT LOGIC.
YEAH.
IT'S NOT LIKE LOGIC CAN MAKE ME DESPISE SOMEONE, EITHER.
I SHOULD SLOW DOWN.
I DON'T WANNA SCREW UP AGAIN.
CRAP, AND I ALREADY TOLD BLOOD "I CAN'T FORGET ABOUT MY TEACHER" RIGHT TO HIS FACE!
HOW CAN I FIX THAT?!

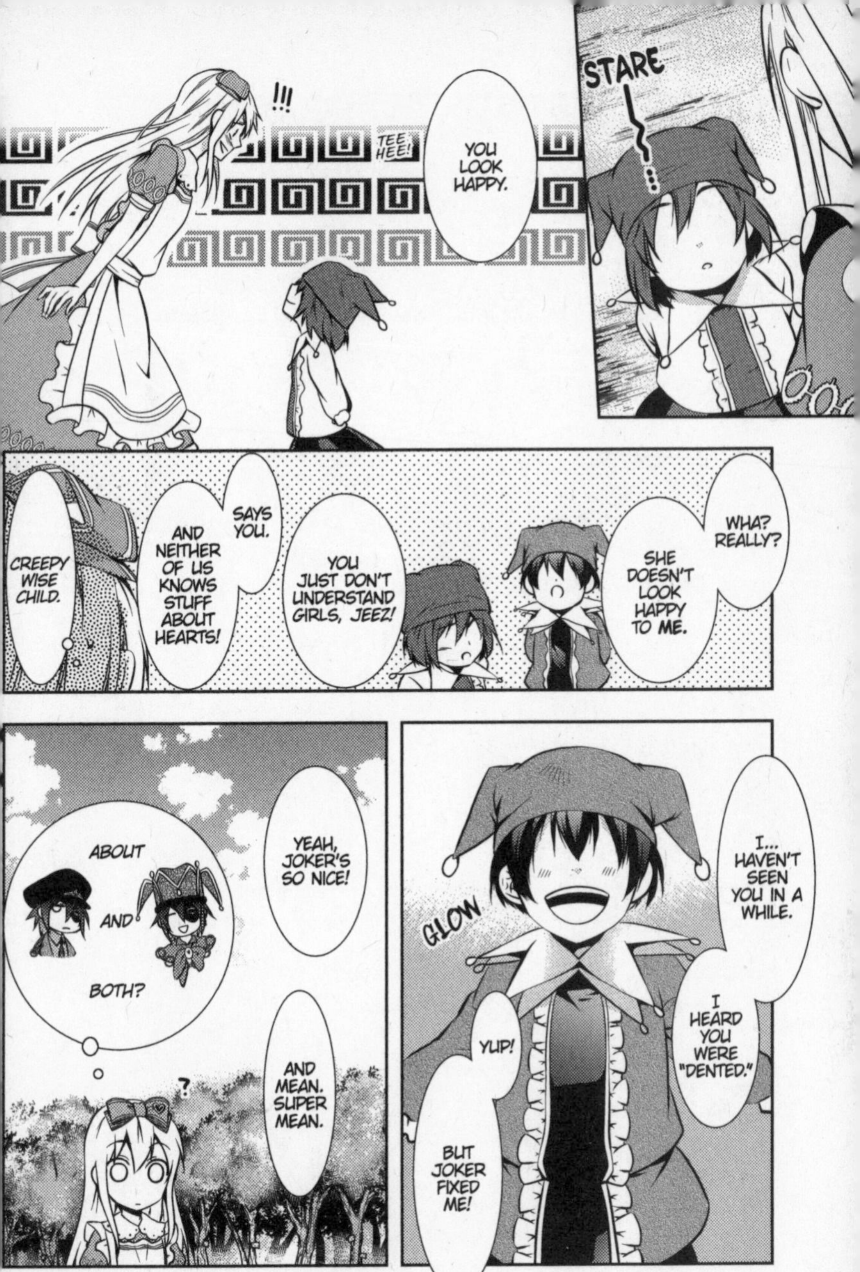
STARE
...
YOU LOOK HAPPY.
TEE HEE!
!!!
WHA? REALLY?
SHE DOESN'T LOOK HAPPY TO ME.
YOU JUST DON'T UNDERSTAND GIRLS, JEEZ!
SAYS YOU.
AND NEITHER OF US KNOWS STUFF ABOUT HEARTS!
CREEPY WISE CHILD.
I... HAVEN'T SEEN YOU IN A WHILE.
I HEARD YOU WERE "DENTED."
GLOW
YUP!
BUT JOKER FIXED ME!
YEAH, JOKER'S SO NICE!
AND MEAN. SUPER MEAN.
ABOUT
AND
BOTH?
?

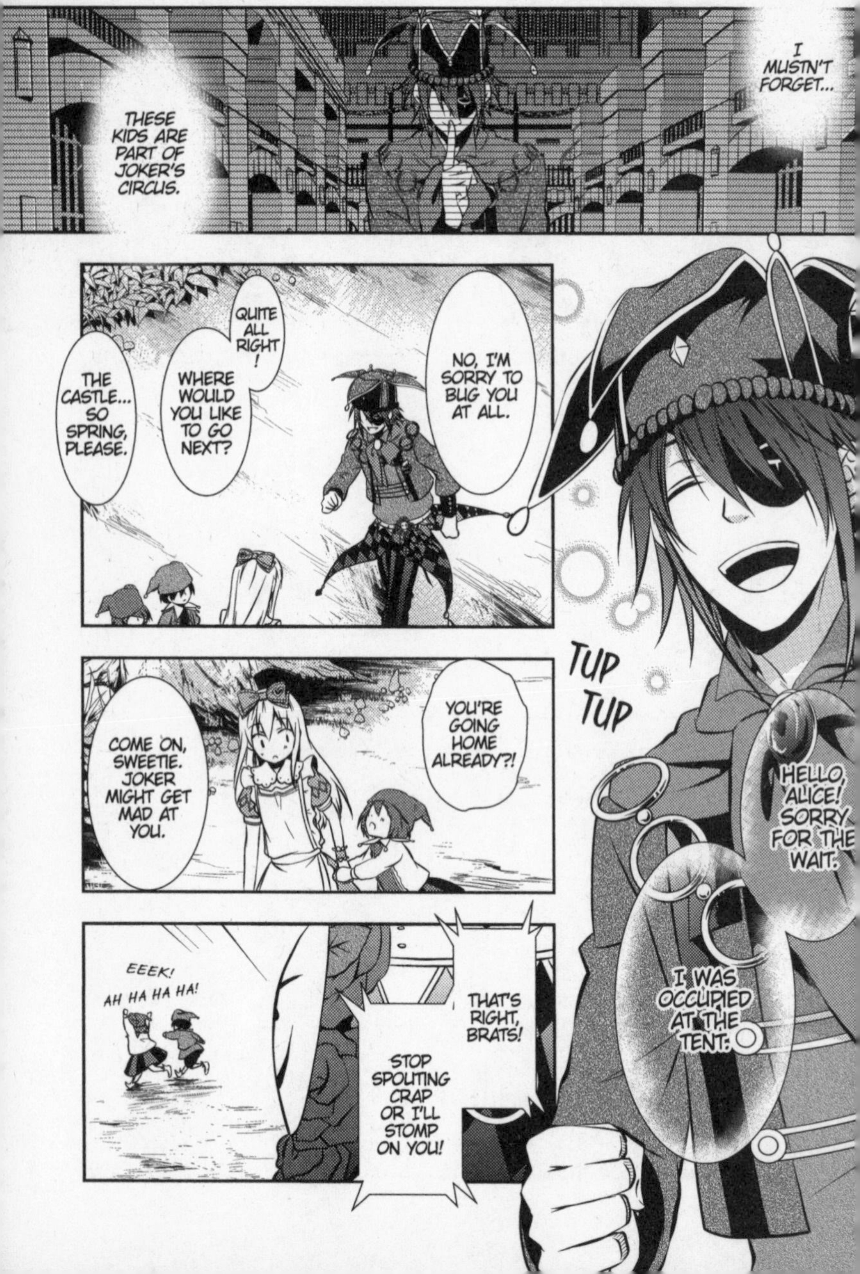
I MUSTN'T FORGET...
THESE KIDS ARE PART OF JOKER'S CIRCUS.
HELLO, ALICE! SORRY FOR THE WAIT.
TUP TUP
I WAS OCCUPIED AT THE TENT.
NO, I'M SORRY TO BUG YOU AT ALL.
QUITE ALL RIGHT!
WHERE WOULD YOU LIKE TO GO NEXT?
THE CASTLE... SO SPRING, PLEASE.
YOU'RE GOING HOME ALREADY?!
COME ON, SWEETIE. JOKER MIGHT GET MAD AT YOU.
THAT'S RIGHT, BRATS!
STOP SPOUTING CRAP OR I'LL STOMP ON YOU!
EEEK!
AH HA HA HA!

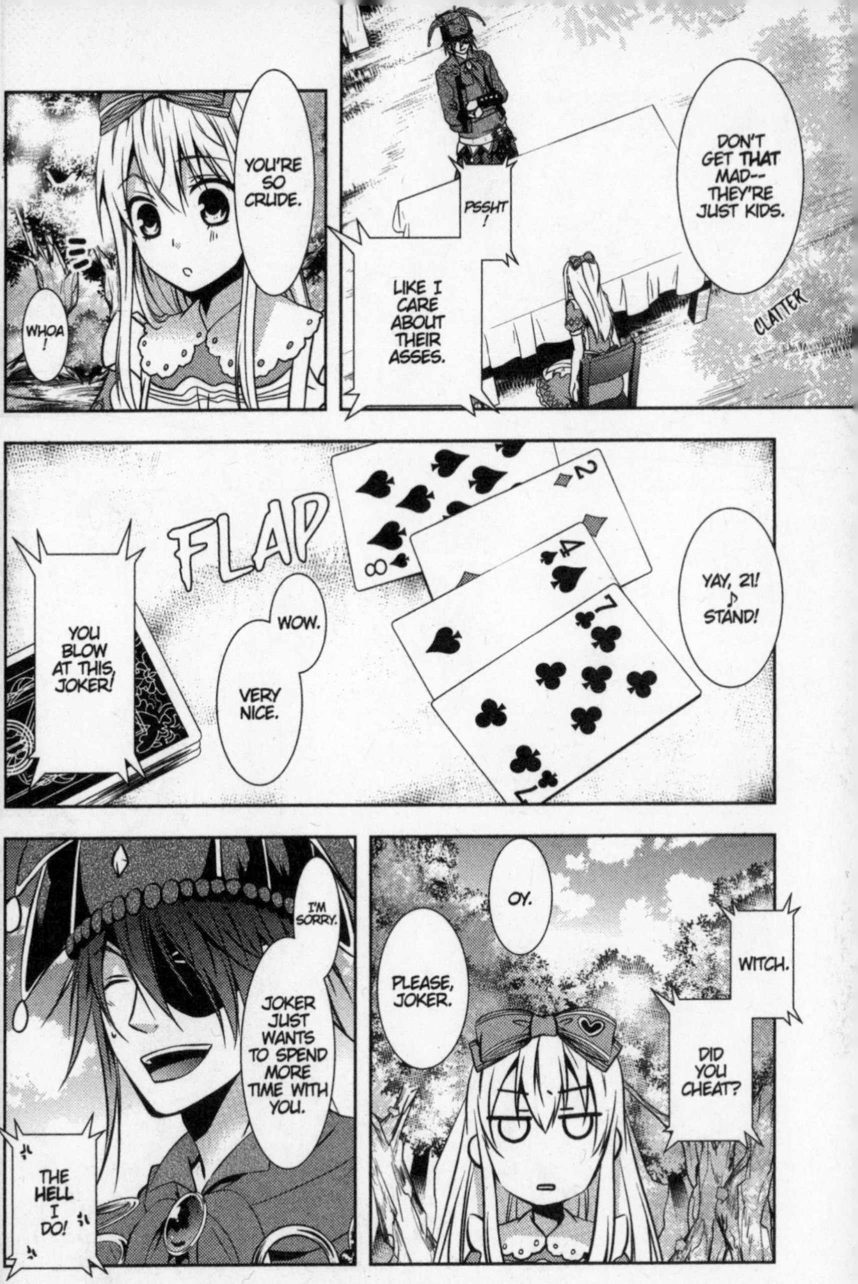
DON'T GET THAT MAD-- THEY'RE JUST KIDS.
CLATTER
PSSHT!
LIKE I CARE ABOUT THEIR ASSES.
YOU'RE SO CRUDE.
WHOA!
YAY, 21! ♪ STAND!
FLAP
WOW.
VERY NICE.
YOU BLOW AT THIS, JOKER!
OY.
WITCH.
DID YOU CHEAT?
PLEASE, JOKER.
I'M SORRY.
JOKER JUST WANTS TO SPEND MORE TIME WITH YOU.
THE HELL I DO!

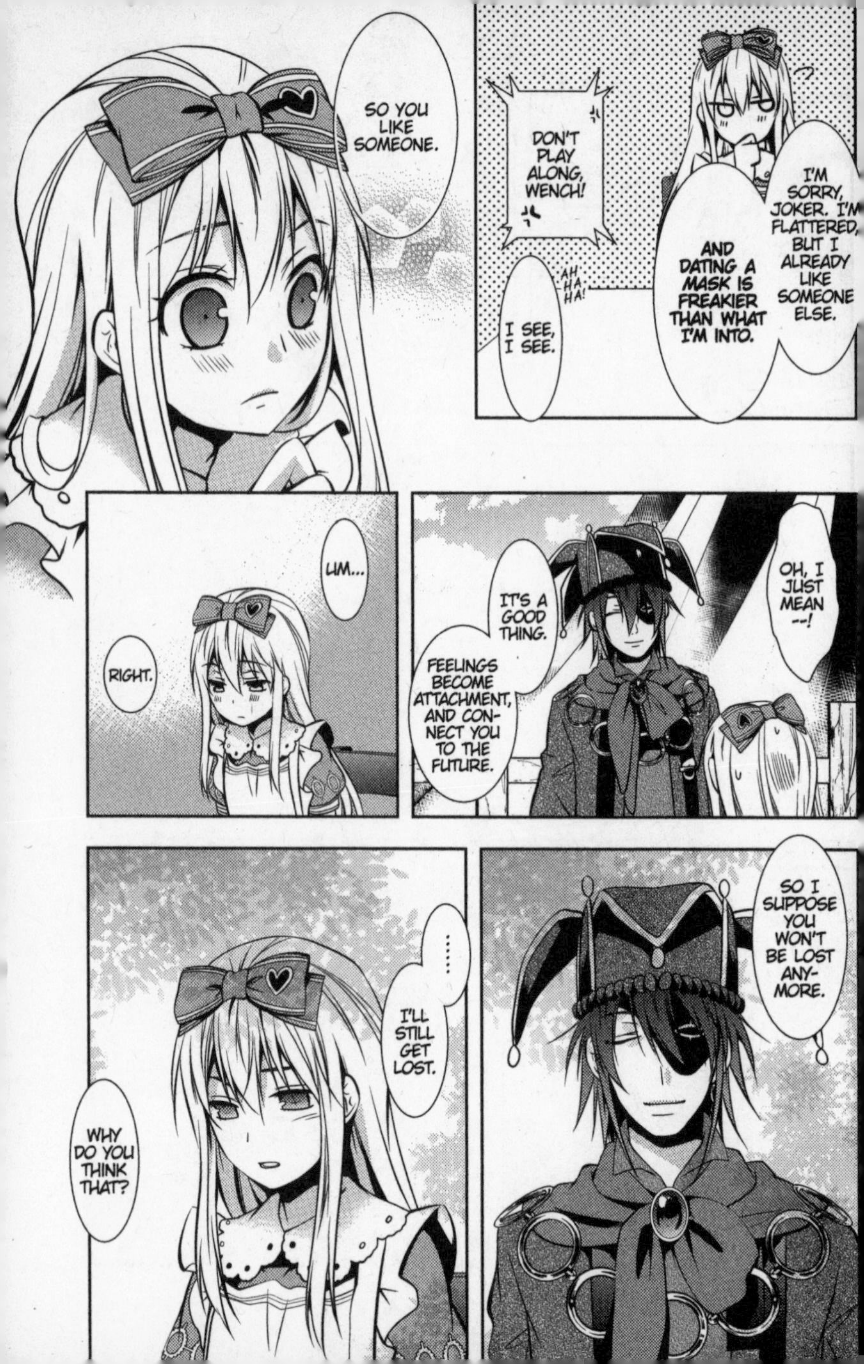
I'M SORRY, JOKER. I'M FLATTERED, BUT I ALREADY LIKE SOMEONE ELSE.
AND DATING A MASK IS FREAKIER THAN WHAT I'M INTO.
DON'T PLAY ALONG, WENCH!
AH HA HA!
I SEE, I SEE.
SO YOU LIKE SOMEONE.
OH, I JUST MEAN --!
IT'S A GOOD THING.
FEELINGS BECOME ATTACHMENT, AND CON-NECT YOU TO THE FUTURE.
UM...
RIGHT.
SO I SUPPOSE YOU WON'T BE LOST ANY-MORE.
......
I'LL STILL GET LOST.
WHY DO YOU THINK THAT?

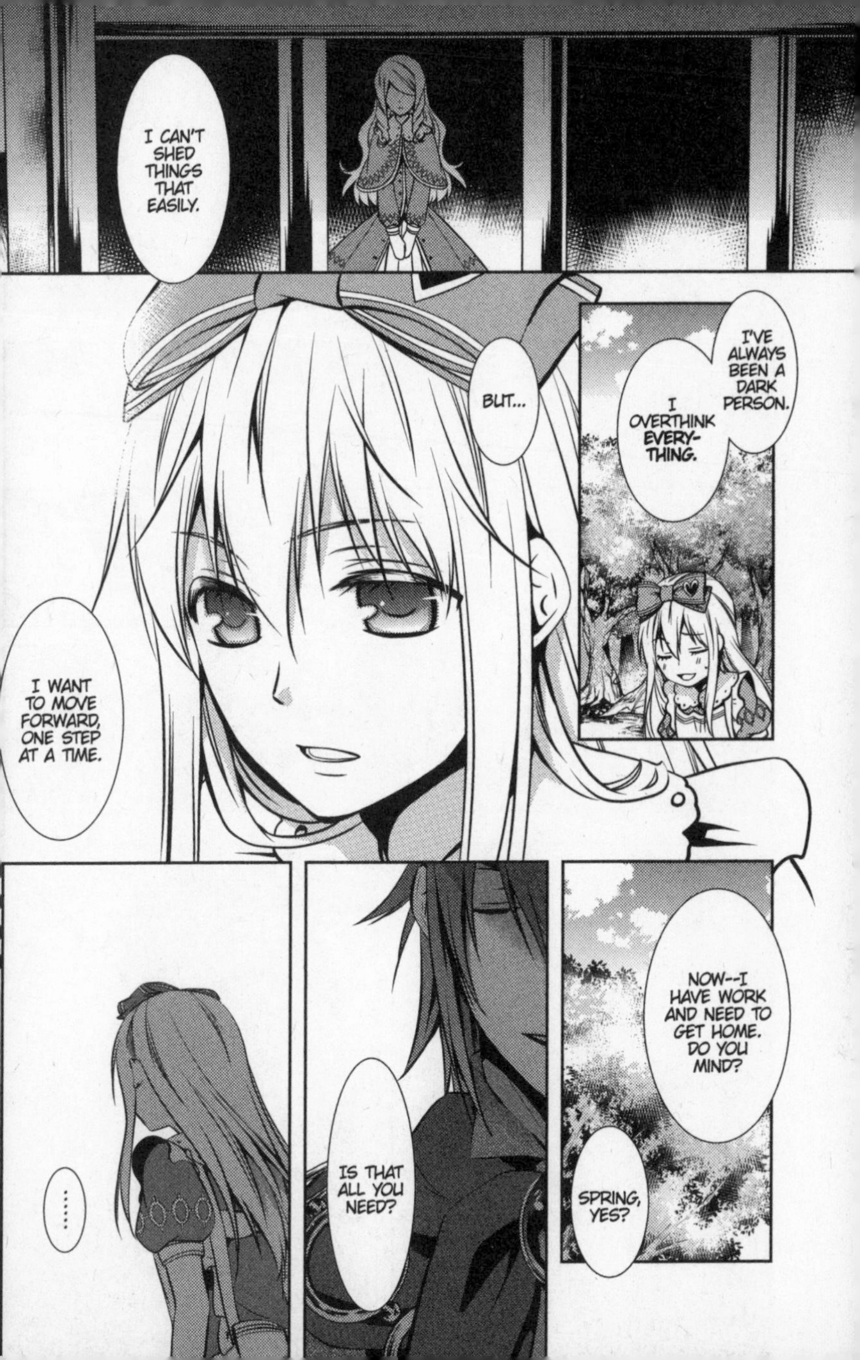
I CAN'T SHED THINGS THAT EASILY.
I'VE ALWAYS BEEN A DARK PERSON.
I OVERTHINK EVERY-THING.
BUT...
I WANT TO MOVE FORWARD, ONE STEP AT A TIME.
NOW--I HAVE WORK AND NEED TO GET HOME. DO YOU MIND?
SPRING, YES?
IS THAT ALL YOU NEED?
......

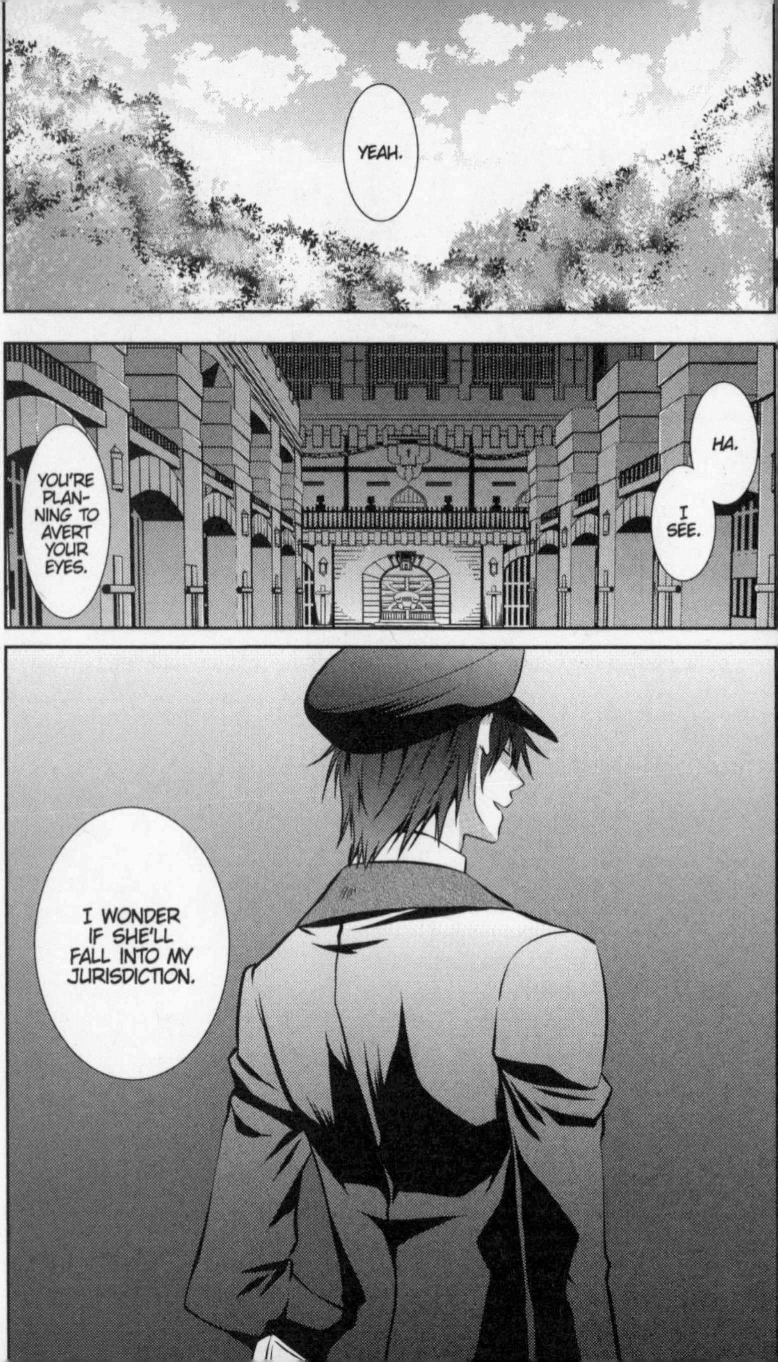
YEAH.
HA.
I SEE.
YOU'RE PLAN-NING TO AVERT YOUR EYES.
I WONDER IF SHE'LL FALL INTO MY JURISDICTION.

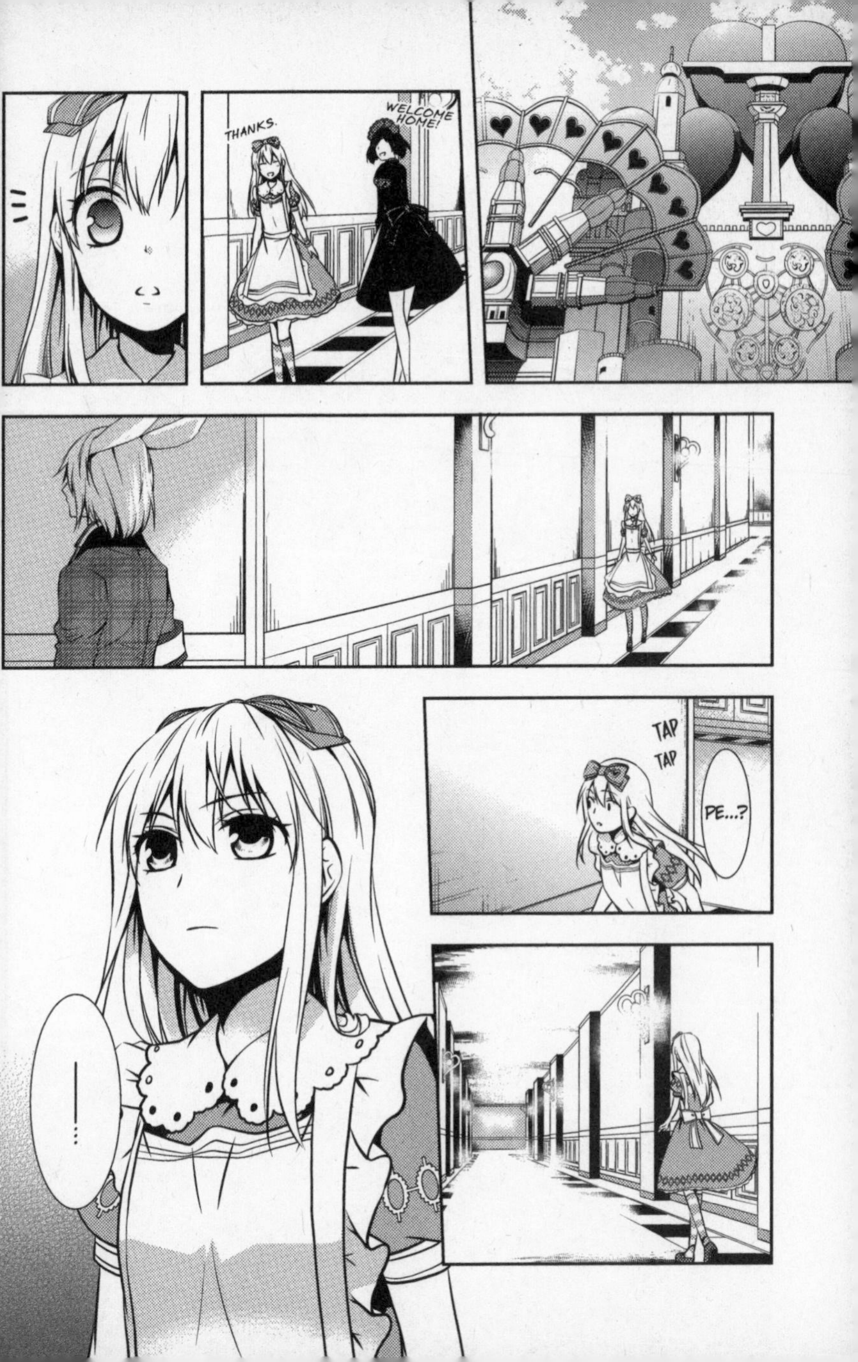
WELCOME HOME!
THANKS.
TAP
TAP
PE...?
—...

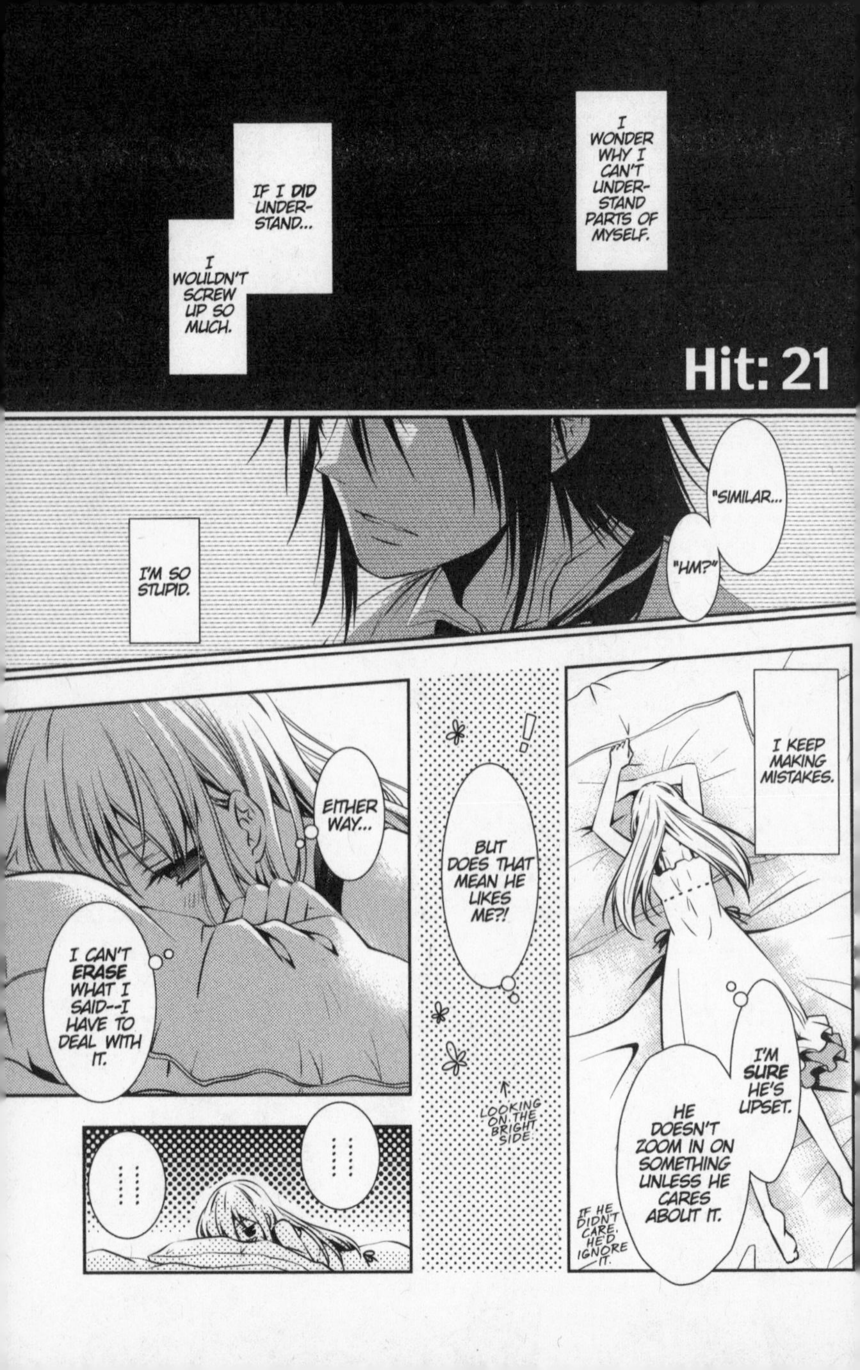
I WONDER WHY I CAN'T UNDER-STAND PARTS OF MYSELF.
IF I DID UNDER-STAND...
I WOULDN'T SCREW UP SO MUCH.
Hit: 21
"SIMILAR...
"HM?"
I'M SO STUPID.
I KEEP MAKING MISTAKES.
I'M SURE HE'S UPSET.
HE DOESN'T ZOOM IN ON SOMETHING UNLESS HE CARES ABOUT IT.
IF HE DIDN'T CARE, HE'D IGNORE IT.
!
BUT DOES THAT MEAN HE LIKES ME?!
LOOKING ON THE BRIGHT SIDE
EITHER WAY...
I CAN'T ERASE WHAT I SAID--I HAVE TO DEAL WITH IT.
......
......

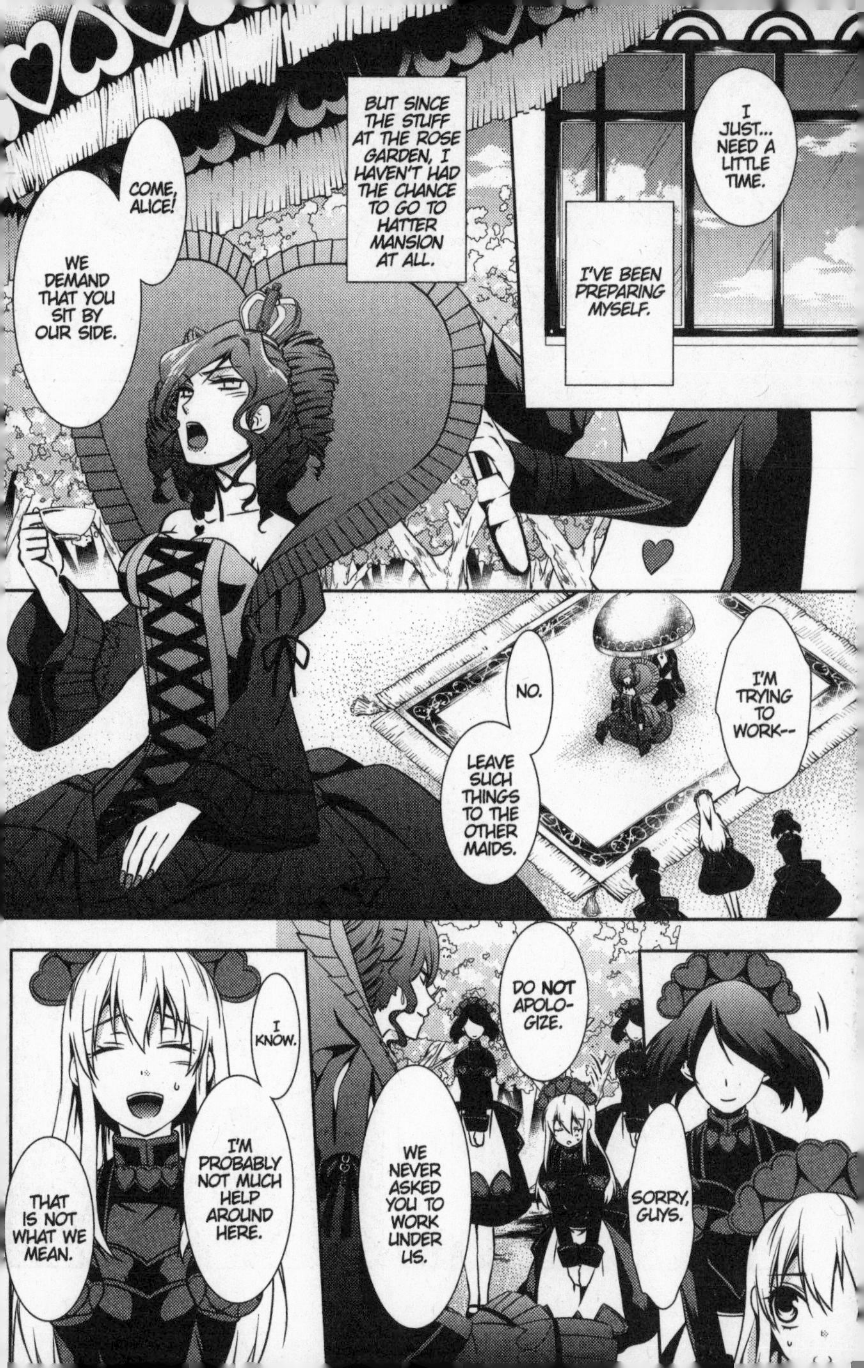
I JUST... NEED A LITTLE TIME.
I'VE BEEN PREPARING MYSELF.
BUT SINCE THE STUFF AT THE ROSE GARDEN, I HAVEN'T HAD THE CHANCE TO GO TO HATTER MANSION AT ALL.
COME, ALICE!
WE DEMAND THAT YOU SIT BY OUR SIDE.
I'M TRYING TO WORK--
NO.
LEAVE SUCH THINGS TO THE OTHER MAIDS.
SORRY, GUYS.
DO NOT APOLO-GIZE.
WE NEVER ASKED YOU TO WORK UNDER US.
I KNOW.
I'M PROBABLY NOT MUCH HELP AROUND HERE.
THAT IS NOT WHAT WE MEAN.

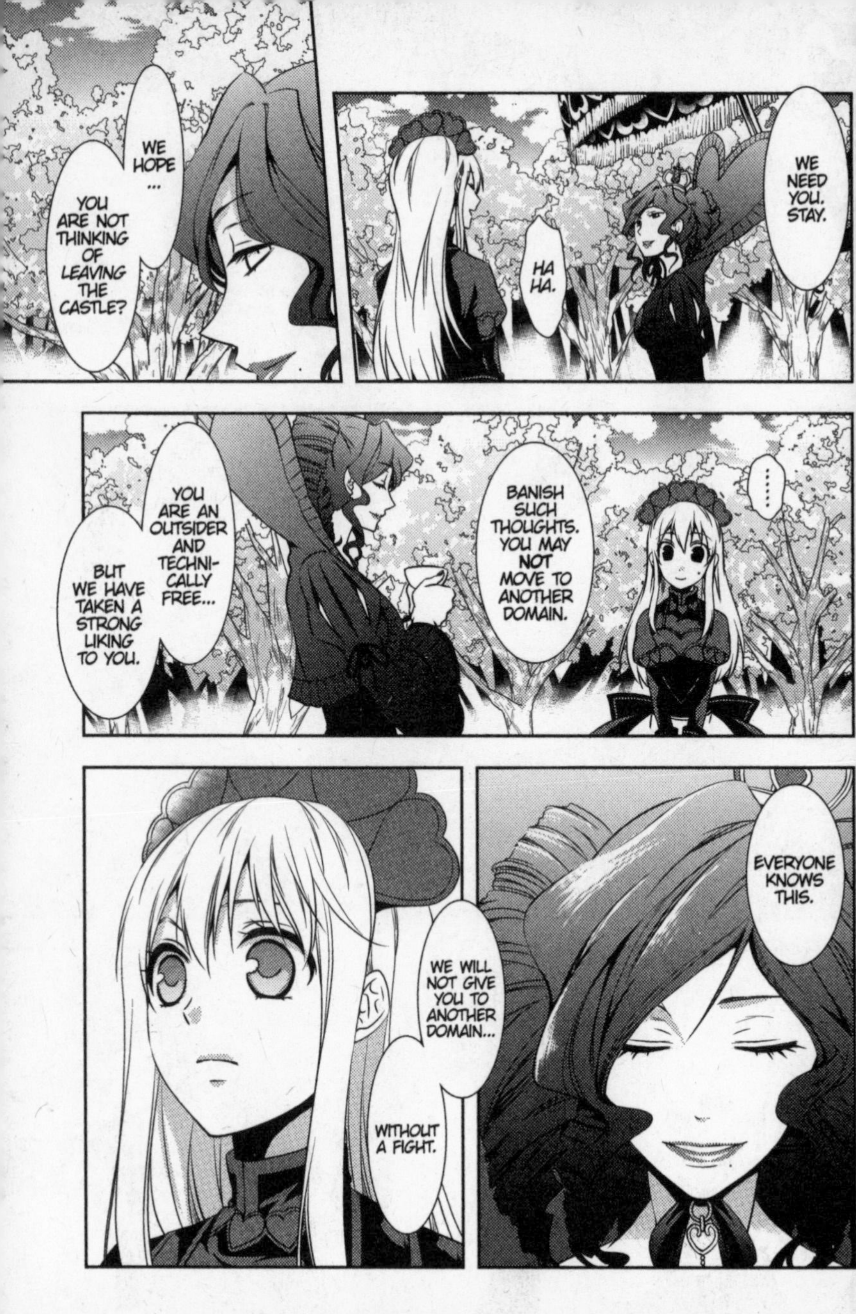
WE NEED YOU. STAY.
HA HA.
WE HOPE ...
YOU ARE NOT THINKING OF LEAVING THE CASTLE?
......
BANISH SUCH THOUGHTS. YOU MAY NOT MOVE TO ANOTHER DOMAIN.
YOU ARE AN OUTSIDER AND TECHNI-CALLY FREE...
BUT WE HAVE TAKEN A STRONG LIKING TO YOU.
EVERYONE KNOWS THIS.
WE WILL NOT GIVE YOU TO ANOTHER DOMAIN...
WITHOUT A FIGHT.

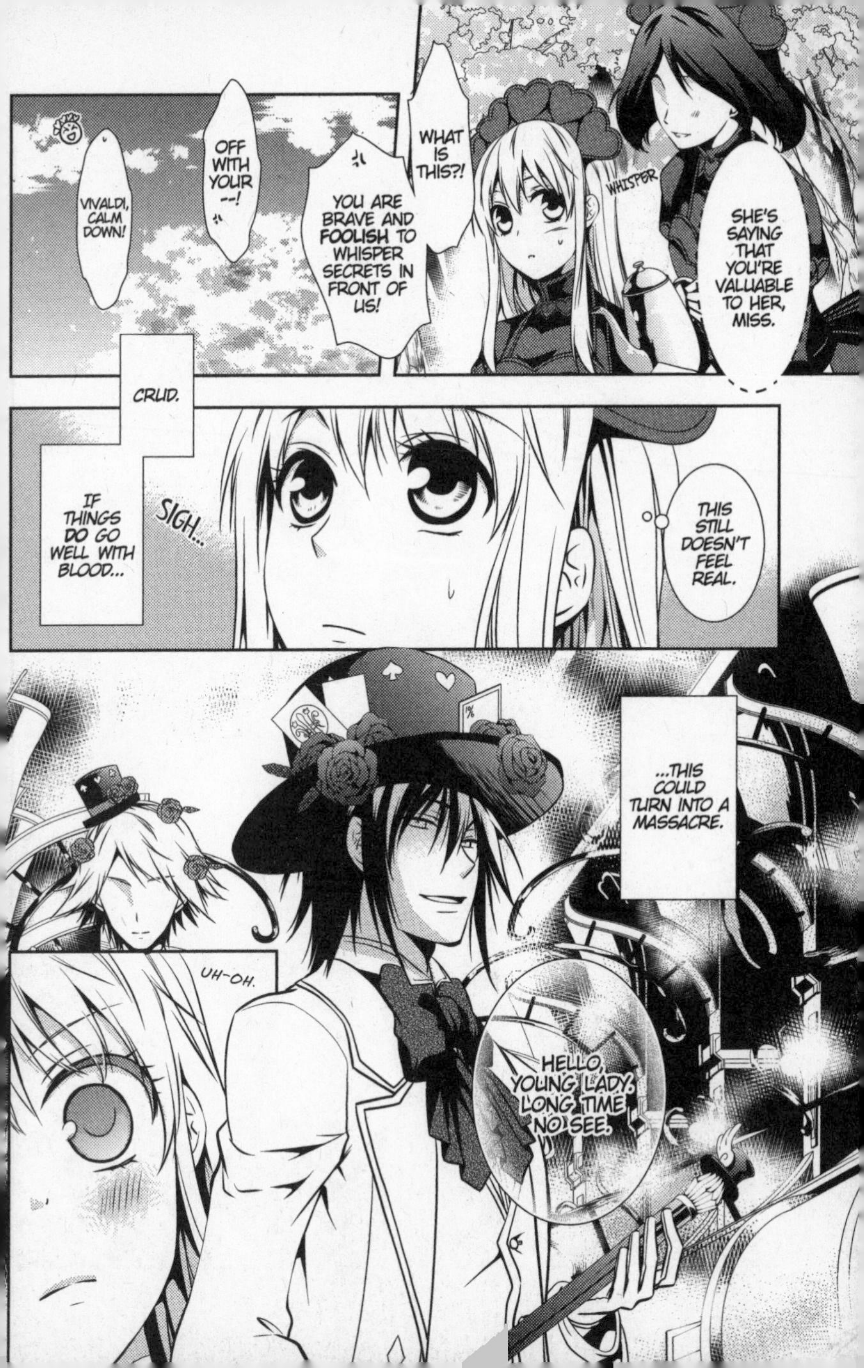
WHISPER
SHE'S SAYING THAT YOU'RE VALUABLE TO HER, MISS.
WHAT IS THIS?!
YOU ARE BRAVE AND FOOLISH TO WHISPER SECRETS IN FRONT OF US!
OFF WITH YOUR --!
VIVALDI, CALM DOWN!
THIS STILL DOESN'T FEEL REAL.
CRUD.
SIGH...
IF THINGS DO GO WELL WITH BLOOD...
...THIS COULD TURN INTO A MASSACRE.
HELLO, YOUNG LADY. LONG TIME NO SEE.
UH-OH.

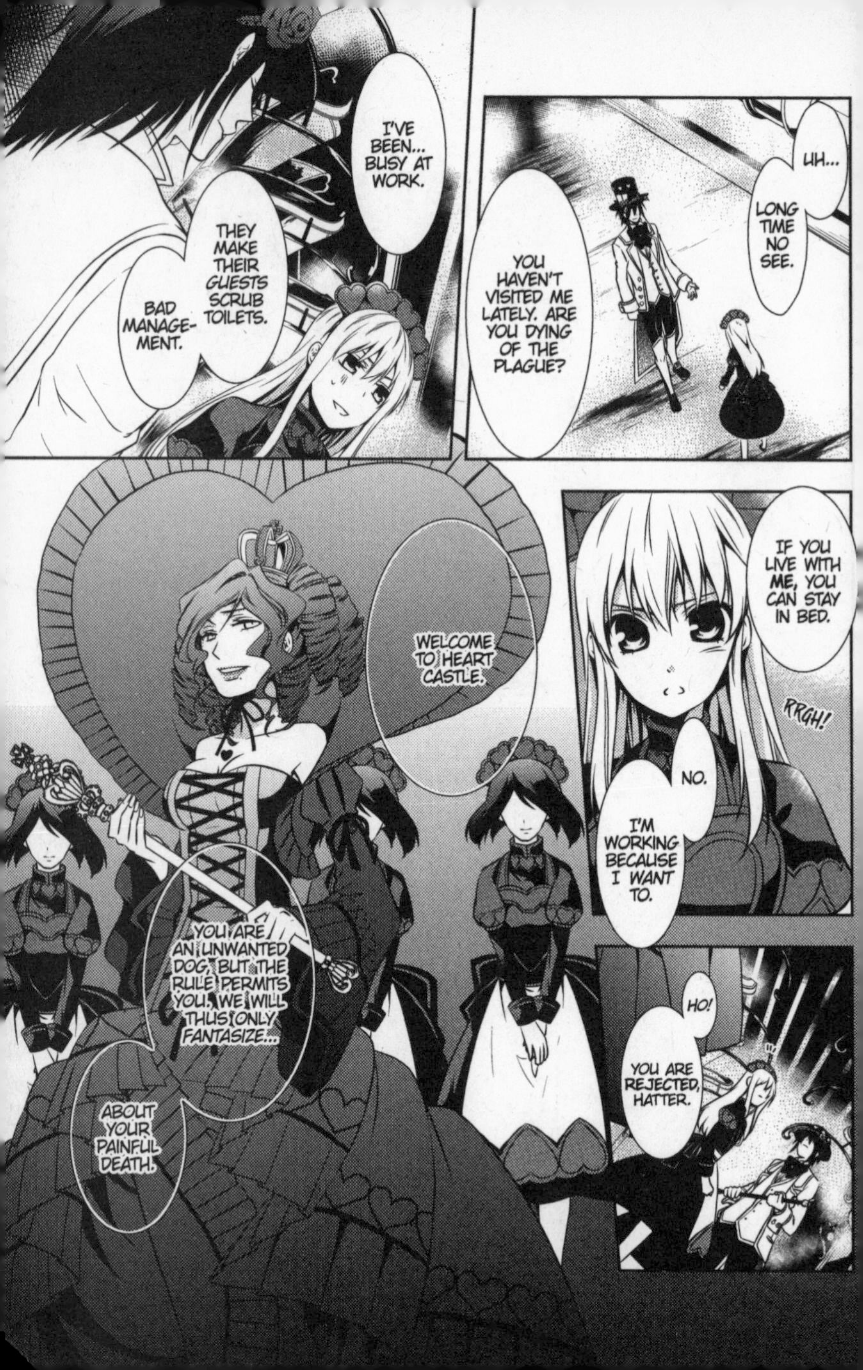
UH...
LONG TIME NO SEE.
YOU HAVEN'T VISITED ME LATELY. ARE YOU DYING OF THE PLAGUE?
I'VE BEEN... BUSY AT WORK.
THEY MAKE THEIR GUESTS SCRUB TOILETS.
BAD MANAGEMENT.
IF YOU LIVE WITH ME, YOU CAN STAY IN BED.
RRGH!
NO.
I'M WORKING BECAUSE I WANT TO.
HO!
YOU ARE REJECTED, HATTER.
WELCOME TO HEART CASTLE.
YOU ARE AN UNWANTED DOG, BUT THE RULE PERMITS YOU, WE WILL THUS ONLY FANTASIZE...
ABOUT YOUR PAINFUL DEATH.

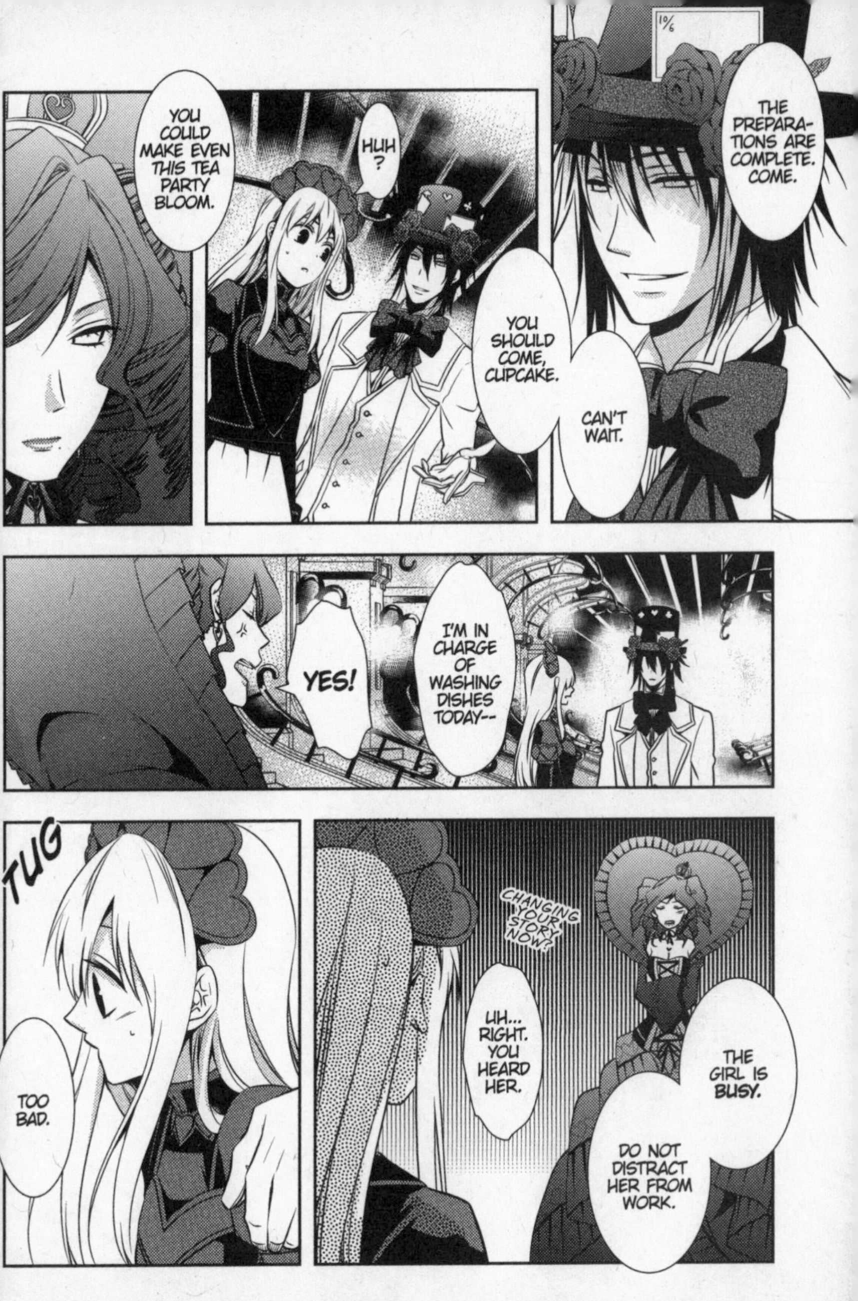
THE PREPARATIONS ARE COMPLETE. COME.
CAN'T WAIT.
YOU SHOULD COME, CUPCAKE.
HUH?
YOU COULD MAKE EVEN THIS TEA PARTY BLOOM.
I'M IN CHARGE OF WASHING DISHES TODAY--
YES!
THE GIRL IS BUSY.
DO NOT DISTRACT HER FROM WORK.
UH... RIGHT. YOU HEARD HER.
CHANGING YOUR STORY NOW?
TUG
TOO BAD.

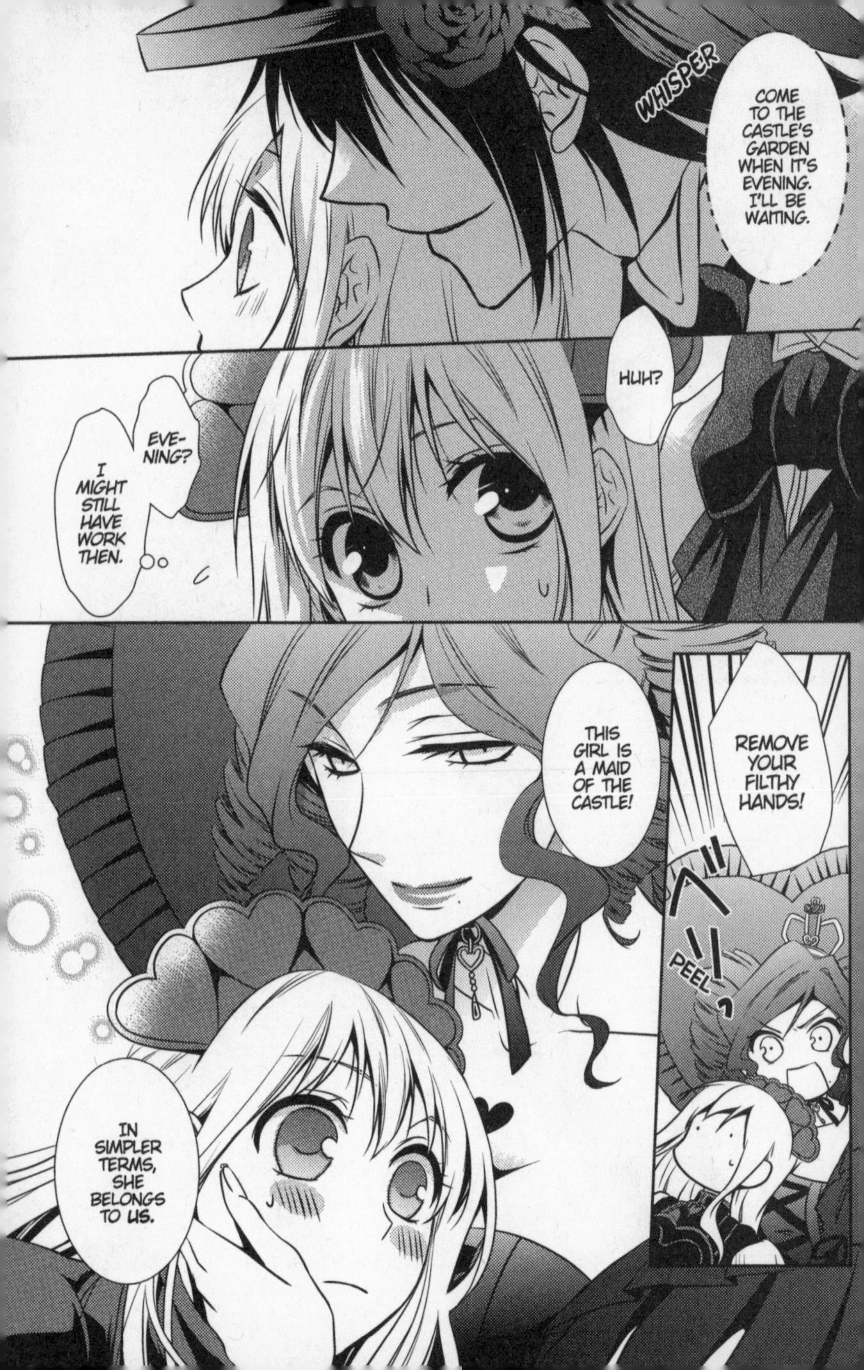
WHISPER
COME TO THE CASTLE'S GARDEN WHEN IT'S EVENING. I'LL BE WAITING.
HUH?
EVE-NING?
I MIGHT STILL HAVE WORK THEN.
REMOVE YOUR FILTHY HANDS!
PEEL
THIS GIRL IS A MAID OF THE CASTLE!
IN SIMPLER TERMS, SHE BELONGS TO US.

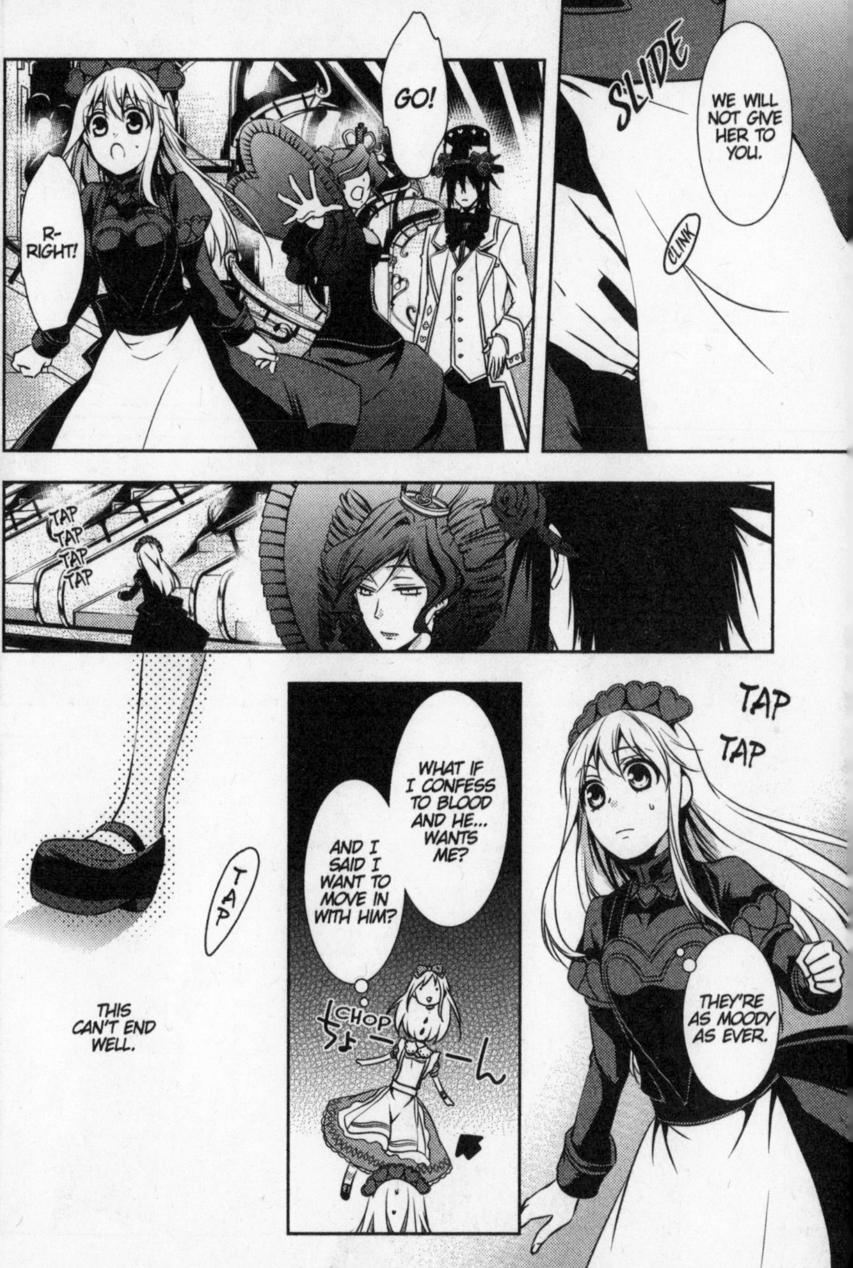
SLIDE
WE WILL NOT GIVE HER TO YOU.
CLINK
GO!
R-RIGHT!
TAP TAP TAP TAP
TAP
TAP
THEY'RE AS MOODY AS EVER.
WHAT IF I CONFESS TO BLOOD AND HE... WANTS ME?
AND I SAID I WANT TO MOVE IN WITH HIM?
CHOP
ちょーーん
TAP
THIS CAN'T END WELL.

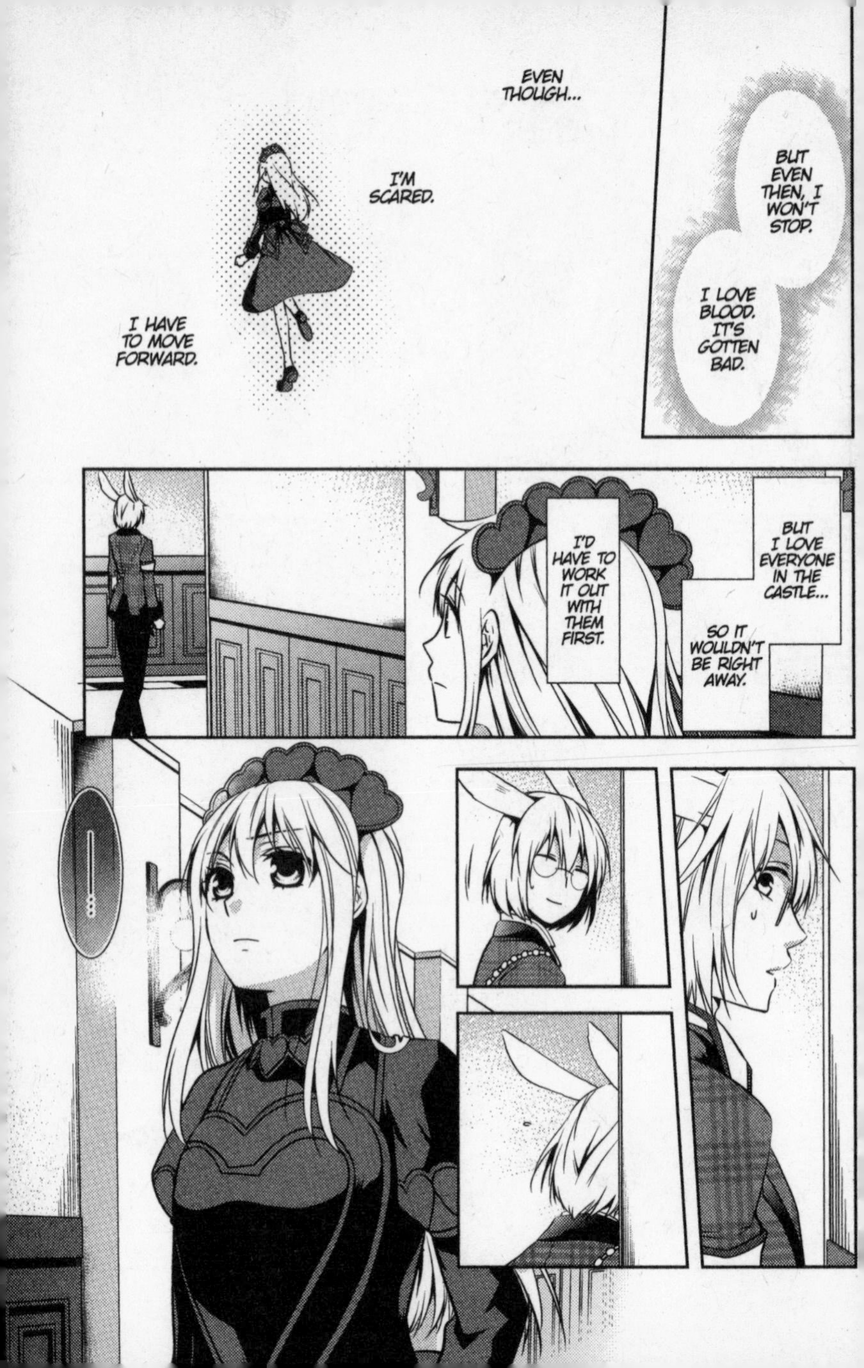
BUT EVEN THEN, I WON'T STOP.
I LOVE BLOOD. IT'S GOTTEN BAD.
EVEN THOUGH...
I'M SCARED.
I HAVE TO MOVE FORWARD.
BUT I LOVE EVERYONE IN THE CASTLE...
SO IT WOULDN'T BE RIGHT AWAY.
I'D HAVE TO WORK IT OUT WITH THEM FIRST.

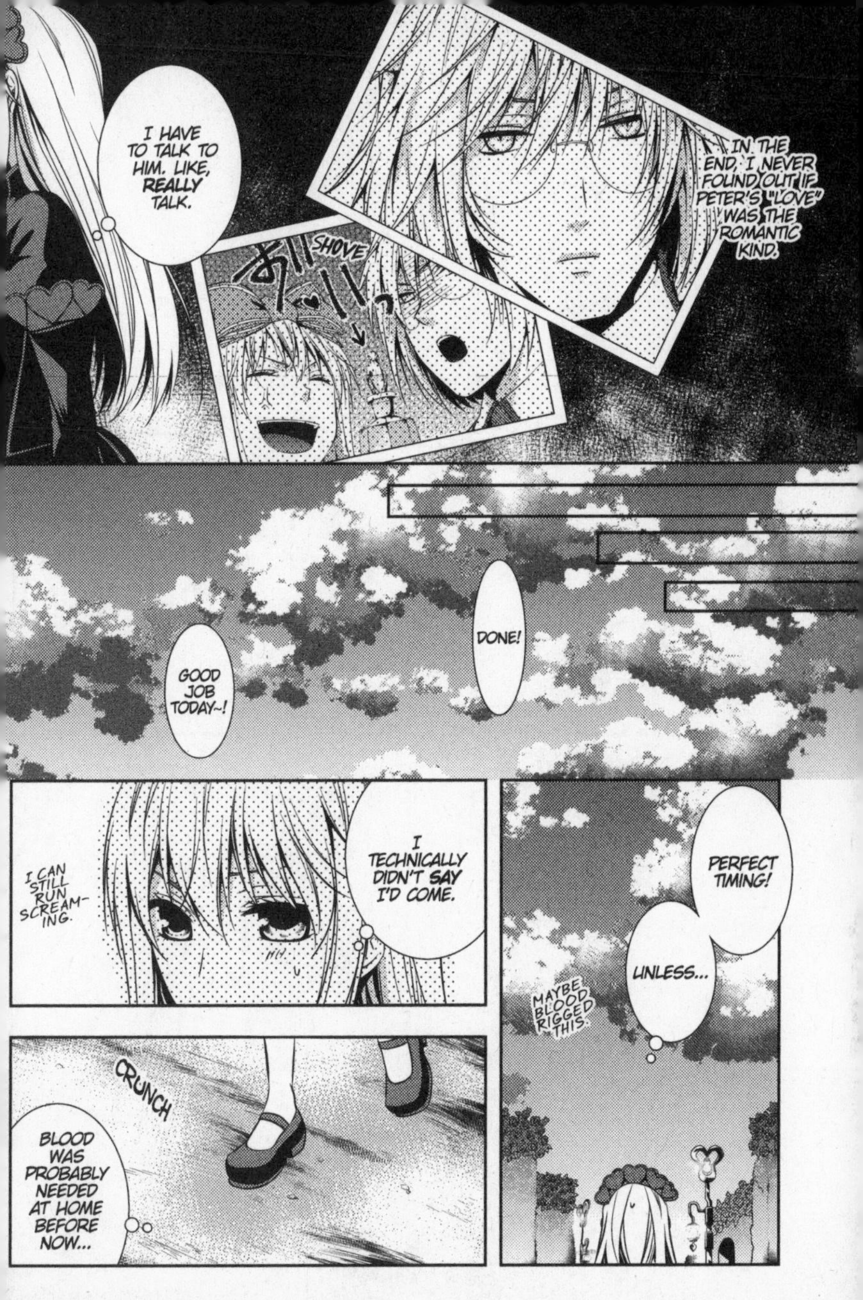
IN THE END, I NEVER FOUND OUT IF PETER'S "LOVE" WAS THE ROMANTIC KIND.
SHOVE
I HAVE TO TALK TO HIM. LIKE, REALLY TALK.
DONE!
GOOD JOB TODAY~!
PERFECT TIMING!
UNLESS...
MAYBE BLOOD RIGGED THIS.
I TECHNICALLY DIDN'T SAY I'D COME.
I CAN STILL RUN SCREAMING.
CRUNCH
BLOOD WAS PROBABLY NEEDED AT HOME BEFORE NOW...

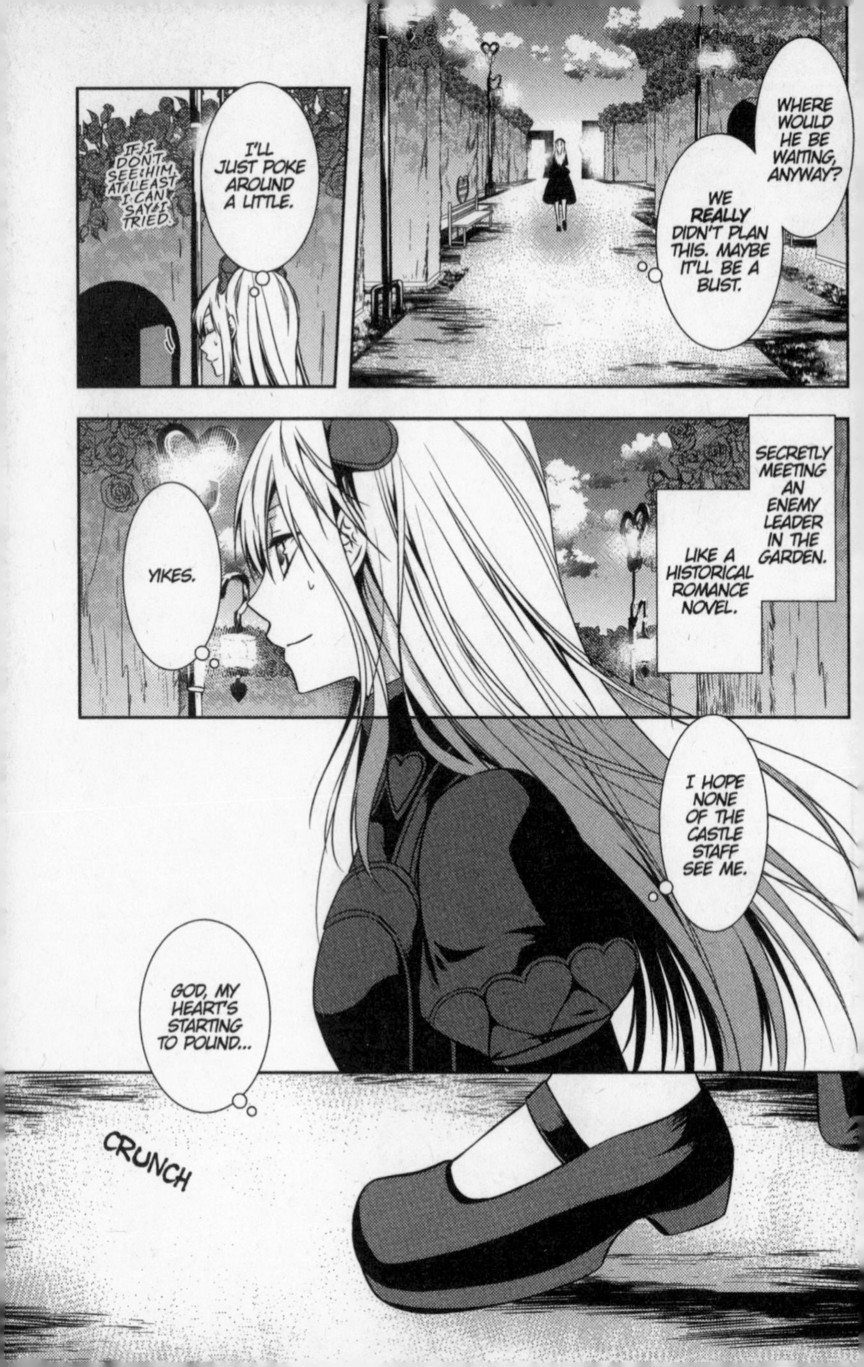
WHERE WOULD HE BE WAITING, ANYWAY?
WE REALLY DIDN'T PLAN THIS. MAYBE IT'LL BE A BUST.
I'LL JUST POKE AROUND A LITTLE.
IF I DON'T SEE HIM, AT LEAST I CAN SAY I TRIED.
SECRETLY MEETING AN ENEMY LEADER IN THE GARDEN.
LIKE A HISTORICAL ROMANCE NOVEL.
YIKES.
I HOPE NONE OF THE CASTLE STAFF SEE ME.
GOD, MY HEART'S STARTING TO POUND...
CRUNCH

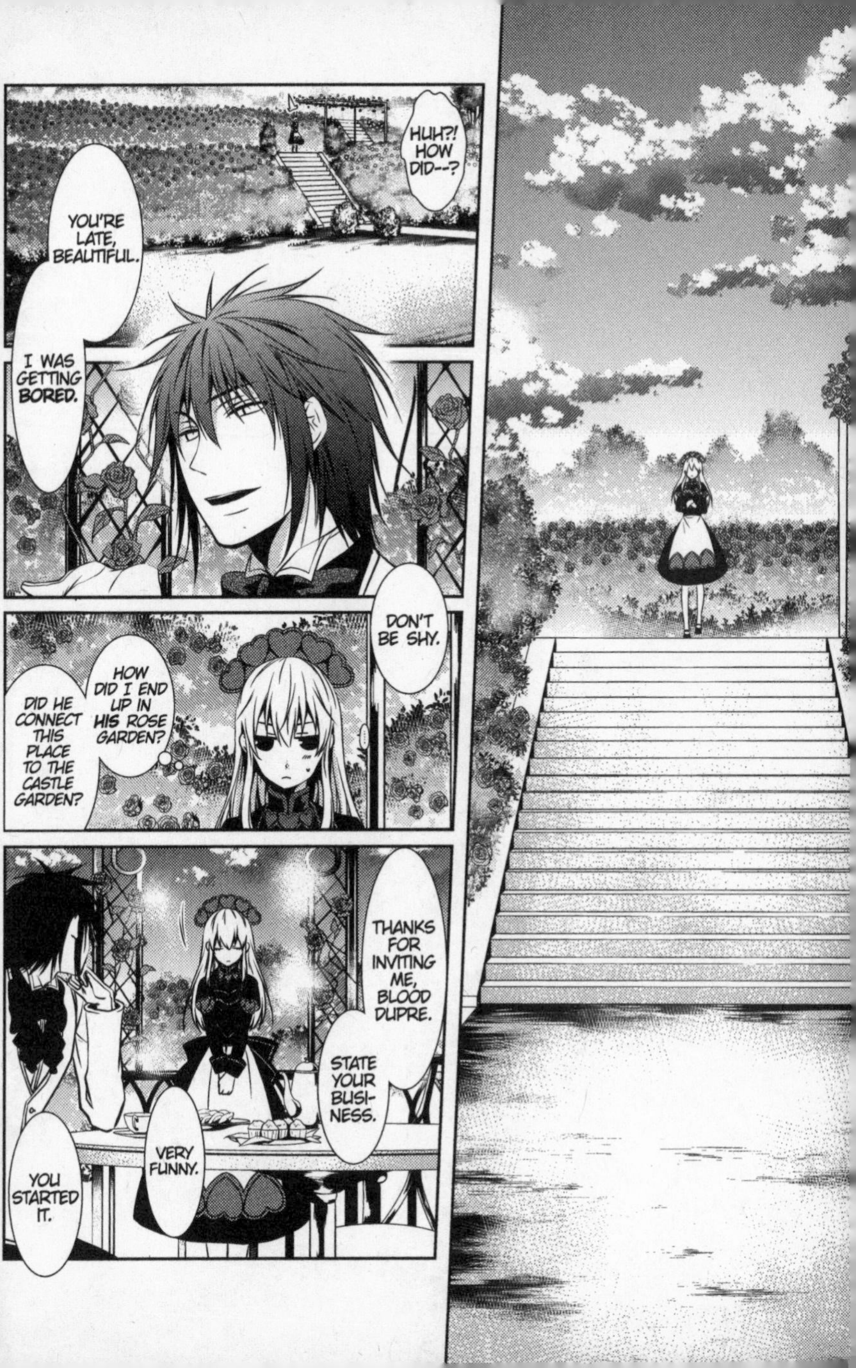
HUH?! HOW DID--?
YOU'RE LATE, BEAUTIFUL.
I WAS GETTING BORED.
DON'T BE SHY.
HOW DID I END UP IN HIS ROSE GARDEN?
DID HE CONNECT THIS PLACE TO THE CASTLE GARDEN?
THANKS FOR INVITING ME, BLOOD DUPRE.
STATE YOUR BUSINESS.
VERY FUNNY.
YOU STARTED IT.

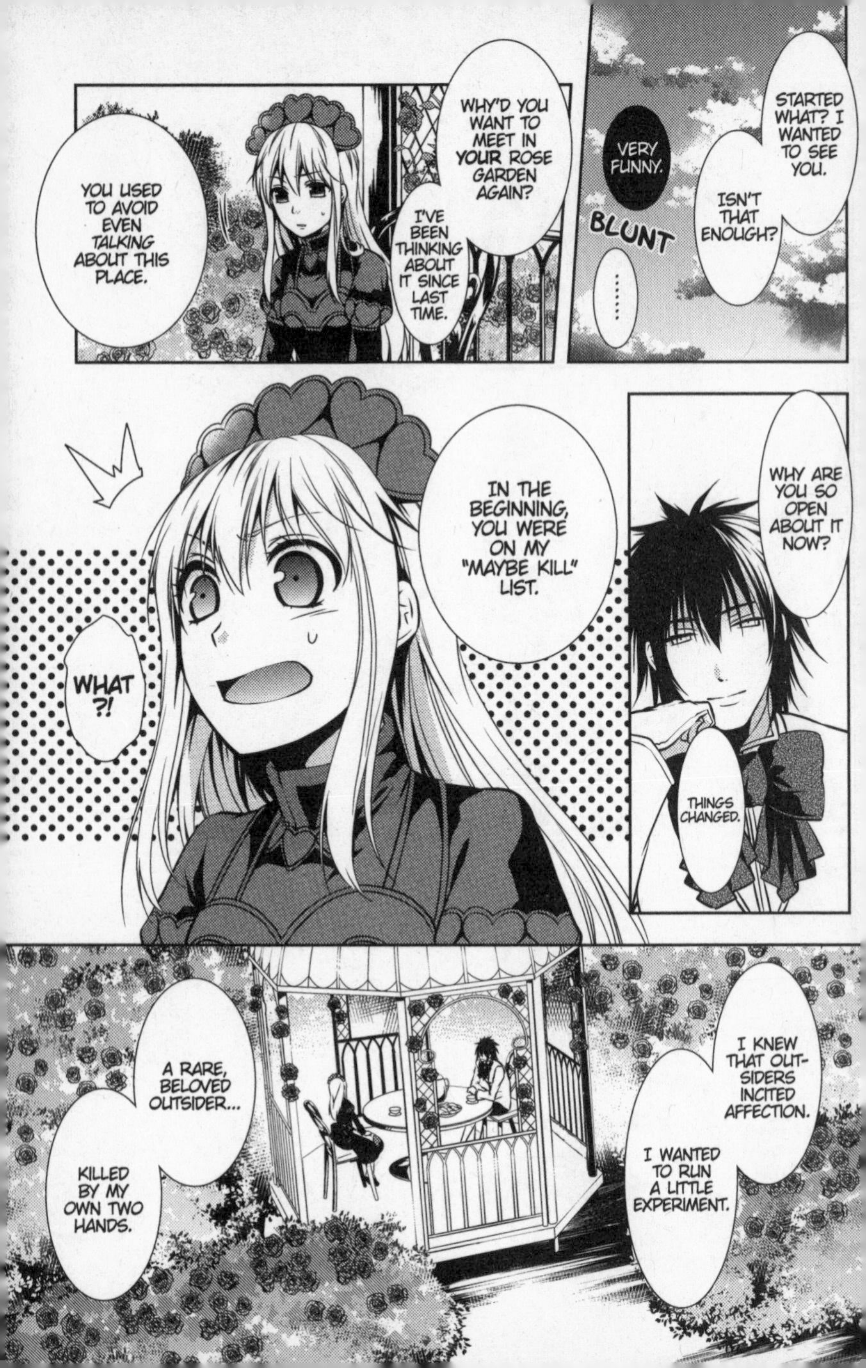
STARTED WHAT? I WANTED TO SEE YOU.
ISN'T THAT ENOUGH?
VERY FUNNY.
BLUNT
......
WHY'D YOU WANT TO MEET IN YOUR ROSE GARDEN AGAIN?
I'VE BEEN THINKING ABOUT IT SINCE LAST TIME.
YOU USED TO AVOID EVEN TALKING ABOUT THIS PLACE.
WHY ARE YOU SO OPEN ABOUT IT NOW?
THINGS CHANGED.
IN THE BEGINNING, YOU WERE ON MY "MAYBE KILL" LIST.
WHAT?!
I KNEW THAT OUT-SIDERS INCITED AFFECTION.
I WANTED TO RUN A LITTLE EXPERIMENT.
A RARE, BELOVED OUTSIDER...
KILLED BY MY OWN TWO HANDS.

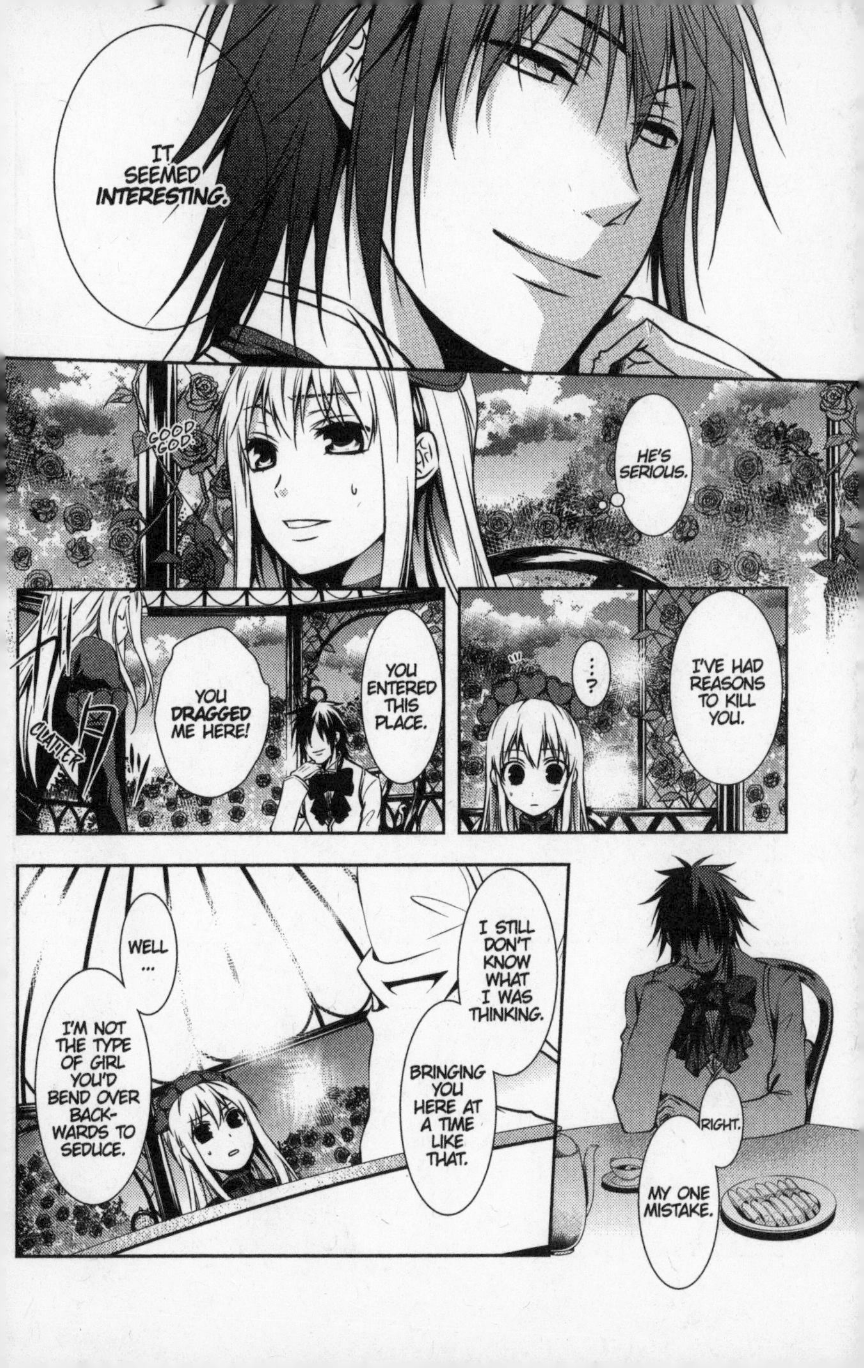
IT SEEMED INTERESTING.
HE'S SERIOUS.
GOOD GOD.
I'VE HAD REASONS TO KILL YOU.
...?
YOU ENTERED THIS PLACE.
YOU DRAGGED ME HERE!
CLATTER
RIGHT.
MY ONE MISTAKE.
I STILL DON'T KNOW WHAT I WAS THINKING.
BRINGING YOU HERE AT A TIME LIKE THAT.
WELL...
I'M NOT THE TYPE OF GIRL YOU'D BEND OVER BACK-WARDS TO SEDUCE.

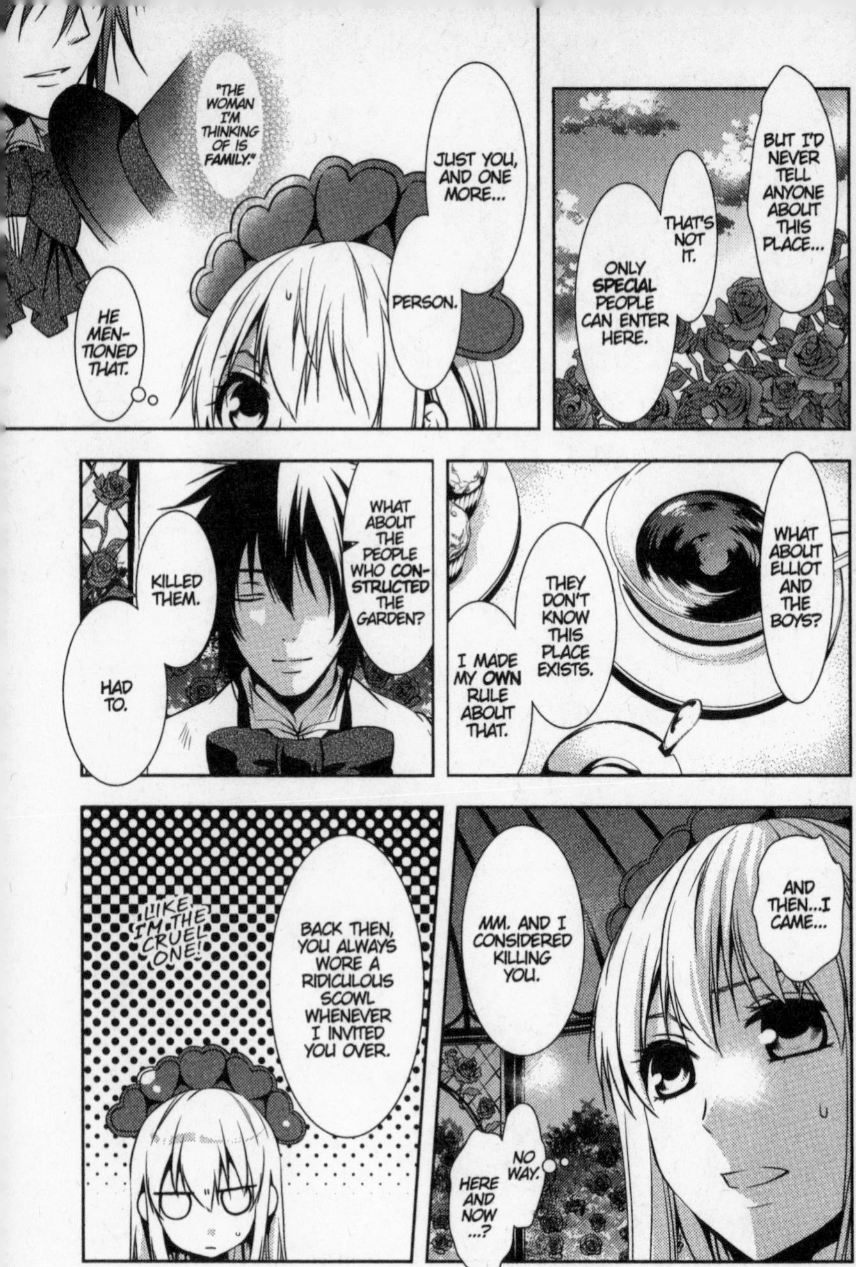
BUT I'D NEVER TELL ANYONE ABOUT THIS PLACE...
THAT'S NOT IT.
ONLY SPECIAL PEOPLE CAN ENTER HERE.
JUST YOU, AND ONE MORE...
PERSON.
"THE WOMAN I'M THINKING OF IS FAMILY."
HE MEN-TIONED THAT.
WHAT ABOUT ELLIOT AND THE BOYS?
THEY DON'T KNOW THIS PLACE EXISTS.
I MADE MY OWN RULE ABOUT THAT.
WHAT ABOUT THE PEOPLE WHO CON-STRUCTED THE GARDEN?
KILLED THEM.
HAD TO.
AND THEN...I CAME...
MM. AND I CONSIDERED KILLING YOU.
NO WAY.
HERE AND NOW ...?
BACK THEN, YOU ALWAYS WORE A RIDICULOUS SCOWL WHENEVER I INVITED YOU OVER.
LIKE I'M THE CRUEL ONE!

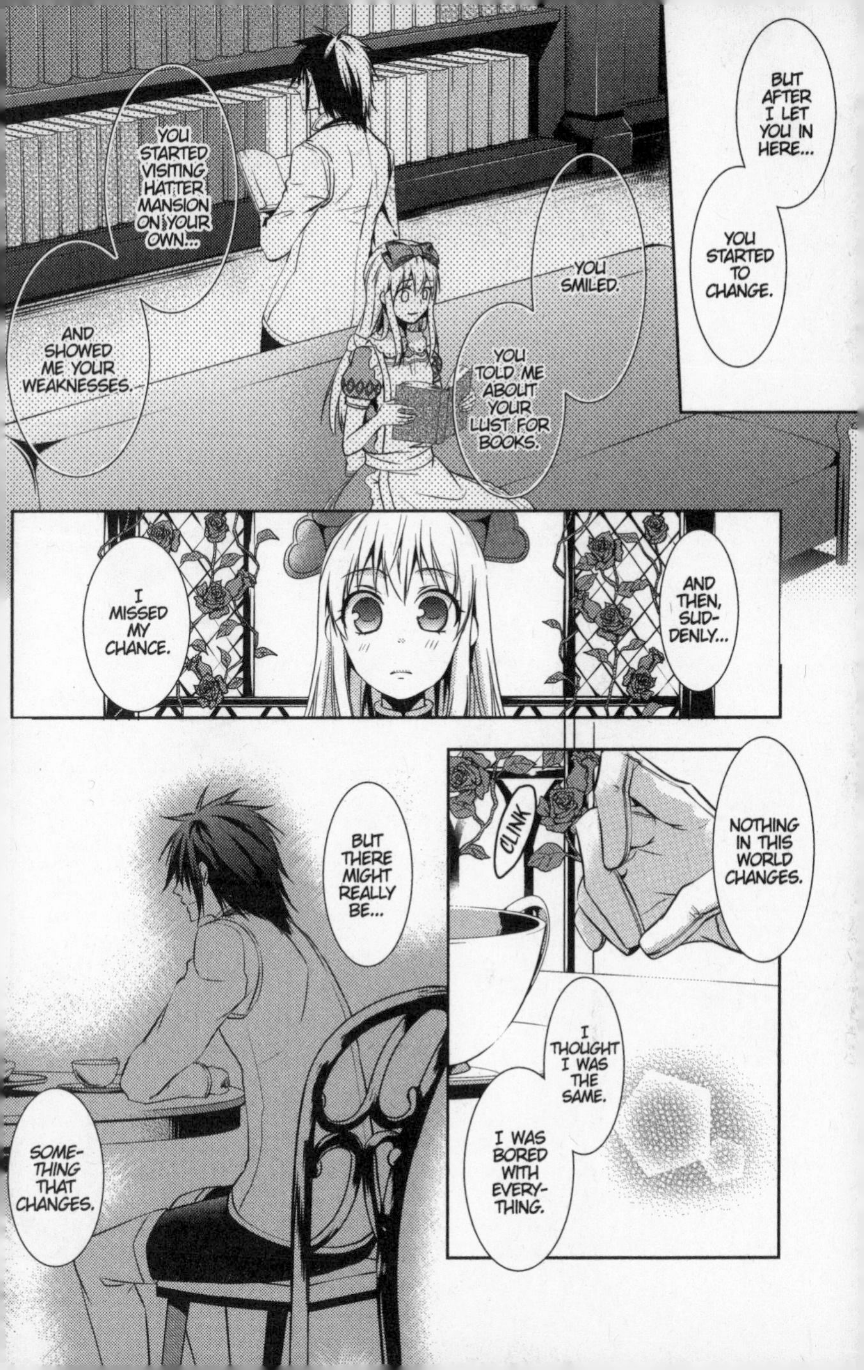
BUT AFTER I LET YOU IN HERE...
YOU STARTED TO CHANGE.
YOU STARTED VISITING HATTER MANSION ON YOUR OWN...
AND SHOWED ME YOUR WEAKNESSES.
YOU SMILED.
YOU TOLD ME ABOUT YOUR LUST FOR BOOKS.
AND THEN, SUD-DENLY...
I MISSED MY CHANCE.
NOTHING IN THIS WORLD CHANGES.
CLINK
I THOUGHT I WAS THE SAME.
I WAS BORED WITH EVERY-THING.
BUT THERE MIGHT REALLY BE...
SOME-THING THAT CHANGES.

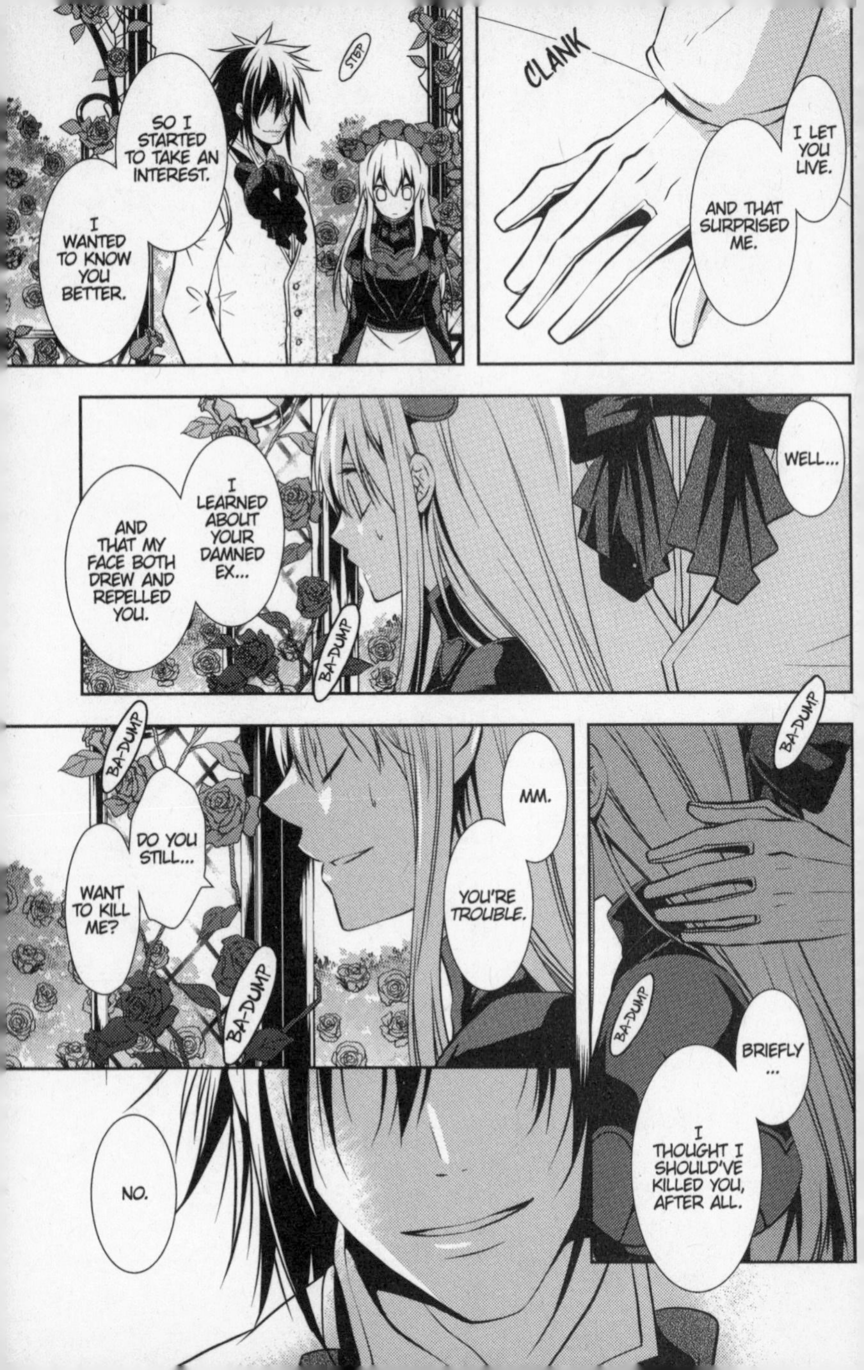
CLANK
I LET YOU LIVE.
AND THAT SURPRISED ME.
STEP
SO I STARTED TO TAKE AN INTEREST.
I WANTED TO KNOW YOU BETTER.
WELL...
I LEARNED ABOUT YOUR DAMNED EX...
AND THAT MY FACE BOTH DREW AND REPELLED YOU.
BA-DUMP
BA-DUMP
MM.
YOU'RE TROUBLE.
BA-DUMP
DO YOU STILL...
WANT TO KILL ME?
BA-DUMP
BA-DUMP
BRIEFLY ...
I THOUGHT I SHOULD'VE KILLED YOU, AFTER ALL.
NO.

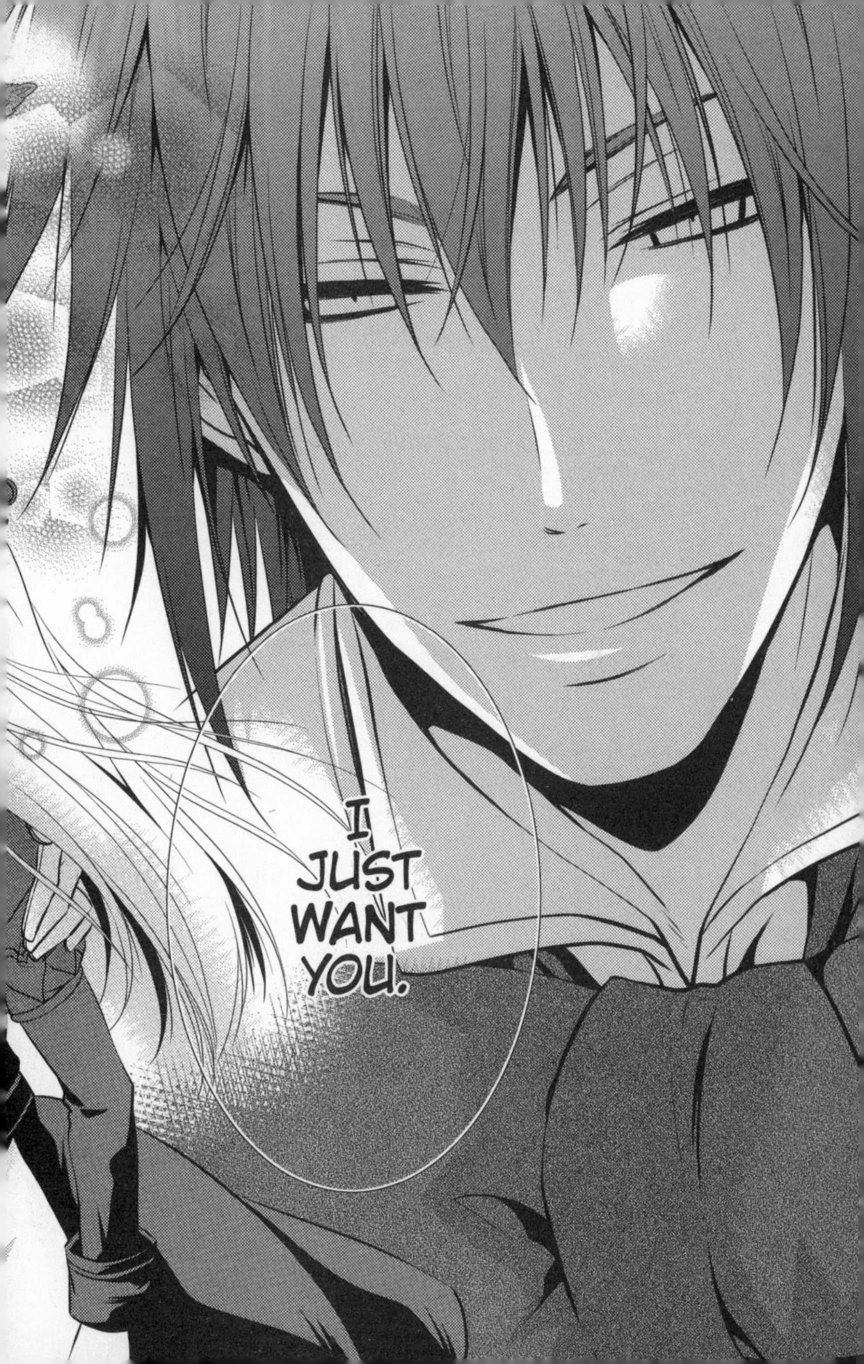
I JUST WANT YOU.

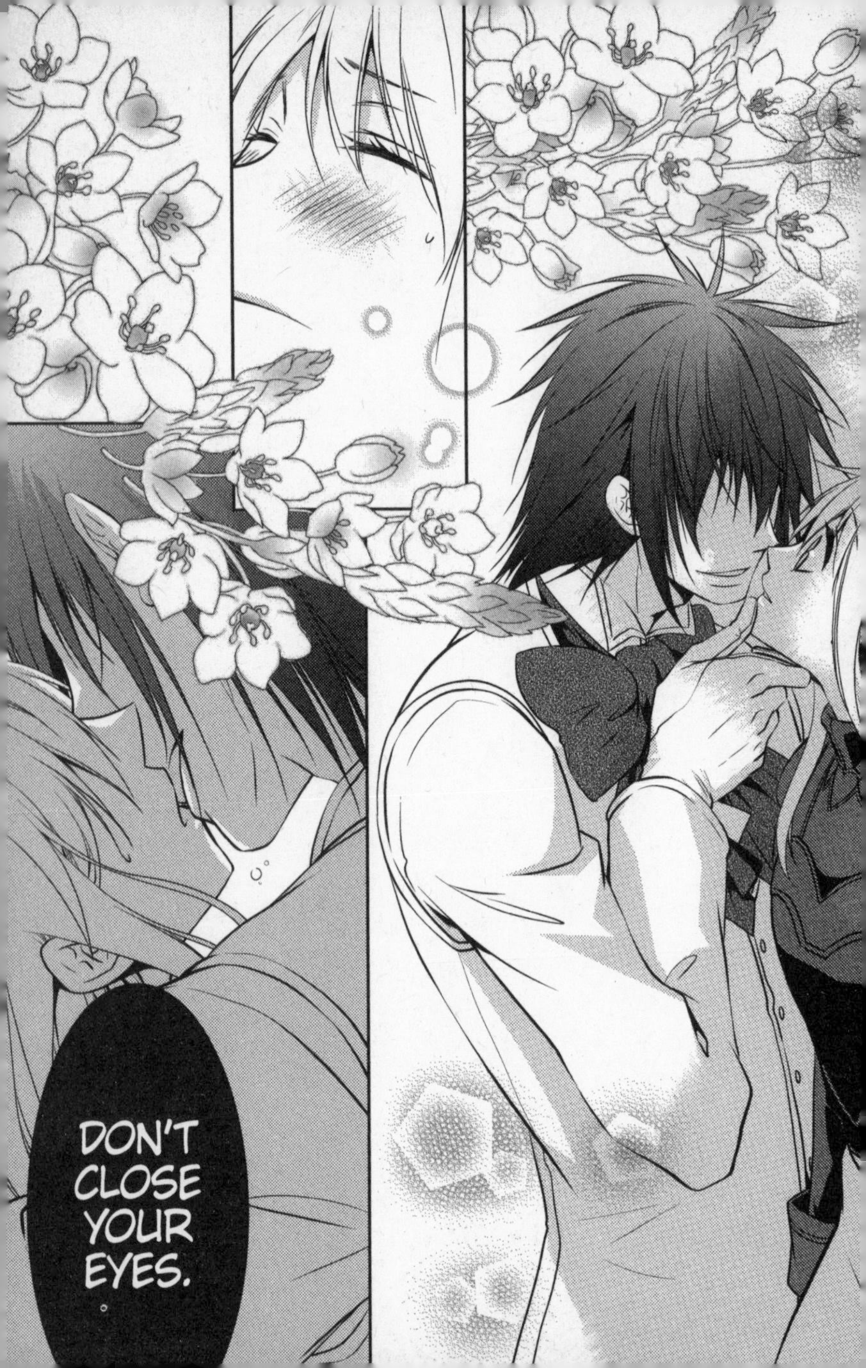
DON'T CLOSE YOUR EYES.

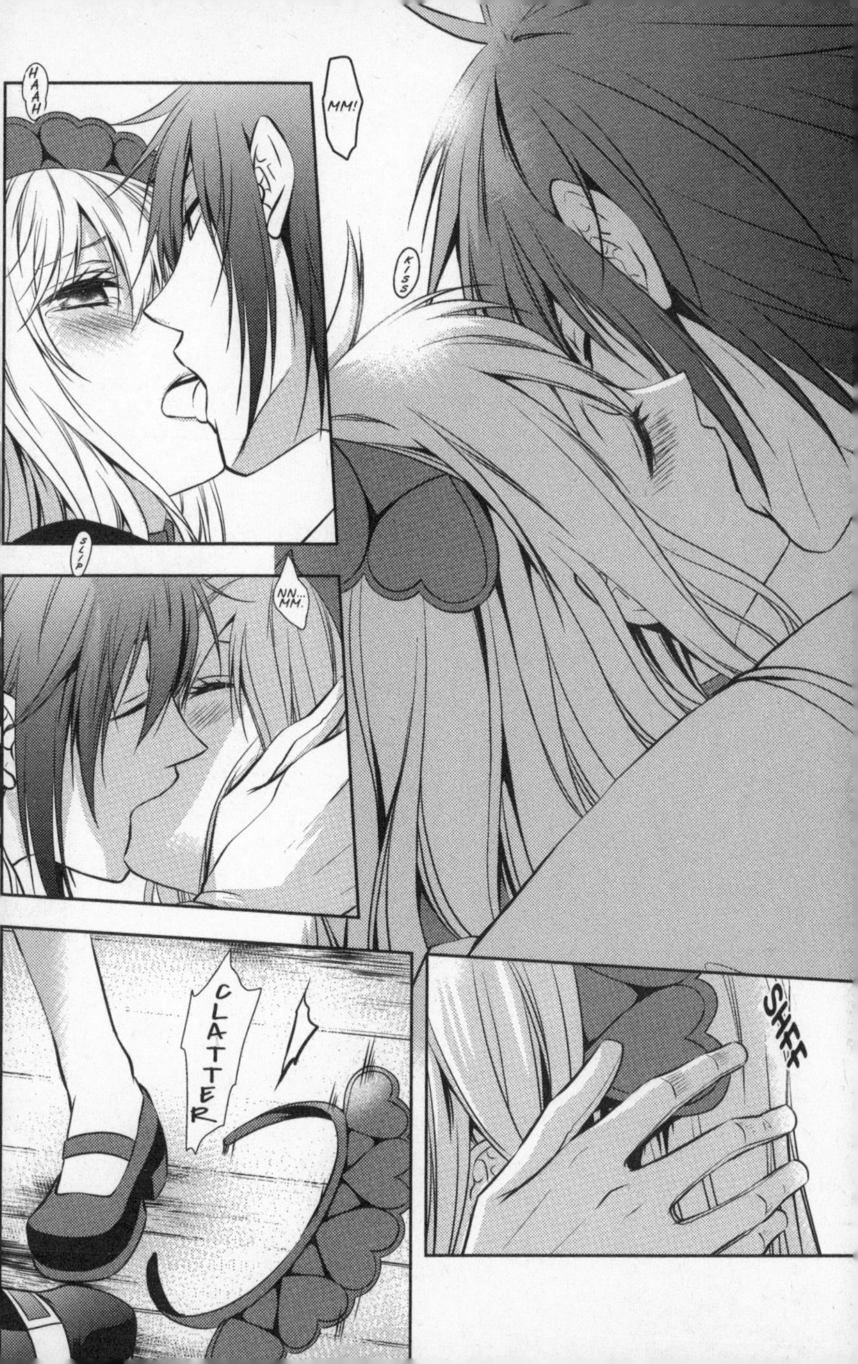
KISS
MM!
HAAAH
NN... MM.
SLIP
SHFF
CLATTER

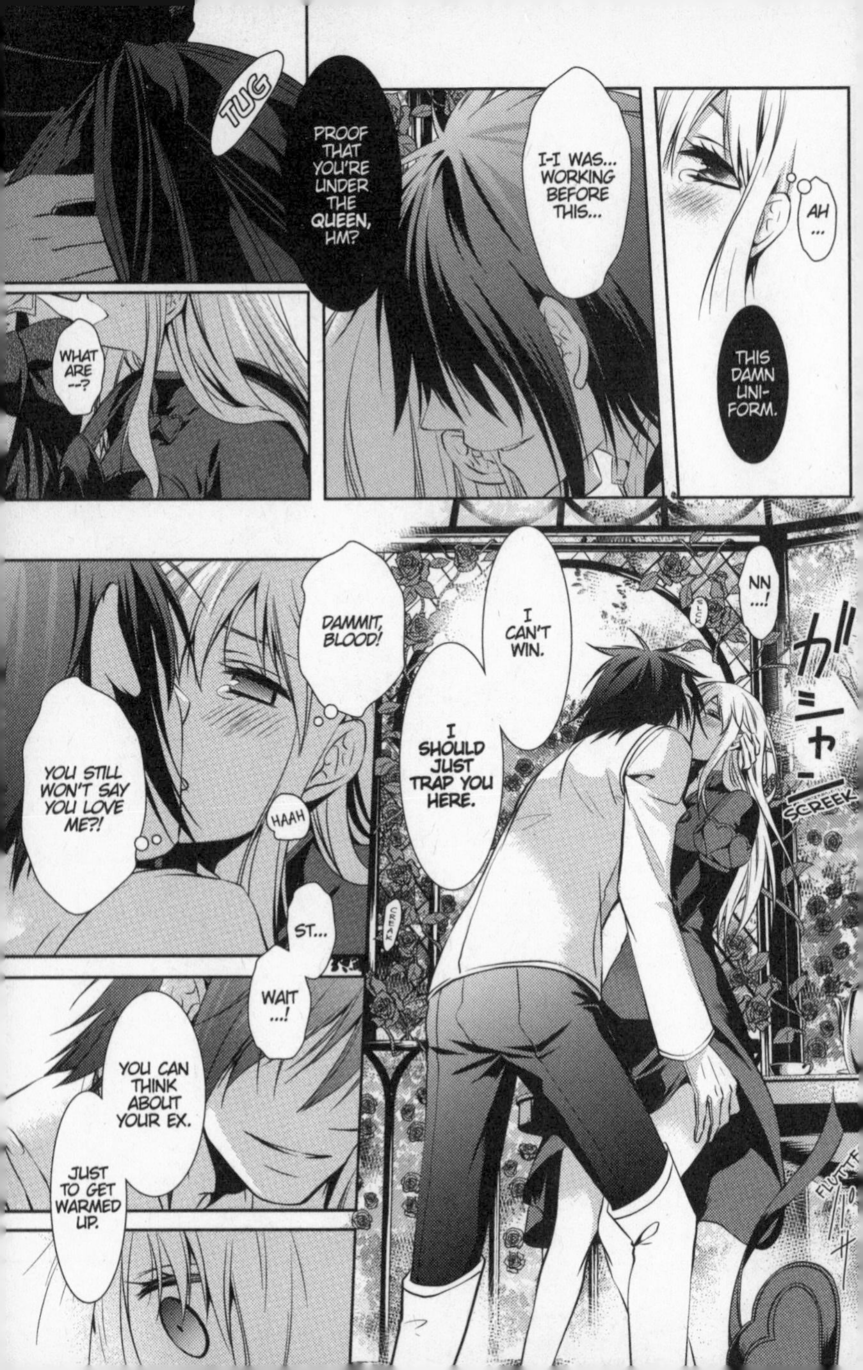
AH...
THIS DAMN UNI-FORM.
I-I WAS... WORKING BEFORE THIS...
TUG
PROOF THAT YOU'RE UNDER THE QUEEN, HM?
WHAT ARE --?
NN ...!
ガシャー
SCREEK
I CAN'T WIN.
I SHOULD JUST TRAP YOU HERE.
DAMMIT, BLOOD!
YOU STILL WON'T SAY YOU LOVE ME?!
HAAH
ST...
WAIT ...!
YOU CAN THINK ABOUT YOUR EX.
JUST TO GET WARMED UP.

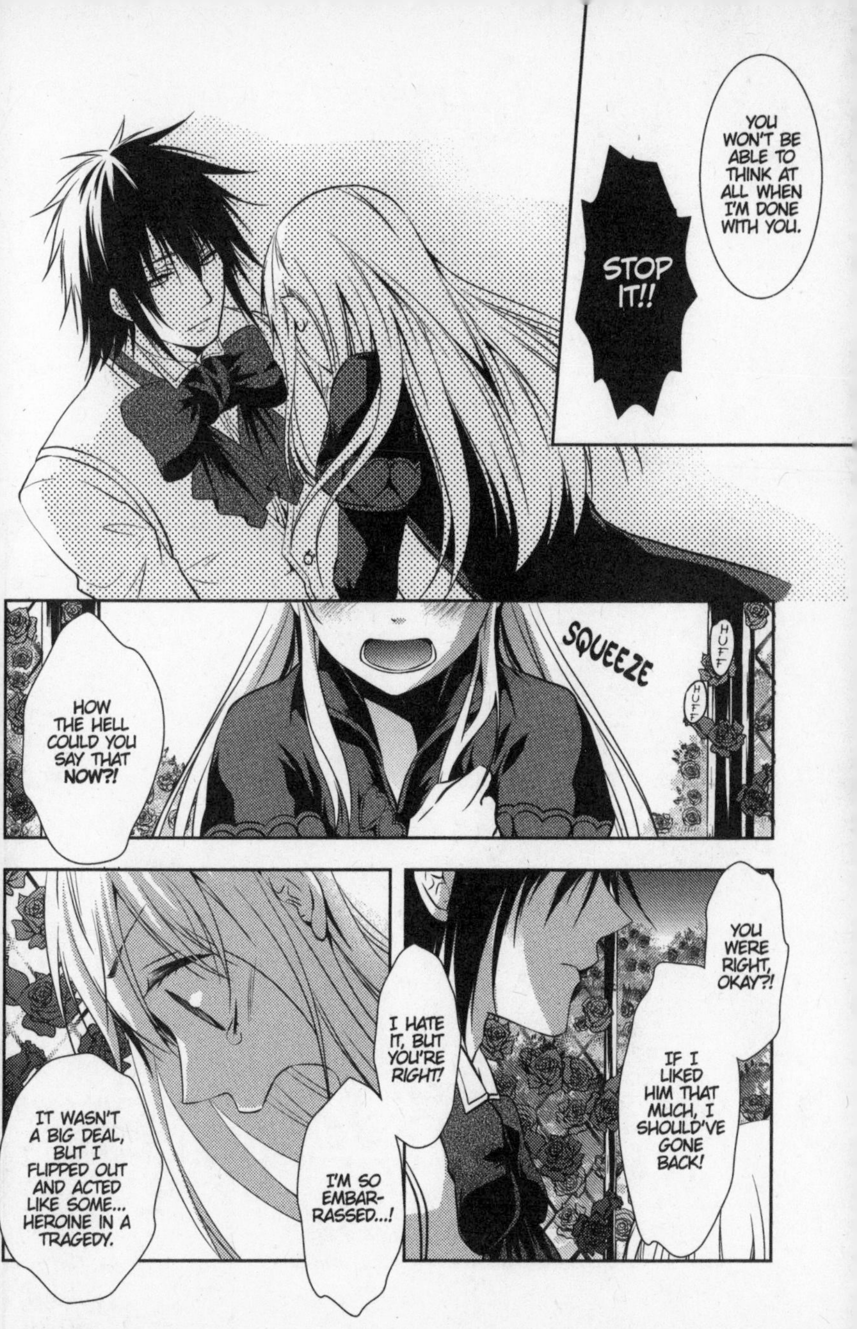
YOU WON'T BE ABLE TO THINK AT ALL WHEN I'M DONE WITH YOU.
STOP IT!!
HUFF
HUFF
SQUEEZE
HOW THE HELL COULD YOU SAY THAT NOW?!
YOU WERE RIGHT, OKAY?!
IF I LIKED HIM THAT MUCH, I SHOULD'VE GONE BACK!
I HATE IT, BUT YOU'RE RIGHT!
I'M SO EMBAR-RASSED...!
IT WASN'T A BIG DEAL, BUT I FLIPPED OUT AND ACTED LIKE SOME... HEROINE IN A TRAGEDY.

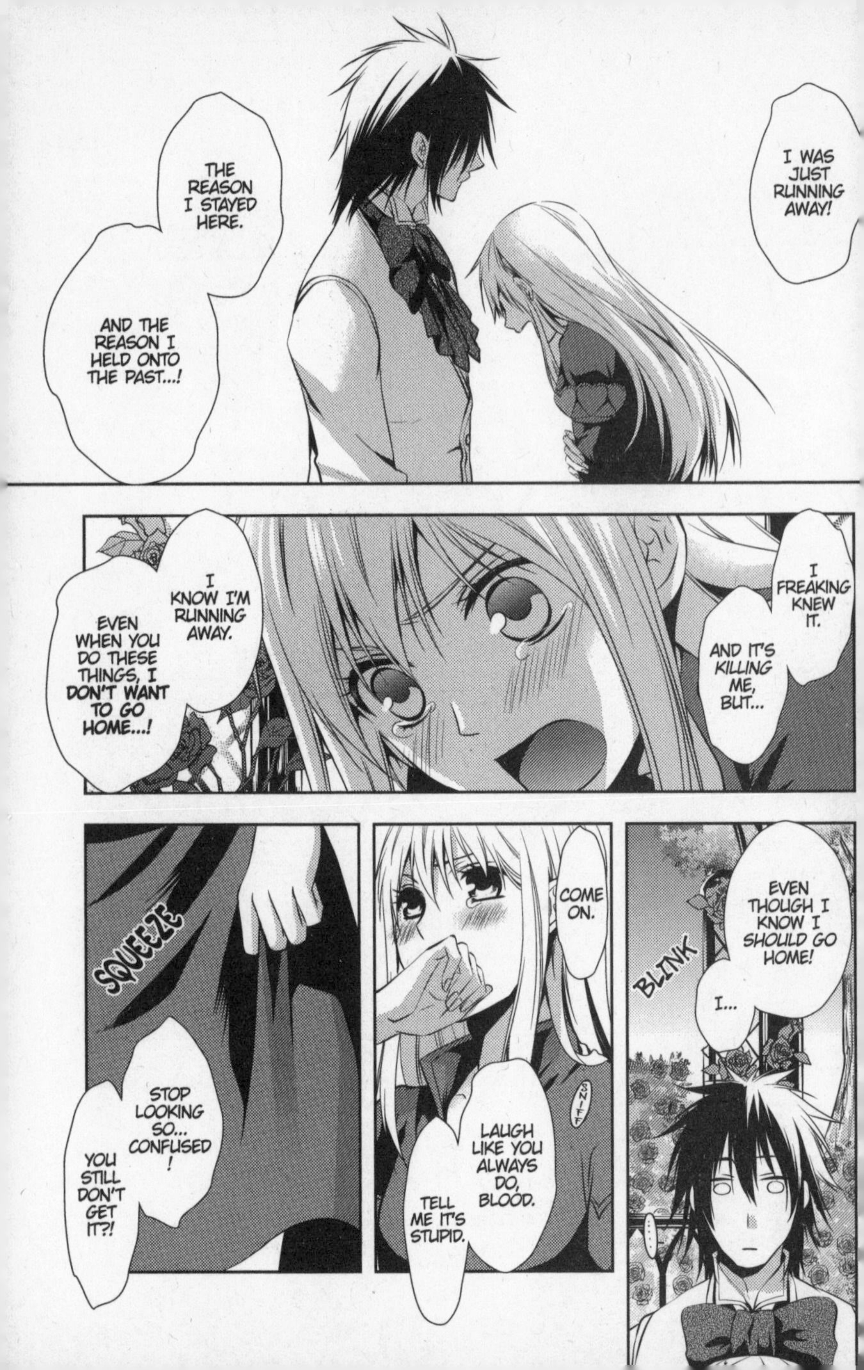
I WAS JUST RUNNING AWAY!
THE REASON I STAYED HERE.
AND THE REASON I HELD ONTO THE PAST...!
I FREAKING KNEW IT.
AND IT'S KILLING ME, BUT...
I KNOW I'M RUNNING AWAY.
EVEN WHEN YOU DO THESE THINGS, I DON'T WANT TO GO HOME...!
EVEN THOUGH I KNOW I SHOULD GO HOME!
I...
BLINK
......
COME ON.
SNIFF
LAUGH LIKE YOU ALWAYS DO, BLOOD.
TELL ME IT'S STUPID.
SQUEEZE
STOP LOOKING SO... CONFUSED!
YOU STILL DON'T GET IT?!

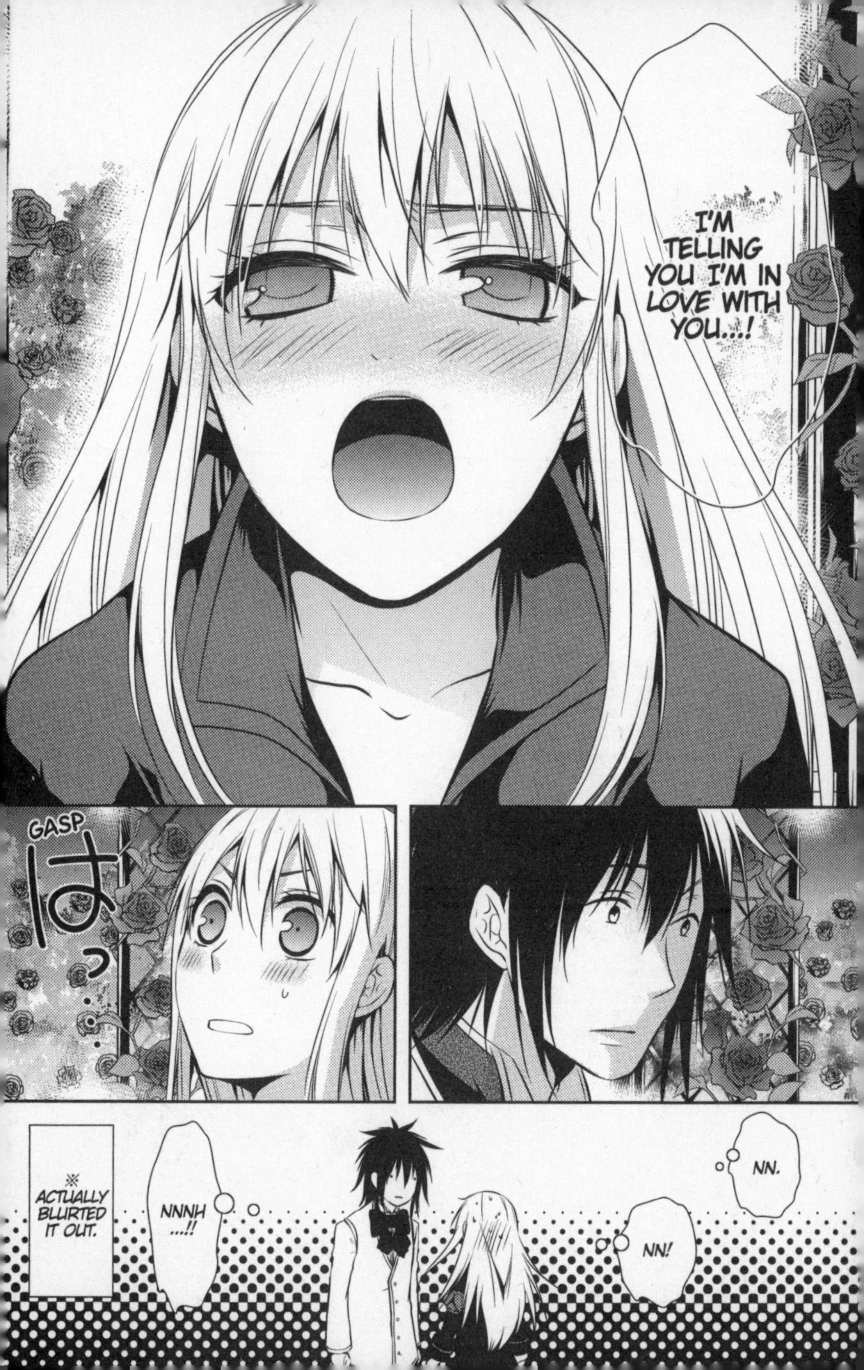
I'M TELLING YOU I'M IN LOVE WITH YOU...!
GASP
はっ…
NN.
NN!
NNNH ...!!
※ ACTUALLY BLURTED IT OUT.

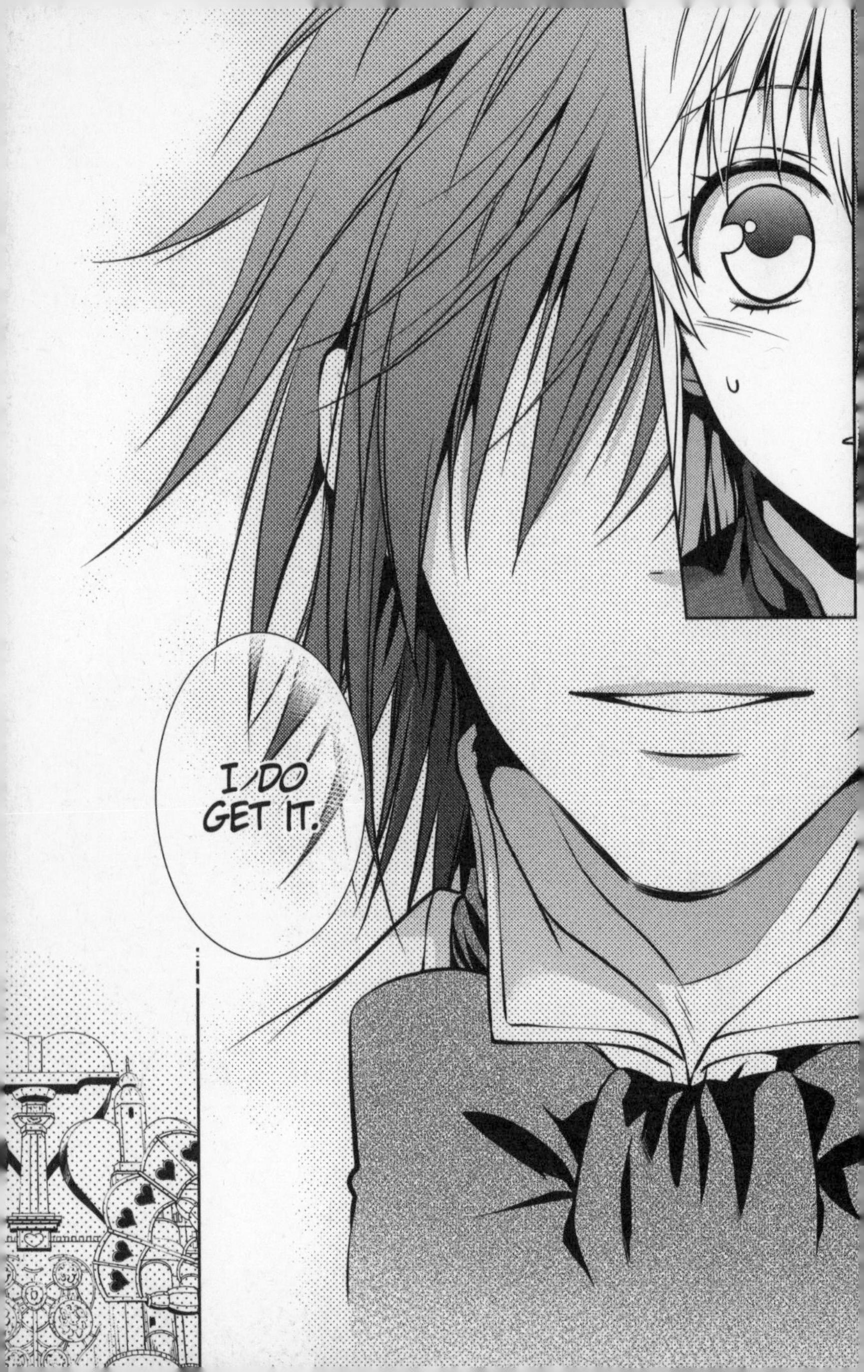
I DO GET IT.

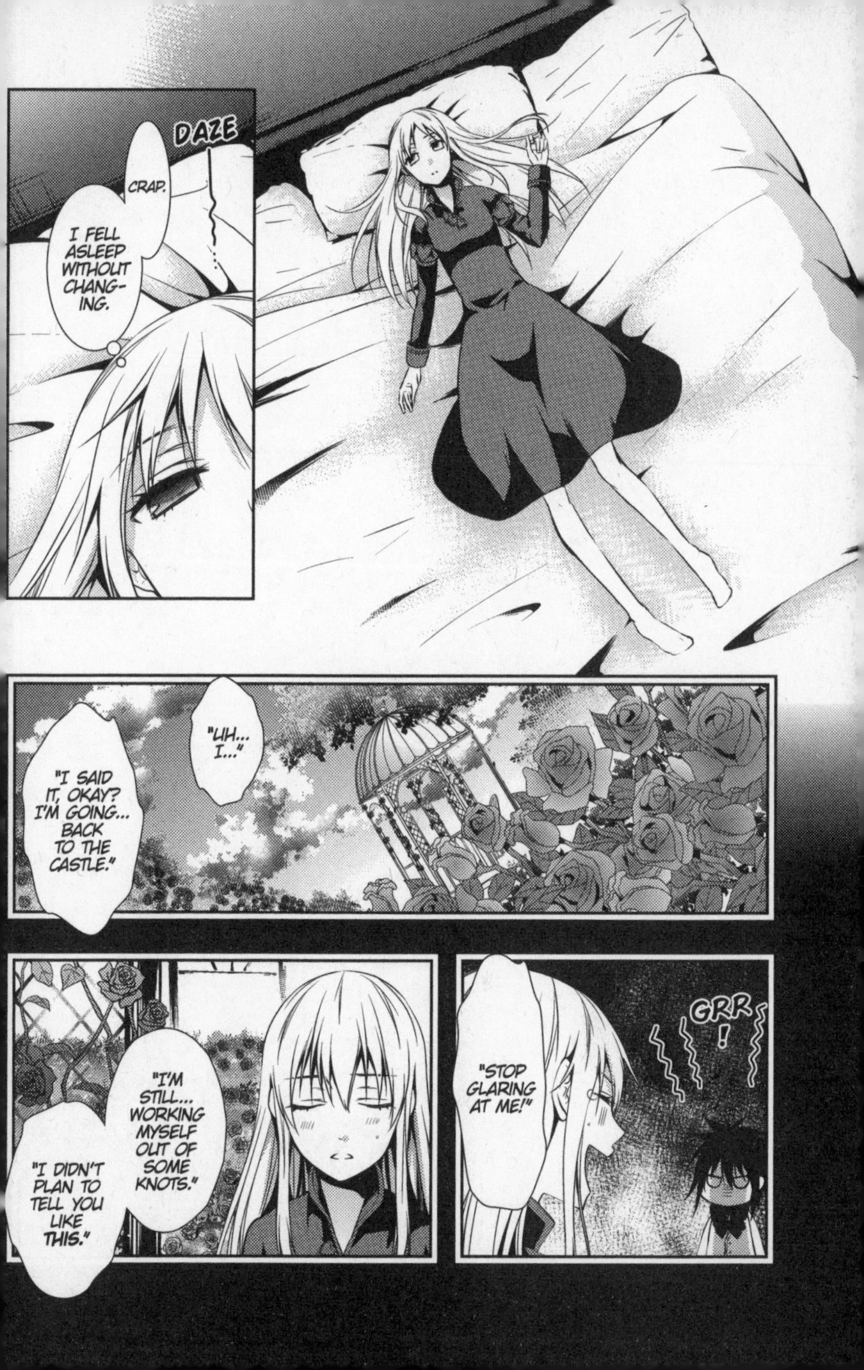
DAZE
CRAP.
I FELL ASLEEP WITHOUT CHANGING.
"UH... I..."
"I SAID IT, OKAY? I'M GOING... BACK TO THE CASTLE."
GRR!
"STOP GLARING AT ME!"
"I'M STILL... WORKING MYSELF OUT OF SOME KNOTS."
"I DIDN'T PLAN TO TELL YOU LIKE THIS."

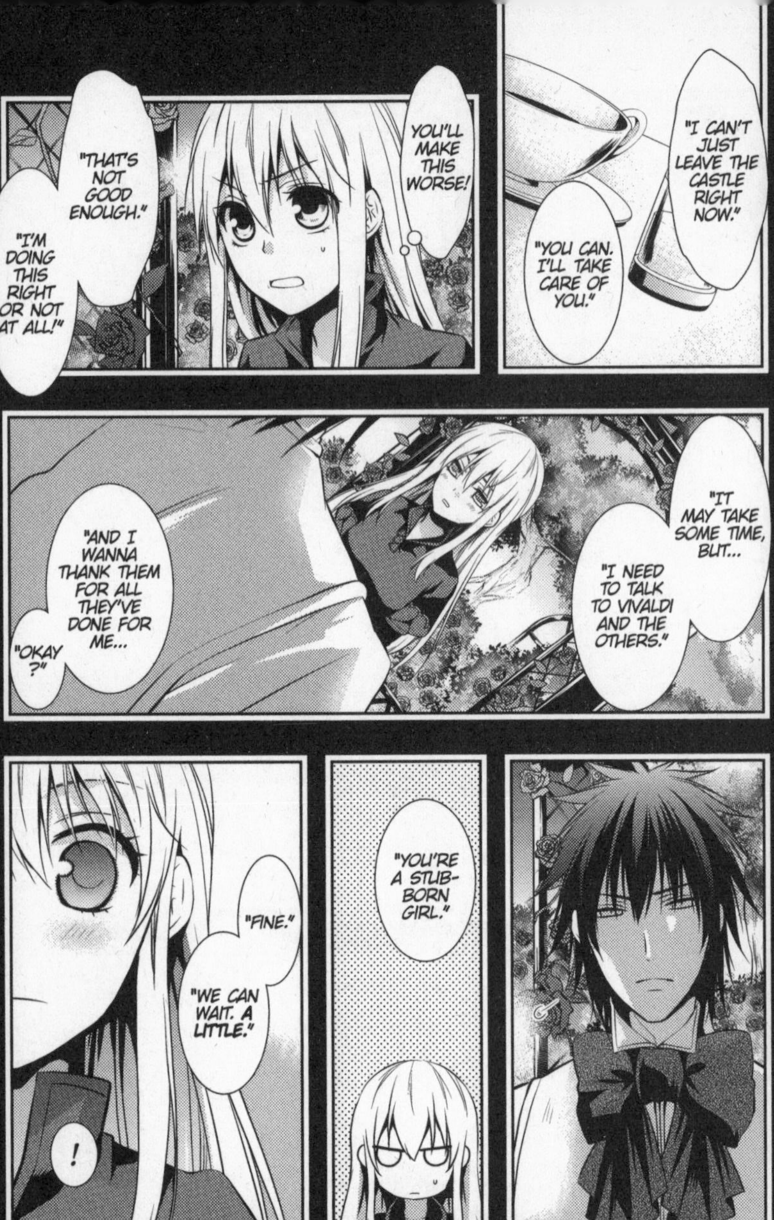
"I CAN'T JUST LEAVE THE CASTLE RIGHT NOW."
"YOU CAN. I'LL TAKE CARE OF YOU."
YOU'LL MAKE THIS WORSE!
"THAT'S NOT GOOD ENOUGH."
"I'M DOING THIS RIGHT OR NOT AT ALL!"
"IT MAY TAKE SOME TIME, BUT...
"I NEED TO TALK TO VIVALDI AND THE OTHERS."
"AND I WANNA THANK THEM FOR ALL THEY'VE DONE FOR ME...
"OKAY?"
"YOU'RE A STUBBORN GIRL."
"FINE."
"WE CAN WAIT. A LITTLE."
!

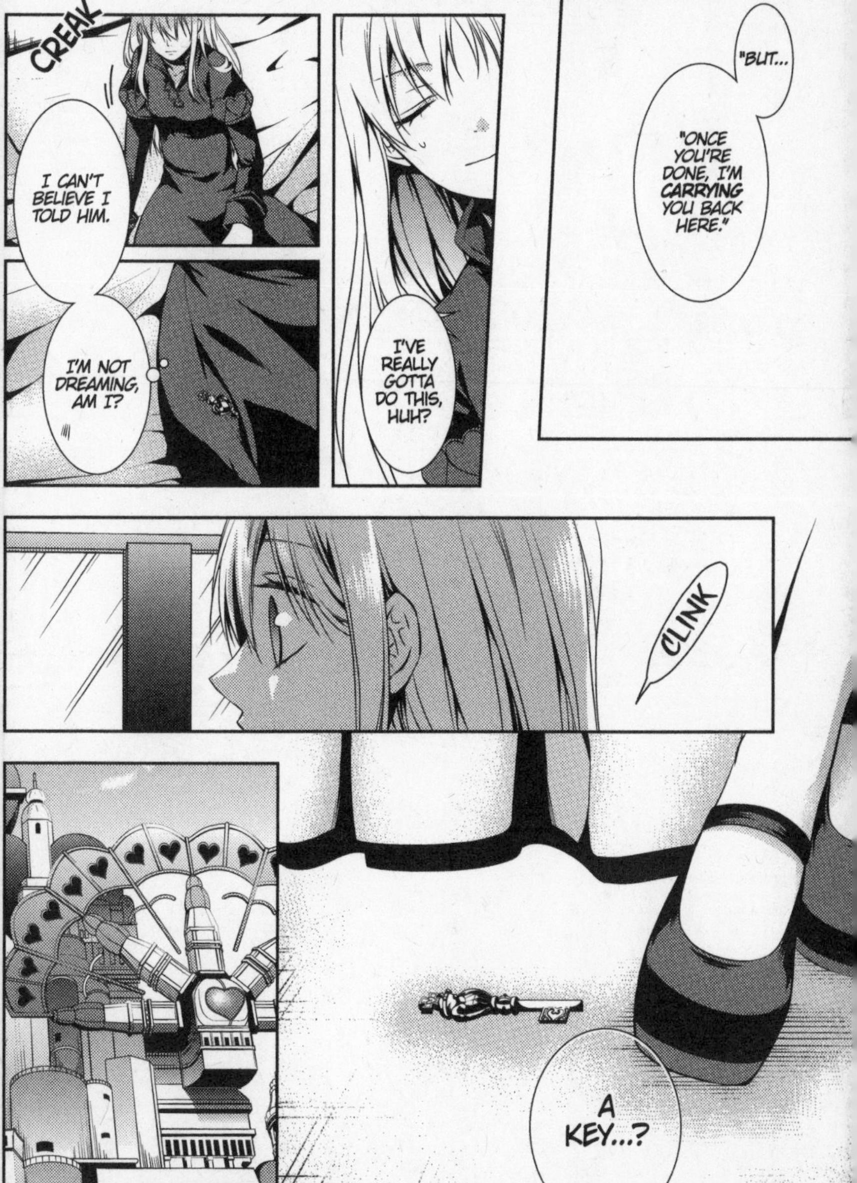
"BUT...
"ONCE YOU'RE DONE, I'M CARRYING YOU BACK HERE."
I'VE REALLY GOTTA DO THIS, HUH?
CREAK
I CAN'T BELIEVE I TOLD HIM.
I'M NOT DREAMING, AM I?
CLINK
A KEY...?

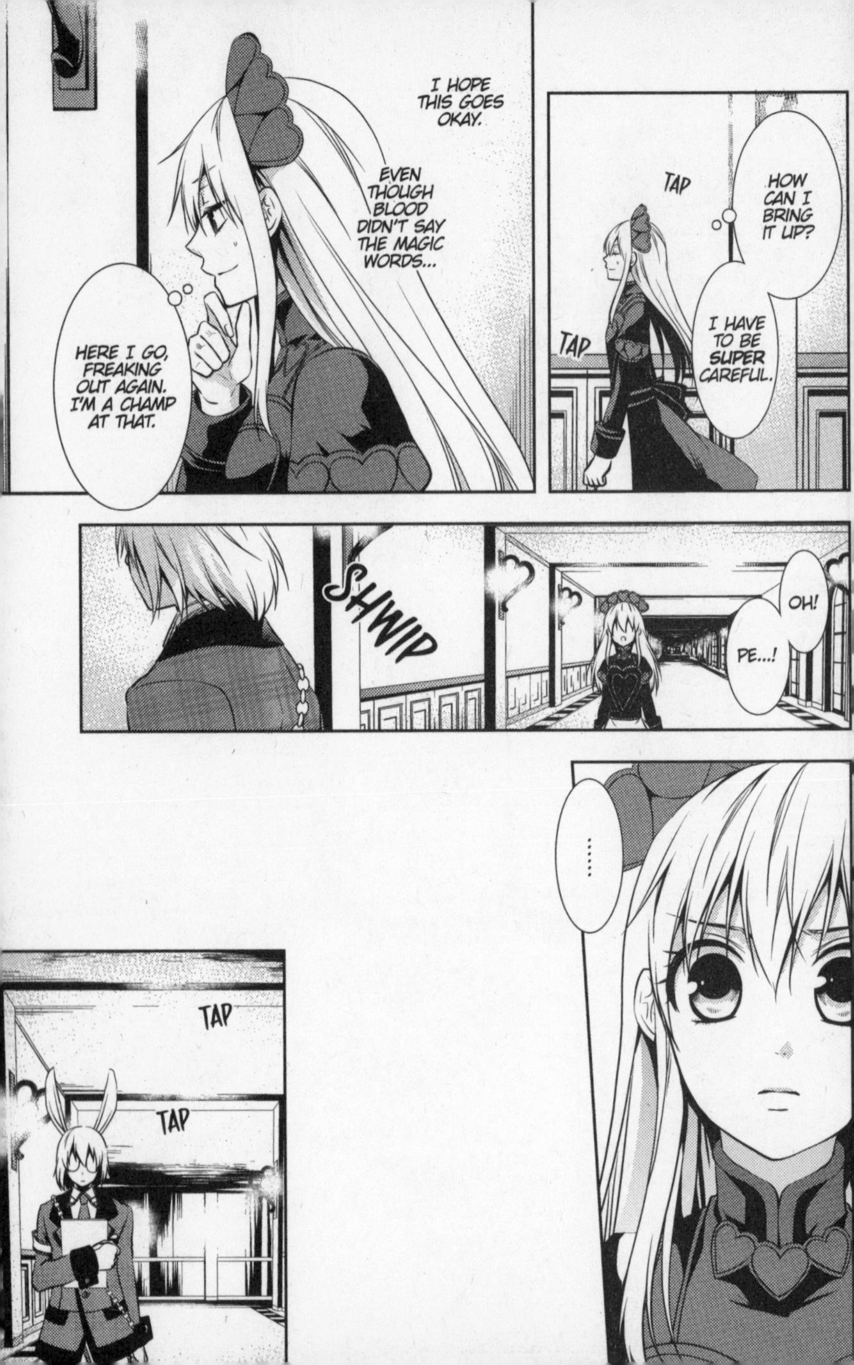
TAP
HOW CAN I BRING IT UP?
I HAVE TO BE SUPER CAREFUL.
TAP
I HOPE THIS GOES OKAY.
EVEN THOUGH BLOOD DIDN'T SAY THE MAGIC WORDS...
HERE I GO, FREAKING OUT AGAIN. I'M A CHAMP AT THAT.
OH!
PE...!
SHWIP
......
TAP
TAP

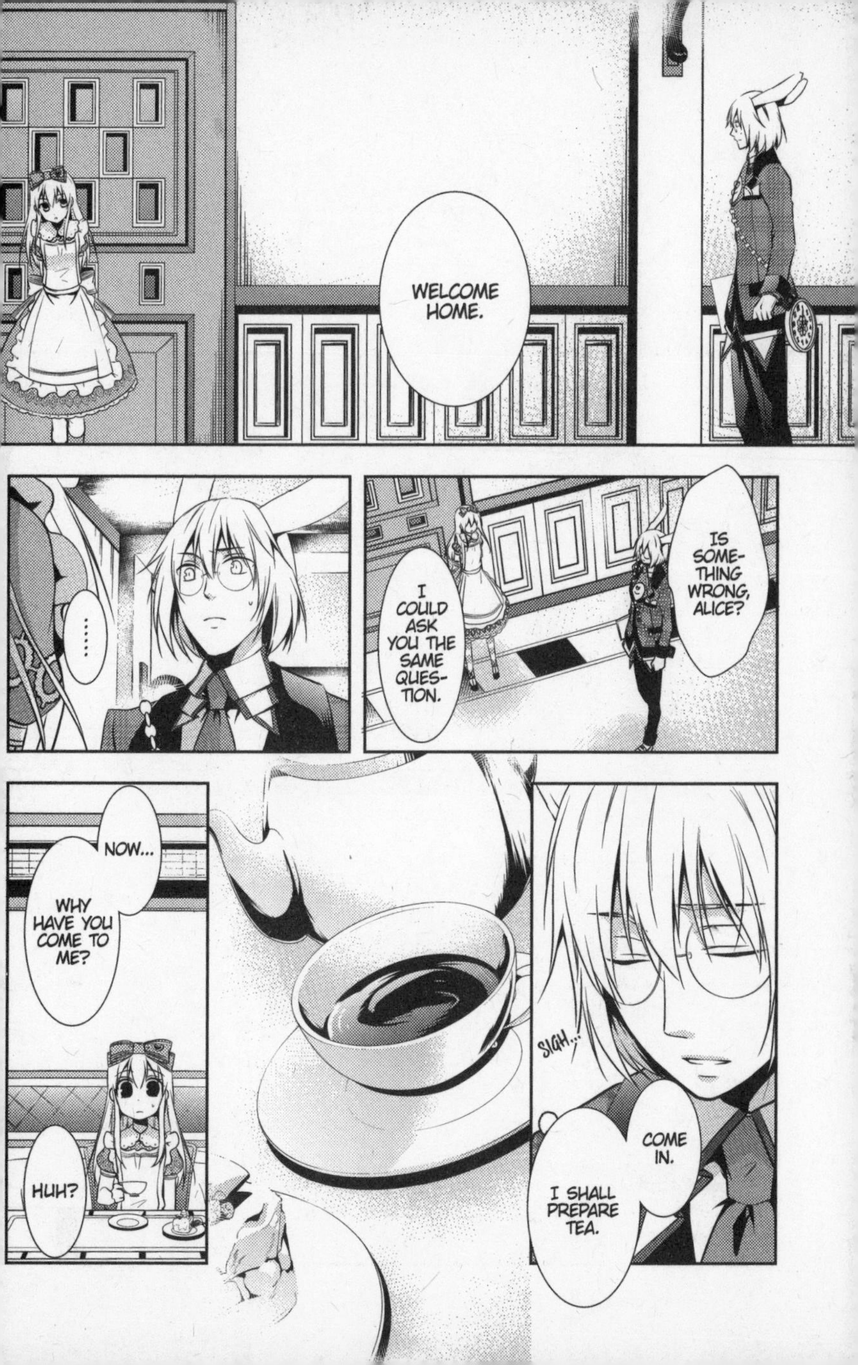
WELCOME HOME.
IS SOME-THING WRONG, ALICE?
I COULD ASK YOU THE SAME QUES-TION.
......
SIGH...
COME IN.
I SHALL PREPARE TEA.
NOW...
WHY HAVE YOU COME TO ME?
HUH?

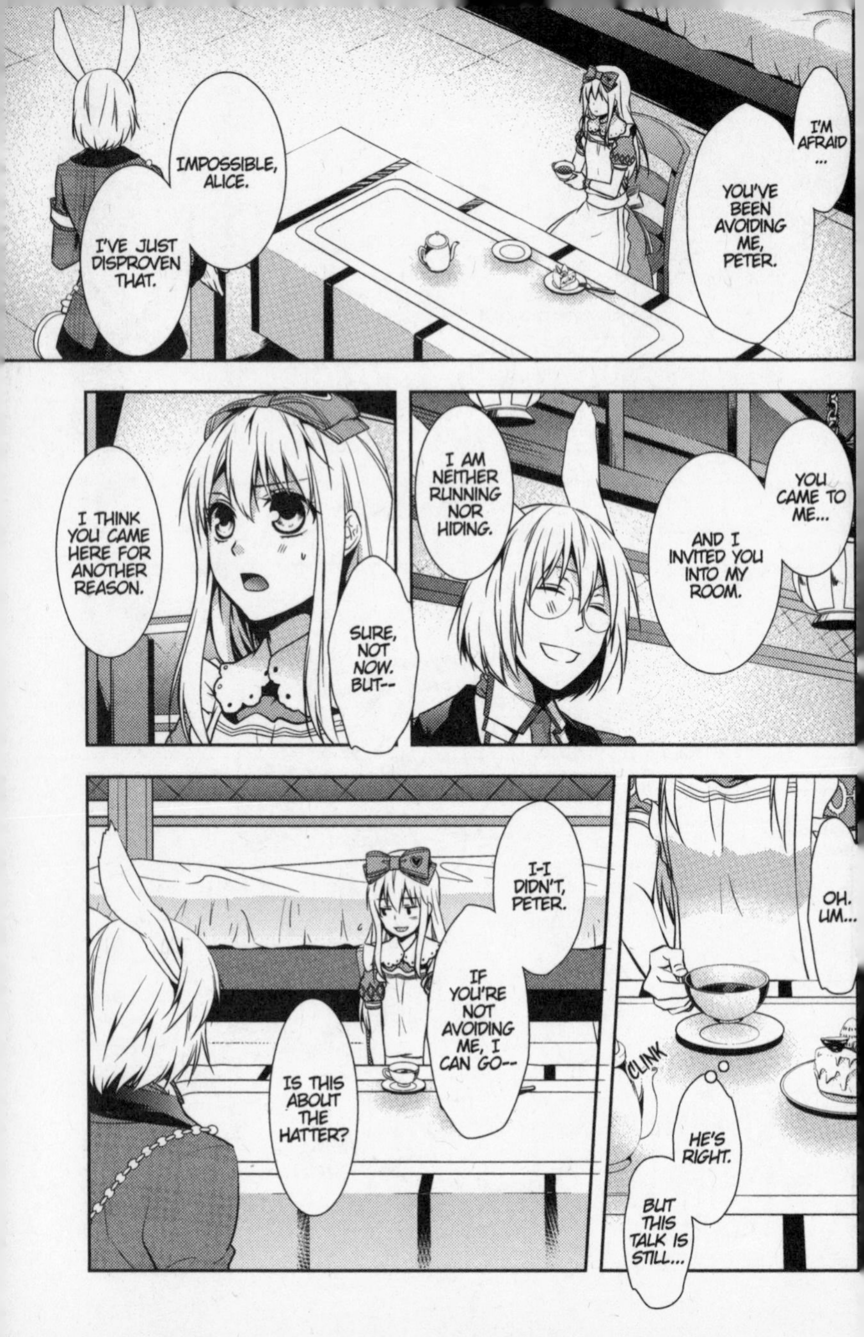
I'M AFRAID...
YOU'VE BEEN AVOIDING ME, PETER.
IMPOSSIBLE, ALICE.
I'VE JUST DISPROVEN THAT.
YOU CAME TO ME...
AND I INVITED YOU INTO MY ROOM.
I AM NEITHER RUNNING NOR HIDING.
SURE, NOT NOW. BUT--
I THINK YOU CAME HERE FOR ANOTHER REASON.
OH. UM...
CLINK
HE'S RIGHT.
BUT THIS TALK IS STILL...
I-I DIDN'T, PETER.
IF YOU'RE NOT AVOIDING ME, I CAN GO--
IS THIS ABOUT THE HATTER?

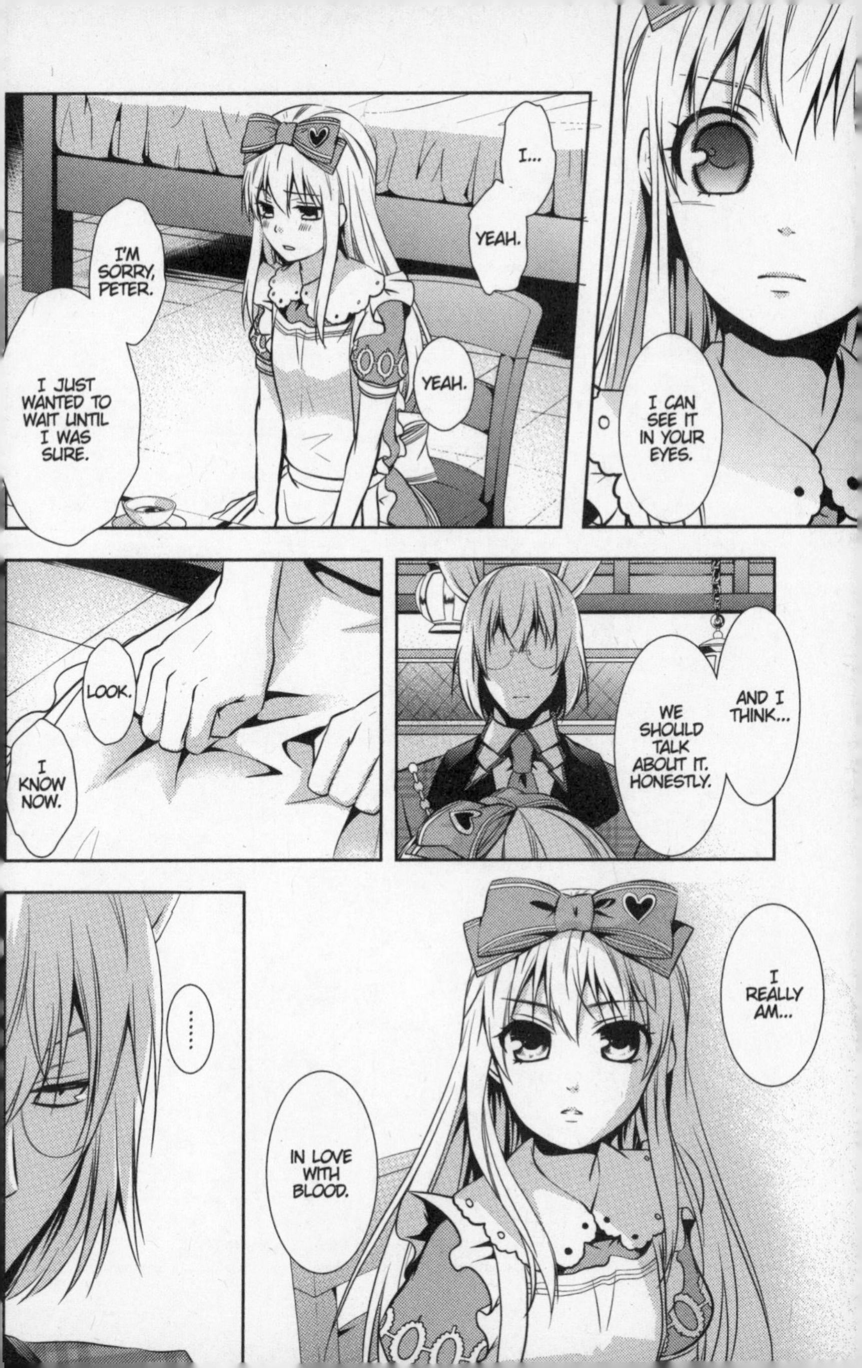
I CAN SEE IT IN YOUR EYES.
I...
YEAH.
I'M SORRY, PETER.
YEAH.
I JUST WANTED TO WAIT UNTIL I WAS SURE.
AND I THINK...
WE SHOULD TALK ABOUT IT. HONESTLY.
LOOK.
I KNOW NOW.
I REALLY AM...
IN LOVE WITH BLOOD.
......

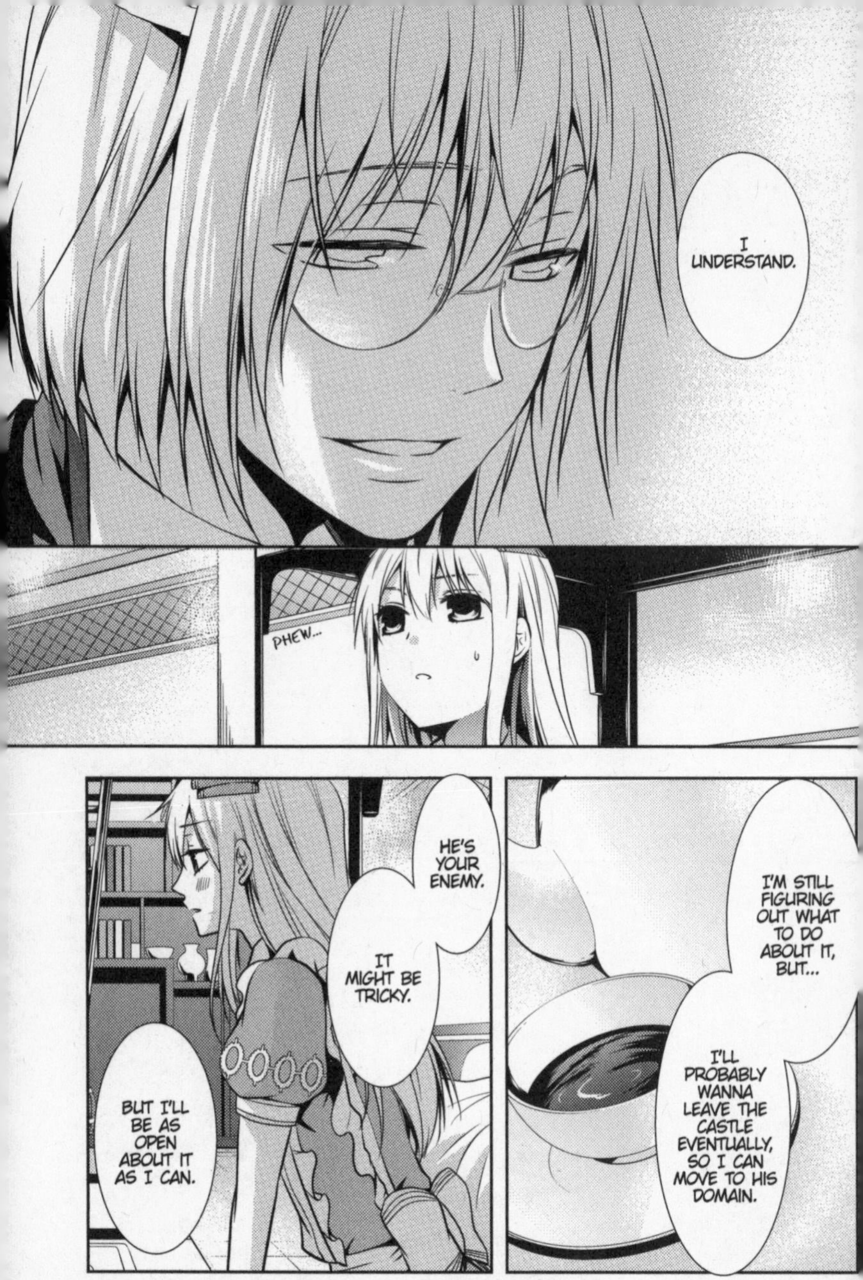
I UNDERSTAND.
PHEW...
I'M STILL FIGURING OUT WHAT TO DO ABOUT IT, BUT...
I'LL PROBABLY WANNA LEAVE THE CASTLE EVENTUALLY, SO I CAN MOVE TO HIS DOMAIN.
HE'S YOUR ENEMY.
IT MIGHT BE TRICKY.
BUT I'LL BE AS OPEN ABOUT IT AS I CAN.

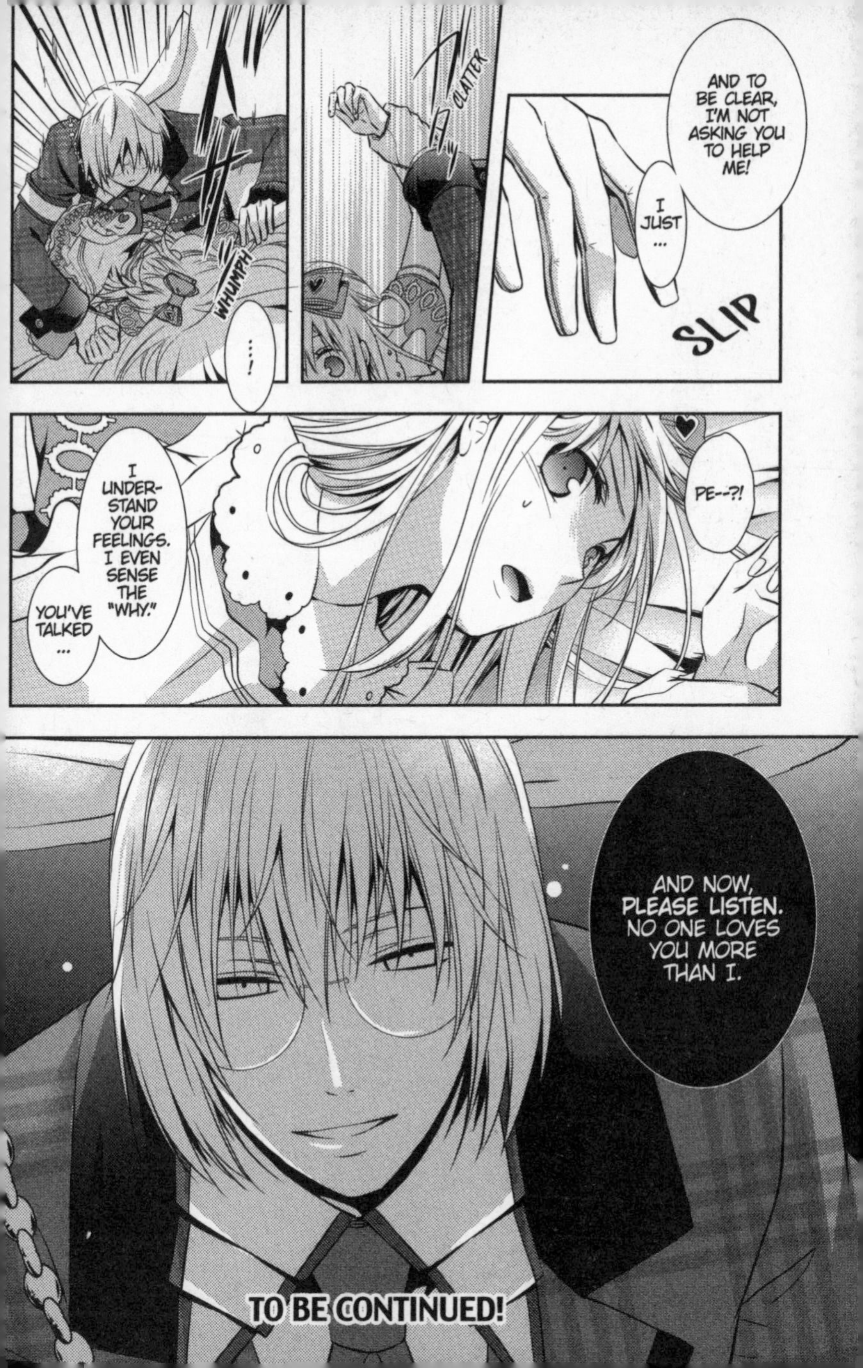
AND TO BE CLEAR, I'M NOT ASKING YOU TO HELP ME!
I JUST ...
SLIP
CLATTER
...!
WHUMPH
PE--?!
I UNDER-STAND YOUR FEELINGS. I EVEN SENSE THE "WHY."
YOU'VE TALKED ...
AND NOW, PLEASE LISTEN. NO ONE LOVES YOU MORE THAN I.
TO BE CONTINUED!

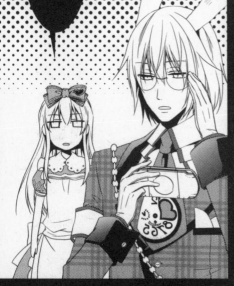

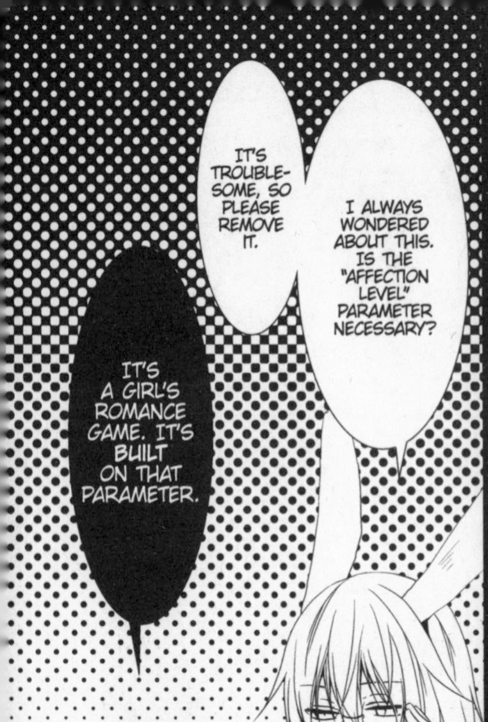

I ALWAYS WONDERED ABOUT THIS. IS THE "AFFECTION LEVEL" PARAMETER NECESSARY?
IT'S TROUBLE-SOME, SO PLEASE REMOVE IT.
IT'S A GIRL'S ROMANCE GAME. IT'S BUILT ON THAT PARAMETER.

Peter's affection level was maxed out from the beginning.

THANK YOU VERY MUCH!

To everyone who helped with the publication

Friends & Family

QuinRose-sama

The Publishers

And most importantly-- the readers!

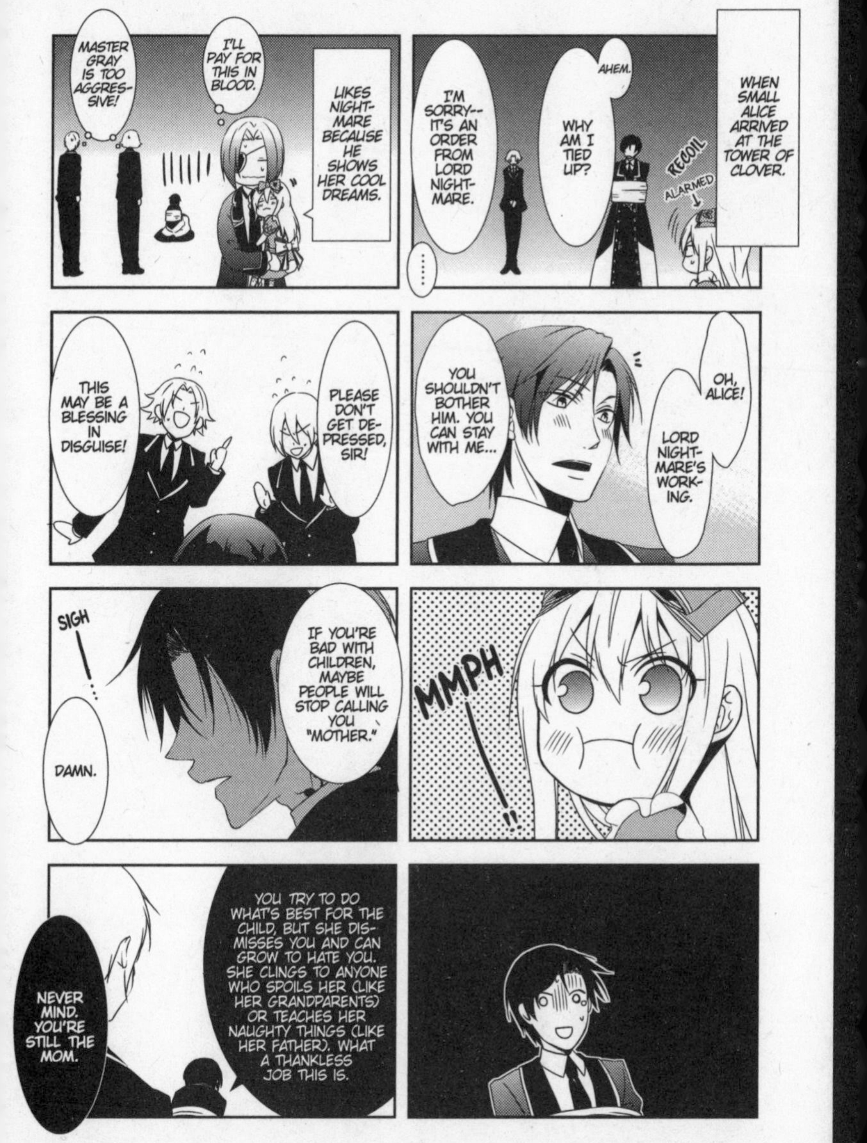
WHEN SMALL ALICE ARRIVED AT THE TOWER OF CLOVER.
AHEM.
WHY AM I TIED UP?
RECOIL
ALARMED
I'M SORRY-- IT'S AN ORDER FROM LORD NIGHTMARE.
......
LIKES NIGHTMARE BECAUSE HE SHOWS HER COOL DREAMS.
I'LL PAY FOR THIS IN BLOOD.
MASTER GRAY IS TOO AGGRESSIVE!
OH, ALICE!
LORD NIGHTMARE'S WORKING.
YOU SHOULDN'T BOTHER HIM. YOU CAN STAY WITH ME...
PLEASE DON'T GET DEPRESSED, SIR!
THIS MAY BE A BLESSING IN DISGUISE!
MMPH !!
IF YOU'RE BAD WITH CHILDREN, MAYBE PEOPLE WILL STOP CALLING YOU "MOTHER."
SIGH ...
DAMN.
YOU TRY TO DO WHAT'S BEST FOR THE CHILD, BUT SHE DISMISSES YOU AND CAN GROW TO HATE YOU. SHE CLINGS TO ANYONE WHO SPOILS HER (LIKE HER GRANDPARENTS) OR TEACHES HER NAUGHTY THINGS (LIKE HER FATHER). WHAT A THANKLESS JOB THIS IS.
NEVER MIND. YOU'RE STILL THE MOM.

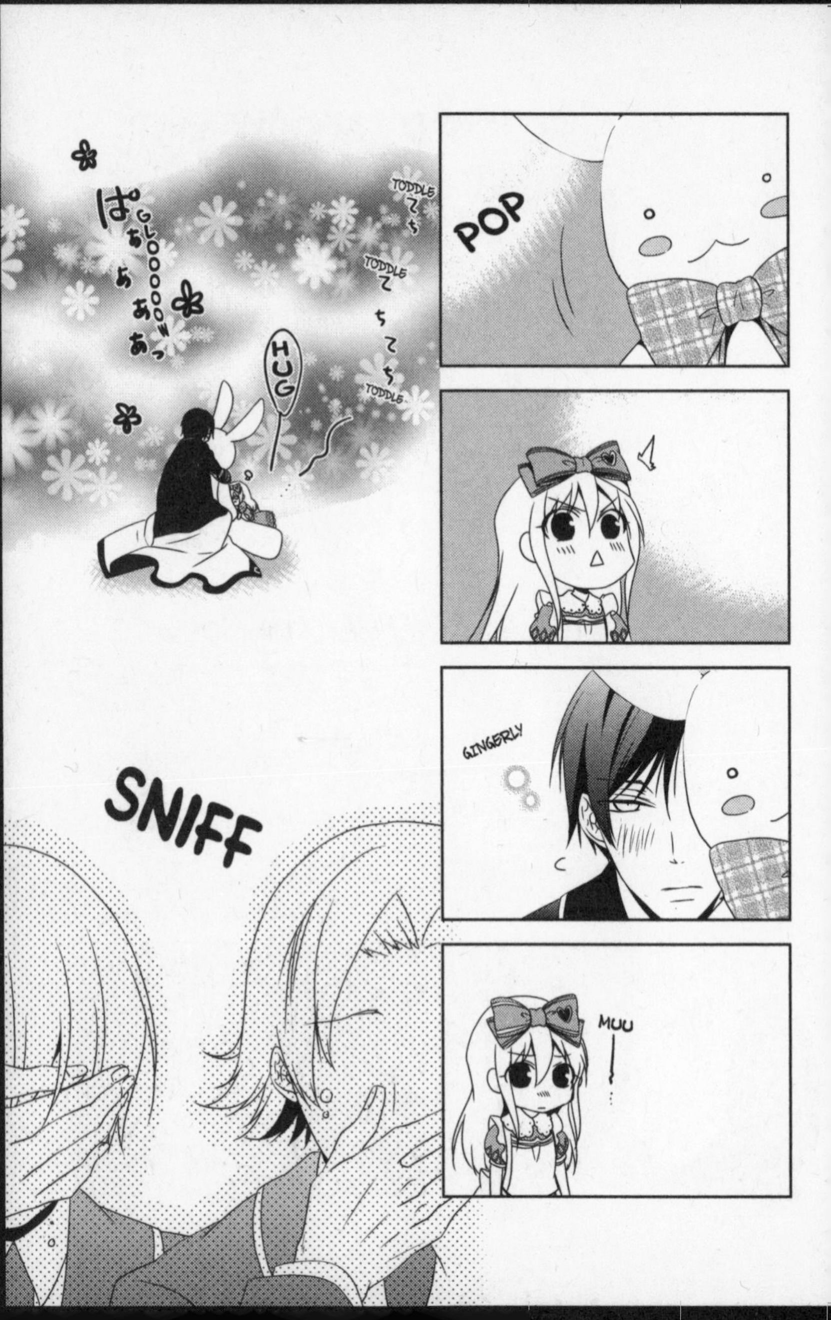
POP
GINGERLY
MUU
TODDLE てち
TODDLE てちてち
TODDLE
HUG
GLOOOOOW
ぱぁぁあっ
SNIFF

COMING SOON

JULY 2014
Alice in the Country of Clover:
Knight's Knowledge Vol. 1

AUGUST 2014
Alice in the Country of Joker:
The Nightmare Trilogy Vol. 1

SEPTEMBER 2014
Alice in the Country of Clover:
Knight's Knowledge Vol. 2

OCTOBER 2014
Alice in the Country
of Diamonds:
Bet On My Heart

SEVEN SEAS ENTERTAINMENT PRESENTS

Alice IN THE COUNTRY OF Joker

CIRCUS AND LIAR'S GAME

art by **MAMENOSUKE FUJIMARU** / story by **QUINROSE** **VOLUME 5**

TRANSLATION
Angela Liu

ADAPTATION
Lianne Sentar

LETTERING AND LAYOUT
Laura Scoville

LOGO DESIGN
Courtney Williams

COVER DESIGN
Nicky Lim

PROOFREADER
Shanti Whitesides
Conner Crooks

MANAGING EDITOR
Adam Arnold

PUBLISHER
Jason DeAngelis

Seven Seas books may be purchased in bulk for educational, business, or promotional use. For information on bulk purchases, please contact Macmillan Corporate & Premium Sales Department at 1-800-221-7945 (ext 5442) or write specialmarkets@macmillan.com.

ISBN: 978-1-626920-55-2

Printed in Canada

First Printing: June 2014

10 9 8 7 6 5 4 3 2 1

FOLLOW US ONLINE: ***www.gomanga.com***

READING DIRECTIONS

This book reads from ***right to left***, Japanese style. If this is your first time reading manga, you start reading from the top right panel on each page and take it from there. If you get lost, just follow the numbered diagram here. It may seem backwards at first, but you'll get the hang of it! Have fun!!

1
2
3
4
5
6
7
8
9

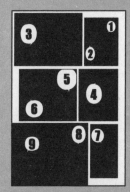